PSYCHOLOGY IN ACTION

This book is dedicated to all my students, past, present and future. To those who take me seriously, but mainly to those who do not take me too seriously.

Psychology in Action

Edited by
DAVID CANTER
University of Liverpool, UK

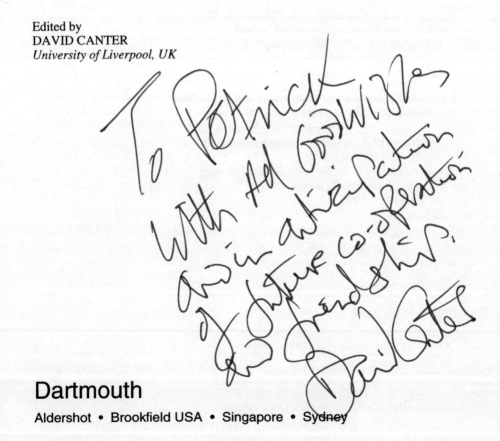

To Patrick
With my Good Wishes
and in anticipation
of future co-operation
and friendship.
David Canter

Dartmouth

Aldershot • Brookfield USA • Singapore • Sydney

Published by
Dartmouth Publishing Company Limited
Gower House
Croft Road
Aldershot
Hants GU11 3HR
England

Dartmouth Publishing Company
Old Post Road
Brookfield
Vermont 05036
USA

British Library Cataloguing in Publication Data
Psychology in action. - (Benchmark series)
1. Psychology 2. Psychology, Applied
I. Canter, David, 1944-
150

Library of Congress Cataloging-in-Publication Data
Psychology in action / edited by David V. Canter.
    p.   cm. – (Dartmouth benchmark series)
    Includes bibliographical references and index.
    ISBN 1-85521-365-6
    1. Psychology. 2. Environmental psychology.
I. Canter, David V. II. Series.
BF121.P826 1996
158–dc20   95-52120
                                                              CIP

ISBN 1 85521 365 6

Printed in Great Britain by Galliard (Printers) Ltd, Great Yarmouth

Contents

COMPLEMENTARY MEDICINE

Also in the Dartmouth Benchmark Series:

Experiments in Social Interaction
Michael Argyle, University of Oxford

Refiguring Self and Psychology
Kenneth J. Gergen, Swarthmore College, Pennsylvania

Louis Guttman on Theory and Methodology: Selected Writings
Shlomit Levy, The Louis Guttman Israel Institute of Applied Social Research

Human Nature: Selected Writings of Hans J. Eysenck
Graham Powell, University of Surrey

Series Preface

Psychologists publish in a wide variety of outlets; many different journals, chapters of readings, conference proceedings as well as their own monographs and books. Even the work of one distinguished scholar is likely to be spread over many different sources. For the serious student this can make the task of locating all the significant work of a prolific psychologist extremely difficult.

The parsimony with which libraries throughout the world now stock journals, and the rapidity with which publishers cause books to be out of print, can mean that key papers in an seminal opus may be hard to obtain.

Psychology is a discipline in which it is often valuable to read the original papers of major contributors. It is also often of great value to be able to study the development in their ideas over their careers. Psychologists, possibly more than in any other discipline, should be able to benefit from exploring how particular individuals have struggled, through their writings, to make sense of human actions and experience.

As an educational device, the bringing together of the writings of one key figure in a single volume, helps students to understand the development of issues, theories and results, whilst being able to relate them directly to the approach of a particular person.

The *Benchmark Series* brings together the key publications of leading psychologists from right across the discipline. Each volume is edited by the author or a close colleague and includes a full bibliography of the work of the author and a brief biography. An introduction reviews the contribution of the work and sets it in its historical and intellectual context.

The books will be valuable adjuncts to many undergraduate courses in psychology, bringing the discipline alive through a deeper understanding of the people who are shaping it. Psychologists specialising in the areas covered by a particular author will find them to be of especial value.

DAVID CANTER
Series Editor
University of Liverpool

Introduction: Making Psychology Count

When the publisher of this *Benchmark* series suggested that I should also contribute a volume, though I was editing the series, I thought that such an act would stretch the limits of even my capacity for *chutzpah*. However, discussions with colleagues and students emphasised for me that by good fortune or necessity I have been able to explore a variety of areas of the applications of psychology that are not widely studied. Furthermore, quite unusually, the results of many of my studies have been acted on. It therefore seemed that there would be some value and general interest in having a selection of publications of this work organised, between one set of covers.

In considering what to include it occurred to me that particular types of academic theories and methods are better suited to practical application than others. So, for this volume I have selected published papers that illustrate those theories and methods that I have found to be of applied utility. However, academic papers in psychology, even in applied psychology, typically do not show the link between research and practice. I have therefore also included edited sections of unpublished reports, written for clients, which illustrate how my approach to the study of human experience in context has led to specific guidelines, which were used in non-academic settings.

In selecting the papers for this book, though, I have not tried to provide a recipe book for the applications of research. That would be an even more challenging task than the present one and could not have been completed by reference to existing writings alone. Instead I have brought together material that illustrates the attempts of my colleagues and myself to connect with questions that are being asked beyond the groves of academe. These connections may sometimes be loose, as in the general explorations of the meanings of places, or very tight, as when trying to locate where an unknown rapist may live. But all of the studies can be seen to have their origins in questions asked of psychologists by practitioners who are not necessarily psychologists themselves; architects, police officers, research engineers, homeopaths and so on.

The papers have been selected to provide a gamut of examples, with only a couple drawn from my studies in environmental psychology. (A more extensive selection of those are planned to appear in the Ethnoscapes series, published by Avebury, under the title *The Meanings of Place*.) The present range of papers, written for a mixture of audiences, also illustrate different stages in the development of connections with ongoing domains of enquiry. Some areas, like that concerned with human actions in fires and related emergencies, are now mature and the papers here are a summary of many years' research. Other areas, notably the study of complementary medicine, have hardly got started and so we are still struggling to define clearly what questions are to be answered.

As a consequence of this range of topics and the variety of stages in their development any neat chronology could be quite misleading. For example, the work on complementary medicine started at the same time as the work on criminal behaviour, yet the latter has already spawned a graduate programme, but the study of complementary medicine is still very small scale. Instead of a chronology, then, the papers have been arranged as a sort of development of themes and variations in different contexts. The opening section may be considered an overture that lays out the motifs that will be taken up and modified in later papers, but as the book progresses the variants become less obviously related to their origins and more exploratory in their form.

The opening chapter was written in response to a request from Irving Altman to write an intellectual biography for his volume of such biographies. It thus provides an introduction to many of the subsequent chapters. I find it noteworthy, though, that five years ago, when I completed that chapter, at least half of the papers in the present volume had not been written. That biography therefore outlines many of the issues which I have studied, attempting to bring out the recurring themes, but without noting the subsequent implications of those themes. In so doing it defines the context of my work in naturally occurring settings, but also shows that an understanding of the significance of any transactions with the environments of those settings relies on study of the social processes and purposes that energise those settings. In other words, the physical environment that was the focus of my early studies turned out to be most readily understood as a social process and a reflection of social processes, no mere set of stimuli to prod a passive organism into life.

The great attraction of studies that seek simple, direct causes of behaviour, or examine psychological processes in the carefully refined environment of university laboratories, is that relatively straightforward, tried and tested methods of study are available which are not sullied by the need to take account of the trials and tribulations of daily life. In order to carry out studies of relevance to non-psychologists who wish to act on the results, rather different sorts of methodologies are necessary.

An opportunity to encapsulate my views about the methodologies that are helpful in doing relevant psychology came when Graham Powell asked me to contribute to the discussions of the core of a curriculum for clinical psychology. In order to increase its generality I have edited that paper, for the second chapter of the present volume. (Readers will also find thorough exploration of many matters that are similar to those covered in that chapter in the book by Robson, 1993, bluntly called *Real World Research*.)

In preparing that chapter on what I called, a little facetiously, 'wholistic, organic' research I realised how far I had strayed from the conventions of hypothesis testing, dependent and independent variables and that whole panoply of procedures that owe so much to the biology of the 1920s and 1930s. In so doing, though, a rather different, but I would claim equally if not more scientific set of research strategies and tactics have evolved of particular utility in applied domains.

The third chapter summarises the general approach to research that I have drawn upon for much of the last fifteen years, the Facet approach. In essence this approach is systemic and structural. It takes as axiomatic that the naturally occurring phenomena that are of interest in an applied context have to be described, their components identified and the relationship between those components established. From these structural models explanations of complex causality may be derived, but often understanding is enriched enough to propose consequent actions without the need for detailed causal models.

But the structural models that emerge from the facet approach are always models of people acting on the world in relation to the sense they make of it. I would therefore not regard my research as psychological if it did not make some connection with the internal mental processes of the people whose actions were of interest. Those processes are also seen as reflecting structural systems that need to be described and analysed. Chapter four describes a procedure that my colleagues and I have found to be enormously robust and valuable for examining people's conceptual systems in a wide range of studies, the multiple sorting procedure.

The most extended development of the theories and methods reviewed in the first four chapters has been in the realms of environmental psychology. Chapter five summarises the formulation of psychological structures relevant to the experience of places. As such it is really an update of my 1977 book *The Psychology of Place*. It extends those earlier ideas by giving much more significance to purposes and roles and by proposing that the apparently antagonistic paradigms that distinguish different areas of environmental research from each other are actually different facets of the same processes of person-place transactions (throwing down the gauntlet for researchers to demonstrate the analogies between these facets).

The study of signposting (or as it is called in the US 'signage') is a particular, focused application of the theory of place that has led to some practical commissions, most notably for the University of Surrey. Chapter six reviews that work and shows how the often seemingly abstract concepts and demanding methods that are described in other publications do have direct relevance for such practical problems as what to signpost and where to put those signs.

The challenge of studying human behaviour in fires, reviewed in chapter seven, contrasts with the work on signposting, although there are some interesting overlaps. One important difference is that virtually all the conventional tools of psychological research are unusable or potentially very misleading if applied without modification to the study of behaviour in fires. Surveys, interviews, controlled experiments, even observational studies are extremely difficult to use for such rare and traumatic events. Instead official reports and statements taken by investigators have to be relied upon. Such accounts have to be treated with great caution but they can be used to explore the patterns of actions that occur and from that to develop an understanding of the processes that give shape to those actions. Perhaps the most surprising result to come out of this work is how the power of existing expectations and networks of influence continue to dominate human thoughts and actions even in the heat of a major disaster.

Validation of the conclusions drawn from the study of behaviour in fires has come from some unexpected sources, perhaps most notably from those rare occasions when cameras were present at fires and recorded precisely those patterns of actions that would have been predicted from the much more indirect records available to the researchers. Some costly, but reasonably realistic simulations, created for television programmes or for commercial developments have also supported the three stage model derived from witness statements.

There have been widespread practical implications of the study of behaviour in fires but in terms of the development of psychological research perhaps one of the most important consequences of that research was the development of a methodology that could be applied to material, such as police statements, that are sometimes the only accounts that are available of significant human activities and experiences. Curiously, the fire research did not draw heavily on the facet approach but it helped to open up a type of data that the facet approach is especially suited to analyse and therefore provided a range of possibilities that turned out to be very productive when considering violent crime.

Most studies of crime have been aimed at explaining why it occurs, or the processes that shape it, very few studies indeed have examined crimes with a view to how psychological research could help identify unknown offenders. Somewhat unexpectedly, then, when I began to consider an investigative psychology I found that questions were raised about identity and individual differentiation that I had not really considered in other areas of application. The study of rape in chapter eight illustrates how one gap in the psychological issues tackled in earlier studies may be filled.

Most of my earlier work was devoid of any recognition of differences between people except for the social psychological differences in their context related role and associated purposes. Yet any psychological theory that attempts to give emphasis to human agency ought to be able to distinguish between people in the form that agency takes. It was in the rather extreme context of studying violent sexual assaults against strangers that I first began to see the possibility for developing a faceted classification of individuals, derived from their actions, that could show us something of their characteristic ways of acting on the world.

The classification scheme developed from that study of rape (later refined and published with more explanation in *Criminal Shadows*, 1994) has subsequently been extended to a number of other types of crime. It is opening up a framework for considering the role that the victim is assigned by the offender. This assignment looks as if it may be a distinguishing characteristic of the offender that may tell us much about his life and ways of dealing with the world.

Such forays into new territory are never totally separate from earlier concerns. Chapter nine provides a bridge between the earlier study of the sense people make of their surroundings and the study of rapists. It does this by exploring the relationship between the residential base of an offender and the area in which he lives. The power of the results that emerge have practical importance for apprehending unknown offenders, but have longer term significance in linking the concerns of investigative psychologists to those of environmental criminologists.

The implications for police officers of knowing the area in which a criminal might live are reasonably obvious, but most research, even when it is apparently applicable, does not openly declare how it is to be acted upon. It took me some time to realise that my lengthy research reports were being virtually ignored by the people who had paid so much for them because I had not taken the trouble to convert the results into Action Plans. As an academic I had mistakenly believed that I was not expert enough in the details of my clients' organisation and activities to be able to interpret what they should do. What I had not appreciated was that, as ignorant as I was, if I could not give some indication of the practical implications of my research then no-one could. However, there are few models available of how such guidance should be given and so I had to develop for myself ways of making these recommendations.

By far the most successful set of recommendations were those made to British Steel to help improve the safety of their workforce. This research grew directly out of the studies of behaviour in fires but moved on beyond overt behaviour to consider the attitudinal precursors of dangerous actions. A number of companies have subsequently followed British Steel's lead with similar achievements. The major strategy document I prepared for them has, however, never been published. For the present volume I have reproduced part of it, in chapter ten, not so much for its content as for its structure. During surveys at British Steel subsequent to presenting them with this action plan, heavily thumbed copies of this report were found in the back pockets of hardened steel workers, clear indication that it made sense to them and provided direct guidance for their actions.

The safety research enabled me to understand some of the reasons why so little practical attention is paid to environmental psychology research. So little attempt has been made to interpret the design implications of its results. I was fortunate to be given a sort of second chance after my early architectural research to carry out some studies that were aimed at direct design guidance. Extracts from the reports that resulted are given as chapters eleven and twelve.

A final paper edited from a number of other papers deals with a new area of research, complementary medicine. This covers those forms of medical treatment that do not have their roots in conventional medical practice and, more importantly, still have no established basis in the biological or physical sciences. These forms of treatment are often called 'alternative', implying a whole other style of medicine, but the term 'complementary' is seen as more liberal in implying that these potions and manipulations are merely adding to our stock of medical understanding. Yet, these forms of therapy cover such a vast range of interventions, from faith healing to osteopathy, that it is unlikely that they will all some day find acceptable scientific explanations in the realms of physiology or chemistry.

When the lack of any firm scientific basis in the conventional medical sciences for any complementary therapies is compared with the huge uptake and strong support for them in the population at large - well over one in ten 'medical' consultations are with alternative practitioners (Fulder, 1984) - then it is a reasonable hypothesis that the processes involved will be revealed, at least in part, by psychological study. But this turns out to be yet another important area of psychological research that has been left virtually untouched.

This chapter explores some of the difficulties of carrying out psychological studies of complementary treatment. It draws upon approaches and methodologies that were found to be relevant in other areas of application to draft out an agenda for research in complementary medicine and to indicate some of the questions to be answered. As in most other areas of applied research the 'presenting complaint' that the psychologist is asked to cure is deceptively simple. In this area the question is most often phrased as 'Does it work?', apparently asking for direct evidence for whether any particular treatment alleviates any particular symptoms. But close analysis reveals that for most complementary therapies there is no simple way of knowing what 'it' is. The treatment varies from practitioner to practitioner, is part of different therapeutic regimes, different diagnostic strategies and so on. Furthermore there is no easy way of establishing what 'works' means. Therapeutic successes can take many different forms, over different time scales, and there is no guarantee that different estimates of success will intercorrelate. Research into complementary medicine thus epitomises all attempts to apply psychology. Many of the practices we wish to influence are as strongly believed in as acupuncture or colour therapy but with as little or less evidence to support them! Architectural design strategies, police investigation procedures, management approaches to safety improvement and even the sacred cows of research methodology itself, all have more parallels to the manipulations of chiropractors and faith healers than their practitioners would like to believe.

Questions of definition are endemic to applied research. If the problem to be solved has its roots in the conceptions of non-psychologists then there is a reasonable chance that help is needed precisely because of a lack of clarity of what exactly the problem is. Resolving these questions can thus never be solely a technical matter of, a problem of measurement. It requires the use, and often the development, of psychological concepts and theories. Real world research, then, is not the mere application of techniques - it is psychology in action.

References

Canter, D. (1977), *The Psychology of Place,* Architectural Press, London.

Canter, D. (1994), *Criminal Shadows,* HarperCollins, London.

Fulder, S. (1984), *The Handbook of Complementary Medicine*, Hodder and Stoughton, London.

Robson, P. (1993), *Real World Research,* Blackwell, Oxford.

Acknowledgements

Most of the chapters in this book have been the result of collaborative work with many different colleagues. Typically, but not always, they have been students turned colleagues. Where co-authorship is clear I have sought to recognise that in the authoring of the chapters, but that gives the mis-leading impression that the names linked to the paper were the only individuals who contributed to that work. Nothing could be further from the truth. Over the last 15 years or more I have always been fortunate to be part of an enthusiastic group of researchers who have willingly shared their ideas and confusions with me and have been ready to comment on mine. Wherever possible I have tried to acknowledge their contributions at the end of each chapter, but I know that I will not have remembered all the names of a generation of people I have had the delight of working with. I hope they will forgive me if they have not been mentioned where they clearly ought to have been (or have been mentioned where they ought not).

There are two people though whose names I do know do not feature as frequently in the following pages as they ought. Ian Donald and Margaret Wilson (very different people who will tolerate me mentioning them in the same breath) have worked with me over many years, far longer than their youthful looks would imply. I know that they have often helped behind the scenes with projects, smoothing the path for students and colleagues who needed detailed, patient help then and there rather than the hurried asides that have often been my stock in trade. I am pleased to have the opportunity of giving this public recognition of their many and varied, valuable contributions.

INTRODUCTORY REPRISE

1 In Search of Objectives: An Intellectual Autobiography

Early Days (1964 - 1968)

The Architectural Context (1967 - 1970)

The Japanese Experience (1969 - 1971)

Emerging Conceptualisations of Place (1970 - 1975)

The Theory of Place (1973 - 1977)

The Journal of Environmental Psychology

Fire Research (1975 - 1984)

Building Evaluations

Facet Theory

A Developing Theory of Environmental (social) Psychology

The Feasibility of Application

Broadening Horizons

Early days

Any account of a natural process must be a simplification. The written word can only sketch the variety that is integral to growth and change. This is true whether it is a garden that is being described or a human career. But for a career there is a further distortion. The sequence of activities that intertwine to make a period in a person's life when written as a history has far more shape and direction to it than it ever has at the time, when it is being experienced.

Certainly, for me, setting out to produce an intellectual history of myself, I am aware that the history I am about to describe, as confused as it may be presented, will appear far less haphazard than it felt at the time. The arbitrariness of the emerging story line may be gauged by considering the research contracts for which I am currently responsible. These range from studies of the experience of homeopathy to examination of the behaviour of serial murderers and rapists and include studies of safety in the steel industry and the design of psychogeriatric facilities. All these current studies have roots in my earlier work in environmental psychology, even though those roots may be confusingly entangled in a disordered undergrowth. The present chapter, therefore, is in part at least, a personal exploration through this undergrowth. It is to be hoped too that any such personal discoveries will also benefit you, the reader.

Office size

The profligate diversity of my current activities all started from an unambitious PhD on the effects of office size on worker performance. What the PhD had in common with nearly all my later work, and all my current research, is a determination to use field based methodologies to develop psychological theories about environmental actions and experience. A predilection for using multivariate statistics as an aid to the development of these theories was also present from my earliest studies.

Curiously, though, I had found my way into the study of office size from an undergraduate degree in psychology at Liverpool University. The psychology department at Liverpool was steeped in the experimental tradition of British psychology, but through the guidance of its head, L.S. Hearnshaw (cf. his history of psychology, 1987) and other members of staff, notably D.B. Bromley (as revealed clearly in his book on case study methodology, 1986) there was a productively eclectic debate about the nature of psychology and appropriate directions for its growth. I had wished to follow my personal interests in art to study empirical aesthetics for a doctorate, but the only opportunity available to me was to join the Pilkington Research Unit in Liverpool University's Department of Building Science. This multidisciplinary team was lead by an architect, Peter Manning who had written on architectural education and systematic design procedures. His objective was to develop appraisals of all aspects of a building's environment. He brought a geographer and a physicist on to the team as well as a psychologist, Brian Wells, who was studying the psychological implications of open plan offices (Manning, 1965). In effect, Brian Wells supervised my PhD, which was nonetheless registered in the Department of Psychology. Thus my existence with feet in more than one university discipline was presaged from my earliest days as a researcher.

The Pilkington Research Unit encouraged me to move away from a focus on aesthetics and look directly at the implications of office size for worker performance. At times I feel that my subsequent research has been a struggle to return to my original interest in how the physical phenomena, that are artistic productions, can have such a significant emotional impact. The office research convinced me that field research explores a different class of phenomena to those studied within the confines of the laboratory. So although there can be fruitful interactions between laboratory and field studies they should not be misconstrued as studying the same thing.

My own interests have always been in what people do in their daily lives rather than in what they can do if a psychologist asks them. I think that this perhaps also has some roots in my experiences in student drama when I was an undergraduate. It became very clear to me that people have a huge flexibility for generating actions under training and instruction. The laboratory experiment really examines the range and limits of this flexibility.

The study of offices taught me this because I had set off to examine directly the impact of office size on the performance of clerical workers. The results showed that people in their own small offices were performing better than people in their own large offices, but that this effect disappeared when people were tested in other people's large or small offices. This was difficult to understand as a direct effect of office size on performance. But when I stopped looking at the results as revealing the effects of the office size on the workforce and started looking at them as an indication of the type of person who would accept, or stay in, a job in an office of a particular size, they made much more sense.

Looking on the subjects of the research as actively part of their context, selecting where they would work (or at least being selected), rather than passively being influenced by the room, made the results quite comprehensible (Canter, 1968). Better, more able workers were more likely to be found in the preferable smaller offices.

Yet this active, context specific, interpretation could have been difficult to glean by an experimental study in which people were asked, say, to rate slides of offices. An experimental study though, could have been touched on the wider significance of design. Its meaning to the respondent as part of their lives, rather than as a 'stimulus'.

Room meaning

My origins in experimental, mechanical psychology did not fade away too rapidly. After the office research, I thought (as many researchers still do) that I could study the meanings, implied by the differences between the people found in different rooms, in a systematic, controlled way. So that when Roger Wools, an architect joined me to do a PhD under my supervision, together we continued with simple laboratory studies. We wanted to look at which aspects of buildings held particular meanings for people and used a classical, factorial experimental design in which types of furniture, ceiling angles and window sizes were modified in drawings and photographs of models (Canter and Wools, 1970).

These studies showed very clearly that people did associate sloping ceilings and easy chairs with room friendliness. But although a few doctoral students attempted to follow this idea directly, they found that it was not really possible to establish a vocabulary of forms, whereby certain physical constituents could be linked to particular responses. One reason was a methodological one. The experimental design quickly becomes very complicated and unmanageable if a large number of aspects of form are explored.

Yet the need to explore interactions between aspects of form mean that a series of simple experiments are likely to prove inconclusive. The other reason was more closely tied to the psychological processes revealed by later studies. The meaning of the forms is probably specific to context and culture as well as relating closely to respondents' reasons for judging meaning. In other words, just as an office worker's responses are a function of their position in the organisation so the ratings of pictures relates to the particular type of experimental/subject role that the rater is taking.

This continues to be a challenging area of environmental research, but it is noteworthy that most of the people who have started to explore this avenue have moved on to quite other research questions, usually more distinctly field based. Even those who set up major laboratories to create simulations of environments to study have changed the way these simulations have been used and distanced themselves from the mechanical stimulus/response examination inherent in looking at which architectural variables 'cause' which semantic differential responses.

It was about 15 years after I supervised Roger Wools' thesis that I was able to work with Linda Groat, who, having a design training initially, asked very similar questions to Roger but who was able to benefit from the work that had been going on in the interim. In supervising her MSc (published in part in Groat,1982, and PhD thesis (Groat, 1985) it was possible to work on non-experimental approaches to architectural meaning. Indeed the work helped to establish an approach very different from the semantic differential and the factorial design models that Roger Wools had worked with (Canter et al, 1985) and gave rise to work that was published in Progressive Architecture (Groat and Canter, 1987), a rare acceptance by the architectural profession of findings from an uncompromising piece of environmental psychology.

The architectural context

We are all conduits for the ideas and actions of others. So that one of the illusions my personal intellectual history could create is that my actions in some way can be clearly distinguished from the actions of others. This, of course, is far from the truth. Peter Manning and Brian Wells both set the agenda for my PhD work, and although I was supervising Roger Wools he taught me much of what an architect strives for in psychological research. The research that was my main activity at the time I was working with Roger was also shaped by the perspectives of others. This was the development of building evaluation procedures and their use in the evaluation of comprehensive schools.

My work on offices was conducted as part of the 'total environment' evaluations of the Pilkington Research Unit at the University of Liverpool. That unit had pioneered the use of building appraisals as a contribution to design. Following on directly from it, Tom Markus established at Strathclyde University, in Glasgow, the Building Performance Research Unit. It was as a member of that unit that I found myself supervising Roger Wools. In 1967 it did not seem as strange as it might to-day for a psychologist to join a school of architecture. The quest for interdisciplinarity was still strong and Tom Markus brought together a team with very varied backgrounds. One member of the team was Peter Whyman, and I had noted how many of the new school buildings we were studying had undergone changes to their fabric and use in the few years since they had been first occupied. He had called these modifications 'improvisations', and had noted for a number of school buildings that the changes varied from major alterations such as the addition of new classrooms to minor changes, such as the redesignation of room allocation, with sealing up doors or moving walls as more intermediary levels of change. We wondered what the consequence of all this improvisation was. A simple environmental effect hypothesis would suggest people were reacting to poor conditions. A more active hypothesis would suggest that they were positively making sense of their buildings.

It was possible to test these opposing hypotheses because we had building evaluations of the schools and we were able to derive scores for the amount of improvisation that had been carried out. The result was very clear. A significant positive correlation between degree of satisfaction and degree of improvisation. I took this to support the active hypothesis. Unfortunately, no-one has been able to replicate this study. It takes a dedicated architect and a large scale survey to make it possible, but if the result could be reproduced it would have enormous implications both for environmental psychology and for approaches to design.

Looking back, towards the end of my time at the School of Architecture at Strathclyde University my research activity had provided me with some basic principles that my subsequent research struggled to make sense of. These may be summarised as follows:

1. Environmental Psychology had to be carried out in existing environments. Too much is left unsaid and unstudied if it is moved into the abstractions of the laboratory.

2. The environment is not just a useful base for research with complex variables. It provides a context for examination that has to be studied in its own terms.

3. The environmental context cannot be approached devoid of any world view or metatheory. A perspective that searches for the role of human agency is more likely to be fruitful.

4. But human agency itself implies that people have some understanding of their environment and its significance. Examination of people's experience of environments must therefore include exploration of what is signified by them as well as how people evaluate their contribution to their own actions.

Psychology for architects

By 1970, I had become convinced that psychology had much to offer architecture, especially architectural education. As part of my job in the school of architecture I had set up a variety of courses, so that students studied various aspects of psychology in every one of their five years. Increasingly, I had found that as the architectural psychology literature had been developing, architecture students needed some background in psychology in order to understand the advancing field of research. But none of the existing psychology texts answered their needs. I therefore set about writing *Psychology for Architects* (Canter, 1974). I mention this because, although I now regard it as being very dated in its account of psychology, it has continued to sell a few copies each year for the almost 20 years it has been in print. It therefore must continue to answer some sort of need, serving to show that psychologists can be too ambitious in what they aspire to give to designers. This book contains virtually no 'environmental psychology', just an account of psychological ideas with architecturally relevant examples.

The Japanese experience

I suppose, in all honesty, I was rather bemused towards the end of the BPRU work as to what direction was appropriate for my research, although with hindsight the seeds of my current work can be seen in the principles and emphases of *Building Performance* (BPRU, 1972) and other publications from the late 1960s and very early 1970s. Certainly, if in those days, I'd been asked if 20 years later, I'd be working with the Salvation Army on hostel design, I'd have said I hope so. But behaviour in fires and emergencies would have been more difficult to foresee and the current involvement with the police on offender profiling would have seemed beyond the scope of our theories and methods.

Two nascent themes already present in the late 1960s, but the significance of which I had not recognised then, can now be seen as directly pertinent to later directions that my work took. One of these themes was the drift from an individualistic to a social psychological context for considering environmental experience and meaning. The other was the need for methods for constructing theories, and the associated analysis systems, that would help in finding patterns in data harvested from 'the field'.

So that when the opportunity arose of spending a year in Japan I was, now I think, already primed to be sensitive to a number of possibilities that later dominated my research. The undemanding fellowship to Japan was of particular significance in that it shocked me into seeing the power of culture on all aspects of behaviour, especially the way people deal with each other and make use of their surroundings. By living in such a different culture it became even more clear to me that the significance of a place was not some reflection of the external physical parameters that characterise that place, but derives from the cultural framework within which people experience a place. These are reflections of the way they see the world and think about it.

Ethnoscapes

Like so many influences of that kind it was a number of years before they really surfaced openly in my publications. It was certainly one of the reasons why I was so keen to include regional reviews in the *Journal of Environmental Psychology*, a development that was clearly seen to be of value because the distinguished editors of the *Handbook of Environmental Psychology* later emulated the practice.

Even more directly the recent series of books I have established with David Stea, *Ethnoscapes: Current Challenges in the Environmental Social Sciences*, (Canter et al, 1988) make explicit the need for environmental research to embrace cultural diversity. This is not just a matter of including cross-cultural comparisons on the research agenda, but of integrating studies in different national and sub-cultural contexts within the framework of research activities. One important example of this approach is allowing research questions, for example, to be defined by local, cultural imperatives, rather than by some reference to the current intellectual fashion in North America.

This series had truly transnational roots, evolving out of meetings I had with David Stea in Indonesia and Venezuela and Martin Krampen in Germany. All three of us were aware that there was a changing mood in environment and behaviour studies being reflected in conferences around the world. Yet the old vocabulary of 'environment', 'behaviour', 'architecture', 'psychology' and so on was masking these changes. We therefore deliberately set out to coin a new term that would reflect the new sensitivities of researchers in many countries and to launch a series of books that could act as a vehicle for publishing this research.
We defined *Ethnoscapes* as:

'scholarly and/or scientific explorations of the relations between people, their activities and the places they create and/or inhabit; historical, psychological or sociological studies of the experience of places, attitudes towards them, or the processes of shaping, managing or designing them'.

Canter et al (1988) page xi

To some extent the growth of our field beyond the North Atlantic basin has naturally lead to a greater cultural diversity in the studies being carried out, with I think enormous long-term benefits to the field. The experience of living in an unfamiliar large city also alerted me to environmental psychology issues at a planning scale, which I had never really explored before. In particular I was aware that Tokyo was such a complex city to find my way around that I became interested in how that was possible. Route finding appeared an inappropriately simple-minded, and practically extremely difficult way of exploring the basis of urban navigation. I therefore started asking people to estimate 'crow flight' distances (although in one study that I supervised in Japanese this got lost in the translation and the respondents ended up giving me shortest walking route distances).

I had begun some similar, tentative explorations in Glasgow before going to Japan, but I was surprised by how accurate people could be in a city as complex as Tokyo. On my return to Glasgow I worked with Stephen Tagg and others to explore this further (Canter and Tagg, 1975) and became aware of the power of dominant features such as the 'circle line' of Tokyo's underground system and the Thames and underground train network in London. Clearly people form some sort of composite conceptualisation of a city that they use to act on. This is more pragmatic and individualistic than Lynch's 'image' although it clearly relates to it.

Conceptualisations of place

On my return from Japan I had a unique opportunity to study the Royal Hospital for Sick Children at Yorkhill in Glasgow. I was able to spend a great deal of time over six months, with assistance from students and colleagues in examining the new building at the request of the *Architects' Journal*. The editor had requested the study because he felt that a children's hospital should not look like a multi-storey office block and he wanted a psychologist to confirm this.

The intensive study I was able to do (Canter, 1972) was close to an ethnographic account of the building and quite unconstrained by any limitations as to how it should be done. I interviewed whoever I could, carried out behavioural mapping studies and got people to complete repertory grids and questionnaires. Probably the most valuable aspect of the work for me was the training it gave me in what a building is and how it is shaped by many forces. I certainly learned more about the real world or architecture in that study than I had in the previous five years in a school of architecture.

The study helped me to develop a number of ideas for which I had been reaching. Three in particular are worth noting at this stage.

Firstly, how a building is created, the social, political and economic processes, as well as the design intentions, is very important in influencing what results. This will seem obvious to any practising architect, but it is a point that is still virtually ignored in the environmental psychology literature.

Secondly, by being able to explore in detail, with a number of people, their views and experience of the building, it became very clear what large differences there were between them in what they saw the building as being and, as a consequence, how they evaluated it. The major difference appeared to be a function of what they wanted to do in the building, what they were in the building for. This I summarised as 'Role differences in conceptualisations'.

The third idea to emerge more strongly from the Yorkhill study had been presaged a few years earlier in a paper entitled 'Should we treat building users as subjects or objects?' (Canter, 1969) in which I argued that, to get a full picture of the implications of a building, we psychologists needed to combine observation of buildings in use with explorations of the significance of those uses to the users. The intensive Yorkhill study, using a mixture of very different methods of data collection, also forced me to accept that the experience of the building was reflected in the combination of actions and conceptualisations.

By carrying out behaviourally oriented studies following Barker's ecological perspective, in combination with personal construct studies following Kelly, it was clear that both had something to offer and any future development must find ways of combining these two very different perspectives. Barker had ignored the interpretations of the people being studied and Kelly's intense clinical perspective seemed inappropriate for the essentially public and social qualities of a building. Taken together they could leaven each other's weaknesses.

The theory of place

Soon after the Yorkhill study I moved from Glasgow to Surrey, where I established the graduate programme in Environmental Psychology, the first entry of which was in 1972.

By the mid-1970s students on the MSc course were pressing for some coherent, theoretical account of where I stood in relation to environmental psychology.

The pressure from students for me to organise my ideas in a way they could grasp, together with the Japanese experience, the Yorkhill study and the distance estimation studies became the basis for an attempt at an outline of an environmental psychology theory, which became my book *The Psychology of Place* (Canter, 1977).

In writing the book it became clear to me there were two fundamental difficulties with which environmental psychology has to struggle. One is the empirical fact that the physical environment can only be shown to have any strong impact at the margins of physiological tolerance. Any other significance of variations in the environment can be readily swamped by social processes and motivation. Yet a great deal of effort and resource goes into shaping our surroundings. One task for environmental psychology is to resolve this paradox of why resources are spent on something that does not seem to produce direct measurable effects on behaviour or performance.

The second difficulty stems from the first. How can psychological involvement contribute to the improvement of our surroundings? If social processes and personal expectations are so much more important than any direct impact of the surroundings, how can we make recommendations about the form, shape or characteristics that those surroundings can take? Talking in general terms about design flexibility, individual variation and social constraints does not really give an architect anything very specific, or concrete, to go on.

In considering these issues they seemed to me to be so fundamentally difficult to resolve that the questions themselves must have some basic illogicality in them. It was out of these reflections that I began to think that taking the environment as an entity distinct from behaviour was the flaw. A unit of focus for research was needed that adjusted the emphasis. The idea of a place as that unit seemed worth exploring. This 'place' became a system that integrated physical and psychological aspects of experience. Research therefore needed to discover the structure of places. Contribution to design became participation in the shaping of these structured systems.

The *Journal of Environmental Psychology*

Writing *The Psychology of Place* and the associated reading and discussion with students had alerted me to the fact that there was a strange hiatus in publications in our field. The only major journal *Environment and Behaviour* deliberately had the important objectives of communicating across disciplines and making direct contact with policy issues. Furthermore, because so many researchers carrying out applied studies, in effect, published mostly for the non-specialist who might act on their results, there were very few opportunities for researchers to present to other researchers intensive, academic accounts of their work.

I believe it is essential that we debate with each other at the most demanding intellectual levels the theories, methods and results out of which our discipline is evolving. After all, it is such internal debate that gives science its strength. But by the late 1970's although there was a reasonably sized, scholarly community in environmental psychology, the pressures to communicate with those who fund our activities tended to mask the equally important communication amongst ourselves.

I therefore proposed to Academic Press that we launch a *Journal of Environmental Psychology*. A sabbatical in 1980, at U.C. Berkeley with Ken Craik enabled us to launch the Journal by 1981. In launching it, though, we were determined that it should not ossify the field but contribute to its evolution. We therefore have been eclectic in what we take Environmental Psychology to be, and have deliberately cherished many forms of communication besides the report of empirical studies. As the Journal enters its tenth year it is curious to ponder why we did not start it 20 years ago?

Fire research

My directly applicable research activities were also given a fillip in Japan when I came across a small study carried out by Masao Inui and his colleagues, which as far as I know was never published. They had interviewed people who had been in buildings on fire. I was struck by the possibility, that these Japanese building science researchers had discovered, of getting people to answer questions about a threatening and traumatic situation. As an undergraduate I had been introduced to the work of Quarantelli (1957) on disasters and learned from his studies that patterns could be found to seemingly bizarre and random behaviour, but I had not appreciated the potential significance of these studies for building design.

In the context of the Japanese Building Research Institute I began to see that the fire regulations governing the design of buildings were based upon assumptions of what people would do in a fire. Yet these assumptions were all derived from major enquiries of very unusual incidents. Very little systematic research had been done.

On my return from Japan I approached the British Fire Research Station and discovered that they, themselves, were developing an interest in human behaviour in fires and so started to support our own endeavours.

This research on fires has provided me with one of the strongest themes to my work over the last ten years. Yet often when I am reviewing my research I forget, initially, to mention it. I think that this is because it is unlike my other research activities in very many ways. It is field research in the most extreme form, in that the only really effective way to carry it out is to follow up incidents that have already happened.

What emerged as quite remarkable from studies of 20 or so incidents, including some very large scale ones, that my colleagues John Breaux and Jonathan Sime and I examined, was the consistency in the overall pattern of actions that occur in fatal building fires (Canter et al, 1980). In order to explain these consistencies it was necessary to ask what are the mechanisms that maintain human actions in these very unusual circumstances? The answer that I propose draws heavily on the idea of place rules and environmental roles (Canter, 1986).

The work also revealed that the early stages in any emergency are potentially very confused. The time it takes to make sense of the rapidly changing events can be what turns an emergency into a disaster. The importance of these findings was recognised by the Fire Research Station, especially because they acknowledged the widely experienced problem that alarm bells are not, usually, taken seriously. A series of studies were therefore commissioned on what we called Informative Fire Warning systems (Canter et al, 1987). Out of this work prototype computer based warning systems have been developed and installed, which have had a large impact on approaches to fire safety in buildings.

It is interesting that this work, with its roots in a fixed engineering view of provision for escape, should have matured into yet another context in which the interpretations that people make of their surroundings, and the opportunities or threats those people find, are paramount. The design developments therefore address directly ways of facilitating effective understanding and consequently more effective plans of action in threatening circumstances. This approach to design for active understanding and control, doubtless has applications to many other aspects of the environment.

Building evaluations

The studies of human behaviour in fires was one strand of the contract research that I was carrying out during the mid-1970's to the mid-1980's. In parallel, my earlier involvement in building evaluations was continuing through a series of studies of housing satisfaction and evaluations of acute wards in hospitals and prison buildings (Canter and Rees, 1982, Kenny and Canter, 1981 and Canter, 1986).

These were all studies that were defined in terms of the methodology most appropriate for them. I found this increasingly unsatisfying for three reasons. One, it was difficult to see any accumulation of approach or knowledge. Each study seemed to exist on its own, in a sort of theoretical limbo. Secondly, the questionnaire methodology sometimes seemed to so structure people's responses that many of the insights apparent in the pilot work were lost by the time that the main study was completed. Thirdly, the implications for action from the evaluation studies were not always apparent.

These three problems lead me to use the evaluation studies, increasingly, as a vehicle for developing new methodologies and a general theory of evaluation. The multiple sorting task (Canter et al, 1985) and the purposive evaluation model (Canter, 1983) were the result of that. Curiously, these rather academic developments opened the way to a much more direct, yet rather distinct, mode of involvement in the design process. These developments required a much more flexible methodology, more subtle in how it could be used to uncover interacting systems. Facet Theory increasingly provided the vehicle for this.

Facet Theory

One of the other coincidences about my stay in Tokyo was that during my time there Louis Guttman visited for a month. I had been interested in the unusualness of the approach to attitude scaling that is named after Guttman and wished to explore possible developments of it with him. To my amazement I discovered that the principles inherent in Guttman scaling had evolved into a major new approach to doing scientific research.

When I met Louis Guttman in Tokyo he had probably not met anyone for a few weeks who spoke fluent English and was prepared to listen at length to his thoughts. I was therefore given the privilege of a lengthy disquisition on his theory about how science should be carried out, which he called Facet Theory. It took me a number of years to digest and understand the implications of what I was told that morning (Canter, 1985). Indeed, looking through my diary and notes for my year in Japan I can find no reference to that meeting, although I remember it clearly and Louis Guttman also mentioned it when I met him again a few years later.

What attracted me to his approach was that it did away with arbitrary levels of acceptability for 'findings' and put the creation of a lucid account of the system being studied at the forefront of scientific activity. My methodological interests, and the search for some sort of theoretical perspective that would capture the essence of an ongoing system, had pushed me further and further away from the experimental models in which I had been schooled, but I did not feel comfortable with a retreat into a type of journalistic, purely qualitative, account rendering. As I worked within the facet framework it became clearer to me that it would provide a sound methodological framework for the type of theoretical accounts I was trying to give.

Facet Theory enables me to generate models that describe initially complex phenomena in quite simple, clearly structured ways. Probably the two most fruitful uses this has been put to so far is firstly in the development of the purposive model of evaluation (Canter, 1983) and secondly in the analysis of multiple sorting procedures (Canter et al, 1985). In both these cases a system of interrelationships is revealed upon which future elaboration is possible without having to start from scratch.

Purposive evaluation

One particular contribution of the facet approach was to enable us to start building a model of environmental evaluation that would evolve from one study to the next. The first large data set we had to work with was drawn from an evaluation of hospital wards (Kenny and Canter, 1983). Initial factor analysis gave us a very patchy picture of the reactions to these wards, but when we carried out non-metric multidimensional scaling, with a faceted framework for interpretation, it became clear that the provision of care at the bedside was the metaphorical as well as the literal focus of ward evaluation. Furthermore, a clear level of interaction facet, showing the different scales of the place, from the bedside to the whole ward, was also found in the results.

This provided a testable system of relationships that was consistent with studies of attitudes in other very diverse fields. We were therefore encouraged to look for evidence of this structure in other areas.The housing satisfaction data we had collected yielded a similar structure (Canter and Rees, 1982) and Donald (1985) found evidence for the same model in office evaluation. However, because each of these studies used different questionnaires they were able to identify quite different foci for the places being studied. Such foci were the central purposes of those places as conceptualised by the respondents.

Place goals

Other studies conducted since, as part of graduate dissertations, have found the model fruitful when applied to places as varied as neighbourhoods, city parks and training centres. This range of applications has enabled us to consider whether there are places in which there is a mixture of purposes that may be in conflict. Such an idea had already been presaged in the work Sandra Canter, a clinical psychologist, and I had done on therapeutic environments.This was summarised in the book we edited *Designing for Therapeutic Environments* (Canter and Canter, 1979). In the introduction to that book we outlined the various goals for therapeutic environments, ranging from custodial to personal enhancement.

More recent student research has shown that different groups within a hospital will have different goals and as a consequence will differ in the designs that they consider appropriate. Some of these goals may also be in conflict. Our research is therefore beginning to use the purposive model of place as a way of establishing the emphases in place goals and how conflicts between them may be resolved by approaches to management and design.

A developing theory of environmental (social) psychology

Once the *Psychology of Place* had been published it became clear in discussions with students that there was a productive, but fundamental, ambiguity in the model sketched out in the book. In striving to develop a research focus that bridged the environment/behaviour divide I had left the 'places' being studied in limbo. It was unclear as to where they were. They were not simply physical locations, but shaped by the actions and experiences of people, but it was also argued that they were not merely mental representations of environments. They clearly have physical components that are integral constituents. So, if they are not just a part of an individual's psyche and they are not simply a physical location, the question emerges as to what they actually are.

To provide any confident answer to this would be to imply that 2000 years of philosophical debate had been resolved, but some interesting possibilities can be gleaned from taking a social psychological perspective (or even a sociological one, depending where you draw the boundaries between the disciplines) on our experience of our surroundings. Within this framework, especially as elaborated by Moscovici (Farr and Moscovici, 1984), it is recognised that many phenomena experienced as having an independent existence, whether they are for example, 'health', 'psychoanalysis', or 'unemployment', all are socially constructed so that their existence is more than the agglomeration of attitudes, or perceptions held by individuals.

My development of this view has been spurred on by the shift in the audiences that have asked me to write for them or make presentations to them. In the 1970s and early 1980s I would guess that the majority of invitations came from architectural sources, but this has given way to far more invitations from psychologists, especially social psychologists. Of course, this shift could be entirely due to what I might be able to comment on with any skill, but I think it is more a reflection of changes in the disciplines themselves. As architects have moved away from a concern with their users to a concern with form and image, so social psychology has become more environmental.

I became most strongly aware of this when Michael Argyle asked me to talk at a seminar on 'situations', which eventually emerged as a book edited by Furnham (1986). Here, at last (I thought), were social psychologists examining the context in which behaviour occurred. Unfortunately, I soon found that their experimental traditions soon destroyed this interesting exploration, treating 'situations' as independent variables to be manipulated and thereby losing the significance of the context to which Barker had drawn attention 30 years earlier.

From this experience I began to look at how the notion of place could be linked to the situational debate in psychology. My paper *Putting Situations in their Place* (Canter, 1986) was a result of this exploration. The conclusion I came to was that the search for situations, and the associated attempt to classify them and systematise their impact was really at too fine a level of detail to reveal any general structures. The concept of place, which could house a number of characteristic situations, was more likely to prove fruitful. Part of the reason for this view was that a variety of studies of place use had produced consistent, eminently interpretable multi-variate structures. We had found, for example, that certain clusters of activities were found in certain rooms. Bedrooms, dining rooms, kitchens and so on can be characterised by what goes on within them, even though the words used to describe these rooms in different languages do not necessarily encapsulate their function as it does in English.

That people should sleep in bedrooms, eat in the room with a dining table in it, should not be too surprising. That there are a whole range of other activities and expectations that also coalesce around these actions is a clear example of the existence of 'place' systems. The questions that reveal these most strongly, though, deal with who is responsible for the furniture or activities in a room, and what is allowed or not allowed in a room. In other words the rules that structure that place.

This awareness, that the interpretable structures we were finding were reflections of place rules, took much longer to emerge than might be apparent from a reading of the Psychology of Place. What might be called the anthropological shift took some accepting.

From the writing of 'putting situations in their place' my attention had been drawn to the actions that are central to the definition of places, but in that paper I was uncomfortable with the apparently static qualities that this model had. Places appeared as givens, yet there are many reasons why they should not be expected to be static. Perhaps the most fundamental is the active nature of human agency in making sense of the environment and the implied coercive qualities of places that structure human experience. Furthermore our daily experience shows change and modification as characteristic of place experience, just as 'improvisation' was so prevalent in the Scottish comprehensive schools. I was therefore puzzled by the need to find a balance between the consistency of place use and experience, necessary for a social sharing, and the dynamic qualities that are part of life as it is lived.

The opportunity to chase these ideas further came from being asked to give a keynote address at the Berlin IAPS conference (Canter, 1985). For that presentation I explored the possibility that it is the interplay between the static quality of places and the dynamic, purposive nature of human action that provides the process out of which both places and actions evolve and change. I suppose this is a model of person/environment interaction shifted to a higher level of complexity. But in moving to this level I am finding that there is much more real possibility of the application of environmental psychology ideas without diluting their subtlety.

The feasibility of application

The fire research was the first set of studies in which I have been involved that led clearly and directly into some aspect of policy formulation. It had the consequence of my being invited to join two government established enquiries into major fires, one for the Bradford City Football ground fire, the other set up to examine the

Kings Cross Station Underground fire. These experiences have caused me to consider what it is that psychologists may contribute. Increasingly, I am coming to the conclusion that it is not some specific facts or findings, but ways of thinking about a problem. This parallels closely the often quoted remark by Kurt Lewin that 'there is nothing so applicable as a good theory'. But there is nothing so difficult to develop and then communicate as 'a good theory'.

This attempt to communicate a way of thinking about an environmental problem domain has been followed through in a book, written as a result of the work on the Football Ground fire, *Football in its Place* (Canter et al, 1989). The book quite deliberately is used as a vehicle to develop a popular account of the relevance of environmental psychology and had as its sub-title *An environmental psychology of football grounds*. As chance would have it the book was planned to be published in the late Spring of 1989, so it was published shortly after the Hillsborough football ground disaster in which 95 people were killed.

Embracing the media

The Hillsborough tragedy brought home to me how inevitable is the contact with journalism and the 'mass media' for an applied field like ours, if we really do have anything to contribute. For although, over the last few years my research activities have increasingly become of interest to Television, Radio and the newspapers it has been easy, from an academic position within a university, to dismiss all this interest as trivial or to see my involvement as merely significant as a form of advertising or self enhancement.

Yet, when our work may contribute towards the saving of lives, we have to consider seriously how our findings can be communicated to those many important audiences, who do not read academic journals or attend professional conferences. We should weigh carefully the implications of media coverage. After all, our research activities are unashamedly aimed at changing relevant actions and decisions.

The applied orientation of person/environment studies has never been in doubt. As Robert Sommer (1988), for instance, has been at pains to point out, the people outside of the academic community whom we wish not only to communicate with but also to influence, do not read articles in the *Journal of Environmental Psychology* or *Environment and Behaviour*. They read newspapers and watch television. In Great Britain they also listen to national radio.

The problem this raises is that once we do have something to say that is of general public interest there is a temptation to shape research in relation to the questions journalists ask. This is wrong. The role of the research community is to formulate ways of thinking about the world that are shaped by empirical scientific processes, not by populist or political ends. I have found the need to constantly examine what the objectives are for my research in the same way that my research has lead me to try and unravel the role of the objectives of others. This search for objectives is the central scientific quest. This is not an easy point to make to journalists who want immediate discoveries to quote for tomorrow's publication deadlines.

Broadening horizons

In writing a personal intellectual history it becomes apparent to me that recent and current research is too close to see in perspective. Its roots can be traced with some confidence, but in all honesty the long term directions in which it is leading are far from clear. Looking back, I did not think at the time and could not have guessed that my PhD research on offices would have taken me so far away from examining the effects of the environment on behaviour. At the time of the Yorkhill Hospital study I did not think that it would have lead me to put such store by role differences. Nor was I aware for at least another ten years that in depth evaluation of a building in use could provide the basis for a participative design procedure.

The studies of behaviour in fires were aimed at the building regulations, so I had not appreciated how they would lead me into considerations of the management of safety in industry (Powell and Canter, 1985). Although that organisational perspective on emergencies and accidents is completely consonant with the social perspective on building design, the emphasis that the safety research has given with regard to place rules was especially unexpected.

Given all the vagaries of previous research, in which personal discoveries have overtaken initial hypotheses, the directions in which current activities will lead are difficult to predict. Nonetheless, they all reflect a drift even further away from the experimental, perceptual tradition to a much more transactional,social psychological framework. Of particular delight is the discovery that the problems of environmental research are so difficult that if some handle can be got on them then this is likely to be of value in other field based studies as well.

As a direct result of the perspectives and methodologies I have mentioned I have become involved in looking at criminal behaviour, with a direct contribution to ongoing police investigations, in some cases even making a contribution to the apprehension of a person who has murdered a number of strangers (Canter, 1989). Thinking about how a criminal may structure his objectives, in relation to the understanding he has of the environment in which he operates, turns out to be a fruitful basis for the application of the facet approach.

Even less obviously related are the studies I have been conducting on the experience of alternative medicine, most notably homeopathy (Canter, 1987). Yet here again it is the understanding and direct experience of the user that is the focus, rather than the medical impact of any particular drug. Not unlike an effective environment, it is also emerging that alternative medicine seems to be attractive because of the control over their illness it gives patients. In other words how it helps them to be more successful in achieving their daily objectives.

It may seem a long way from studies of the effect of office size on worker performance to the experience of homoeopathic medicine, but the strands tying them together are unbroken. The search for how active, human agency interacts with the world of physical experiences is the problem of why art exists, that I was curious about as an undergraduate. Seeing these 20 years of research in this light makes me feel that, at last, I am probably ready to begin.

References

Barker, R.G. (1965), 'Explorations in Ecological Psychology', *American Psychologist,* Vol. 20, pp. 1-14.

BPRU (1972), *Building Performance,* Applied Science Publishers, London.

Bromley, D.B. (1986), *Case Study Method in Psychology and Related Disciplines,* Wiley, Chichester.

Canter, D. (1966), 'On Appraising Building Appraisals', *Architects' Journal,* 21st December, pp. 881-888.

Canter, D. (1968), 'Architecture Office Size: An Example of Psychological Research', *Architects' Journal,* pp. 881-888.

Canter, D. (1969), *Should We Treat Building Users As Subjects Or Objects?*

Canter. D. (ed.), RJBA Publications, London, 'Need for A Theory of Function in Architecture', *Architectural Psychology,* pp. 11-17.

Canter, D. (1972), 'A Psychological Analysis of The Royal Hospital for Sick Children: Yorkhill Glasgow', *Architects Journal* 6th September.

Canter, D. (1970), *Journal,* 4th February, pp. 299-302.

Canter, D. (1974), *Psychology for Architects,* Applied Science, London, pp. 11-17.

Canter, D. (1977), *Psychology of Place,* Architectural Press, London.

Canter, D. (1983), 'The Purposive Evaluation of Places: A Facet Approach', *Environment and Behaviour,* Vol. 15, No.6, Sage Publications, pp. 659-698.

Canter, D. (1985), *Facet Theory,* Springer-Verlag, New York.

Canter, D. (1986), 'Putting Situations in their Place: Foundations for a Bridge between Social and Environmental Psychology' in Furnham, A. (ed.), *Social Behaviour in Context,* Allyn and Bacon, London.

Canter, D. (1987), 'Research Agenda for Therapy Studies that Consider the Whole Patient', *Complementary Medicine Research,* pp. 101-113.

Canter, D. (1988), 'Action and Place: An Existential Dialectic' in Canter, D. et al (eds), *Ethnoscapes: Current Challenges in the Environmental Social Sciences Volume 1 - Environmental Perspectives,* Avebury, Aldershot, pp. 1-17.

Canter, D. (1989), 'Offender Profiling', *The Psychologist,* January, pp. 12-16.

Canter, D., Breaux, J. & Sime, J. (1980), Environmental Perspectives, *The Psychologist,* pp. 12-16.

Canter, D. (1980), 'Fires and Human Behaviour - An Introduction' in D.Canter (ed.) *Fires and Human Behaviour,* Chapter 1, pp. 1-12, Wiley, Chichester.

Canter, D., Brown, J. & Groat, L. (1985), 'A Multiple Sorting Procedure for Studying Conceptual Systems' in *The Research Interview: Uses and Approaches,* Academic Press, London.

Canter, M., Brown, J. & Brenner, M. (1985) (eds), *The Research Interview: Uses and Approaches*, Academic Press, London.

Canter, D. & Canter, S. (1979) (eds), *Designing for Therapeutic Environments: A Review of Research*, Wiley, Chichester.

Canter, D., Comber, M. & Uzzell, D. (1989), *Football in its Place*: *An Environmental Psychology of Football Grounds*, Routledge, London.

Canter, D., Dramper, M. & Stead, D. (1988) (eds), *Ethnoscapes: Current Challenges in the Environmental Social Sciences, Vol. 1 - Environmental Perspectives*.

Canter, D., Krampen, M. & Stea, D. (1988) (eds), *Ethnoscapes: Current Challenges in the Environmental Social Sciences, Vol. 3 - New Directions in Environmental Participation*, pp. 144-152, Avebury, Aldershot.

Canter, D., Powell, J. & Booker, K. (1987), *Fire Warning Systems*.

Canter, D. & Rees, K. (1982), 'A multivariate model of housing satisfaction' *International Review of Applied Psychology*, Vol. 31, pp. 145-151.

Canter, D. & Stringer, P. (1975), *Environmental Interaction*, International Universities Press, New York.

Canter, D. & Tagg, S. (1975), 'Distance Estimation in Cities' in *Environment and Behaviour*, Vol. 7, March.

Canter, D. & Wools, R. (1970), A Technique for the Subjective Appraisal of Buildings, *Building Science*, Vol. 5, pp. 187-198.

Donald, I. (1985), The Cylindrex of Place Evaluation in Canter, D. (ed.), *Facet,* Springer-Verlag, New York.

Farr, R.M. & Moscovici, (1984) (eds), *Social Representations*, Cambridge University Press, Cambridge.

Furnham, A. (1986) (ed.), *Social Behaviour in Context,* Allyn and Bacon, Boston.

Groat, L. (1982), Meaning in Post-Modern Architecture: An Examination Using the Multiple Sorting Task, pp. 3-23.

Groat, L. (1985), *Psychological Aspects of Contextual Compatibility in Architecture: A Study of Environmental Meaning*, PhD Dissertation, University of Surrey, England.

Groat, L. & Canter, D. (1979), 'Does Post-Modernism Communicate?', *Progressive Architecture*, Vol. 12, pp. 84-87.

Hearnshaw, L.S. (1987), *The Shaping of Modern Psychology*, Routledge, London.

Kelly, G.A. (1955), *The Psychology of Personal Constructs,* Norton, New York.

Kenny, C. & Canter, D. (1981), A Facet Structure for Nurses' Evaluations of Ward Designs, *Journal of Occupational Psychology*, Vol. 54, pp. 93-108.

Manning, P. (1965) (ed.), *Office Design: A Study of Environment*, Department of Building Science, Liverpool.

Omotayo, F.B. (1988), *A Cross-Cultural Comparison of Space Use in the Hausa, Ibo and Yoruba Families of Nigeria*, PhD Thesis, University of Surrey, England.

Peled, A. & Ayalon, O. (1988), The Role of the Spatial Organisation in Family Therapy: Case Study, *Journal of Environmental Psychology*, pp. 87-107.

Powell, J. & Canter, D. (1985), 'Quantifying the Human Contribution to Losses in the Chemical Industry', *Journal of Environmental Psychology*, Vol. 5, pp. 37-53.

Sommer, R. (1988), The Behaviour of Panic Participants, *Sociology and Social Research*, Vol. 41, pp. 187-194.

2 The Wholistic, Organic Researcher: Central Issues in Clinical Research Methodology

The problem of 'methods'

A challenging look at research methodology is necessary because of the confusion of terminology that has come about by the accretion over the last century of research methods and the vocabulary for describing them.

Probably the most ambiguous term of all is the term 'methods' itself. Many different meanings of this word can be found within the literature. Indeed, one text book that has a title 'Research Methods in Psychology' may be totally different in its coverage from another book. The term 'methods' can be used to describe statistical manipulations. By contrast it can be seen as an exploration of the issues of research planning and design. Yet another usage is to describe the instruments that are utilised to collect the actual data that is at the heart of the study. There are yet other usages that put the term 'method' into a more ideological framework by contrasting phenomenological methods, for example, with positivist ones. Many other different usages can be found in the literature, but even these few serve to illustrate that there is no clear framework as to what really is the appropriate focus to any discussion of research procedures.

Research questions

At the heart of research is the answering of questions. This rather looser form seems to me to be fruitful, instead of 'the testing of hypotheses', because the hypothetico-deductive approach assumes a very particular framework for scientific investigations. In a situation in which the research study may be aimed at formulating policy guidelines, or for example disentangling the particular constituents of a therapeutic activity or clarifying the most useful ways of combatting memory deficits, there will usually not be any formal hypotheses in the conventional scientific sense. What hypotheses was Darwin setting out to test when he went on his voyage on 'The Beagle'? If he was just exploring the varieties of

Note: This chapter is based on many years' experience of teaching post-graduate students research methodology. My notes for that teaching were written into a chapter for Clinical Psychologists. For this volume I have edited that chapter to bring it back to its general perspective on research of relevance to all areas where psychology is applied.

animals around a loosely formulated notion of speciation is it right to dismiss his work as 'unscientific'?

If research is about answering questions, methodologies need to be considered in terms of how appropriate they are for answering a particular question. To understand the appropriateness of a methodology, it is useful to recognise the many different types of research questions that can be asked.

Five broad types of research questions can be distinguished.

Causal explanations

These are research questions of the classical form in which distinct influences on particular outcomes are to be identified. A lot of therapeutic research is formulated in these terms, on the lines of 'does a particular therapy really produce a change in the patient'. Psychophysiological studies are also typically of this form, whereby the effects are examined of particular mechanisms on behaviour. However, such formulations often come unstuck when the complexity of the ongoing situation is explored, for example the ways in which alcohol interacts with cultural expectations to produce its effects. As a consequence, the strongest causal questions would appear to come from highly controlled, laboratory based, biologically oriented studies in which the impact of particular organic or pharmacological states are being examined.

Probative influences

The term probative is stolen from the legal framework because this describes studies in which the specific causal mechanisms are not open to study but some indication of the directions of influence can be disentangled. This is the type of research question that is typically studied using 'field experiments'. Changes are introduced into some component of an ongoing system and their effects monitored. This is a model that is frequently upheld as appropriate for studying the effects of therapy, environmental design, or changes in training and other organisational practices. However, the amount of control that it is necessary to introduce into a field situation - in order to get clear indications of the broad influences of a particular type of intervention - are usually so demanding that they are likely to distort the organisations to the extent that the results may not be generalisable. As a consequence practical constraints tend to make extensive field experiments very rare and those that are done tend to be small scale or superficial, with a few noteworthy exceptions.

Relational studies

Here we have questions about the patterns of relationships between variables. Surveys of the relationship between IQ and school achievements, stimulus complexity and preference, or what sorts of patients seem to be benefiting from what sorts of treatment would fall into this category. Curiously this framework for research is often despised by people with an experimental frame of mind who are looking for direct causal links, yet it is by far the most common approach especially for applied research. I think the reason for its common use is that not only is it essentially cost effective, but the strategy can also establish relationships on which predictions can be based. Predicting which group of patients are most likely to benefit from what sort of treatment or what level of IQ is appropriate for university education, is often of more immediate utility than knowing why such effects may actually be occurring.

Descriptive studies

When I was taught research methods as an undergraduate, the word description was used as a term of insult commonly associated with the term 'merely'. However, anybody who has studied anthropology, the law or many areas of management science, or of course medicine and large areas of biology, will realise that giving a clear and coherent description is challenging and often crucial. To know exactly what is being delivered in a particular service, the sorts of people who are making use of it and what they are actually experiencing may be the key to understanding how that service can be improved or what its general values are. Just as a full description of a habitat can help us to understand how animals may survive within it, or the identification of memorising strategies can help in establishing how people cope with reduced memory capability.

Consultancy (action research)

The first four questions are truly research questions in the sense that they can be answered independently of any detailed understanding of what is likely to be done with the results. However, there are many important research challenges in which the research is being conducted precisely to change the organisation, or individuals on whom the studies are being conducted. I prefer to call this 'consultancy' because it implies a very different mode of relationship to the research activity than 'action research', which still implies the researcher has some distance from the organisation. The crucial point about consultancy is that it must be carried out in a way that enables the organisation to act on the results of the work. It therefore needs to take into account the way in which the organisation does indeed act. Consultancy is always a part of the decision process and therefore has a quite different relationship to the topics of study from the other types of research activity. In effect, the central question of consultancy is 'how can we enable the people who we are advising to change for the better?'

My proposal is that all five types of research question imply different types of research framework, which might be called research strategies. I use the term strategy very deliberately taking it from the military metaphor in which the strategy is the overall framework for describing how the war is to be conducted. It covers the overall planning and logistics of the research activities, embracing what is often thought of as research design, but really going beyond that to cover all the related issues of how the research is to be approached. This will take account of the major limitations on research which are carefully hidden from undergraduates. The published literature always describes research as if it happens in an unconstrained universe. The limits of time, money, the particular skills and resources available, that are all necessary to conduct the research are never ever indicated. The whole operation is described as if it were still being carried out by nineteenth century gentlemen of private means who could do whatever was necessary to achieve their particular objective. However, an appropriate research strategy would take very real account of the cost effectiveness of different approaches to answering the research questions as well, of course, as establishing what is the appropriate set of research design procedures for answering the particular question.

Another important point about recognising that each type of research question has its own appropriate form of strategy is that it also recognises that there is not one pure form of research design - the laboratory, controlled experiment - compared with which all other research designs are more primitive and less effective. The general discussion of good and bad research that puts so much emphasis on control groups and experimental groups, dependent and independent variables, tests of the null hypothesis and so on, are, within the framework I am outlining, only one type of research design and a very limited one, really only appropriate to experimental studies of causality.

Once it is accepted that there are other questions that it is legitimate to answer, beyond focused questions about cause and effect, then it can be seen that each research strategy has its own rules and procedures. There are good and bad ways of doing descriptive case studies, or surveys of relationships, or field experiments, just as there are good and bad ways of doing controlled, laboratory based experiments. What researchers need to understand are the different criteria that are relevant for evaluating each of the different strategies. Not the narrow view that all studies are some form of experimental test.

This broadening of the consideration of the criteria for evaluating research also broadens the range of psychological theories that can be developed. The experimental study of causality really assumes more or less mechanical models of cause and effect. However, if it is accepted that we are often trying to build up an account of interrelated systems of influence, then a research strategy that allows us to identify what the major constituents of the system are, is going to be more productive. The experiment has the distinct limitations of only testing influences at a few levels and usually only on a few output, dependent variables. Furthermore, we often want to know how a system operates in its natural setting. It is, therefore, necessary to be sure that the research procedure does take account of naturally occurring psychological and social processes.

As well as the different criteria, that can be brought into to play for evaluating different research strategies, there is also a possibility for identifying more clearly the skills that are needed for answering different research questions. The most important and obvious example of this is that the skills associated with consultancy, in which some change is desired in an organisation, clearly relate to persuasion and communication, not solely to computer literacy or ability with arcane statistics. A commanding presence may be the difference between a piece of consultancy having some influence on an organisation and that same advice falling on stony ground.

All five types of research question interrelate and therefore all the different strategies need to be drawn upon in different circumstances. There may even be an evolution of stages in the explanatory process that is relevant to formulating large research programmes. But until these issues are carefully and fully debated within the framework of applied psychology methodology, we will continue to have a lot of neat experiments published in our journals by a few academic researchers, but which have very little impact on policy and practice. By contrast there will continue to be a whole range of rather poorly conducted pieces of action research that are taken notice of by health authorities, government departments, commercial organisations and newspapers, but which embarrass academic psychologists . 'We didn't have much time and just did what we could' is usually taken as an excuse or defence for work that the psychologists believe is not as neat and tidy as the paradigm models of controlled experiment that they think they must be aiming for. My argument is that these limitations should always be understood within the research framework and that studies should be conducted in full knowledge of what is the most effective way of answering the question *within* the resources available.

Research tactics

Just as the *strategies* for research imply a formulation of the types of psychological theory that are appropriate to develop, so research *tactics* carry implications for the models of human beings that it is assumed legitimate to formulate.

Putting it at its most extreme, studies that use instruments that observe the individual at a distance, or test some performance that the person can produce under specific conditions, are assuming models of humanity that has people as essentially mechanical objects that can be understood from 'the outside'. By contrast, any procedure that involves a direct questioning and interaction with a respondent, not only assumes that the individual has a special perspective on his or her own experiences but also that individual is able to understand the framework that the researcher is bringing to the situation. The respondent, furthermore, must understand the questions well enough to be able to answer appropriately. It therefore follows that at the one extreme we are likely to have theories of behaviour that are biological in orientation and look for processes that are beyond the individual's control or awareness, whereas at the other extreme, we have theories that give pride of place to the interpretation and understanding of the person who participates in the research. There are, of course, gradations in between these two extremes, but they all carry with them implicit assumptions about the nature of people. Research tactics are no more neutral about the types of theories to which they pay homage than are research strategies.

It therefore is no surprise to find that the research strategies which are essentially mechanical and simply causal in the types of questions they attempt to answer, also tend to draw upon research tactics that equally look for direct and relatively straightforward causal mechanisms within the individual. By contrast the strategies that look for the complex interrelationships between existing systems of experience are likely to use tactics that put the subject of research into the position of expert on the process being studied. Of course, there are many hybrid procedures and there are many attempts to break through these different barriers, but I believe that it is only from an understanding of the theoretical assumptions that are implicit within strategies and tactics that really innovatory procedures and theories will be able to evolve.

Appropriate use of resources

In order to understand more fully the ways in which research strategies and tactics can be harnessed to the resolution of the many problems faced by psychologists doing research, it is useful to consider more directly some of the constraints and possibilities that are prevalent in most areas of psychological research.

I think it is productive to characterise a fruitful approach here as one of 'organic data collection'. What I have in mind here is the notion of understanding fully the context within which the data is being collected and drawing upon that context in a clear-sighted way, rather than planning research in relation to pure and abstract notions of elegant design.

There are many issues in developing organic research projects, but three points are illustrative of the general approach that I believe is worth considering.

The first is the most obvious organic notion of developing research in a way that makes it natural to its context. Setting up special procedures that can only be operational under particular experimental conditions with specialist resources needs to be very carefully evaluated. In contrast, taking advantage of circumstances that already exist will often have greater potential. This means for example that physiological studies using extensive equipment may be more appropriate within hospitals that have such equipment regularly in use, but is less appropriate when trying to study people in their own homes or to take another example, getting coal miners to complete a lengthy questionnaire at work may prove far more artificial than asking civil servants in a tax office who are used to filling in forms.

A second aspect of the 'organic' approach is to think of the possibilities of recycling existing materials; reusing old data. Most organisations are now buried under large amounts of records and other summaries of activities and experiences. Furthermore, there exists large amounts of data that has never been either fully analysed or reanalysed in the light of new understandings of psychological processes, and ways of studying those processes. It might even be suggested that there ought to be a moratorium on all new data collection until we have really made proper use of all the data we have already collected! But even the possibility of this as an approach to research has implications for research strategies and tactics, because it pushes the research in the direction of description and understanding and away from the study of precise causal mechanisms. One spin off of this way of thinking about research data is that the records that are kept can be developed in a more systematic way so that they are of more utility to the organisation as well as being of value to the research process itself.

A final aspect of organic research, that may seem a little paradoxical, is the proposal to avoid 'operational' definitions of what is being studied. By defining what is being studied in terms of the procedures that are used to study the phenomena we are quite directly separating the issues being studied from their context. Issues being studied need to be defined in terms that relate to the context and then procedures found which are valid and reliable ways of exploring the issues that have been identified as being relevant. Perhaps the classic example here is the study of intelligence. As long as it was defined in relation to abstract measurements from IQ tests theoretical progress was slow and application dogged with confusion. It was only by looking at what the intellectual demands were on people in a variety of situations that the study of intelligence took a leap forward.

This point, of putting emphasis on the definition of what is being studied, is a plea for a much closer link between the theoretical formulations of research and the ways in which measurements are being made. This emphasis on the closer link between the theoretical formulations and the procedures also, perhaps again paradoxically, makes it much more possible for the research to have an impact. An understanding of the ways in which the conceptualisation of the research problems are the basis for the effectiveness and utility of the research, can best be gleaned by considering the research process and how it integrates with decision making. It is to this linking of research and action that I shall now turn.

Linking research to action

If we think of research as having three broad stages, namely

1.   the formulation of a research problem
2.   the collecting of data and information to help answer that problem
3.   the results and conclusions of research

then it can be seen that the most usual model for the application of research findings is one in which the results and conclusions are fed to which ever group may be interested in those results. However, if it is recognised that decision makers who must act on research also go through a sequential process then a more integrated link becomes feasible.

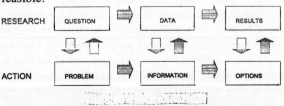

Integrating research and action

Decision makers must also identify the task that they have to deal with. They must further collect appropriate information to help deal with that task. Finally, they must make decisions about the most appropriate ways of dealing with the task given the information that they have.

In the simple model, then, the conclusions are fed in to the decision choice phase, or may possibly be part of the information that is drawn upon. So, for example, knowing that certain classes of phobic patients may benefit from a typical type of intervention may be a research conclusion that is drawn upon when service provisions are being considered.

However, psychological research shows us over and over again that people absorb into their conceptual systems those constructs that connect with their existing framework of understanding. It therefore follows that the research questions themselves should be formulated in ways that connect directly with the salient conceptualisations with which the decision makers have to deal. This will then allow a much closer integration between the research and the action.

Similarly, the data that researchers collect may or may not have links to the sorts of information that the decision makers feel appropriate. For example, where the researcher may wish to have very precise measurements about the detailed impact on behaviour of particular forms of treatment, the policy makers may only be interested in the number of people who make use of that treatment and how much it costs to deliver.

One consequence of these considerations is that the formulations of research questions and their mode of test needs to be open to a variety of presentations and to allow different emphases to be drawn out for different purposes.

In relation to the strategies and tactics discussed above the implications here are that descriptive material that provides a coherent account of what is happening in a situation may often have more utility then a more precisely controlled experimental study. Furthermore, the possibility of illustrating the conclusions with graphic examples cannot be underestimated. Policy makers who need to take information from a variety of disciplines, who will not be specialists in any one particular discipline, will nonetheless make judgements based on their own understanding of the material presented to them. Graphic examples will often enable them to understand the implications of any conclusions, even though those examples cannot be taken as strong empirical evidence within the strict framework of scientific hypothesis testing.

It is worth emphasising that it has been well established, in the realms of expert testimony in the courts, that visual summaries of research findings often carry far more weight with non expert audiences than do numerical, and especially statistical, summaries of those results. As psychologists we all therefore need to become more adept at representing our ideas visually if we are to get our message across.

The increasingly available family of multi-dimensional scaling techniques may offer a new range of ways of summarising research material that allows decision makers to conceptualise the results in a form that is salient to them, while still staying close to the original empirical results. These visual summaries of relationships within sets of data, though, often demand a broader range of explanatory systems than the cause and effect explanations that might be typical of studies modelled on laboratory experiments.

Problem definition

In order to embrace effective research activities that will connect with policy making, it is helpful to consider more closely the three constituents of effective integration. The first is the issue of how the research question should be defined.

The traditional approach is to define problems solely in terms of the existing literature and the hypotheses that might be derived from it. But in order to contribute to the activities of policy making it is fruitful to look at other issues that may limit and give shape to the definition of any research question.

1. Where can solutions be found?
   Most organisations have only the possibilities of acting in a relatively small solution space. It is, therefore, necessary to have some idea of the range of solutions to problems that may be feasible in order to draw on those to shape the questions that may be asked.
2. Are there other ways of considering the problems?
   Often the problems posed by an organisation or by the research literature can be regarded in many different ways. A flexibility of attitude towards what is the real nature of the problem can therefore be very productive. For example, rather than looking at the successes of different therapies it may be more feasible to look at the mechanisms by which patients get assigned to different therapists. It may not be possible to change therapists' approaches to the therapy that they provide but it may be possible to assign patients to different therapists.
3. What are the limits within which the solution(s) must be established?
   This deals with the question of whether there are implicit restraints on costs or time scales that are crucial to solving the problem.
4. Acceptable forms of explanation?
   Some forms of explanation of the phenomena under study may be acceptable within an organisation, for example, those relating to the physical layout or the use of resources, but others may be quite unacceptable, even if scientifically more valid, such as incompetent management or inappropriate training. However, changes in layout or location may require new management procedures that are acceptable and bring in a discussion on training.

There is a central difficulty that comes out of these considerations. Significant psychological research usually implies organisational change. It implies comments on *how* things are done not on *what* is done. But organisations typically prefer options that require them to continue doing things the way they always have. This means that advocacy and indeed rhetoric are important skills in summarising research and its strengths.

Appropriate information

One of the key ways in which the results of research can be advocated is around the information that is presented to support the work. I have already mentioned the value of strong visual summaries and powerful images and have indicated the implication this has for doing at least some qualitative research that will generate good, memorable examples. But there are other aspects of the way the information is presented that are worth consideration.

One of the strong components of the information is the fact that it can be presented as relating to very special preferably unique, 'expertise'. Decision makers will often regard themselves as capable and well informed. They need to be convinced that some extra and additional forms of 'expertness' are being presented to them if they are to take note of it.

However, this expertness cannot be seen as too esoteric or unavailable to direct understanding, otherwise not only is it psychologically threatening to many people who must act on the information, but there will often be some real doubt as to its veracity. The material must therefore be presented as having some degree of face validity. As psychologists know, what seems obvious to a recipient of a piece of information depends to a large extent on the context within which that information is presented. Research findings should, therefore, make a connection with what is seen to be obvious so that its impact can be absorbed.

However, this obviousness should push understanding beyond 'what we know already'. Often there will be a few key findings and a few key illustrations that are a little surprising, although quite understandable in the context presented. It is this balance that enables the policy maker to feel that the research really has moved forward but not too far to be threatening.

Evaluating outcome

The other set of considerations that need to be part of the whole research programme are those relating to the way in which the research itself will be evaluated and especially the results of the research. The criteria do also relate directly to the evaluation of the outcome of any other process such as the delivery of a particular service or a particular type of treatment.

Salience of criteria

As I have mentioned the ways of thinking about the problem, and the room for manoeuvre that is considered to be available, will be brought to bear when looking at the criteria that have been used to reach any conclusions. These criteria therefore have to be carefully evaluated to ensure that they are appropriately salient to the people who will make the decisions. Average life expectancy of patients who have gone through major surgery is often not considered nearly so important, for example, as the proportion of them who live for one or two years after the operation. The number of people who complete a course of training may be more important than the grade they obtain on completion.

Risks of failure

Another important way of evaluating the conclusions of research is to consider what the risks would be that are associated with any failures that result from implementing the research. Most people are cautious in their actions especially if they are in senior civil service positions. The main things that they want to avoid is failure. Successes carry less weight in terms of their future progress through the administrative hierarchy than having particular failures on their career reviews. This essential conservatism is therefore brought to play when evaluating whether major new systems should be implemented.

Need for 'structural' change

Once again it is worth pointing out that organisations, like people, are very reluctant to make major changes in their internal structures, how they think about things or how they do things. Proposals that lead to suggestions that they should do more or less of the same are therefore much easier for them to work with than radical recommendations of entirely new systems of working.

Inherent difficulties of psychological research

Some difficulties of doing psychological research go beyond the practical demands of research within organisations, especially when that research studies the activities and experiences of individuals. There are other problems that are inherent to the whole process of applying psychology. Four of these are worth considering in any research activity.

Individuals count

One of the central demands of much person-oriented psychological activity is to form a judgement about what is appropriate for a particular individual. Being able to demonstrate that there are broad differences on average between different groups of individuals is less valuable than knowing what to do about a specific person. Research procedures, therefore, need to be able to give findings precise enough that they can be linked to a particular individual. Often this means having a strong theoretical formulation that can be applied to the particular person, rather than group averages. It is often difficult to know how to relate the particular person that is the centre of the concern in therapy, selection, training or management to the 'normative' group on which the average was calculated.

Group heterogeneity

Many experimental studies assume that the variability in the sample is not of such a large scale that it will totally mask important differences between sub-groups. However, the ways in which people may differ from each other are legion. Therefore research has to define very carefully the sample to which the results may apply. Otherwise major variation in a particular population may unknowingly negate the relevance to other samples of the effects found in a particular study.

Practical constraints

As I have mentioned, in order for research to be possible it has to be carried out within the resources of time, skills and costs that are available to the researcher. It is, therefore, very critical to the success of a study that it is formulated within the possible practical constraints that exist. This will include access to appropriate data and appropriate contexts for doing research, as well as other limitations that come from the views of ethical committees and the particular points in time at which certain sorts of research is possible. It is one of the great practical problems of postgraduate courses that most studies are planned to be conducted during the summer months. This is precisely the time when many services are not fully operational or when there are limited levels of staffing because of people being away on holiday. As a consequence there are often not people available to help the research forward.

Qualitative concerns

For many real world problems there is not usually a concern with how *much* of a problem exists but rather *what* the problem is that can be described. Quantitative measurement procedures may therefore be very convenient for the desired levels of sophisticated analysis, but the real answers to pressing problems may be best answered by an indication of the mixture and variety of experiences that relate to the problems to be solved.

Conclusions

Central to all my comments above has been the desire to draw upon general psychological ideas to guide thinking about psychological research. One of the curiosities of research methodology teaching in psychology is that it is often devoid of consideration of the psychological issues that would be central to any other teaching in the curriculum. Typically, statistics are dealt with as a branch of mathematics and research design is treated as a cunning game of logic. Even the modes of data collections are usually presented as standardised procedures that have their own inner power, quite independently of any theoretical formulations which may have contributed to their creation.

The central themes I have emphasised for thinking about methodology for psychology has been that psychologists need to use their psychological skills in thinking about the research process. They need to consider why they are doing the research and what the likely consequences of this research will be. In effect, this is moving away from a purist, abstract approach to research and towards a more context aware approach. In advocating that people should understand the potential implications of their research I am not saying that they should avoid the strict logic of science. The opposite is the case. I am advocating a richer understanding of the ways in which scientific method has its impact. Science is not only about disentangling causal influences under controlled conditions. It is also scientific to examine the structure of relationships that exist in natural settings or to give a detailed description of particular patterns of behaviour.

The essence of science is the building of generalisable, theoretical models. It is first of all a clear and, wherever possible, formal, statement of the nature of the hypotheses that are being examined and the test of those hypotheses against appropriate data that makes a study scientific. But the test of hypotheses against data requires a clear sighted understanding of the contextual and resource limitations that are put upon the research.

The teaching of research methods in applied psychology, therefore, should be anything but dogmatic. I believe that it is most productive when it explores the issues I have listed above and many others. This will provide students with a rich, conceptual system that will provide them with a flexible enough range of ways of thinking about research to still be of value to them when they are commissioning their own research projects well into the next century.

METHODOLOGY

3   The Potential of Facet Theory for Applied Social Psychology

Introduction

In order to illustrate a relatively new approach to research methods and data analysis, most commonly referred to as facet theory (Gratch, 1973), the present paper describes three examples of the approach in use. The range of data types and variety of modes of analysis which can be accommodated by this approach are exemplified, starting with a simple example dealing with energy conservation in universities, then moving on to examine differences between prisoners and staff in their evaluation of prison buildings, and finally considering the more complex methodological issues involved in establishing the structure of housing satisfaction. However, whilst this paper essentially concerns research procedures, especially the use of multivariate statistics, I wish to make the case that the facet approach holds particular potential for applied social psychology.

The value of the facet approach derives from the fact that it provides a metatheoretical framework for empirical research. Guttman (1979), a major advocate, has recently summarised its promise as follows:

> Facet theory is proving to provide an effective approach for fruitful design of content, leading to appropriate data analysis techniques, and producing laws of human behaviour in a cumulative fashion. One byproduct is the establishment of more solid bases for policy decisions.

This 'byproduct' is one important reason for my interest in facet theory. For whilst it does not guarantee application, the facet approach does facilitate the exploration of applied problems and generates results which are potentially more open to application: more open in the sense that they have a form and structure which is more synomorphic with the form and structure of decision-making than are the results of conventional approaches to research.

Some of the limitations of conventional psychological research strategies and modes of data analysis have recently been summarised by Bynner (1980). He indicated that these deficiencies are a product of the inappropriateness for psychology of the agricultural examples upon which Fisher (1935) based his original work on analysis of variance. Adding to these criticisms, Bartram (1980) has argued for the insignificance of tests of significance and Guttman (1977) has launched an attack on many habitual usages of statistics, showing, for example, that

39

the mean is not a measure of central tendency and pointing out that analysis of variance does not analyse variance.

Multi-dimensional scaling

One recent methodological development which seemed to offer hope for providing valid descriptions of the more complex sets of variables found in applied research is that which sits under the broad label of multidimensional scaling (MDS) (Romney et al, 1976). Unfortunately, with a few notable exceptions, this approach appears to have been limited to developments in statistics. In general, ways of summarising the issues being explored as well as the results of MDS research have not moved far beyond mathematical descriptions. Furthermore, the plethora of techniques being used frequently encounter many of the pitfalls of earlier approaches in relying on psychological assumptions which are neither explicit nor demonstrably valid.

The facet-theory perspective on social science research has emerged out of the MDS literature. This perspective, whilst certainly not free of its own deficiencies, promises to provide a new approach which will produce more applicable results, both because it leads to precise definitions of the issues studied, and because it is an unashamedly non-metric, multivariate approach. Such approaches to research are certainly not new, although their use in applied research has been limited. Nonetheless, an established expert, Coombs (Lingoes, 1979, p.vii), is now calling for approaches to multivariate research which recognise that 'the analysis of data inevitably implies a theory'. The facet approach provides a framework for presenting that theory.

Introducing facet theory

Facet theory, as an approach to the design of research projects, measuring instruments and data analysis, developed out of the work of Guttman (1954) and his colleagues (Foa, 1953). They were concerned with the selection of items for test construction and with weaknesses in factor-analytic procedures (Guttman, 1954), as well as with the lack of clarity of existing approaches to the definition of research problems. This approach has now evolved into a research orientation with the explicit aim of revealing 'laws' (Shye, 1978).

Facet theory utilises three major constituents of scientific activity: (a) formal definition of the variables being studied, (b) hypotheses of some specified relationship between the definition and an aspect of the empirical observations, and (c) a rationale for the correspondence between (a) and (b).

The definition is provided by the specification of the facets from which the variables are derived, and the conceptual relationships they bear to each other. A facet may be, in essence, any way of categorising observations so long as the elements of the category scheme are mutually exclusive. For example, sex or intelligence can each form a separate facet because no observation of a person can show him/her to be of different sexes or levels of intelligence at the same time. The sex facet normally has two 'elements' - male and female. The intelligence facet could have as many elements as there are different test scores. On the other hand, classifying people in terms of their personality profiles would be a facet approach only if each aspect of personality (e.g., extraversion, neuroticism, psychoticism) were treated as a separate facet.

Recent reviews of facet theory, such as those of Borg (1978) and Shye (1978), have all emphasised its wide range of modes of use. For example, Payne et al. (1976) used it as a basis for classifying and ordering job-satisfaction variables. It was used by Elizur and Guttman (1976) to formulate and then test hypotheses concerning relationships between attitudes towards work and technological change.

Above all, facet theory is a set of related ideas about how to do research and why it should be done in that way (Runkel and McGrath, 1972). As a consequence, it is difficult to present the richness and potential of the approach briefly, except through the discussion of examples. This paper, therefore, describes increasingly complex examples of facet theory in use, taking the opportunity, along the way, of illustrating the more formal properties of the approach. Of course, facet theory has a number of important weaknesses, but for the sake of clarity of presentation an examination of them is left to the concluding section.

Towards applicability

My own conversion to the use of facet theory grew out of my disquiet with the applicability of my own work, when that work made use of conventional approaches to research. I found, for example, that decision-makers were not interested in a significant difference between two levels of a variable if that variable was not under their control, or if the actual size of the difference was so small that it was not worth the administrative upheaval to change things. It became apparent to me that it is often more important for a manager to make sure that he or she has not forgotten some crucial issue than to focus on the precise details of any particular situation. Clearly stating the concerns with which the world faces them seems to be a critical consideration for most senior managers and policy-makers. This can be seen in a perusal of management guides, briefs to policy-makers, or programmes for architects. Essentially, they consist of lists.

I remember my own initial dismay on finding that systematic design procedures in architecture consist almost entirely of checklists specifying what to do and when. The hypothetico-deductive system on which I had been schooled, the axioms, hypotheses, theories and tests of what was happening, were nowhere to be found. How could this be 'systematic'? It was only when I was faced, as a consultant myself, with directly guiding decision-making that I began to appreciate the real complexities of the world we operate within and that the applied scientist's task is to provide a coherent resume of that world so that it can be understood and acted on. Simplifying the problems to be studied, in advance of studying them, for the sake of some notional 'scientific rigour', seemed to me to be like the joke about a person searching for something he had lost where it was easy to see, rather than in the area where he had lost it!

It began to dawn on me that in shaping research so as to increase its potential for use by decision-makers, a number of aspects of the 'real world' in which problems are solved are especially significant for research methodology. In summary, they are as follows.

The categorical nature of policy-making and action-taking. After any deliberations a decision is made whether to proceed or not, to reconsider at a later date, or to forget the whole issue. These are categories of action, not amounts or degrees of action. As a consequence, research results which derive from assumptions about continuous variables and present those results as graphs, correlations, means or any other summary of undifferentiated variables, require conversion into discrete, categorical forms amenable to action. Methods which are derived from non-metric procedures thus have more potential for producing applicable results.

The multivariate structure of human experience and action. The complexity of the physical and social environment outside of the laboratory is the main reason why those interested in the rigorous testing of theories have typically shunned field-studies. The converse of this, however, has not been so logically followed. This is the requirement of field-based research, especially if it is problem-oriented, to incorporate a number of variables into its explorations in any study. The process of isolating variables for examination in the field by controlling the conditions under which they occur, say by selecting sites in which potentially 'contaminating' variables are absent, ignores the fact that to the person wishing to act upon the results of research those theoretical 'contaminants' may well be the very reason for requiring research assistance.

Often action is facilitated if the options available can be specified. This in turn requires that the problems and their component parts be determined and unequivocally labelled. Research procedures which relate directly to the definition of the variables being studied thus have greater potential for application than those which result in purely numerical outcomes.

The concepts being examined need to be specified in other than operational terms. The pertinence of any definition to a policy-maker is often ignored because social scientists appear to learn that definition is a technical rather than a theoretical problem. They are provided with the notion of 'operational' definitions and then resolve the problem of specifying what is being measured by reference to some other measuring device similarly defined. Not surprisingly, decision-makers become impatient with advisors who insist that the devices being used 'measure what they measure'.

These four aspects of applied problems, which must be recognised if the results of research are to be applicable, each find a response, to differing degrees, in the facet approach, as is illustrated through the examples to be presented.

An example from energy conservation: facets of action

The first example illustrates a simple use of facet theory to provide an ordered set of categories of behaviour. The example gives an insight into some of the fundamental principles of the theory, using as its vehicle a study of the actions taken by British universities when attempting to increase energy conservation. These actions provided us (Miles and Canter, 1976) with an opportunity to study the structure of energy-conservation actions within British universities. The data were provided by writing to the Registrars of all 50 institutions and asking them for details of the energy-conserving activities carried out by their universities. A direct content-analysis of the responses from the 43 replies provides the basis of our illustration.

When the energy crisis of the mid-1970s began to be felt, most British universities considered what they should do to conserve funds by conserving energy. I was intrigued, but not surprised, to learn that in the traditions of university autonomy each institution was carrying out its own conservation activities independently from, and in virtual ignorance of, the actions of all the other universities. It was therefore of interest and of potential value to establish whether there were any similarities in the actions taken by different universities and whether any pattern could be discerned, within their activities, which would reveal an underlying consistency to university decision making. A lack of consistency would raise questions about administrative idiosyncrasies. The existence of a common framework could be used to guide concerted action.

The objective, then, was to provide a coherent account of the actions being taken by the universities and to establish the nature of the relationships among these actions. Of course, by providing university administrations with an indication of what other universities were doing and how their own behaviour fitted that general framework, we could not guarantee that taking any given action would inevitably have the desired effects. Nonetheless, at the very least we could enable an administration to know whether their actions were unusual. Furthermore, knowledge of what comparable administrations are doing in response to commonly experienced conditions can be taken as a form of guidance.

However, in order to get beyond a series of anecdotes, or further than a simple list of what was happening, it was important to establish the structure of the actions taken. For example, if it could be demonstrated that some actions were the usual precursors to others then this would suggest that jumping ahead of the sequence might carry unwelcome costs. The significance of any structure revealed will depend on the particular form it takes, so further consideration must follow the presentation of the results. The properties of the problem being investigated can now be specified in order to show the particular value of a facet approach.

1.   We are operating upon the content analysis of a set of recorded events. The data are categorical.
2.   Any categories derived from the data will form the actual content of any summary model produced. Analysis techniques are therefore required

which will not arbitrarily categorise the data. In other words, we must be able to see exactly what is happening to the data so that any substantive manipulations can be controlled.

3.   It is necessary to go beyond univariate cross-tabulations of each category of action with every other. It is the overall pattern of relationships which is being sought.

4.   It is implicit that there will be some sequence or direction to the actions being studied most probably in the direction of earlier or later actions, or of greater or lesser amounts of action. Any analytical procedure should reveal this.

Whilst a number of statistical procedures will cope individually with each of the four problem characteristics above, the facet approach is able to respond to all four. As indicated earlier, it also goes further by providing a systematic, formal procedure for describing and, in effect, defining the variables being examined.

Generating the facets

In the present case the facets are the classes of actions taken by British universities. Any method for classifying a university's actions, derived from a conventional content-analysis of the responses from Registrars, could from a facet, provided that each sub-category (or 'element' of the facet) is mutually exclusive and that it is possible to classify all universities on all facets. A facet is thus different from a 'variable' in that it is one way of categorising the observations. In some studies a number of variables may be so similar that they are all derived from the same facet elements, or pre-defined facets may not be represented by any of the variables being measured. Technically, a facet is 'any set playing a role of a component set of a Cartesian space, this set being called a facet of that space' (Canter, 1977). A 'Cartesian' space is one for which the co-ordinates are simply distances, not angles or specific dimensions. The reference to Cartesian space here also indicates that no assumptions are being made about the dimensionality of the facets. It further implies that the observations are being classified on all the facets. A facet applicable to any observation is applicable to all (Runkel and McGrath, 1972, p. 19).

Three sources were drawn upon to generate facets for the energy-conserving actions. One was a consideration of the actions available to the universities. A second was examination of the replies from the Registrars. The third was a consideration of the existing literature and other sources of concepts for classifying energy-conservation actions (cf. Arbuthnot, 1977; Pallack et al, 1980). In order to present this material as a simple example, only those major facets of immediate interest are discussed. The four main classes of action, which constitute the four facets, were *(A) overall measures, (B) establishing committees, (C) appointing officers, and (D) examining alternative sources of energy.* These four are of especial interest because they range from actions taken by central administrative authorities to those which are carried out by individuals peripheral to those authorities, a sequence which reflects the essentially autocratic, hierarchical structure of British universities. I return to this relationship between the types of action after considering each in a little more detail.

(A)   *Overall measures:* procedures carried out by central university authorities on systems directly under their control, such as lowering the general temperature, reducing the number of lights available for use, and reducing the use of water.

(B)   *Committees:* one or more bodies created specifically to consider aspects of energy use and conservation within the university.

(C)   *Conservation officers:* people appointed or elected to monitor/promote/explore energy use and conservation within their own departments or the university as a whole.

(D)   *Alternative sources:* encouragement or active sponsorship of specified individuals to carry out studies of, or research into, alternative modes of energy production or conservation [I].

Having established these categories of action, each university can be classified in terms of whether or not it has carried out each of the actions within a class, the facets being dichotomous (containing the elements of occurrence and non-occurrence of actions). In effect, a profile can be created for each institution across the four facets of action. Potentially every possible combination ($2^4 = 16$) of action and inaction could combine to provide a characteristic profile. This full set of all possible profiles describes the range of types of energy-conservation activity which is possible within the definition provided by our four facets.

A mapping sentence for energy-conserving actions

One way of summarising the complete set of all possible action profiles is by means of a 'mapping sentence' (cf. Levy, 1976; Borg, 1978). Shye (1978, p. 413) defines a mapping sentence as 'a verbal statement of the domain and of the range of a mapping including connectives between facets as in ordinary language'. In the present case the domain is the set of actions being considered. The range (indicated by -[]) in this instance is taken, for simplicity, as dichotomous : the occurrence or not of an action.

Mapping sentence 1

Energy-Conserving Actions in British Universities (after Miles and Canter, 1976)

Whether *(A) Overall Measures,*	*(B) Special Committees,*
[1. Do not][a]	[1. Do not]
[2. Do]	[2. Do]

(C) Appointed Officers and   *(D) Search For Alternatives*

[1. Do not]   [1. Do not]

[2. Do]   [2. Do]

occur in a given university (x) →   [Do not]

                                          [Do occur]

[a] The [] indicate the facets being utilised to provide the definitional system for the population of each x, i.e., a British university.

The complete set of all possible profiles indicated by the mapping sentence above would number 16, each facet being dichotomous. This is a theoretical set of types of energy-conserving actions which universities might perform. If all the facets are labelled *A-D* and the existence of an action indicated by a 2 and the lack of it by a 1, then the profile for a university which carried out all four sets of actions would be represented by *A2 B2 C2 D2*. An institution which carried out no energy-conserving actions at all would have the profile *A1 B1 C1 D1*. The empirical question, and one concerning which hypotheses can be put forward, concerns which of all the possible profiles actually exists. Furthermore, there is the question as to whether there is any heuristic device which effectively summarises the profiles which actually do exist and their relationships one to another.

In the present case the first point to note is that each of the four facets has a direction to it which can be equated to the direction in the other facets. The 2, denoting the occurrence of an action, has a similar meaning for every facet. As a consequence it is logical to say that the more 2's any university has in its profile, the more active it is in energy conservation. Furthermore, if the simplest possible count of amount of action is taken, all universities can be put in order on the basis of the number of 2's they have in their profiles. The greater the number of actions they have taken, the more 'energy-conserving' they are. This makes minimum demands on the data by giving equal weight to each facet. It also, of course, takes no account of the success of the actions (an issue not explored by the universities).

Of the 16 potential action profiles there are many which would show the same amount of 'energy conservation' but in quite different ways. For example, *A2 B2 C1 D1* would have the same 'score' as *A1 B1 C2 D2*, even though it represents virtually opposite actions. As a consequence, on a directly numerical basis the 16 profiles can be only partly ordered, because there are many profiles whose orders, being qualitatively different, cannot be quantitatively compared with each other (cf. Shye, 1978, p. 265). Yet it is frequently possible to put forward a psychological hypothesis which predicts that the full number of mathematically possible combinations will not actually exist. In the present case this can be done by referring back to the possible relationships among the facets.

A cumulative scale

It was pointed out earlier that the four facets were possibly reflections of four steps of action away from the central authority of the university. Indeed it was the representatives of this authority, the Registrars, who provided an account of the institutions' actions. Let us posit, then, that it is considerably easier for an autocratic organisation such as a British university to carry out central measures, less easy to establish special committees, even less easy to appoint officers, and difficult to encourage particular individuals to explore alternative sources of energy. Under such circumstances the number of potential profiles of conservation actions would be greatly restricted. The easiest way to appreciate these restrictions is by considering that an institution which has carried out a 'difficult' act such as appointing an officer is also likely to have carried out the other 'easier' acts. Hence profiles including a C2 (conservation officer) would be expected also to contain A2 (overall measures) and B2 (committees).

An examination of the 16 possible profiles in the light of the most strict interpretation of the order amongst the facets reveals that only five profiles would be likely to actually exist, as shown in *Figure 1*.

Figure 1 represents a cumulative, 'Guttman' scale, first presented by Stouffer et al (1950). Such a scale is one type of theoretical structure which provides a heuristic device for summarising the relationships among facets and the basis for a more formal hypothesis of the structure inherent in a set of observations. As the present paper proceeds other forms of structural hypothesis will be presented.

In the case of energy conservation all but one of the 43 responding universities had profiles the same as one of those in Figure 1. In other words, if those profiles are taken to be a hypothesis then it can be shown to account for 98% of the observations. Depending upon the use to which the results are to be put this figure will be acceptably high or not. Certainly for most psychological activity it is respectable, within the limits of the sample and the data-collection procedure. For the present purposes the structure certainly seems to describe the relationships among the set of energy-conservation events sufficiently well to allow this example to be taken one stage further.

A1	E1	C1	D1
A2	E1	C1	D1
A2	B2	C1	D1
A2	E2	C2	D1
A2	B2	C2	D2

Figure 1 Cumulative scale for energy-conserving actions represented as facet profiles. These four profiles account for the actions of 42 out of the 43 universities that responded (see mapping sentence 1 for key).

Some consequences

What I wish to argue is that a set of actions structurally related in the way described might well be considered as a flow diagram with prescriptive as well as descriptive properties. The four facets can be thought of as part of a series of possible actions which could be initiated by a university administration, the easiest action, the implementation of central measures *A*, being done first, followed by *B, C* and then *D*. This is not to suggest that this is inevitably the optimum sequence, only that it presents a feasible sequence. The order of the actions certainly raises some questions. For example, why are central actions typically taken before any group has been appointed to oversee those actions? Further, what is the institutional nature of energy conservation which creates situations in which individuals or groups are appointed (*C, D*) only once more general actions have been taken (*A, B*)? The answers which any particular university gave to these questions would carry implications for future actions.

The structure, then, and its interpretation as a sequence of actions, throws light on the organisation of British universities in response to the perception of an energy crisis. It also helps to illustrate how structural hypotheses of defined domains of concern can be explored. Yet in the present example the possibility for application derives from the fact that a simple structure has been identified: a cumulative ordering of the facets. The simplest consequence, therefore, is to use the model as a sequence of actions to take. However, this would virtually accept current practice. More profound consequences would follow from questioning the patterns revealed, for example by exploring why the investigation of alternative sources (*D*) is such a late stage in administrative actions.

An example from prisons: regional hypotheses for people

The second example illustrates the accommodation of more diverse sources of information and the development of more complex structural models than in the preceding energy-conservation example, for which only the actions performed were considered. In one sense, therefore, all the facets were drawn from what Guttman has called the same 'universe of content' (cf. Borg, 1978, p. 66). Other ways of thinking about universities, such as in terms of their age or their size, were not part of the original mapping sentence. In the language of traditional experimental psychology, relationships among 'dependent' variables were being considered. However, many important research questions have always concerned relationships among 'independent' and 'dependent' variables. As Guttman and Levy (1980) among others have pointed out, whether a variable is recognised as dependent or independent is arbitrary in the sense that it is determined by the phrasing of the research question. Nonetheless, there are many occasions when it is clear that the way in which variables are measured, defined or controlled distinguishes them from each other to the extent that they can be considered as deriving from different domains of concern. On such occasions the pattern of the relationships among the variables is likely to be more complex than that illustrated in the preceding example, requiring more sophisticated computing procedures.

The difference between the present example and the previous one is analogous to that between the statistics of association and the statistics of differences. Conventionally, the relationships among energy-conservation actions across universities would be studied using bivariate measures of association, such as chi square. The second example, from prisons, would be analysed by examining differences in the effects of 'treatments' using, say, analysis of variance.

A further distinction between the second example and the first is that the actions chosen for study in the previous example were such that a limited number of actions could be readily identified. It was therefore possible to include them all in the definition of the problem, through the mapping sentence. The structure which then resulted from an examination of the action profiles provided, as a consequence, a description of how all the facets actually related one to another. Although the rationale was presented only briefly, the reasons for the structure found were shown to derive from a consideration of each of the facets themselves and the nature of their coexistence with the other facets.

Many applied problems do not reveal themselves as a clearly defined set of facets. Indeed, as discussed earlier, policy questions are frequently of the form: 'What are the critical issues here? On which entities should I focus?'. The social psychologist is called upon to describe observations so that effective distinctions between elements of facets are revealed. Traditionally this is done by the analysis of variance, to establish 'significant' effects. This approach not only has a number of theoretical weaknesses (as discussed, for example, by Guttman, 1977) , but it also has difficulty in dealing with the non-metric, multivariate data with which applied research must so often contend.

To illustrate a facet approach to these issues I draw upon a recent study of prisons (Ambrose and Canter, 1979). This study was oriented towards the development of procedure for the evaluation of prison buildings. On the basis of previous work in other institutions, to be discussed later (Canter and Kenny, 1979; Rees and Canter, 1979), it was considered feasible to develop, together with other procedures, a standard questionnaire which could be completed by inmates and staff. As part of this development task it was also important to establish that there were consistent differences between prisons, which could be revealed from user responses to the questionnaire.

Questions about the development of an evaluation tool can be expressed in facet terms, as to whether two distinct facets can be identified. In this case, one would be a facet distinguishing responses in terms of the prison which a respondent is describing. The other would be a facet distinguishing respondents independently of their prison. The most obvious elements of the second facet would be derived from a distinction between prisoners and prison officers. However, these are not facets which we expected to operate in the abstract. They are facets which we wished to explore within the context of user responses to their surroundings.

Environmental role

I now introduce briefly some issues of a more theoretical nature which help to clarify the directions in which the empirical observations will be explored.

The first point is that in examining the reactions of individuals to the place in which they live or work, it can be assumed that their mode of interaction with that place will be a significant source from which their response will be derived. This idea has been developed elsewhere (Canter, 1977, 1979) in relation to the concept of 'environmental role'. In essence, it is proposed that it is the use to which people put their surroundings, the extent to which their environment enables them to achieve what they want from it, that determines their evaluation of it.

Prisons which have differing purposes (catering for short as opposed to long prison sentences, for example) may be expected to give rise to differences in the reactions of staff or inmates. Furthermore, it is important for methodological as well as administrative reasons to establish whether prisoners and staff hold distinct conceptualisations of the prison. It is certainly possible that the totality of the institution is such that, together with the time spent within it, the distinction between institutions is greater than the distinction between individuals, even when they perform such different roles within it.

If these differences among people were to be explored by means of a standard questionnaire then there would be a grave risk that, by presenting ready-made concepts for use by the respondents, only a pale reflection of their own conceptual system would be obtained. A number of people have elaborated upon this idea, drawing frequently on Kelly's (1955) personal construct theory, and this led us to develop a procedure which allows individuals to reveal their own concepts while still enabling comparisons between individuals and groups to be made. We have called it a multiple sorting task (Groat, 1979; Groat and Canter, 1979), derived from Sherif and Sherif's (1969) own-categories procedure and Vygotsky's (1934) sorting task.

Method

Forty-six staff and prisoners in three institutions were each presented with 23 cards. On these cards were words describing places in which people might reside, such as 'hotel', 'hospital', 'night shelter'. One card had 'this prison' written on it. Each of the respondents was asked to consider each card and think of a place they knew to which the description applied. They were then asked to sort the cards into as many categories as they wished so that all the places in any given category had some important quality in common. Notes were taken of their description of what it was that the places had in common.

Our concern here was for respondents' conceptualisations of their particular prison. We wished to examine how that institution was related, in their sortings, to all the other places listed. In other words, a matrix can be created for each person indicating whether or not his or her current prison was put in the same category as each of the other 23 places. It is this profile of yes/no associations which provides the account of the respondent's conceptualisations of their establishment. We thus obtained a set of responses, provided by the sorting task, which can be incorporated with descriptions of the people and their institution for analysis. Returning again to the formalities of facet theory, a mapping sentence for the research question can be presented:

Mapping sentence 2

Conceptualisations of prisons. Whether or not respondent (*x*), where (*x*) is an individual describing the place in which he or she is resident or works,

being a	[(*A*) 1. Prison officer] in a	[(*B*) 1. Local prison]
	[2. Prisoner]	[2. Training prison]
		[3. Borstal This)]

indicating his or her present prison to be	[(*N*) 1. Similar to]	{each of 23 }[a]
	[2. Different from]	{other places}

[Does]	indicate his prison to be
→	similar to each of 23
[Does not]	other places

[a] The 1 indicates that N is a facet composed of 23 subfacets, one for each card in the sorting task.

The principle of contiguity

One property of the cumulative scale, not mentioned when it was illustrated (Figure 1), is that it can be regarded as a representation of the relationships among profiles in a spatial configuration. In the preceding example, the most similar institutions (or profiles) were next to each other in the list, the least similar furthest apart. Interestingly, contours can be drawn across the list of profiles corresponding to each of the original facets. *Figure 2* illustrates this by showing how each profile can be represented as a point in a space and that space can then be 'partitioned' to reveal regions associated with elements of the facets. *Figure 2* does, of course, represent a very simple example, because only one dimension is really needed to represent a cumulative scale. However, it does reveal the general principle that regions of a space can provide evidence for facet structure. This is a principle, as will be seen, which can be generalised to a space of any number of dimensions. Thus one of the general tests employed in facet theory is to establish whether a spatial representation of the observations can be created such that the similarity between profiles is directly reflected in their closeness in space. This has been referred to as Guttman's principle of contiguity (Lingoes, 1979, p. 38). All multidimensional scaling procedures are ways of providing geometrical representations of relational data (Lingoes, 1968), but it is the use of the principle of contiguity and the examination of differences between profiles which are derived from facets which distinguishes the facet approach.

In the data from the prison study each profile represents a *respondent*; therefore a spatial configuration is sought such that the more similar the pattern of sorts made by any two people, the closer together they will be in that plot. In other terms, the empirical question posed by mapping sentence 2 is whether or not contiguous regions can be found in an appropriate spatial configuration which correspond to the elements of the facets. At present we focus on facets A (role) and B (location), and wish to know whether a space which accommodates all 23 subfacets of N as well as A and B would indeed reveal areas identifiably related to $A1$ and $A2$, or to $B1$, $B2$ and $B3$.

Profile	Type		Example of configuration				
A1 B1 C1 D1	I						
A1 B1 C1 D1	II		:			:	
		region	: I			:	
A2 B2 C1 D1	III	for B1	:			:	
			:	II		:	
A2 B2 C2 D1	IV		:			:region	
			:		III	:for C1	
A2 B2 C2 D2	V	region	:			:	
		for B2	:		IV	:	
			:			:region	
			:		V	:for C2	

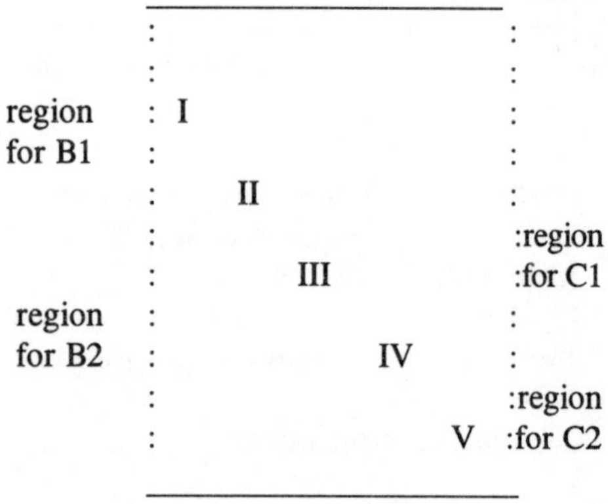

Figure 2   The relationship between the cumulative scale (from Fig. 1) and the spatial representation of individuals. Two ways of partitioning the configuration of profiles are indicated, for Facets B and C (see mapping sentence 1 for key).

Multidimensional scalogram analysis (MSA)

In order to create a configuration of respondents it is necessary to use a procedure which will operate on the dichotomous categories and which, while representing each of the respondents as a point, will nonetheless allow an examination of the regions associated with each facet. Multidimensional scalogram analysis (MSA) is a procedure uniquely suited to these requirements. It operates entirely on categorical differences. Full details of the algorithm have been provided by Lingoes (1968), and other examples of the procedure in use have been published by Jordan (1978), Guttman and Guttman (1974) and by Bloombaum (1970).

The procedure creates a configuration of points, where each point represents a respondent, and the regions of the space reflect the categories of each variable (in the present case, the variables correspond to the facets in the mapping sentence, including both the description of the person and his or her location as well as his or her sorting of places). MSA creates an optimum configuration of points which satisfies as many as possible of the regional limitations set by each variable. Inevitably, for some data, a configuration cannot be found in which for each variable there are regions of the space corresponding to the categories of that variable. In other words, in many cases not all variables actually give rise to regions within the configuration, especially if a two-dimensional configuration is specified. However, the computer program does provide plots for each variable. These can be used to establish whether contiguous regions of the space can be found for any given variable and hence whether it is functioning as a facet in a particular set of data. MSA, then, is a general solution to the problem of representing individuals as points in a space for which each of the variables is a way of partitioning that space and each of the categories of a variable is a region of that space. A cumulative scale is a special case of MSA, as illustrated in Figure 2.

One further advantage of MSA as a general computing procedure is that facets from different domains can be readily accommodated in the same analysis. In the present case it is possible to include the classification of the people, their prisons, and their sorting responses all in the same analysis, and thus establish whether the people (*A*) and prison (*B*) facets do indeed lead to partitions of the total configuration, which is also constrained by the sorts (*N*). In effect, the MSA printout can be examined for direct evidence for the mapping sentence. In the present example we focus on facets *A* and *B*, so only the partitions for those two facets are presented.

Results

Figure 3 presents the configuration of points derived from a two-dimensional MSA. Each point represents an individual respondent, coded to indicate whether the respondent is a member of staff or an inmate. *Figure 4* shows the same configuration, but in this case the points are coded to indicate the prison in which the respondent was.

The intriguing thing about Figure 3 is that there are no clear regions of the space which can be identified with whether a person was an inmate or not. By comparison, in Figure 4 there are clearly defined regions for each of the different prisons.This lends support to the role of facet B in the mapping sentence, but no real support for facet A. One consequence of this finding is that the development of separate evaluation instruments for each set of respondents might not be necessary. Indeed it is possible that the staff share quite closely with prisoners their views on the purposes of the establishments. On the other hand, it is clear that reactions to prisons occur against the background of exactly what type of prison is being studied. Any evaluation, therefore, is meaningless unless it incorporates an understanding of the goals and purposes of each *particular* institution.

MSA has been used in this example as a way of identifying which facets are operative in a given context. It has thus enabled us to move a step further in the direction of using the facet approach for generating a category scheme which has functional utility. It has also illustrated a direct facet theory parallel to the conventional quest to establish which variables have a 'significant' effect. In the present case 'significance' is revealed by the existence of non-controversial partitions of the multi-dimensional spatial representation of the similarities between individuals in their card-sorts.

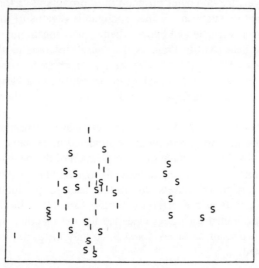

Figure 3   MSA1 of staff (a)[b] and inmates (i) based on their card sorts[c].
[a] *Points represent people.*   [b] *This is coded for Facet [A] of mapping sentence two. (s is A1, i is A2).   No clear regions for these elements can be found, hence no support for facet [A] is provided by this plot.*

An example from housing satisfaction: portraying multivariate structures

So far facets have been identified as part of the definition of the research question and few actual facets have been dealt with at any one time. We have also been concerned mainly with the differences between individuals in the population being studied (universities or inmates). All these limitations to the examples so far are present because we have ignored the structure of the relationships which exist *among* the 'content' variables. In dealing with universities, prisoners and prison staff, it has been assumed that each of the ways of categorising the observations (i.e., the actions and the different sorting categories) could be given equal and qualitatively similar weights in the description of the population for which data were available. Yet we had no information concerning the relationships among the descriptions (their structure). The third example illustrates this most widely utilised aspect of facet theory.

The quest for a facet structure can be seen as the problem of identifying the most

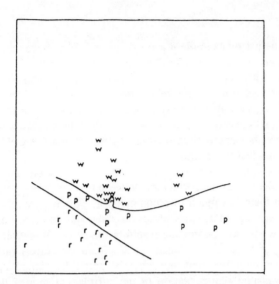

Figure 4 MSA1[a] of respondents showing the prison[b] they are from.
[a] The configuration is the same as for Fig. 3. [b] The plot is coded for facet [B] of mapping sentence two (B1 is p, B2 is w, B3 is r). The regions in which these elements are found have been drawn in by hand.

pertinent classification of variables: the one which will best portray the pattern of correlations among them. One situation in which it is essential to understand this pattern of correlations among variables and identify a facet structure is when using questionnaires. To illustrate this I draw upon a study of the satisfaction people have with where they live, derived from the work of Rees and Canter (1979). *Table 1* presents a set of 13 questions which were asked of 1102 people. Each of these questions was answered separately by husbands and wives, who were each sent an identical questionnaire through the post, as described by Canter et al (1980). Thus, for each *family* responses were obtained to 26 questions.

Of course, these questions can be taken strictly at face value and percentage differences or whatever can be examined for each question across various response groups. However, this avoids the issue of what definitional framework can be provided which will allow a fuller understanding of what these satisfaction questions are about. For example, consider question 1 in Table 1. This may be thought of as a question which has to do with 'neighbourhood', as well as a question which has to do with 'convenience'. In other words, considering all questions, each can be assigned to a category scheme which distinguishes between, say, house questions and 'neighbourhood' questions, a facet of 'environmental scale'. What, then, are some of the facets which can be used to classify the questions in Table 1?

Method of analysis

In the MSA for the prison example it proved very useful to have the observations represented in some spatial form so that, following the principle of contiguity, regions associated with elements of facets could be identified. Thus the partitioning of a spatial representation of the relationship between variables holds many heuristic advantages as a way of portraying facets. In a case such as the present, the size of a correlation between two variables will reflect the similarity of their facet constituents. Hence the pattern of correlations between variables will be examined in order to see what facets it suggests.

To provide an account of a pattern of correlations it turns out that a procedure which represents the size of the correlation between two items as the inverse of the distance between them has much to recommend it. This is precisely what many multidimensional scaling (MDS) procedures do, the major difference in the present case being that we wish to examine the resulting spatial configuration of variables by considering partitions of the space (its 'regional structure') rather than by identifying clusters or dimensions as such. The particular computing procedure used to create a spatial representation of the correlations among the 26 house satisfaction items was SSA1 from the Guttman-Lingoes series of non-metric MDS procedures (Lingoes, 1979). This procedure is now described in a little more detail.

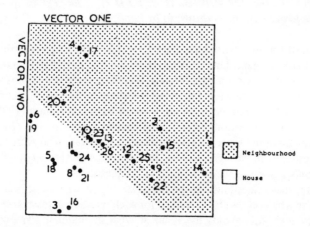

Figure 5   SSA1[a] for 26 questionnaire items showing regions[b] for house and neighbourhood items.
[a] *Points represent items. The axes are arbitrary, hence unlabelled.* [b] *The regions are identified from item content (see Table 1) and drawn in by hand.*

SSA of housing questionnaire

Figure 5 represents the 26 questionnaire items as points and the correlations between items (across the sample of 1102 households) as the inverses of the distances between those points. In essence, the computing algorithm rank-orders the correlations between all items. It then generates a spatial representation of those items, with points representing items, and rank-orders the distances between the

Table 1

Questions from Housing-Satisfaction Questionnaire (from Rees and Canter, 1979)

Reference number in Figs. 5-7		Item
Husband	*Wife*	
1	14	How conveniently located are the shops in your neighhourhood?
2	15	Is your neighbourhood friendly?
3	16	Are you happy with the decor in your house?
4	17	How convenient is it for visitors to park near your house?
5	18	Do you feel satisfied with your house when you have visitors?
6	19	Are you satisfied with the spaciousness of your kitchen?
7	20	How happy are you with the distances between houses near you?
8	21	Is the heating system in your house satisfactory?
9	22	Generally, how convenient is your neighbourhood?
10	23	How pleased are you with the style of houses in your neighbourhood?
11	24	Generally, how do you feel about your house?
12	25	Generally, how convenient do you find your house and the area in which you live?
13	26	All things considered, how would you rate your house and its location?

points. An iterative procedure is used which compares the ranks of the correlations with the ranks of the distances, altering the configuration until the best fit is achieved between the two sets of ranks. A limitation is set by the researcher on the dimensionality of the space in which the configuration is generated. In the present case a four-dimensional configuration was found to be adequate.

A direct comparison of the results of the SSA1 computation with those of a factor analysis is presented later. For the purpose of understanding the following discussion it should be borne in mind that, unlike the case for factor-analytic procedures, the axes of the configuration are arbitrary. Because the plot is developed from the relationships among the items, not from their relationships to some notional 'dimension' or 'factor', the pattern of points (their regional distribution) can be examined directly.

In relation to their facet make-up, any items which have facet elements in common will be found in the same region of the space. It follows that if items are not found in the same region of the space there is no evidence for their having facet elements in common. So the fact that a partitioning of the space can be found which distinguishes house from neighbourhood items, as shown in Figure 5, provides empirical evidence for that facet.

Another ordered facet

However crude or refined the facet of environmental scale is taken to be, It does have the interesting property of being 'ordered'. The elements can be seen to move from smaller scale to larger scale. A quite different type of facet ordering has also been found in other studies (Lingoes, 1979): the order produced when one facet modulates another. This other type of ordering derives from the possibility of classifying questions in terms of how specific they are. For example, some questions such as numbers 12 and 13 use the word 'generally', or the phrase 'all things considered'. They can be contrasted with more focused questions. For example, question 3 deals directly with the decor of the house. Hence an ordered facet of different 'degrees of focus' may be proposed.

The spatial representation of this second ordered facet, however, will respond to its being a modifier of some other facet, because generality or specificity must be a variation of some other set of entities. Furthermore, general items would be expected to have higher average correlations with all the other items than would specific items. Putting these two points together, any region relating to the general items would be expected to be central and a region for specific items to be peripheral to them.

Evidence for this second facet can be found in another projection of the multidimensional space produced for all the questionnaire items. *Figure 6* shows this projection. Therein a circle can be drawn around the general items which is in the middle of the configuration. Other questions such as those dealing with decor, parking space and other specific issues are then seen to be on the periphery of the configuration. A further level of this degree of focus facet, between the central and peripheral, can also be identified in Figure 6.

A non-ordered facet

Considering the items in the peripheral regions of Figure 6, three distinct segments can be identified,. For example, questions 4, 6 and 7 all deal with issues relating to space, whether it be of house or neighbourhood. Items 2, 5 and 3 all have a quality which reflects status. The remaining segment relates to the convenience of the services in the house and neighbourhood. These segments are depicted in *Figure 7*.

The three elements of this facet do not have any linear order. They present a qualitative distinction: different *kinds* of focus to the question, rather than different degrees. It is such differences in kind which form the fabric of social discourse and policy-making. Yet it is precisely such differences which are hidden by conventional, dimensional analyses such as factor analysis, as will be illustrated.

Of course, a three-fold division of 'services', 'status' and 'space' would be of little interest or applied value if the only evidence for it came from the questionnaire being considered at present. Replication of it using other instruments and observations, as well as a theoretical explanation, would be necessary. One power of the facet approach is that it readily allows such tests. Those that we have carried

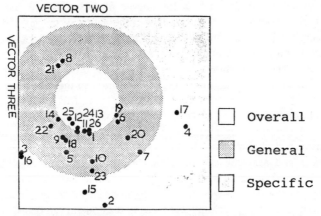

Figure 6 A projection of SSA1 for questionnaire items showing regions relating to generality of the questions (see Table 1).

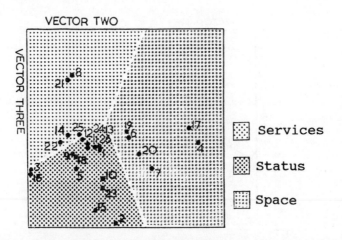

Figure 7 A projection[a] of SSA1 for questionnaire items showing a non-ordered facet (see Table 1). [a] This is the same projection as for Figure 6.

out have revealed a remarkably consistent occurrence of this structure in evaluation data (cf. Canter et al, 1980).

A radex

One strength of working with regional structures is that elegant models of quite complex relationships can be developed. By putting the modulating facet of degree of focus together with the qualitative facet, an interesting spatial representation emerges. This model, shown in *Figure 8*, represents the idea that the ordered facet contains a core in which all the different aspects of satisfaction combine to make a general overview. It shows how the degree of focus facet is modulating the different foci of housing satisfaction. This combination of an ordered and a non-ordered facet has been labelled a 'radex' (Lingoes, 1979).

The radex is a potent structure because it summarises both ordered and non-ordered facets. Yet it also shows the way in which the ordered facets are modifying the non-ordered ones. Furthermore, the juxtaposition of these two facets provides a definition of the 'core' of the domain which can prove fruitful in the development of even richer models.

From the decision-maker's point of view, the clarification of any structured set of relationships can be of value. In the present case, for example, knowledge that space, status and services can be effectively distinguished, provided that the appropriate level of specificity is used, can guide both discussion and the establishing of priorities. However, if the research leads towards a radex then there is the added bonus that a psychological focus to the domain can be established, with the consequent policy focus that implies.

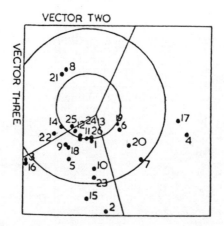

Figure 8 A projection of SSA1[a] showing the ordered and non-ordered facets superimposed - a radex.

A cylindrex

The radex in Figure 8 was represented in the projection of vector **2** against vector **3**. The ordered facet of environmental scale is orthogonal to this, in the projection of **1** against **2**. It is therefore possible to combine these two projections into a cylinder-like model. Each cross-section of the cylinder is a radex, one being for houses, the other for neighbourhoods. Indeed, with hindsight, one projection of this cylinder can be seen in the projection of vector **1** against **2**.

The purpose of presenting the three-dimensional model is to show how it summarises elegantly many aspects of the relationships among the variables and of the structure of the facets. It has also been presented because, like the radex, there are a number of examples of such structures in the literature and, as Canter and Kenny (1979) have pointed out, a number of general implications for applied problem-solving can be derived from such a structure. However, the power of the approach is such that for the present example this model can be taken one step further, by introducing another facet into it.

Higher-order dimensionality

In the study considered, questions were answered separately by husbands and by wives. Yet in all the configurations examined so far the pairs of identical items are typically close together in the space (this can be quickly verified for example by considering in Figure 5 the locations of items 1 and 14, 2 and 15, 3 and 16, and so on.) Nonetheless, common experience would suggest that it would be remarkable if husbands and wives saw eye-to-eye so totally. Some viewpoint could be anticipated from which the differences between them might be apparent. In other words, *Who* answered the questions would operate as a facet. As it happens, in the present data the correlations between the pairs of items are quite high (cf. Rees and Canter, 1979) . Most forms of analysis would therefore not reveal the differences that might be expected. However, using SSA1 higher dimensionality can be considered.

Figure 9 shows vector **2** against vector **4**. There a neat partitioning of the space between the questions answered by husbands and those answered by wives can be seen. Yet it should be noted that this facet is orthogonal to the cylinder which has already been discussed. In other words, a cylinder adequately summarises the structure of the satisfaction of either husbands or wives although Figure 9 suggests that there might be subtle nuances which distinguish them. Interestingly this lends support to the finding of the prison study, which also deemphasised the differences in role, the focus of the conceptualisation.

Although the housing-satisfaction questionnaire has been approached as an exploration, we have, in effect, emerged with a definition of what it covers. It has been seen that this requires a multidimensional model which starts to stretch the powers of our visual imagery, being essentially four-dimensional. Hence the value of summarising the structure of the observations as a mapping sentence, both to help those who wish to act on the data and for those who wish to develop the theoretical aspects further.

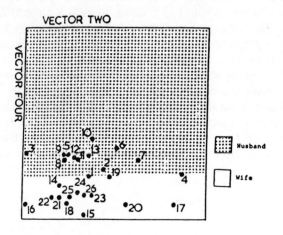

Figure 9   A projection of SSA1 coded for respondent (see Table 1). A mapping sentence for housing satisfaction

Mapping sentence 3

Housing satisfaction. The extent to which the [Husband] of family (*x*), where (*x*) are drawn from

[Wife]

owner-occupiers living in Great Britain,

is satisfied   [Overall]   with the   [Space]
                   [In particular]   [Services]
                                                        [Status]

of   [The house itself]   by stating that they are
                   [The neighbourhood]

                   [Very satisfied indeed]
→   to
                   [Not satisfied at all]

Comparision with factor analysis

The typical approach to analysing a questionnaire is by use of one of the variants of factor analysis, or principal-components analysis (Mulaik, 1972). Therefore, to facilitate comparison with SSA1 a principal-components analysis with varimax rotations was performed on the housing-satisfaction data. The relationship of the factors derived to the SSA1 configuration can be seen graphically by indicating on the SSA1 plot, for each factor, those items having a loading higher than 0.50 on that factor. *Figure 10* is the same projection of the SSA1 space shown in Figure 9 with the highly loaded items and their factor membership indicated.

The way in which the factors relate to small regions of the overall space in Figure 10 is typical of the emphasis of factor-analytic procedures on a large number of unrelated factors. In effect, a factor usually corresponds to what we called earlier a 'profile': a particular combination of facet elements. It is for this reason that it is relatively easy to identify a number of factors in most studies, but difficult to define them precisely or to create an overall model to which they all relate.

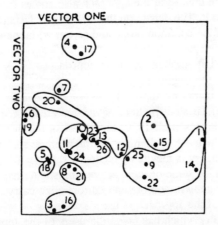

Figure 10 An SSA1 projection[a] of questionnaire items with the results of a factor analysis[b] superimposed. [a] Same projections as Figure 6. [b] All those items which have a factor loading greater than 0.5, on a given factor have a bubble drawn around them. Eight components had eigenvalues greater than unity. Three items (5, 7, and 18) do not load greater than 0.5 on any factor.

Conclusions

Facet theory in use

My own commitment to the facet approach emerged gradually. It was through trying the approach in a number of different studies that I began to appreciate the potential it had. However, it was the consistencies which emerged across different sets of data which turned me into an advocate; the personal discovery, which is a product of its strength, was that its formal properties (the mapping sentence, regional hypotheses, etc) tend to hide, in publications of research, exactly what it is that a researcher does when using a facet approach. Intriguingly this is a common criticism of the use of 'Guttman scales' made by methodologists. They complain that there is no obvious way of finding items for a cumulative scale during its stages of development. Similarly, the facet literature is vague on how to 'find' facets, prior to data and analysis.

My experience has been that the identification of facets relies upon the same procedure as does the emergence of any other research idea: the literature is studied, pilot data are scrutinised, and lengthy discussions are held about the logic of the facets that are proposed. Two processes speed up this quest. One is the pre-existence of a mapping sentence for a similar domain. For example, mapping sentence 3 above, dealing with housing satisfaction, has been used in evaluations of offices, prisons and restaurants as a first approximation for developing pilot questionnaires. Help in the use of the approach also comes from membership of a group who understand it. The debate on the meaning of facets and their elements, on the exact nature of the common range and so on, is, in the early stages, a very lively one. Because the approach demands the clarification of aspects of the study which are typically left implicit in other approaches, it is difficult for many researchers to do this thoroughly in isolation.

The difficulties of using the approach are compounded by a diffuse and often inaccessible literature. These difficulties have been greatly reduced by two recent books of readings (Lingoes et al, 1979; Shye, 1978), but these still remain rather technical accounts which are challenging to the average social psychologist. The vocabulary of facet theory is inevitably technical (although in the present paper I have deliberately avoided some of the more neologistic terms), yet it seems to me that until it is widely known, authors and editors alike carry a special burden of clarifying the nature of the approach in use.

One further difficulty which has faced the users of the approach has been the uncoordinated range of substantive topics which facet users have explored. The tendency has been for researchers to take one topic, such as worries about job deprivation (Shye and Elizur, 1976), and, after having found an interesting structure, to move on to other issues. There are clearly pressures from within the institution of academic psychology which foster this magpie activity, but it has led to a very piecemeal development of facet theory. However, as more examples amass, consistencies across different topic areas are emerging (cf. Shye, 1978).

Given that a key question is what a researcher actually does when making use of the approach, in the spirit of clarification, I now summarise the major stages involved, using the housing-satisfaction study as a vehicle.

(1)   We had decided that we wished to study the basis of housing satisfaction. We therefore conducted a number of open-ended interviews with typical respondents, in the traditions of survey research.

(2)   The answers were summarised in terms of the major themes which were present. This summary was influenced by previous research interests and

certain theoretical formulations.

(3)   The themes were examined for their potential facet structure. Earlier ideas had made us sensitive, for example, to the environmental scale which a question addressed.

(4)   A preliminary mapping sentence was created. From earlier studies we had some ideas as to what form this might take, but in many cases this first mapping sentence is a leap into the dark.

(5)   A questionnaire was then developed from the mapping sentence. At this stage a number of things tend to happen at once:

(a) those facets, or facet elements, which are so ambiguous that questions cannot be readily derived from them, are clarified;

(b) the facets, or elements, which seem of least interest are dropped, so that a questionnaire of reasonable length can be produced; if no such priorities are possible then a sampling of facets and elements is made using a specific sampling framework;

(c) the initial questions which are generated from the facets are frequently ponderous and difficult to comprehend. (For example, a [particular], [social], [neighbourhood] question might have started life as:

'to what extent does your neighbourhood satisfy your particular purposes of getting into contact with other people?'

Eventually, we decided to substitute a different form of words:

'Is your neighbourhood friendly?'

Later checks and tests will indicate whether the facet structure of a question has been radically changed in making it comprehensible.)

(6)   The preliminary questionnaire was administered to a pilot group and the responses subjected to SSA. Frequently the results of this first analysis lead to a radical reformulation of the facets and to revision of the questionnaire.

(7)   Further development depends upon resources and the ultimate objectives of the project. My own experience is that once various internal checks have been made on the pilot data, subsequent questionnaires and data do not usually need radical revision. Instead a process of evolution occurs whereby the facets are enriched, either by adding to the elements or by adding new facets. Because the questionnaire now contains few redundancies this is possible without making it of unmanageable size.

Studies which are based upon categorical analysis of open-ended data, such as the present energy-conservation and prison examples, tend to emphasise the earlier stages in this sequence. Nonetheless, whatever the data source, the use of the facet approach does involve a commitment to a developing, evolving orientation to problem-solving. A process of successive approximations is used rather than the testing of hypotheses which are seen as being in any sense final or definitive. The results are always consciously open to another interpretation if it can be shown to be fruitful. It is possibly this creative ambiguity which has led to the approach taking so long to find advocates.

Facet theory in practice

Two themes have been intertwined throughout this paper. One has been the introduction of a set of research methodologies not widely utilised. The other has been an argument for the practical value of certain ways of doing research and presenting the results. In order to do the former it has been necessary to use varied examples which are simplifications drawn from major projects. Thus although some of the practical implications in these cases have been indicated, it has not been possible to elaborate this aspect of the work. Nonetheless it has been possible to illustrate the way in which the approach leads to an elucidation of the problems being examined and makes manifest the options available.

My personal vindication that policy-makers welcome the approach has come from the reactions I have had to reports of our work. For example, a number of British university energy conservation groups requested detailed copies of our report to distribute to their members. Reactions to proposed or developed mapping sentences have also been encouraging. Non-psychologists have grasped them readily and been prepared to add facets, or elements to facets, as a means of clarifying for us what problems they face. We even had one official research contract specified in facet language. The public review of the work produced by the Israel Institute of Applied Social Research summarises most of its projects in the form of mapping sentences (cf. Gratch, 1973), with official approval.

Of course, many gaps remain to be filled during the further development of the approach. One gap which has most significance for application is the absence of models which combine the power of descriptions of individuals, as in our energy-conservation and prison examples, with the power of the description of content domains, as in the housing-satisfaction example. The development of partial-order scalogram analysis (POSA), as illustrated in the work of Shye and Elizur (1976) or Canter and Brown (1979), appears promising. Nonetheless, there are still major conceptual hurdles to surmount, as well as technical ones, if the approach is to be widely used. Furthermore, the full implications of the multidimensional models which are emerging have yet to be clarified. A start has been made on investigating the practical consequences of a cylindrex model for design evaluation (Canter and Kenny, 1979), but it is clear that some general model of praxis must eventually emerge so that the practical implications can follow with the same elegance as the theoretical ones.

Acknowledgements

The material in this chapter has grown out of the activities of the Environmental Research Group at Surrey University. I am grateful to all my colleagues there for their help and criticism. The comments of Jennifer Brown and Cheryl Kenny have been especially significant. The encouragement given to our efforts by Louis Guttman and his colleagues, at the Israel Institute of Applied Social Research in

Jerusalem, has also been an important stimulus to our activities.

References

Ambrose, I. & Canter, D. (1979), 'The design of Total Institutions; Organisational Objectives as Evaluation Criteria', paper presented to *ICEP, Guildford, July 1979.*

Arbuthnot, I. (1977), 'The Roles of Attitudinal and Personality Variables in the Prediction of Environmental Behaviour and Knowledge', *Environment and Behaviour,* Vol. 9, pp. 217-232.

Bartram, D. (1980), 'Do You Really Need Your Null Hypothesis?", *British Psychological Society Bulletin,* Vol. 33, pp. 318-321.

Bloombaum, M. (1970), 'Doing Smallest Space Analysis', *Journal of Conflict Resolution,* Vol. 14, pp. 409-416.

Borg, I. (1978), 'Some Basic Concepts of Facet Theory', in J.C. Lingoes (ed.), *Geometric Representations of Relational Data,* Ann Arbor, Ml: Mathesis.

Brown, J. (1979), 'Motives and Moving House', paper presented to *ICEP Guildford, July 1979.*

Bynner, J. (1980), 'Some Problems with Psychological Research Practice', *British Psychological Society Bulletin,* Vol. 33, pp. 315-317.

Canter, D. (1975), *Environmental Interaction,* Surrey University Press, London.

Canter, D. (1977), *Psychology of Place,* Architectural Press, London.

Canter, D. (1979), 'Are There Laws of Environmental Interaction', paper presented to *IAAP Conference Louvain, 1979.*

Canter, D. & Brown, I. (1979), 'Explanatory roles', in C. Antaki (ed.), *The Psychology of Ordinary Explanations,* Academic Press, London.

Canter, D. & Kenny, C. (1979), 'Implications for Hospital Ward Design from a Multi-dimensional Model for User Evaluation', paper presented to *ICEP Guildford, July 1979.*

Canter, D. & Lee, K.H. (1974), 'A Non-reactive Study of Room Usage in Modern Japanese Apartments', in D. Canter and T. Lee (eds), *Psychology and the Built Environment,* Architectural Press, Tonbridge, Kent.

Canter, D. & Walker, E. (1980), 'Environmental Role and Perceived Housing Quality', *Architectural Research Paper Symposium on Housing Quality, IAAP Munich, 31 July 1978.*

Canter, D., Kenny, C. & Rees, K. (1980), 'A Multivariate Model for Place Evaluation', Mimeo, University of Surrey.

Fisher, R.A. (1935), *The Design of Experiments,* Oliver and Boyd, London.

Foa, & U.G. (1958), 'The Contiguity Principle in the Structure of Interpersonal Relations', *Human Relations,* Vol. 11, pp. 229-238.

Freedman, I. (1975), *Crowding and Behaviour.* San Francisco: W.H. Freedman.

Gratch, H. (1973), *Twenty-five Years of Social Research in Israel,* Jerusalem Academic Press, Jerusalem.

Groat, L. (1979). 'Post-modernism and the Multiple Sorting Task', paper presented to *ICEP Guildford, July 1979.*

Groat, L. & Canter, D. (1979), 'Does Post-modernism Communicate?', *Progressive Architecture*, Vol. 12, pp. 84-87.

Guttman, L. (1954), 'A New Approach to Factor Analysis: the Radex', in P.F. Lazarsfeld (ed.), *Mathematical Thinking in the Social Sciences*, Free Press, New York.

Guttman, L. (1977), 'What is Not What in Statistics', *The Statistician*, Vol. 26, pp. 81-107.

Guttman, L. (1979), 'New Developments in Integrating Test Design and Analysis', paper presented to the *40th International Conference on Testing Problems, Educational Testing Service New York, October 1979.*

Guttman, R. & Guttman, L. (1974), 'Non-metric Analysis of Genetic Relationships Among Inbred Strains of Mice', *Systematic Zoology*, Vol. 23, pp. 355-362.

Guttman, L. & Levy, S. (1980), 'Two Laws for the Structure of Intelligence' *Behavioural Science Quarterly,* Vol. 25.

Hewitt, J.A. (1979), 'The Ecology of the Home: Differences and Similarities Among Families with One, Two or Three or More Children', MSc Thesis, University of Surrey.

Housing Research Unit (1978), *'Descriptive statistics on house buying'*, University of Surrey, Guildford.

Jordan, J.E. (1978), 'Facet Theory and the Study of Behaviour', in M. Shyes (ed.), *Theory Construction and Data Analysis in the Social Sciences*, Jossey-Bass, San Fransisco.

Kelly, G.A. (1955), *The Psychology of Personal Constructs*, Norton, New York.

Kenny, C. & Canter, D. (1979), *'The Multivariate Structure of Design Evaluation: A Cylindrex of Nurses' Conceptualizations'*, submitted.

Levy, S. (1976), 'Use of the Mapping Sentence for Coordinating Theory and Research', *Quality and Quantity*, Vol. 10, pp. 117-125.

Lingoes, J.C. (1968), 'The Multlvariate Analysis of Qualitative Data', *Multivariate Behaviour Research*, Vol. 3, pp. 61-94.

Lingoes, J.C. (ed.) (1979), *Geometric Representation of Relational Data*, Ml: Mathesis, Ann Arbor.

Miles, H. & Canter, D. (1976), *'Energy Conservation in British Universities'*, mimeo, University of Surrey.

Mulaik, S.A. (1972). *The Foundations of Factor Analysis*, McGraw-Hill, New York.

Pallack, M.L., Cook, D.A. & Sullivan, J.J. (1980), 'Commitment and Energy Conservation', in L. Bickman (ed.), *Applied Social Psychology Annual 1*, Sage, Beverley Hills.

Payne, R.L., et al. (1976), 'Organizational Climate and Job Satisfaction; A Conceptual Synthesis', *Organizational Behaviour and Human Performance,* Vol. 16, pp. 45-62.

Rees, K. & Canter, D. (1979), 'Comparing Married Couples' Satisfaction with their Housing Environment', paper presented to *ICEP Guildford, July 1979*.

Runkel, P.J. & McGrath, J.E. (1972), *Research on Human Behaviour; A Systematic Guide to Method,* Holt, Reinhart and Winston, New York.

Saxe, L. & Fine, M. (1980), 'Reorienting Social Psychology toward Application: A Methodological Analysis', in L. Bickman (ed.), *Applied Social Psychology Annual 1,* Sage, Beverley Hills/London.

Shapira, Z. & Zevelun, E. (1978), 'On the Use of Facet Analysis in Organizational Behaviour Research; Some Conceptual Considerations and an Example', *Working Paper No. 10-78-79 Graduate School of Administration, Carnegie - Mellon University,* Pittsburg, PA.

Sherif, M. & Sherif, C. (1969), *Social Psychology,* Harper and Row/John Weatherhill, New York/Tokyo.

Shye, S. (ed.) (1978), *Theory Construction and Data Analysis in the Behavioural Sciences,* Jossey-Bass, San Fransisco.

Shye, S. & Elizur, D. (1976), 'Worries about Deprivation of Job Rewards Following Computerization; A Partial Order Scalogram Analysis', *Human Relations,* Vol. 29, pp.63-71.

Stouffer, S.S., Guttman, L., Suchman, E.A., Lazarfeld, P.F., Star, S.A. & Clausen, J.A. (1950), *Measurement and Prediction,* Princeton University Press, New Jersey.

Vygotsky, L. (1934), *Thought and Language*, Massachusetts Institute of Technology, Massachusetts.

4 A Multiple Sorting Procedure for Studying Conceptual Systems

Constructs and categories

Many psychologists have emphasised that the ability to function in the world relates closely to the ability to form categories and to construct systems of classification by which nonidentical stimuli can be treated as equivalent (e.g., Miller 1956; Bruner et al, 1956; Rosch, 1977). As Smith and Medin (1981) have recently reiterated, if we had to deal with objects, issues, behaviour, or feelings on the basis of each unique example, then the effort involved would make intelligent existence virtually impossible. Thus, an understanding of the categories people use and how they assign concepts to those categories is one of the central clues to the understanding of human behaviour. As consequence, one of the important questions for many investigations is the nature and organisation of the concepts that people have, specific to the issues being explored.

In the present chapter, a procedure for exploring the categories and systems of classification that people use in any given context will be described. It is known as the *multiple sorting procedure* and it allows a flexible exploration of conceptual systems either at the individual or the group level. The rationale for the procedure will first be discussed and then examples of its use for answering a variety of different research questions will be presented.

In this discussion of the nature and organisation of people's conceptual systems, an important distinction must be made between the underlying categorisation processes and the 'ordinary' explanations that people give for their actions. It is the former that is the focus of this chapter; the latter will be discussed in another chapter by Brown and Canter.

As Brown and Canter argue, many research questions are best answered by reference to 'ordinary' explanations, especially when the expertise of the individual being questioned and the unique understanding that he or she can bring to the situation are central. Alteratively, in those studies where the research questions focus on the general conceptual processes underlying the explanations people might give, it is frequently fruitful to explore the categorical organisation of those conceptual processes.

For example, if the research were questioning the compromises involved in administering a prison, then the explanations of the prison governor would be

°We are grateful to Judith Sixsmith for her comments on this chapter crucial to the study. On the other hand, if the differences in the experiences of inmates of different prisons were being explored, then it would be important to examine the classification schemes which prisoners applied to their prison experience.

The study of personal systems of classification and of explanations are not inevitably distinct. They are both part of the general psychological approach that places an emphasis on understanding the individual's own framework for dealing with and making sense of the world. They do, however, place an emphasis on different aspects of people's conceptualisations, and are consequently of particular relevance for different types of research question.

Thus, although the study of the personal categorisation processes people use in thinking and acting can be recognised as being part of the general exploration of meaning, it does focus especially on subjective or personal meaning. In the book they edited, *Personal Meanings*, Shepherd and Watson (1982) show with many examples that in both a clinical and a scientific mode of operation, practitioners need to construe the personal meanings of others. This construal requires, they argue, the development of a framework for describing the professional understanding of the meanings utilised by others. For such a framework to be authentic, Shepherd and Watson insist, following Harré and Secord (1972), that it must draw upon an intensive rather than extensive approach to data collection. This involves working directly with individuals in their own terms, respecting their ability to formulate ways of thinking about the world and their experience of it. This contrasts with the use of standard questionnaires or structured interviewing procedures in which the researcher has formulated views on what the respondent will wish to comment upon, and so the researcher is, in effect, checking the extent to which the respondent will endorse the experimenter's speculations.

The intensive study of personal meanings also has strong parallels in the studies of *subjective meaning* carried out by Szalay and Deese (1978). They argue for a clear distinction between 'lexical' and subjective meaning. The former being an attempt to define in the public forum (as in a dictionary) the commonly held meanings of words, the latter being an account of what is salient to an individual together with an indication of its affectivity. They see the study of these meanings as being crucial to the understanding of culture.

It is their focus on culture that leads Szalay and Deese to refer to *subjective* meaning, and the client-oriented perspective of Shepherd and Watson which leads them to deal with *personal* meaning. Yet they both have much in common. They both emphasise the need to understand the conceptual system of the individuals being studied or helped. The conceptual framework of constructs and the categories on which the respondent draws are seen by both as the starting point for understanding the respondent's actions in the world.

In Britain, at least, the concern with understanding the personal conceptual systems of individuals was spurred on by the writings of Kelly (1955) and helped along by the prolific enthusiasm of Fransella and Bannister (e.g., Fransella and Bannister, 1977). Yet, the view that each individual had a unique way of construing the world was not alien to William James many years earlier (1890) and was emphasised in some of Allport's writings (1937), when he argued for the value of an idiographic approach. Anthropologists and sociologists, especially those with a structuralist orientation, have also emphasised throughout the present century the importance of understanding individuals' systems of meaning (cf. Douglas, 1977). Furthermore, social psychologists, in studying the role of situations in human behaviour, have established the importance of the interpretations people make of those situations in which they find themselves (Argyle et al, 1981).

Restrictive explorations

The brief review above reveals that there are two common themes in many disparate writings on psychology. One is the need to explore the view of the world as understood by the respondents in any enquiry. The second is the recognition that world view is built around the categorisation schemes people employ in their daily lives. Yet, unfortunately, psychologists have been influenced by a further consideration, which has tended to dilute the impact of these two themes: the desire for quantitative, preferably computer analysable, results. Most computing procedures have limitations that are so fundamental that they are taken for granted and rarely challenged, thus influencing the data collection procedures in ways so subtle that researchers are unaware of them. A self structuring cycle is then set in motion. Data are collected in a form that fits known methods of analysis. Standard analytical procedures gain in popularity and are easy to use because they fit the usual data. Data are then commonly collected in the form appropriate to the standard procedures. Thus the existing capabilities of readily available computing procedures help to generate standard forms of data collection, even if those computing procedures are inappropriate for the psychological issues being studied. Without going into a lot of technical detail, a number of restrictions imposed by conventional, widely used, statistical procedures can be summarized:

1. The most commonly used statistics tend to limit data to those having a strong, clear, linear order. Categorical data are seen as being difficult to accommodate. Thus, rating scales (e.g., 7-point) are much preferred to qualitative categories.
2. The procedures limit the structure of the set of variables, so that there are the same number for each respondent. Furthermore, the number of divisions into which each variable is coded is constrained, so that it is the same for all people. Analysis is limited to the manipulation of arithmetic means and correlations over large groups, but this requires that the actual organisation of the data for each respondent is identical.
3. Because of their computational efficiency and mathematical elegance, statistical models have tended to be restricted to those that are based on assumptions of underlying linear dimensions and that consequently generate dimensional explanatory models. Qualitative models, although increasing in popularity, are still rare.

These constraints on the analysis of data have become more apparent with the increasing availability of other computing procedures that do not have these limitations and with the strengthening of the idiographic perspective. Indeed, it is being recognised that the popularity of procedures such as the semantic differential (Osgood et al, 1957) are due to the ease of data analysis rather than any conviction that they are measuring important aspects of human experience. The semantic differential with its 7-point scales, standard set of items, and factor analysis of results, has been shown to be insensitive to differences between cultures (Osgood, 1962), and, although this may be of interest to cross-cultural psychologists, it does not suggest itself as a technique that will reveal important differences between individuals.

In effect, the semantic differential constrains the concepts people can reveal by providing them with a set of terms to which to respond and by giving precise instructions as to how that response can be structured. Procedures that allow some possibility for the respondent to frame his/her own answers are essential if the essence of any given individual's conceptual system is to be established. Thus, open-ended procedures, especially those built around the interaction potentials provided by the one-to-one interview, recommend themselves to the student of conceptual systems.

Many researchers (unaware of the range of analyses now available) are fearful of embracing open-ended procedures because they are concerned that their results will be difficult to interpret and the report or publication they seek will be difficult to structure. Thus, even when they are interested in their respondents' understanding of the world, they explore it through multiple-choice questions or very constrained rating procedures. Yet, serious researchers will still insist on what is usually termed 'good pilot research'. This does involve talking to people in a relaxed, open-ended way and learning from them about the concepts they use in a particular context. It is often at this stage that the real objectives, and in effect the major findings, of the research emerge. Subsequent research frequently only clarifies a little, or provides numerical support for, the insights gained at this 'pilot' stage. This is a curious state of affairs when data comes from one part of the research activity and insights from another. Research would be more effective if procedures allowed the interviewees to express their own view of the issues at hand, in their own way, whilst still providing information that is structured enough for systematic analysis and reporting.

Beyond the repertory grid

The interview, with its potential for subtle interactions and its concern with the interviewee's understandings, is a fruitful context in which to explore people's concepts. Over the past few years a number of procedures have emerged for generating and examining people's conceptual systems within that context. One of the most popular is Kelly's repertory grid (Kelly, 1955). As many authors have noted (e.g., Fransella and Bannister, 1977; Adams-Weber, 1979; Bonarius et al,

1981), the repertory grid, deriving as it does from a theory of people that puts emphasis on their conceptual systems, does have much to recommend it; yet the Role Repertory Test, which has evolved from Kelly's original proposals, is often used with less sympathy for Kelly's Personal Construct Theory than might be expected. Furthermore, the forms of statistical analysis known to Kelly limited the forms of development in grid analysis procedures, which has had direct consequences for the forms of grid which he and his followers have developed.

Fransella and Bannister (1977) comment on many of these weaknesses of the grid as used. They point out:

1. The grid 'has been turned into a technology which generates its own problems and then solves these problems. Such problems do not necessarily relate to any attempt to understand the meaning which the person attaches to his universe' (p. 113).
2. Grid use has been limited by the 'requirement that the subject present his judgements in handy grid statistical format before we can analyse pattern' (p. 116).
3. It is a fair guess that it is the mathematical ingenuity of the grid which has attracted psychologists rather than its possibilities as a way of changing the relationship between 'psychologist' and 'subject' (p. 117).

Recent developments in computing procedures have weakened some of these criticisms, especially interactive on-line computing, which allows a much more flexible exploration of construct systems (cf. Shaw, 1982), but the main point made by Fransella and Bannister, that the grid technology as such has masked other possibilities for exploring personal constructs, still remains.

The repertory grid technique is neither as unique in its contribution nor as definitively special to personal construct theory as its users often claim. Kelly himself traces the origins of the grid to the sorting procedures used by Vygotsky (1934) and others, and thus puts his grid technique firmly in the realm of the exploration of categories and concepts. He writes:

> Methodologically the Repertory Test is an application of the familiar concept formation test procedure. It uses as 'objects' those persons with whom the subject has had to deal in his daily living. Instead of sorting *Vygotsky blocks* or *BRL objects* the subject sorts people. The technique bears some resemblance to the sorting employed in the Horowitz Faces Test. It is also somewhat similar to Hartley's later procedure in which he used pictures in a sorting test. Rotter and Jessor have also experimented tentatively with the formation of 'social concepts' in the sorting of paper dolls of the Make a Picture Story (M.A.P.S.) Test. (Kelly, 1955, Vol. 1, pp. 219-220)

He emphasises that his test differs from these other procedures in two ways. First, it is concerned with content, 'how the items are dealt with', as well as the more usual concern for the level of abstraction involved. Second, it is 'aimed at role constructs'. This latter emphasis was seen as being relevant to clinical practice, not an inevitable emphasis for all studies of personal construct systems.

Instead of Q-sorts and paired-comparisons

The Q'-sort' technique was, like the repertory grid, developed as a way of examining the critical concepts people hold about role figures or events of significance to them (Stephenson, 1953). But, while this method enables people to assign elements to categories, the categories themselves are specified, usually as increments of an adjectival scale. Moreover, the Q-sort is typically used in a form whereby the interviewee is required to assign elements to the categories in a specified (almost always an approximately normal) distribution (Pitt and Zube, 1979). The use of an enforced distribution is defended, in part, on the grounds that the procedure provides data that is more conveniently processed (Block, 1961), and eliminates the problem, inherent in rating scale procedures, of different individuals calibrating the scale in different ways (Palmer, 1980). These restrictions on the interviewee's sorting behaviour thus make the Q-sort more akin to the semantic differential technique than to the intensive one-to-one interview procedure we are advocating.

Other highly restrictive sorting procedures have recently been developed as an alternative to paired-comparison judgements of similarity. For example, Ward (1977) and Ward and Russell (1981) have used sorting procedures, in which both the sorting criteria and the number of categories are specified, as a means of generating similarity matrices. Although Ward argues that the process of sorting is probably more 'natural' for the interviewee than similarity judgements, the key argument for its use seems to be that it is less time consuming than paired-comparisons while at the same time provides equivalent similarity data that is suitable for multidimensional scaling procedures.

Indeed, the development of multidimensional scaling procedures grew out of the analysis of similarity judgements of pairs of stimuli. Schiffman et al, (1981) see similarity judgements as 'the *primary* means for recovering the underlying structure of relationships among a group of stimuli' (p. 19). They go on to state that they think that similarity judgements are to be preferred to verbal descriptors because such descriptors are 'highly subjective and often conceptually incomplete' (p. 20). The view of the authors of the present chapter is that, whilst there may be some validity to this contention in the experimental study of perceptual stimuli, to which Schiffman and her colleagues repeatedly make reference, such a view of all human conceptualisations is unnecessarily restrictive and has not been defended with any theoretical strength.

It is our contention that perceived similarity is a more complex phenomena than can accurately be described by a single rating. Perceived similarity may, in fact, be defined by a set of multiple categorisations based on a wide variety of criteria. In many cases it is the overall patterns that emerge as a result of the concepts people themselves naturally apply to the objects or elements that is of psychological concern. Even when people are unable to put words on their categorisation of elements, it is the structure they impose on the world that should be the starting point for the psychologist, rather than any general mathematical theory.

For, although interview-based sorting procedures do have a long history, it is only recently that the full possibilities of this approach have become apparent. These possibilities attempt to avoid the limitations of earlier procedures. The multiple sorting procedure does not impose a view of the likely structure and content of an individual's conceptual system on the interviewee. It minimises the 'technique for its own sake' syndrome by allowing the exploration of both the nature and the organisation of concepts about any issue, maintaining the freedom and open-ended qualities considered so essential by many researchers, yet still providing for systematic analysis of individuals or groups. The use of the multiple sorting procedure and systematic analysis of data from it is possible, in part because of developments in nonmetric multidimensional scaling procedures, the use of which will also be illustrated later in this chapter.

Sorting as a focus for an interview

As has been noted, many of the explorations of which interviews are a part are aimed at coming to grips with the conceptualisations of the interviewee, whether it is a market research study, such as that looking at the corporate image of banks (Frost and Canter, 1982), or a more theoretical exploration of architects' use of stylistic terms (Groat, 1982), or even research of a more pragmatic nature, looking at why people move house (Brown and Sime, 1980). In all cases it is the particular categories and concepts people use that is at issue, as well as the way in which they use them. The interview is especially suited to these types of exploration, because the interviewer and the interviewee can explore each other's understandings of the questions being asked and because the one-to-one situation can accommodate a more intensive interaction.

Unfortunately though, the potentials of the interview are frequently its pitfall. Asking open-ended questions in the relaxed way thought to increase rapport is the formula for unanalysable material. What is needed is a way of providing a focus for the interview to guide and structure the material produced without constraining the interviewee unduly. Bruner et al (1956) were some of the first to show clearly the possibilities for exploring the nature of the concepts people have by studying how they assign elements to categories. Such a procedure provides a focus for the interview, allowing other related material beyond that generated by the sorting to be noted. Yet few have followed this lead out of the laboratory by using as elements material of direct significance to the responding individuals.

Sorting procedures of various types have probably been used most frequently in the environmental psychology field, perhaps because they enable researchers to use illustrations and other visual material which are difficult to accommodate within other procedures. Specific applications of sorting technique within environmental psychology have ranged from those used simply to generate similarity matrices

(Ward, 1977; Horayangkura, 1978; Ward and Russell, 1981) to those seeking to integrate the sorting process with the verbal descriptions and explanations inherent in a one-to-one interview situation (Gärling, 1976; Palmer, 1978; Groat, 1982). In the case of the latter, the researchers have intentionally used the sorting technique precisely because it is free of the limitations discussed earlier.

In the case of social psychology, one of the earliest approaches to the sorting stimuli is found in the work by Thurstone and Chave (1929), who used the judgements people made of questionnaire items as a basis for assigning weights to those items. It was the discovery that the attitude of the judges influenced the pattern of judgement that lead Sherif and Sherif (1969) to develop the 'own categories' procedure and direct measure of 'ego-involvement' in attitudinal issues. In the 'own categories' procedure, judges assign attitudinal items to categories in terms of how extreme the attitudes expressed are thought to be. The distribution of the items in the categories is then used as a measure of the intensity of the judge's own attitudes. This differs from the clinical object sorting procedure, which Kelly discussed, in that the distribution of items to categories in a predetermined sorting concept is the main concern.

Contemporary psychologists such as Eckman (1975) have also used free sorting procedures in their work on normal verbal communication. In a related manner, Tajfel (1981) developed a theory of social categorisation to explain 'in' and 'out' group behaviour. Tajfel (1978) states: 'The role of categorisation in perceptual and other cognitive activities has been for many years one of the central issues in psychological theory' (p. 305).

Tajfel's work involves organising information in certain ways, examining differences and similarities between the content of categorisations. The chief function of this process resides in its role as a tool in systematizing the environment for action. However, Tajfel argues that assigning items to categories is influenced by the other categories in the structure of a person's experience. His experimental work was aimed at unravelling the complexities of prejudice through the process of category assignments.

Clearly then, in using the sorting procedures as an interview focus, the interviewer's task is to identify the interviewee's salient categories and the pattern of assignments used to relate categories to elements. The more freedom the interviewee can be given in performing this task the more likely that the interviewer will learn something of the interviewee's construct system rather than just clarifying his own. Such freedom should extend to the range and structure of the categories, of which the constructs are composed, as well as to constructs and elements sorted.

The multiple sorting procedure

The multiple sorting procedure advocated here asks little of the interviewees other than that they assign elements to categories of their own devising; it differs from the other previously discussed response formats in that no limitations are necessarily placed on how the sorting is to be done. In fact, the respondent is encouraged to sort the elements, using different criteria, a number of times. The rationale for this less restrictive version of the sorting process is the belief that the meanings and explanations associated with an individual's use of categories are as important as the actual distribution of elements into the categories.

The actual act of sorting items is a common activity. For example, in choosing a house, people will literally sort through the particulars sent to them by estate agents. In many other areas of choice, whether it be clothing, books, partners, or political parties, there is an explicit selection on the basis of a personal categorisation scheme. But even when a selection is not overtly involved, such as in evaluating how successful a given setting is likely to be for a given activity, or an essay in gaining a good mark, the judgement is based on an implicit categorisation scheme. The multiple sorting procedure aims to bring to light these personal schemes.

To carry out the multiple sorting, a person is presented with a set of elements and an introduction and instructions as follows:

> I am carrying out a study of what people think and feel about *children* [A] so I am asking a number of people *chosen at random* [B] to look at the following *pictures* [C] and sort them into groups in such a way that all the pictures in any group are similar to each other in some important way and different from those in the other groups. You can put the picture into as many groups as you like and put as many pictures into each group as you like. It is your views that count.

> When you have carried out a sorting, I would like you to tell me the *reasons* [D] for your sorting and what it is that the pictures in each group have *in common* [E].

> When you have sorted the pictures once I will ask you to *do it again* [F], using any different principles you can think of and we will carry on as many times as you feel able to produce different sorts. Please feel free to tell me whatever occurs to you as you are sorting the pictures.

The items underlined and indicated with letters in [] are those components of the instructions that are likely to change for different procedures in relation to different research questions. It must be emphasised, however, that these instructions are only a general statement of what is possible. The flexibility of the procedure is such that many different variations of the instructions are possible. Pilot work is always essential in order to discover what particular instructions are appropriate for each study, although typically all components [A] to [F] must be explicitly dealt with.

The elements to be sorted ([C] in the instructions), depending on the research question, may be generated by the interviewee or the interviewer; they may be labels, concepts, objects, pictures, or whatever, as will be illustrated. The person is usually asked to look through the elements to familiarise him/herself with them; also, the purposes of the research enterprise are explained (relating to instructions components [A] and [B]). In particular, it is pointed out that the interviewer is interested in the interviewee's ways of thinking about the elements presented. The interviewee is then asked to sort the elements into groups so that all the elements in any given group have something important in common, which distinguishes them from the elements in other groups. Thus, a number of groups are produced which may vary in the number of elements in them, and of course the number of groups produced may also vary from person to person and from one set of elements to another.

After this initial sort, further sorts may be carried out by the same individual, a number of times. But let us consider the initial sort before moving to multiple sorts.

An individual example

Consider a preliminary example, here drawn from a multiple sort carried out with a gambler we will call Ace. We were interested in Ace's views of various casinos, as part of a larger project to study what it was that gamblers enjoyed about gambling. The particular purpose of the sorting procedure was to see the basis on which a gambler selects which Casino to visit and to get some understanding of his view of the Casinos available. We wanted to know what sort of world a gambler moves around in, what type of choices he sees as being available to him.

Ace was asked to list on cards all the casinos he knew in any detail and to assign names for his own convenience. For the researcher's convenience, each card was numbered on the back. On his first sort, Ace chose to divide the cards into three groupings. These groupings were recorded as shown in *Table 1*, by the simple process of noting under each group the letter for the card.

At this stage, the researcher has an indication, without any verbal labelling, of one category scheme for the respondent. Such information can be very valuable, especially when working with groups of people who are not especially articulate. But there are a number of further developments of the procedure possible within the same framework. The verbal concomitants of the category scheme can be explored by asking the interviewees to indicate the basis on which they have carried out the sorting, as in the instructions [D] and [E]. This generates two levels of description. The first is a superordinate description of the principle for the sorting, from instructions [D], for example, 'whether the casinos have frills or not, or 'the amount of money to play the lowest stake'. The second is a set of category labels for each of the groups (instructions [E]), for example, for the 'frills' sort, Ace's categories were 'places with no frills', 'places with sedate dining', and 'vaudeville'; for the 'stakes' sort, Ace's categories were 'less than £5,' 'between £5 and £25', and 'greater than £25'.

A useful way of recording this verbal information shown by reference to Ace's sorting of casinos is also in Table 1. The categories are summarised with a description of the category scheme for the sort as well as labels for each of the groups within this sort. Other comments and points of clarification made by the respondent can easily be accommodated within this format, as well as any order that might be given to the category groupings. Given the value of the procedure as a focus for exploring a content domain, these comments may generate material of considerable value in their own right. Thus, the researcher need not reduce the responses to bipolar scales, which are often ambiguous when considered at some time after the interview.

Table 1

Record of Ace's Sorts

First Sort: 'Class of Casino'
    1. 'Gaming Halls': G, H, D, A
    2. 'Middle Class': B, C
    3. 'High Class': E, F
Second Sort: 'Type of Frills'
    1. 'Just Gambling': A
    2. 'Baudeville': B, G, H
    3. 'Sedate Dining': E, D, C, F
Third Sort: 'Size of the Stake'
    1. 'Less than £5': A
    2. 'Between £5 and £25': G, H, B
    3. 'Greater than £25': C, D, E, F
Fourth Sort: 'Most likely place for me to make money at'
    1. 'Most likely': A, G, H
    2. 'Not so much': B
    3. 'Too expensive': C, D, E, F
Fifth Sort: 'Preference'
    1. 'Most preferred': A, G, H, E
    2. 'Solid Casinos': C, D
    3. 'Bit Quiet': F
    4. 'Did not like at all':B

---

[a]Casinos: A-Golden Nugget; B-Playboy; C-Park Lane; D-Palm Beach; E-Hereford; F-Park Tower; G and H-Las Vegas casinos.

Unlike the analyses discussed by Schiffman et al (1981), and used, for example, by Ward and Russell (1981), the multiple sorting data need not be reduced to association matrixes, typically aggregated across groups. Both the superordinate description and the category labels can be subjected to content analysis and to multivariate statistical analyses, but it should be noted that no structure or order to these descriptions is initially assumed or implied. This is particularly important for the category labels. The bipolar dichotomies of rating scales are not assumed, nor is the order of items from ranking or scaling. If the interviewee specifies a particular order, as in the 'amount of the stake' example, then note can be taken of that, but if any order might be more obscure, as in the 'frills' example, then that can be utilised as well. Indeed, category schemes frequently emerge that are not simply bipolar; and this raises important questions about the extent to which such bipolarity, assumed in much research, is an actual feature of psychological processes or an artifact of the structured measuring instruments used. Furthermore, in some cases an interviewee may choose to sort some of the elements and leave others as irrelevant to the overall sort taken into account. This irrelevant group is treated as forming a further category and can be incorporated in the subsequent analysis without any loss of information or imposition of a superordinate categorisation on all the elements.

Having produced one sort of the elements, it is of value in many projects for the multiple sorting to continue by asking people to examine the elements again and to try and produce another category scheme with new descriptors (instructions [F]). Table 1 gives a summary of all five sortings produced by Ace in the interview conducted with him. Analysis of this will be discussed later. It should also be noted that the number of elements sorted here (eight casinos) is limited by the number of casinos to which anyone has ready access in London, and might not give the richest picture possible. The process can continue as many times as the interviewee feels able to sort the elements. In research carried out to date, two or three sorts are common, but up to seven or eight are frequently possible, with 15 or more occurring in some cases. The number of elements that it seems fruitful to use is in the region of 15 to 25. Depending on the individual, of course, a complete set of sorts may take anything from 10 minutes to well over an hour, which may also be extended insofar as the sorting is used as a focus for other issues explored in the interview.

Hypothesis testing

The example used so far, from the casino sortings, is simple enough to illustrate the procedure in use with one person, as a basis for getting to understand some particular aspects of that individual's conceptual system. But the power of the multiple sorting task as a means for testing hypotheses of conceptualisations common across a number of people can also be readily illustrated. Let us consider, for example, the work of Bishop (1983).

Bishop had as a central concern the role the age of buildings played in people's views of their surroundings. However, he was aware that his own fascination with the age of buildings might have given him a particular perspective and that this way of thinking about buildings might not have been very important to most people. However, since it is clear that people can comment on a building's age, any direct questioning about age or its significance might have given a spuriously high weighting to the role of age. Bishop therefore carried out a multiple sorting with a number of respondents. He did this by preparing a set of photographs of buildings which differed in age and gave them to people to carry out a set of free sorts, as described above.

Bishop's hypothesis was strongly supported. Thirty of the thirty-five people he asked used age as a basis for sorting, although only eight used it as the basis of their first sort. Bishop went a step further and classified his respondents in terms of the type of age sorting they made, showing quite convincingly that their understanding of architectural age varied very greatly, although they spontaneously used the concept. This differentiation of his groups laid the foundations for the development of his study.

To see the potential range of uses of, and variation on, the multiple sorting procedure and ways of analysing data from it, we will now turn to other specific examples.

Variations in elements sorted

The types of elements that can be used for sorting are limited only by the imagination of the investigator and the practicalities of what can be carried about and sorted on the surfaces available. Indeed, the development of microcomputers offers some intriguing possibilities for increasing the range and variety of elements that can be sorted; for example, moving objects, even for monitoring the process of sorting by recording the hesitations and false starts that might otherwise get lost in a paper and pencil record. From the initial uses of sorting procedures, as noted earlier, a great number of different objects have been sorted. But in the more recent explorations of the content and structure of free, multiple sortings, a variety of representations of objects, or simulations, have also been used. Groat (1982), for example, used *photographs* of buildings taken from architectural magazines, books and slide collections, to explore how architects' ways of thinking about famous buildings compared with the conceptual systems of accountants. Oakley (1980) used *labels* of places to stay such as hotel, parents' home, or hospital, to examine the views residents had of Salvation Army hostels in which they were living. Grainger (1980) had architects and their clients sort the *activities* a proposed building might house, in order to establish their different understandings of what the building's functions were to be.

Focus of the elements

In general, the more concrete and specific the elements are and the more familiar the respondent is with the elements, the more likely it is that they will be able to produce a number of rich and varied sorts. Abstract labels of possible emotions, for example, are likely to encourage relatively few sorts, whereas a set of detailed descriptions of actual places a person has direct experience of is likely to lead to the generation of a great many sorts from each respondent. The selection of elements will always need to be guided by an awareness of what the respondents are normally used to considering and whether the research is best served by a simulation, a representation of some entity, or by reference to the actual phenomenon itself.

A further consideration in selecting the range of elements to use is how big a variation to select. If general stereotypic sorts are of interest, then a very broad range across the element domain is advisable. For example, a study of conceptualisations of medical specialities among medical students would possibly be best studied using a list of all the specialities as organised in a medical text book. On the other hand, if students' individual choices of future careers were being explored, then a subset of specialities described in relation to their working context and with reference to the students' direct experience may well generate more specific sortings, revealing the idiosyncrasies of particular individuals' conceptual systems.

Generation of the elements

In considering how the elements should be generated, two matters need to be considered: (1) whether the elements are to be generated by the investigator or not, and (2) whether the elements will have a specified structure or be a sample of some identified population.

If the researcher is setting out to test some hypotheses about people's conceptual systems, then it is likely that the elements will be identified by the researcher. For example, Groat (1982) chose photographs of buildings to test her particular hypotheses about architects' conceptions of styles. On the other hand, in the example with Ace described above, it was essential to elicit the casinos of which he had direct experience. Similarly, Groat ensured that her set of photographs included three specified styles and four building functions, whereas for the gambler, all the casinos he had actually visited were used.

The generation of the elements thus has a direct bearing on whether the sorting procedure is to be used for exploratory, heuristic, or descriptive purposes or hypotheses testing. This procedure then has potential at many different stages and in many different areas of research endeavour.

Construct elaboration

As has already been mentioned, the sorting procedure allows constructs to be elaborated in many different ways, depending on the goals of the research activity and on the capabilities of the respondents. If the research is aimed, for example, at identifying whether residents of a hostel think of its function differently as a consequence of how long they have been there, then a knowledge of which other places of residence they think are similar to their own hostel may be of great value. For instance, Oakley (1980), in his study of hostel residents, generated data from the sorting procedure without probity for labels of the categories being used. His respondents did find verbalisation difficult, but the groupings of the elements themselves provided him with some useful basic data, which enabled the Salvation Army to clarify some of the principles on which to consider the provision of new hostels.

On the other hand, if the aim of the research had been to look directly at the processes of individual rehabilitation, it would have been necessary to uncover the concepts residents use for deciding where they are going to stay. In this case, labels associated with each category, or group of elements, would have to be elicited. It is likely that a different set of elements would have been of use in such a study, so that respondents with few verbal skills could be encouraged to express their understanding of what is available to them.

Foci of analysis

The reluctance of earlier researchers to use procedures as open ended as the multiple sorting task, may to some extent be due to the difficulty they perceive in analysing the data generated. However, besides the developments in content analysis, discussed by Barbara Mostyn in an earlier chapter, all of which can be directly applied to the category descriptions generated during the sorting, it is possible to use nonmetric MDS procedures. These enable the analysis to be focused on different issues depending on the research question.

What is meant here by 'focusing' is that the research procedure can be tuned to any of a number of different aspects of the material potentially available. The researcher can, for example, choose to deal with differences between groups or to concentrate on particular sorting criteria within individuals. The multiple sorting procedure as such has no special limitation as to the research enterprise for which it is appropriate. It is simply a data generating procedure which can be harnessed to the goals of a wide range of projects.

First, we shall consider studies of group differences, looking at the relationships between elements and then the relationships between categories. Second, we shall consider studies of differences within individuals.

Group differences

Elements, concepts, and people. In any study of conceptual systems there exist three broad ways in which the data can be examined: by considering differences between the people, differences between the elements, or differences between the concepts and categories to which the elements are assigned. The data matrix that is always possible can be thought of as a cube, as shown in *Figure 1*.

The importance of the data cube is that it shows the variety of possibilities there are for data analysis. In essence, each of the planes of the cube, A, B, or C, provides a different analysis possibility by aggravating combinations of the dimensions. For example, in the prison study described below only one aspect of the concepts was dealt with - similarity to 'this prison'. Thus, it was plane A, elements across people, which was the focus of analysis. A study centring on the structure of the concepts a group of people have across one or many elements would be dealing with the data in plane C, because it would require the differences between people to be ignored. A study comparing people in their conceptualisations would be drawn from plane B.

Figure 1 can be used as a guide to help clarify the research question by showing which 'slice' through the cube is being used and what 'collapsing' of data from another dimension is necessary. It is extremely complex to carry out analyses that combine all three aspects of the data in one operation. It is usually more appropriate to proceed through the analysis in stages, working with one plane of the data cube at a time.

One of the most obvious uses for the multiple sorting procedure is to compare the conceptual systems of different groups. There is now a large literature showing how different groups of individuals addressing the same topic may have quite different conceptualisations about it, which in turn give rise to different evaluations of the issues at hand and related actions. However, as Canter (1977) pointed out, studies using standard response formats, such as the semantic differential, tend to underestimate the difference in perspectives between individuals. Indeed, such procedures tend only to indicate small differences in emphases rather than revealing the radical differences in conceptual systems commonly present when different groups interact in relation to some common object.

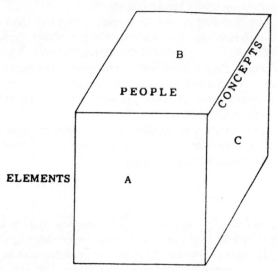

Figure 1 The data cube

The repertory grid is commonly used for group comparisons and frequently with some success (Adams-Webber, 1979); but it does have severe practical limitations, both in the number of elements that can be dealt with in any given study and in the overall time taken to complete a grid (Canter et al, 1976). For comparisons of groups it is also frequently the case that much of the detail generated by the grid is superfluous and not used in analysis. An open, free sorting procedure often has the advantages of individual sensitivity without the procedural disadvantages of the grid.

Ambrose showed the value of a sorting procedure for revealing group differences in a study reported in Canter (1980). In a study of different prisons, inmates and members of staff were asked to sort labels describing places in which people might live. One of the labels to be included in this sort was 'this prison'. A matrix was derived for each respondent showing which other card was put into the same sort as the cards specifying 'this prison'. This matrix, in effect, consists of a series of profiles for each individual indicating whether or not they saw their particular prison as similar to all the other places listed. A multidimensional scalogram analysis (MSAI; see Lingoes, 1973, and Zvulun, 1978 for details) was carried out to see whether there were any similarities or differences between the different respondents and their different institutions. *Figures 2 and 3* reveal the results.

Figure 2 shows the partitioning of the space for the prisons and Figure 3 the partitioning of the space for the prison staff and the prisoners. Each point in this space represents an individual. The closer together any two individuals are the more similar are their profiles in the data matrix. The advantage of the MSA procedure is that it only deals with each response as a categorical one comparing the categories with each other. No order is assumed between the various categories, nor is any similarity of meaning assigned to the categories for each of the variables. The variables in this case were created by each of the cards used in the sort.

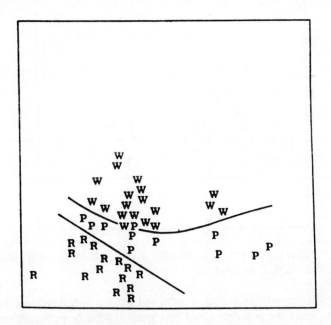

Figure 2 MSAI of card sort of residential setup by respondents in three prison establishments. W, satellite design prison in a rural location with a regional catchment area; R, block design prison in an urban location with a regional catchment area; P, radial design prison in an urban location with a local catchment.

Looking at these MSA results, it is clear that there is no difference between staff and inmates. No clear regions of the space can be identified for these two different groups. In other words, there is not an effect of role on their perceptions of the particular prison. On the other hand, there are clear regional partitions for the different institutions. Furthermore, the order of the three regions through the space places the institutions in a sequence, from those that are most strict in their regime to those that are least strict. This shows that the strictness of the regime can be recaptured from the assignment of the institutions to the place categories. It is also interesting to see here that through individuals' free sorts, the perspective shared by prisoners and staff on the nature of the institution is revealed. In this particular case the role groups may well be assumed to be individuals who would not necessarily be expected to work together. Nonetheless, the sorting demonstrates that they do share an understanding of the nature of the institutions.

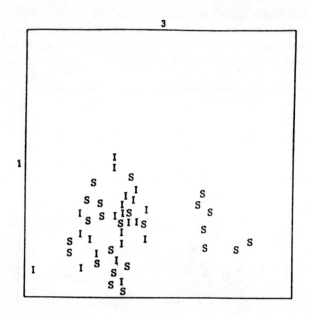

Figure 3   MSAI card sort of residential settings showing staff and inmate respondents: S, staff; I, inmates.

The significance of this finding is increased when it is realised that there is no easy way in which the prisoners could have guessed what the prison officers would have done in a free sort, especially across three different institutions. Yet, in a conventional questionnaire it would have been very difficult to remove social desirability bias from such a situation. Furthermore, the language requirements in terms of fluency and vocabulary that would have been necessary to question people about these subtleties would also have been demanding on many prisoners. However, in the present circumstances a simple assigning of cards to sorting categories appears to have been sufficient to reveal some intriguing differences. Of course, a detailed understanding of the conceptual basis of these differences would not be achieved without a further analysis of the concepts used by staff and inmates. Unfortunately, because of the constrained nature of what was possible within the prison system, the details of the conceptualisations were not explored fully by Ambrose. We will therefore turn to another example to illustrate these more elaborated studies.

The structure of the elements. In some situations it is of particular interest to try and identify the type of conceptual system groups are using. In other words, the structure and content of elements shared by groups of individuals need to be established. With the prison example this was less possible because only one sort was made by each individual, and the particular analysis carried out (reported above) focused on the relationship of one element to all the others. However, it is also possible to carry out analyses that look at the comparison of every element with every other element. Hawkins (1983) did just such an analysis using labels of a variety of possible places with residents of different psychiatric day centres.

Hawkins asked each individual to sort a set of cards labelling places where they might spend their day. Three different day centres were involved in this study, and Hawkins was able to compare the structure of the elements for each of these. She did this by creating an association matrix containing the frequency with which every element was assigned to the same group as every other element, across all sorts and respondents (plane A in Figure 1). A Smallest Space Analysis was carried out on each of the association matrixes created for each of the day centres (cf. Lingoes, 1973; Shye, 1978 for details).

This analysis generates a plot showing that elements more similar to each other in the pattern of sortings to which they are subjected are closer together. *Figure 4* shows the SSA plot for the three different hostels; to aid interpretation regions have been indicated on these plots. It can be seen that the overall structures have a number of similarities. They all show the existence of five groups of elements: work, leisure, service, therapy, and residential. They also show that these groups are qualitatively sequenced, around a circle, rather than having a simple, quantitative linear order to them. Yet, there are some clear differences in the way the residents of the three day centres see the various places. In other words, it is not solely their view of the location of their own particular hostel that is different, but the residents of each day facility actually have a different system of thinking about other possible locations. For example, to the residents of centre C the therapeutic group, including 'this day centre' is seen as being between leisure and residence, whereas for the people in centre A it is between work and residence. This reflects a differing emphasis on rehabilitation to work in the various centres. For centre B, 'this centre' and the other therapy elements are confused with residential items coming close to hotel and house. This relates to the fact that the residents of these day centres have typically been using them for up to eight years and they are more chronic and indeed settled into their daily use of these places as somewhere to go.

This is particularly important for both design and development of therapeutic programs. If the whole regime of a particular psychiatric day centre relates to the way the residents conceptualise the opportunities available to them, and this consequently differs from one centre to another, then any generalised guidance suggested for use in all day centres, which aimed to help people to move into the community, would be ineffective if it did not take into account the conception of 'the community' particular to any given day centre. The results indicate that the attempts to move individuals from their centre out into the community require subtle understanding of how those individuals actually conceive of the community itself.

The structure of constructs. Another focus for analysis is the establishment of the underlying constructual processes the individual brings to bear on a pattern of elements. This issue is particularly well illustrated by the work of Groat (1982) to which reference has already been made. She was concerned with whether or not architects would conceptualise works of architecture in different ways from accountants. She was able to establish quite clearly, using procedures like those described in earlier sections, that the actual sorting of the elements was different for the two groups. However, it was important to Groat's work that she should establish what types of conceptual issues were actually paramount in the judgements being made.

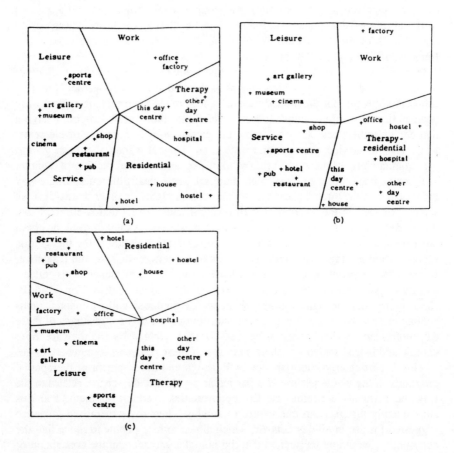

Figure 4 Position of each place on SSA-I plot looking at the frequencies from (a) centre A, (b) centre B, and (c) centre C.

In order to examine the conceptual issues, she developed a matrix based on the categories within similar sorts. In other words, she first identified, through context analysis, the types of sort used by each of her groups of respondents. For example, both groups contained a number of individuals who referred to both the function and the style of the building. Two separate matrixes were produced, one for the function categories, and one for style. In each of these matrixes, the categories were the columns and the 24 buildings sorted were the rows (plane C of Figure 4). The cells of this matrix were a dichotomous score indicating whether that particular building was ever assigned to that category. Smallest Space Analysis of this data showed that the structure of the 'function' categories was very similar for both groups. They both divided the photographs into domestic and non-domestic buildings and within each of these groups distinguished the buildings in terms of scale. However, the style categories were quite distinct. The accountants made a big distinction between what they saw as 'traditional','modern', and 'futuristic' buildings, whereas architects used a classification scheme clearly drawn from the literature of architectural criticism, distinguishing 'Expressionist', 'Brutalist', and 'Post-Modern'.

Groat's study thus shows very well how a detailed analysis of the structure of the conceptualisations of the two groups can reveal subtle differences and similarities in their category schemes. Such differences would normally be hidden by structured questionnaire and interviewing procedures and would be extremely difficult to establish with repertory grids, unless separate grids were developed for each respondent with the consequent time consuming analysis that would involve.

Differences within individuals

In our initial example of a multiple sorting we referred to Ace, a gambler. As part of the same study, a casino manager also went through a sorting procedure using the casino and parts of casinos of which he had direct experience. The results of these sortings are given in *Table 2*. The sortings from these two people, taken together, serve to illustrate the way in which very specific foci can be developed for analysis, dealing directly with the unique, idiosyncratic conceptualisations of particular key individuals.

When individuals carry out detailed sorts on elements that are special to themselves, there is always a possibility that over a variety of sorts they repeat similar categories, simply assigning different labels to each categorisation. Thus, an individual who is fluent but not especially cognitively complex may generate a large number of apparently different sorts, which on closer examination are found to have little in the way of variation between the different sortings.

This is an especially important point if comparison is to be made of individuals, because it is the key aspects of their conceptual systems that we need to understand, not simply how many words they can string together. Thus, it is necessary to do an analysis for each individual and to reveal the main conceptual structure within which the individual is working. In regard to the gambler and the manager separate

Table 2

Record of Casino Manager's Sorting[a]

First Sort: 'Staff Recruitment'
1. 'Career Staff': A, B, C, F
2. 'Recruit from outside': E, D, G
Second Sort: 'Staff Training'
I. 'Little training': A, B, C, F
2. 'More training': E, D, G
Third Sort: 'Staff Benefits'
1. 'Mainly for senior Staff': A, B, C, F
2. 'Also for lower Staff': E, D, G
Fourth Sort: 'Sex of Staff'
1. 'Male only': A, B, C, E, D
2. 'Male and Female': F, G
Fifth Sort: 'Staff Contact with Customers'
1. 'None': A
2. 'Good with company support': G, E, D
3. 'Good with no company support': F
4. 'Unclear': B, C
Sixth Sort: 'Staff Experience'
I. 'Trainee Staff': A, B, C
2. 'Mixed': E, D
3. 'Inexperienced Staff': F, G
Seventh Sort: 'Whether Takes Cheques or Cash'
1. 'Cash': A, B, C
2. 'Mixed': E, D
3. 'Cheques': F, G
Eighth Sort: 'Concern for Customer Quality'
1. 'Quantity only': A, B, C, E
2. 'Quality and Quantity': D
3. 'Quality': F, 6

[a]Casinos: A-Golden Nugget; B-Palm Beach; C-International; D-Hereford; E-Park Lane; F-Curzon House; G-Gladbroke.

analyses for each was carried out and a schematic representation prepared to facilitate a comparison of their two conceptual systems.

The analysis here again used MSA1. In this case each of the sortings acted as a separate variable and each individual had a separate matrix. The matrix consisted of the elements as rows and the sortings as columns (a slice through plane B of Figure 1). The cells of the matrix are numbers indicating the sorting categories to which the different elements were assigned. Each matrix was put into a separate MSA analysis. The analysis, in this instance, generates a configuration in which each element (in this case, casinos) was a point in the space. The closer together any two casinos are in this spatial representation the more similar they are in terms of the categories that are assigned to them over the number of sorts carried out by each individual.

Table 3 shows the data matrix derived from the sorts illustrated in Table 1. *Figure 5a* shows the MSA for the gambler and *Figure 5b* shows the MSA for the manager.

The partitioning of these figures is derived from an examination of the way in which each individual sort contributes to the spatial configuration. Thus, it is clear that the manager divides casinos up on the basis of how they deal with the clientele and how the overall casino management deals with their staff. This gives a two-way classification of casinos: those that select their staff carefully but are not too selective of their clientele; those selective about their clientele but not so careful of their staff; and those not especially careful about how they chose their staff or their clientele. This reveals the division the manager makes between the staff and the clientele and the way in which his perspective relates to selectivity and overall standards. At first sight, the gambler's MSA reveals a very different sorting.

Table 3

Data matrix derived from the sorting produced by age[a]

Elements (Casinos)	First	Second	Third	Fourth	Fifth
A	1	1	1	1	1
B	2	2	2	2	4
C	2	3	3	3	2
D	1	3	3	3	2
E	3	3	3	3	1
F	3	3	3	3	3
G	1	2	2	1	1
H	1	2	2	1	1

[a]Number in cells are categories derived from sortings as shown in Table 1.

Essentially, there is a two-way division between those casinos that are very up-market and those casinos that are more general. The gambler makes a more precise distinction within the more general casinos between those that have added frills like the famous Playboy Clubs, or those that are just large gaming halls with little extra, and a group in between. Clearly, the gambler makes much more refined judgements about the nature of the action going on within the casino than does the manager. However, they both share the superordinate categorisation of how selective the casinos are.

This selectivity of casinos throws an interesting light on the whole gambling experience. It shows that an individual, in effect, is playing himself into some sort of exclusive club. These casinos, then, unlike those in the United States, may gain some of their important qualities from the way in which both the management and the gamblers draw lines between who can afford to be in which places. Certainly, further discussion of these conclusions with the respondents here as well as with other management groups would be necessary to test that hypothesis more fully.

Again, it would be difficult to see quite how such a result could be derived from a conventional questionnaire procedure. Open-ended interviews could well have revealed the same sort of material, but they might have hidden the underlying structures in people's conceptualisation, while of course emphasising other aspects of casinos that may well be important.

Complex comparisons of categories and construct systems

As a final illustration of the foci of analysis that can be derived from sorting procedures, the work of Grainger will be briefly mentioned. Working from a model of place (Canter, 1977), Grainger asked a variety of individuals associated with the design of a fire station to carry out sortings of three groups of elements, each of which was generated by the individual in the course of discussion. One group of elements was the activities that were to be housed in the building; the second group, the physical properties the building required; and the third group, the concepts that would be associated with the design - the concepts of the design objects. Grainger asked individuals to do this at different stages in the design process and carried out a series of analyses to show the way in which the conceptual systems of the individuals changed over time in relation to one another. What emerged was that the activity constructs, which were initially very similar in the architects' minds to their physical constructs, became more distinct, and in so doing they became similar to the clients' conceptualisation of the activities the building was to house. Grainger was thus able to reveal the dynamic evolution of the design brief by showing how the discussion between client and architect about both the intended activities and physical form can generate a common understanding of the building's future character.

Some important questions for the future

The examples presented so far have served to illustrate the variety of possible uses for the multiple sorting procedure. They have shown that the multiple sorting procedure derives from a variety of psychological techniques and a melding of approaches to psychological problems. However, the use of the multiple sorting procedure as a focus for open-ended interviewing is relatively recent and still only rarely utilised. There are a number of questions about the use and analysis of the multiple sorting procedure that remain unanswered. Some of the more important ones will now be considered. All of them are amenable to empirical tests drawing on the data collection and analysis procedures that have already been described.

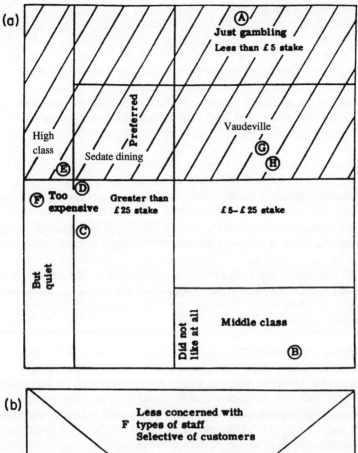

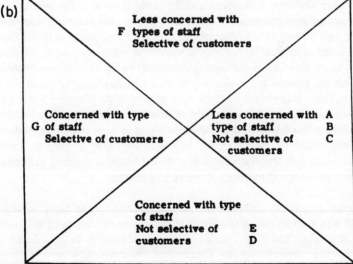

Figure 5 Summary MSAI of (a) Ace's sortings (see Tables 1 and 3 for basis), and (b) Casino Manager's Sorting (see Table 2 for basis).

Questions in analysis and use

Category salience. One aspect of the categories employed in sorting that is especially amenable to exploration, but not as yet examined, is the salience or significance to the individual of the categories used. The role of any categorisation scheme in the overall sorting structure has been explored, as discussed above, but the importance to the individual of one sort over another has not been scrutinised. Yet, the sorting procedure does lend itself to such examinations by virtue of a number of properties that potentially might reveal salience.

The range of sort convenience. One way in which the importance of different concepts can be examined is in relation to the appropriateness of those categories for all the elements involved. Kelly (1955) discusses the importance of establishing what he calls the 'range of convenience' of a construct, which he defines as covering 'all those things to which the user found its application useful' (p. 137). In the sorting procedure, it is always possible for the respondent to produce a sort which only covers a subset of the elements and for the remaining elements to be assigned to a general class indicating their irrelevance to the sorting criteria. Measures and content analyses of the range of items to which different category schemes were applied would help to clarify the salience of different sorting categories.

The significance of sort order. In a multiple sorting task it is clear that sorts follow each other in a distinct order. The question is therefore raised as to what the significance might be of the order in which sorts are elicited. In their study of different numbers of sorts Rosenberg and Kim (1975) came to the conclusion that sort order carried no significance. Unfortunately they only examined the first two sorts rather than looking at a larger number. Informal discussion with respondents does suggest that there may be contexts in which the order does carry significance and relates to the salience of the sorting categories being used. Some instructions may heighten this possibility, particularly instructions emphasising the use of sorts that the respondent believes reveal 'important aspects of the elements being sorted'.

Studies asking the respondent directly what importance they attach to different sortings are quite feasible as well as content analyses of sorts in terms of sort order. Such studies would be of value not only because little is known about the significance of sort order, but also it may reveal some interesting properties of conceptual systems not illuminated by other procedures.

The relevance of category distribution. As discussed above, an early version of a sorting task was used by Sherif and Sherif (1969) in the development of Thurstone attitude scales. They had judges assign attitudinal statements to an ordered set of categories. They argued that the distribution of items in a sorting revealed something of the intensity of the sorter's judgements; the more skewed the distribution of categories the more extreme the judges' views. In other words, if people assigned a similar number of elements to each category, then they were likely to hold much less extreme views than someone who put most of the elements in one or two outlying categories.

Although the Sherif and Sherif 'own categories' procedure, as they called it, is different in a number of important respects from the multiple sorting task, it does point to the possible value of studying the number of categories used and the number of items assigned to each category. Simple indexes of the distribution of items per category could easily be devised and used as a basis of this study. Such indexes could be directly related to the literature on cognitive complexity (Bieri, 1971; Streufert and Streufert, 1978) and thus provide an important link to the discussion of the role of cognitive structure in attitude change.

Theoretical clarification

As discussed, the multiple sorting procedure has evolved out of a variety of origins in clinical, experimental, environmental, and multivariate psychological research. It is consequently inevitable that some of the differences of opinion between practitioners in these areas has provided a basis for some confusion in the theoretical issues underlying the use of the multiple sorting procedure. All of these issues require debate and open up interesting areas of possible research.

Categories and constructs. Kelly (1955) makes it very clear that constructs are distinct from category schemes, although the labels given to categories may usefully identify constructs in certain circumstances. He even writes that he uses the term construct 'in a manner which is somewhat parallel to the common usage of "concept" ' (p. 69). One important assumption about constructs in Kelly's terms is that they are dichotomous. They enshrine bipolarity of aspects of the similarity and differences between elements.

In this sense, categories to which elements in a sort are assigned are the constructs of the user, although only one pole of the construct may be specified. However, in Kelly's terms, the bipolarity of the constructs is an assumption of his theory, it is not open to test within his theory, nor as a consequence can it be tested using a repertory grid. This is not the case for multiple sorting. If a person assigns elements to categories that can be ordered from least to most along a single bipolar concept, then that category scheme reveals a construct (e.g., Ace's sorting according to size of minimum bet). If, however, the sorting produces a set of categories that are multipolar, then it would be inappropriate to regard this category scheme as consisting of constructs (e.g., Groat's architects' classification of building styles as Brutalist, Post-Modern, Expressionist, etc).

Thus, the multiple sorting procedure does allow one of Kelly's fundamental assumptions to be tested. Indeed, it is the emergence of classification schemes that are not obviously constructs which is one of the starting points for considering the multiple sorting procedure rather than the repertory grid. But this leads to the question of the conditions under which people use constructs as opposed to multipolar category schemes and the possibility of converting one system of classification into the other.

Individual differences in sorting competence. Anyone who uses the multiple sorting procedure will come across respondents who will find the task difficult and challenging to complete. This raises the question of how natural the task is to all people and of what differences there might be between people in their ability to carry out a multiple sorting task. Of course, the specific nature of the task itself does need to be considered. A sorting of abstract concepts is likely to be more difficult than a sorting of places to go on holiday. It is also necessary to distinguish between difficulties people may have in understanding what they are to do and difficulties in actually doing it.

These individual differences are of interest because the procedure does have roots in clinical psychological concerns with understanding the difficulties people have in coping with the world. If there are circumstances in which respondents find it difficult to form categories stable enough to describe, then the reasons for this should be searched out. The comments people make when carrying out sorts can give a valuable clue here to the difficulties they are facing and these can be related to measures such as the number of sorts and the time taken to complete a sort. The exploration of who finds what type of sorting difficult and why is likely to repay the effort involved.

Should sortings be reliable. The sorting task is likely to be a self-exploration for the individuals doing it, a learning process in which they come to understand more about their own conceptual system. As a consequence it is possible that an individual would not give the same sortings twice. Certainly the order in which he/she carried out his/her sortings is likely to vary from one session to the next. What is being studied is the overall conceptual system a person uses. It is likely that using two parallel sets of elements, in analogy with parallel forms of reliability testing, would not obviate the effects of the increase in self-understanding associated with a sorting task.

No published studies can be found dealing directly with these issues, but advocates of repertory grid procedure (e.g., Fransella and Bannister, 1977, Chapter 6) have gone to some length to argue that reliability can easily be a measure of the insensitivity of a procedure to changing circumstances rather than a valuable psychometric property. With respect to the multiple sorting procedure, it is likely that stable individuals would generate reliable responses over two or three sorting sessions, but only if the procedure itself did not contribute to a fuller understanding of their conceptual systems or their personal growth. Only direct tests of these important questions can help answer them. Here, as with the other questions, the comments people make during the sorting procedure could provide valuable clues.

Exploring face validity. The validity of a sorting must depend a lot on the conditions under which it is carried out. The essence of a sorting task is to establish the individuals' own understanding of their personal conceptual system. The extent to which individuals will feel able and be able to generate that system will depend on how they understand the instructions, the personal relevance of the elements, and so on. Thus, as much as any other data collection procedure, the conditions under which the data are collected need to be carefully reported and interpreted, in terms of how the procedure was experienced by the respondent.

In this framework, face validity is given considerably more prominence than in other psychometric procedures. This is because one very important meaning to the validity of a sorting task is the extent to which the respondent and the investigator have a shared understanding of what the procedure is measuring. In this respect the details of the results, both in content and structure, can be examined to see what they reveal of the respondent's understanding of the task as presented. For example, consider the situation in which the sortings generated are all based on objective, physical aspects of the elements, such as their weight and size, yet the investigator was apparently looking for emotional significance of the elements. This suggests the procedure was not tapping what the investigator thought it was, and so careful scrutiny of the details of the procedure and its context may reveal the basis of this lack of apparent validity. For instance, perhaps the investigator introduced himself as a designer and thus set up expectations as to the type of sorting that would be appropriate.

The consequences of subtle changes in the instructions or context of a multiple sort for the results produced are directly amenable to empirical study. Here the vast literature on interviewing procedure and threats to its validity would have many points of relevance. The consequences of interviewer sex and experience are obvious examples from this literature, but there are many others mentioned throughout the present volume.

Modifications and developments of the sorting procedure

The following are possible ways in which the sorting procedure can be developed and modified in order to answer some research questions more directly:

1. The creation of element sets to sort can be taken a number of steps. The selection of a carefully matched set of elements, possibly factorially designed is one step. But by adding other descriptors, experimentally varied sets of elements can be produced.

2. Sorting procedures in which one set of elements is sorted into another set offer a number of prospects for exploring the relationship between different conceptual domains. If both sets of elements are sorted independently as well as together, there is the possibility of a very close analysis of the fit between domains.

3. Asking people to sort elements into provided category schemes as well as free sorts generates links to studies using other methods of concept exploration.

4. Ranking and rating of sorts against different criteria such as importance provides the opportunity for the development of classifications of sorts themselves - higher-order sorting.

5. Group sorting procedures have been used from time to time and can add

greatly to the cost effectiveness of data collection. However, these procedures are likely to be limited to groups that are quite sophisticated or to very simple aspects of sorting, such as paired comparisons.

Values and contraindications

As mentioned throughout this chapter, the sorting procedure has the flexibility to be applied to answer a wide variety of research questions, but there are some types of questions for which it may be inappropriate. Only further use will help to clarify the boundaries of advantageous and disadvantageous uses, but a few pointers can be given now.

The multiple sorting procedure clearly has strength when the elaboration of the meaning of a concept is central to the research question. Studies of how people use the word 'home', or whether 'post-modern' architecture has an identifiable public recognition, or the conditions under which people will describe their actions as 'panic', all lend themselves to exploration using a sorting procedure. If these concepts have a common but highly ambiguous currency, then the demands of the sorting procedure may well help to disentangle the different meanings. Also, when conceptual systems are being explored with groups whose verbal fluency may be restricted such as children or psychiatric patients, then a sorting procedure may be especially useful.

There are two types of research questions, however, for which multiple sorting may be less appropriate; they fall into two general classes. The first are those questions in which a very personal, idiosyncratic perspective is what is being sought. The indepth psychotherapeutic interview can never be replaced by sorting tasks. The second class of research questions are those concerned with a direct understanding of processes, especially sequences of action. For example, studies of how people make decisions under stress or cope with bereavement are less likely to prove fruitful if built around a study of personal category schemes than if they focus directly on the stages through which people go and what moves them from one stage to the next.

Conclusions

This chapter has presented a detailed account of multiple sorting procedures, with respect to both their theoretical origins and their numerous applications to open-ended interview situations. As the first section of the chapter has demonstrated, the multiple sorting procedure has roots in both the early clinical object sorting techniques and the paired comparison procedures advocated recently by multidimensional scaling enthusiasts. But more important, the multiple sorting procedure derives from two parallel concerns in psychology: the significance of the respondents' own view of the world, and the recognition that world view is built around a pattern of categorisations. In this respect, the multiple sorting procedure reveals theoretical links to Kelly's work in the development of the repertory grid and to other more recent research in social and clinical psychology.

With respect to its applications to the interview process, the second portion of this chapter has provided examples of its adaptability, and ease of administration. However, it is clear that one of its primary virtues may also be a burden to the researcher: it probably makes even greater demands than the repertory grid on the intellectual stamina of the investigator, forcing her or him to clarify exactly what it is that he/she is looking for and why. In this respect it serves as an appropriate complement to other forms of the interview procedure, such as the use of ordinary explanations. The multiple sorting task thus takes its place amongst the family of interviewing procedures, but only future developments and use will establish the role it is to play.

References

Adams-Weber, I.R. (1979), *Personal Construct Theory: Concepts and Applications,* Wiley, Chichester.

Allport, G.W. (1937), *Personality: A Psychological Interpretation,* Holt Saunders, New York.

Argyle, M., Furnham, A. & Graham, I.A. (1981), *Social Situations*, Cambridge University Press, London.

Bieri, I. (1971), *Cognitive Structures in Personality*, in H.M. Schroder and P. Suedfeld (eds), *Personality Theory and Information Processing*, Ronald Press, New York.

Bishop, R. (1983), *The Perception and Importance of Time in Architecture*, Ph.D thesis, University of Surrey.

Block, I. (1961), *The Q-sort Method in Personality Assessment and Psychiatric Research*, Charles C. Thomas, Springfield, Illinois.

Bonarius, H., Holland, R. and Rosenberg, S. (eds) (1981), *Personal Construct Theory: Recent Advances in Theory and Practice*, Macmillan, London.

Brown, I. & Sime, I. (1980), 'A methodology for accounts', in M. Brenner (ed.), *Social Methods and Social Life*, Academic Press, London, pp. 157-188.

Bruner, I., Goodnow, I. & Austin, G. (1956), *A Study of Thinking*, Wiley, New York.

Canter, D. (1977), *The Psychology of Place*, London Architectural Press.

Canter, D. (1983), *The Potential of Facet Theory for Applied Social Psychology, Quality and Quantity*, Elsevier Scientific Publishing Co, Amsterdam.

Canter, D., Ambrose, I., Brown, I., Comber, M. & Hirsch, A. (1980), *Prison Design and Use, Final Report to the Home office,* University of Surrey.

Canter, D., Brown, I. & Richardson, H. (1976), *Constructs Without Tears: Is There Life Beyond the Grid,* paper presented to the British Psychological Society Annual Conference, Exeter.

Douglas, M. (ed.) (1977), *Rules and Meanings*, Penguin, Harmondsworth.

Eckman, P. (1975), 'Unmasking the Face', Prentice Hall, New Jersey.

Fransella, F. & Bannister, D. (1977), *A Manual for Repertory Grid Technique*, Academic Press, London.

Frost, A. & Canter, D. (1982), 'Consumer psychology', in S. Canter and D. Canter (eds.), *Psychology in Practice: Perspectives on Professional Psychology*, Wiley, Chichester.

Gärling, T. (1976), 'The Structural Analysis of Environmental Perception and Cognition, *Environment and Behavior*, Vol. 8(3), pp. 385-415.

Grainger, B. (1980), *A Study of Concepts in the Building Design Process*, Msc. Dissertation, University of Surrey.

Groat, L. & Canter, D.V. (1979), 'Does Post-modernism Communicate', *Progressive Architecture*, December, pp. 84-87.

Groat, L. (1982), 'Meaning in Post-modem Architecture: An Examination Using the Multiple Sorting Task', *Journal of Environmental Psychology*, Vol. 2(3), pp. 3-22.

Hane, R. & Secord, P. (1972), *The Explanation of Social Behaviour*, Blackwell, Oxford.

Hawkins, C. (1983), *Differing Conceptualisations of Users of Three Psychiatric Day Centres*, MSc Dissertation, University of Surrey.

Horayangkura, V. (1978), 'Semantic differential structures', *Environment and Behaviour*, Vol. 10(4), pp. 555-584.

James, W. (1890), *Principles of Psychology*, Holt Saunders, New York.

Kelly, G. (1955), *The Psychology of Personal Constructs*, Norton, New York.

Krampen, M. (1979), *Meaning in the Urban Environment*, Pion, London.

Lingoes, I. (1973), *The Cuttman-Lingoes Nonmetric Program Series*, Ann Arbor, Mathesis Press, Michigan.

Miller, G. A. (1956), 'The Magical Number Seven, Plus or Minus Two, *Psychological Review,* Vol. 43, pp. 81-114

Nasar, J. (1980), 'On Determining Dimensions of Environmental Perception', *Edra*, Vol. 11, pp. 245-256, Environmental Design Research Association, Washington.

Oakley, R. (1980), *Profiles and Perspectives of Hostel Residents*, Msc. Dissertation, University of Surrey.

Oostendorp, A. & Berlyne, D.E. (1978), 'Dimensions in the Perception of Architecture', *Scandinavian Journal of Psychology*, Vol. 19, pp. 145-150.

Osgood, G.E. (1962), 'Studies in the Generality of Affective Meaning Systems', *American Psychologist*, Vol. 17, pp. 10-28.

Osgood, G.E., Suci, G.I. & Tanenbaum, P.M. (1957), *The Measurement of Meaning*, University of Illinois Press, Urbana.

Palmer, I. (1978), 'Citizen Assessment of the Coastal Visual Resource', in *Coastal Zone 78,* New York American Society of Civil Engineers.

Pitt, D.G. & Zube, E.H. (1979), 'The Q-sort Method: Use in Landscape Assessment Research and Landscape Planning', in G. H. Elsner (ed.), *Our National Landscape*, Pacific Southwest Forest and Range Experiment Station, Berkeley.

Rosch, E. (1977), 'Human Categorization', in N. Warren (ed.), *Advances in Cross-cultural Psychology (Vol I)*, Academic Press, London.

Rosenberg, S. & Kim, M. P. (1975), 'The Method of Sorting a Data Gathering Procedure in Multivariate Research', *Multivariate Behavioral Research*, October, pp. 489-502.

Schiffman, S.S., Reynolds, L.M. & Young, F.W. (1981), *Introduction to Multidimensional Scaling*, Academic Press, London.

Shaw, M.L.G. (1982), 'The Extraction of Personal Meaning from a Repertory Grid', in E. Shepherd and I.F. Watson (eds), *Personal Meanings,*Wiley, Chichester.

Shepherd, E. & Watson, I.P. (1982) (eds), *Personal Meanings*, Wiley, Chichester.

Sherif, M. & Sherif, G. (1969), *Social Psychology*, Harper and Row/John Weatherhill, New York/Tokyo.

Shye, S. (ed.) (1978), *Theory Construction and Data Analysis in the Behavioral Sciences*, Jossey-Bass, San Fransisco.

Smith, A.E. & Medin, D.L. (1981), *Categories and Concepts*, Harvard Press, London.

Stephenson, W. (1953), *The Study of Behavior: Q-technique and its Methodology*, University of Chicago Press, Chicago.

Streufert, S. & Streufert, S. (1978), *Behavior in the Complex Environment*, Holt Saunders, New York.

Szalay, L.B. & Deese, I. (1978), *Subjective Meaning in Culture: An Assessment Through Word Association*, Hillside, NJ: Erlbaum.

Tajfel, H.G. (1978), *The Structure of our Views about Society* in H. Tajfel and G. Fraser (eds), *An Introduction to Social Psychology*, pp. 302-321, Penguin, Harmondsworth.

Tajfel, H. (1981), *Human Groups and Social Categories*, Cambridge University Press, Cambridge.

Thurstone, L.L. & Chave, E.J. (1929), *The Measurement of Attitudes,*University of Chicago Press, Chicago.

Vygotsky, L. (1934), *Thought and Language*, MA: MIT Press, Boston.

Ward, L.M. (1977), 'Multidimensional Scaling of the Molar Physical Environment',*The Journal of Multivariate Behavioral Research*, Vol. 12, pp. 23-42.

Ward, L.M. & Russell, I.A. (1981), 'Cognitive Set and the Perception of Place', *Environment and Behaviour*, Vol. 13(5), pp. 610-632.

Zvulun, E. (1978), 'Multidimensional Scalogram Analysis: The Method and its Application' in S. Shye (ed.), *Theory construction and Data Analysis in the Behavioral Sciences*, pp. 237-264, Jossey-Bass, San Fransisco.

ENVIRONMENTAL
PSYCHOLOGY

5 The Facets of Place

Contents

This chapter will outline one theory aimed at integrating aspects of environmental psychology with issues in architectural design. The theory to be reviewed is broad in those characteristics of theory that Moore (1987) called their 'form and scope'. This broad brush, top down approach is intended as a contrast with bottom up attempts to specify the behavioural effects of specific aspects of design, such as lighting levels or size of spaces. It also contrasts with models that seek to answer immediate design problems. However, in Moore's (1987) vocabulary, the theory to be outlined is more than an 'orientation', or 'framework'. It is an 'explanatory theory' that has been found to have considerable scope, open to direct empirical test.

At the heart of the theory to be presented is the struggle to create schematic models of the experience of places. These models are offered as general summaries that reflect many current explorations of the phenomenology of places (e.g., Stea and Turan, 1990; Fishwick and Vining, 1992), but have a statistical, empirical basis rather different from the overtly anti-positivist proposals of earlier studies of place experience (most notably Relph,1976).

Although the length of the present chapter does not allow a full exploration of the issues, the premise of it is that in order for empirically sound environmental psychology theories to have the potential for being absorbed into the heartland of architectural decision making they must enrich our understanding of the experience of places. It is only in this way that they will connect with those aesthetic objectives that are such a dominant component of creative design.

In order to elaborate such a wide ranging theory of place, connections will be explored between the major facets of design (what it is that designers manipulate), and the paradigms for environment and behaviour research (what it is that researchers study). A framework will be sketched that links these two realms. In building these links it will be argued that many of the different areas of environment and behaviour research - such as building evaluation, environmental meaning and studies of space use may fruitfully be regarded as sub-sets of a larger matrix of related processes. They are particular combinations of a family of possible combinations of design issues and psychological issues. It is proposed that because they all come from the same family these issues have a basis in the same environmental psychology processes. It is therefore hypothesised that similar underlying structures will characterise results from these different areas of research.

In some senses then, the theory to be discussed can be classified as what Moore (1987) calls a 'structuralistic theory'. This chapter responds to his point that 'the tendency to date has been to argue the [structuralistic] position but show little supporting evidence' (p.1377). The present chapter will both argue the position and provide evidence in support of it.

The framework to be outlined is built upon the theory that place experience combines individual, social and cultural processes. Furthermore, the different paradigms of environment and behaviour research, rather than covering distinct, independent theories and processes, may be fruitfully regarded as exploring different aspects of the same process. It is hypothesised that these different aspects will be found to co-exist when studies of place experience are appropriately conducted. In other words, it is hypothesised that the appropriate analysis of studies of place meaning or use, or of building evaluations or cognitions, will reveal similar components of place experience. Results, to be presented from a variety of studies, support these central hypotheses.

The studies reported recognise that the theory makes special demands on research methodology. These demands are answered, in part at least, by the facet approach to research. This approach will therefore be briefly described. It will be shown that this does offer the possibility for the elaboration and test of hypotheses derived from the theory of place. Examples of such research will be presented as illustrations of the potential of studies of the facets of place for integrating many currently diverse issues in environment, behaviour and design.

Function, form and space

In order to develop detailed psychological theory that can be integrated into design a framework is needed for what it is that designers can have an influence over. What it is that designers actually manipulate has to be specified. Furthermore, if it is to be open to integration with psychological research, such a framework needs to have a real possibility of connecting with human experience. For example, a view of design as the manipulation of financial resources would be relevant to economic input. Conceptualising a building as the structuring of static and dynamic forces would be relevant to research in engineering. Neither of these, equally valid, perspectives would be helpful in building bridges to behavioural research.

What are the major components of the designer's task that are relevant to psychological considerations? One stimulating answer to this question has been offered by Markus (1982, 1987). He has presented a clear argument for there being three recognisable realms of architectural discourse that each reflect different aspects of what he calls 'primary experiences of buildings.' He referred to these as

a) the *function*, which is the experience of the explicit or implicit activities which a building houses,
b) the *form*, which are 'the geometric properties, the proportions, articulation, colour, ornamentation, and surface treatment .... summarised under the term 'style', and
c) the *space*, which embraces 'the number and location ... sequence and linkage of spaces'. (Markus, 1987, p. 469)

Markus' model is especially relevant for the integration of environment and behaviour research because he has argued that each of these architectural discourses, that are primary for the experience of a building, enshrine ways of classifying human action and experience. These classification process all derive from the same social milieu and therefore the discourses are expected to have common roots. He has argued, as a consequence, that although the discourses can be distinguished from each other there

> '... appear to be some basic, memorable, and *typical* conjunctions of form, function and space which seem more powerful, more appropriate and more dominant than others ... such conjunctions could ... be called "building types" and, further, classification could ... be the device which is the basis for the origin and development of building types'. (Markus, 1987, p. 484, his italics)

He thus has presented, as central to the main aspects of architecture, forces that coalesce to give conceptual structure to ways of thinking about buildings. Markus' three aspects therefore facilitate many considerations of how decisions relating to those aspects can be integrated with psychological research. However, before returning to these issues it is necessary to look at the research side of the equation.

Paradigms for E & B research

The range of approaches currently employed in environment and behaviour research is very wide indeed, but the recent review by Saegert and Winkel (1990) is helpful in mapping out the levels of complexity that need to be addressed. They have identified what they have called three 'paradigms' for research in person-environment studies. These are types of research question and associated modes of studying and answering those questions. Their argument is that each of these paradigms presents a virtually distinct realm of discourse, separate domains of activity.

The first of their paradigms is concerned with *environmental adaptation*: studies of the ways in which people cope with the pressures inherent in physical settings.

> '... In the adaptation paradigm the goal of biological and psychological survival motivates behaviour. The biological and psychological individual attempts to cope with threats, to meet basic biological needs and to restore and expand capacities for coping and flourishing'. (p. 446)

Saegert and Winkel did not describe these adaptation processes as passive assimilation by people of the world around them but as active managing of environmental transactions. This requires the utilisation of environmental knowledge in ways that helps to reduce stress and strengthen survival possibilities. The individual's cognitive processing of environmental experiences in order to survive or live more comfortably is therefore central to this paradigm.

The second, *opportunity structure* paradigm, embraces all those studies that deal with the opportunities the environment provides for the achievement of goals.

> ' ... the relationships between the behavioural requirements of the active and goal-directed person and the qualities of the environment ... selecting the best options within a system of socio-physical constraints and opportunities'. p. 452

Here the focus is on the options for action that the environment makes available and how people can select or manipulate settings to make possible patterns of behaviour, or styles of life, to which they aspire. An important distinction between the adaptation paradigm and the options paradigm is that the former is couched in individualistic terms, emphasising a person's own distinct reactions to their surroundings, whereas the latter carries strong implications about the social milieu in which a person is operating. Therefore, rather than being distinct and unconnected paradigms, it is worth considering the possibility that these two realms of study are different perspectives on a common system of experiences. One focuses on the individual, complemented by the second focus on the social.

The third paradigm recognised by Saegert and Winkel is the *socio-cultural* one.

> '... The person as a social agent seeks and creates meanings in the

environment'. (p. 452)

'... The paradigm ... explicitly recognises that environmental meanings and actions are not solely individual constructions. The individual both defines and is defined by the groups in which he/she participates'. (p. 465)

Here studies explore the ways in which the environment is a part of processes that define and enhance group and cultural identities. The symbolic and representational qualities of physical settings are the locus of attention for researchers operating within this paradigm. It also encompasses examinations of the historical processes by which the environmental images gained their significance. Research of this third type therefore elaborates the individualistic and social perspectives by adding a dimension that goes beyond the immediate person or group, giving special emphasis to the shared meanings of environments. By recognising that environmental meanings and symbols have an existence beyond the direct experience of individuals, Saegert and Winkel are drawing attention to those environmental psychology studies that explore *cultural* processes.

Saegert and Winkel present three distinct paradigms for research, arguing that more emphasis should be given to the third than is currently the case. However, there is logic to proposing a more closely integrated model. This integration is implicit in the account given by Saegert and Winkel because they present all three paradigms as capturing essentially dynamic transactions between people and their settings. The adaptation paradigm explores how people strive to cope with actual and potential threats; the options paradigm has people creating and selecting opportunities, and the socio-cultural paradigm sees people searching for significance and meaning. The dynamic interplay between these three different aspects of person/environment transactions is a logical assumption.

It is proposed that these three perspectives rather than being merely research paradigms are, in effect, three features of person-environment transaction, from the individualistic through the social and on to the cultural. Consequently, all three aspects are an important element in environmental transactions. A reasonable hypothesis is therefore that these three coalesce in our experience of places, although they are different aspects of it. We adapt, seek to enact opportunities and draw personal significance from the environment, all at one time. Our environmental experience is essentially multi-faceted.

A theory of place

The integration of paradigms

For the theory being developed in the present chapter 'Place', will be used in a slightly different sense from the ways in which Seamon and Mugerauer (1985), Relph (1976) and others have used it. It is proposed as a technical term for describing the system of experience that incorporates the personal, social and culturally significant aspects of situated activities.

The reason, then, for using 'place' as a neutral, technical term rather than implying a quality of a location is to make available a unit of study that encapsulates the mixture of processes that create our experience of our socio-physical surroundings. There are some senses in which this is a development of Barker's (1968) concept of the 'behaviour setting'. It differs from that conceptualisation by including much more directly the understanding and expectations that participants have of the place in which they find themselves, together with the qualities that the physical shape and perceptual properties of that location have. Indeed Barker's ecological psychology tends to focus on the social aspects of the Saegert and Winkel model at the expense of both psychological and cultural processes.

In essence then, a theory of place is being proposed. The following points summarise the main hypotheses of the theory that have been presented so far:

1. There are focused units of environmental experience, 'places'.
2. These aspects of experience incorporate personal, social and cultural constituents of person-place transactions.
3. Each of the constituents will be reflected in the functional, spatial and formal aspects of a place.
4. For any given place there will be structural similarities in the ways in which psychological constituents are reflected in the aspects of a place.

Place as a focus

The first hypothesis implies that there will be core aspects of places. In general, there will be some coherence, or consistency, in the overall goals that a place is seen to serve for a particular group at a particular point in time. This central hypothesis proposes that a place will have a focus that helps to define its characteristic nature. A subsidiary hypothesis is that such core aspects of places will be consistent across places which house similar sets of objectives.

Conflicting goals for place use

Perhaps the strongest challenge to the theory of place outlined here is the recognition that many places will be required to house conflicting goals. Different groups of people may wish to use the same location for competing activities, as when fishermen and watersports enthusiasts wish to enjoy the same area of water. Or the same person or group may have opposing conceptualisations or uses for the same place as when a study bedroom must be used for semi-public entertainment or private sleep or study. The theory of place prediction is that any such conflict or competition is inherently unstable. Processes will be set in motion that will tend towards one or other usage becoming the dominant one. Indeed in his earliest writings Alexander (1964) argued that a central objective of the design process was to help resolve such conflicts. But, it is hypothesised that, even without direct design intervention other modifications will occur in how the place is construed or used so that the setting ends up being one type of place.

The evolution of places

The move to a clear definition of a place implies a constant evolution in those places that already exist. As a consequence one of the strongest tests of the central hypothesis of a theory of place, i.e., that places tend to change towards a focus of experience, may be derived from historical examination of the evolution of places. The argument here is that if distinct places, with identifiable foci exist then there should be historical evidence of the continuing emergence and refinement of places, an evolution of places that is analogous to the evolution of species. One early, amorphous, all encompassing place would be proposed which then evolved into ever more specific places, each place taking on a significance of its own out of which new types of place would emerge.

The essentially dynamic, changing experiences of places inherent in this Theory of Place has already been briefly outlined (Canter, 1985), but evidence for these evolutionary processes in the creation of places has been long recognised, most notably by the social architectural historian Girouard (1978, 1985, 1990). He has presented numerous examples of how places evolve into ever more specific forms.

As is so often the case in science it is difficult to specify the details of research without some understanding of the methodology by which the research is to be conducted. The theory of place puts special demands upon the methodology. So, before detailed empirical studies can be reviewed it is necessary to summarise one approach to research that does appear to respond to many of the demands of the theory.

The facet approach

Demands on methodology

The theory of place draws attention to the essentially multi-variate nature of that experience. This is central because the personal, social and cultural aspects have to be studied together. Furthermore, the studies have to be carried out in such a way that it is possible to identify any existing dominant core of such experiences for any particular setting. Another demand of the theory is that comparisons can be made, from one architectural discourse to another, between the patterns of relationships between components. This is a comparison of what Seamon (1987) called 'structures'.

The theory of place is also sympathetic to the phenomenological objective of establishing '... the actual nature of everyday environmental experiences...' (Seamon, 1987, p. 6). This is taken to mean that the *methodologies* employed do not make any prior assumptions about the structures that will become apparent. The constituents discussed are hypothesised to be naturally present, underlying place experience. No strong prior assumptions are made about how they relate to each other, i.e., their structure. Thus, although the theory of place discussed here does share with the phenomenologists a desire to describe experiences as they exist, it does eschew '... the main vehicle ...' of '... *intuitive insight* directed towards the phenomenon studied ...' (Seamon, 1987, p. 7, his italics), because of the arbitrary nature of the driving of such a vehicle. Application of such insights without any firm basis on which to draw are difficult to evaluate or to incorporate into archival scholarship (Sixsmith, 1983). However, as will be demonstrated, such intuitive insights can be harnessed with profit to the appropriate empirical analyses.

Facet theory

One approach to research that has some potential for responding to these demands is known as *facet theory* (Canter, 1985). This approach can be used to *test* hypotheses about place experiences as in much conventional experimental science. In these circumstances the theory to be tested will have already been formulated, say from previous research or logical examination of the environmental literature. More importantly for the theory of place the approach can be harnessed to the *generation* of hypotheses, i.e., the discovery of naturally occurring systems of place experience, in which loosely formulated 'intuitive insights' can be explored, elaborated and tested through replication. It is in this latter mode that the approach shares some common ground with other strategies, for the *description* of existing systems of action and experience.

Although the term 'theory' is quite accurate in referring to facet theory, in the sense that hypotheses can be derived and tested from it, the term is a little misleading because the theory being espoused is about how theories may be best formulated and tested. In other words it is a *meta-theory*. As such it specifies with some degree of rigour the constituents of theories and ways in which the hypotheses derived from those constituents may be tested. In summary, it can be seen to combine:

a) a rationalist scientific epistemology, in which the scientist is seen as the creator of accounts of the world rather than the discoverer of platonic truths, together with,

b) formal ways of specifying the constituents of a theory with,

c) strategies for deriving and testing hypotheses about the relationships between those constituents, and

d) modes of data analysis.

Such a mixture of procedures and techniques, in effect, provide a whole approach to research so that the term 'facet approach' whilst being looser is more readily understandable.

Central to the facet approach is the proposition that the building blocks of any theory are ways of categorising phenomena. Such categories may be qualitative as when categorising activities into rest, recreation and work, or they may be quantitative, e.g., frequency of place use. These categorisations are known as 'facets'. The specification of facets is the central, formal process for developing any facet theory. The only limitations on what may be regarded as a 'facet' are:

a)   facets exhaustively cover all the phenomena under consideration, i.e., every example being considered is covered by one sub-category of the categorisation scheme, e.g., a facet of twentieth century architectural styles would need to include sub-categories covering both modern and post-modern styles,

b)   each of the sub-categories is mutually exclusive of all the others in that categorisation, e.g., every design would have to find a place in only one style sub-category, but

c)   all the phenomena under study can be categorised into as many facets as the researcher wishes, so for example, buildings could be categorised into primary functions, such as dwellings, offices, shops etc as well as styles. Indeed the values of facet theory derive from the fact that all studies are inherently of multi-faceted phenomena.

Following usage in mathematical set-theory, the sub-categories of a category scheme (the facet) are referred to as the *elements* of that facet.

    The approach is profoundly multi-variate because it is based upon the principle that every entity under study, and thus every associated observation, will be classifiable on every facet the researcher identifies. The metaphor of different perspectives on the phenomena being examined, looking at different faces, or facets, of them is central to the whole theory. Science is seen as the bringing together of particular ways of looking at the world and showing how these different perspectives form an integrated structure. A theory is a related set of such facets together with empirical evidence for their existence and relationships.

The facets of place

Having:

a)   summarised the central thesis of the theory of place by drawing attention to the ways in which Saegert and Winkel's (1990) review and Markus' (1982, 1987) reviews can be seen to suggest hypothesised constituents of places and the importance of identifying their focus, and

b)   sketched out the facet approach as a way of formally specifying those constituents of place experience in a way that is open to empirical elaboration and test,

it is now possible to provide a more precise account of the constituents of places. These constituents are defined as facets. The specification of facets is therefore a first step in producing a testable theory of place. In a nutshell, the theory of place therefore can be seen as the proposition that the following facets of place commonly exist and have consistent relationships with each other i.e., 'invariant structures.'

Facet A: functional differentiation. This first facet derives from the central proposition that places will tend to have a distinct character, what was called earlier a 'focus'. For instance, in studying the use of space in houses, looking say at what happens in each room in the home, it is hypothesised that there will be some activities that will typically take place anywhere in the home. These are the activities that are characteristic of the homes in general. These are the *central* or core elements of activities in the home. Exactly what they are depends upon the particular place and is therefore a descriptive question of some interest. The hypothesis is a structural one. It proposes that when a range of components of any particular type of place are considered some of those components will share common features. Another example can be drawn from evaluation of the functioning of houses, what is often called residential satisfaction. Here the hypothesis is that there will be some general aspects of satisfaction that relate highly to all the others. These general issues will go some way to help define what it is that gives satisfaction with a home of distinct qualities, distinguishing it from satisfaction with other types of place such as offices or hospitals.

If a central hypothesis is that some aspects of a place will be typical of all aspects of such places (conceptually central) then it follows that there will be other aspects of the place that are not typical of all aspects, being conceptually *peripheral*. Two types of 'peripherality' are possible. One is a random, unstructured collection of possible constituents of the different components of places. To take the activities in the home example again. The first type of peripherality would, therefore, predict that beyond the core activities that take place in most locations there are other activities that tend to happen in few locations, but where those locations are varies arbitrarily from one home to the next. The second possibility is a structured sets of constituents, each sub-set being associated with one sub-set of components. This second type of peripherality would predict that there would be groupings of activities associated with each room in the home.

The theory of place is much more comfortable with the second type of peripherality because this implies a structure for the whole pattern of activities that make up the home. It also implies that each room could be treated as a type of place with central activities that could take place anywhere in that room and other activities associated with different parts of it.

The elements of centrality and peripherality have been described, for simplicity, as a dichotomy, but it is logical to assume that they are conceptually distinct poles with various gradations between these two extremes. The degree of precision with which the different gradations can be identified will depend upon the clarity of the data.

One further point of clarification is also important to understand. Because Facet A is an hypothesis about the structure of relationships between components of places the content of the facet, i.e., what it is that is central or peripheral, will be defined by other facets under consideration. This relationship between facets serves to emphasise that any theory derived using the facet approach is a systems theory, it is a theory about the structure of constituent components. In the context of places this structure is seen as derived from the consistent *process* that lead to the differentiation of places.

Facet B: place objectives. This second facet can be identified from the earlier considerations of Saegert and Winkel's (1990) review of research paradigms. In considering those paradigms it was proposed that they were distinct because they studied different aspects of a coherent system of place experience. It was argued that, in essence, each paradigm dealt with different types of objectives for considering the effectiveness of places. In other words, different aspects of the *goals* that a person has in a place. The distinct constituents each lead to a proposed distinct element i.e., *individual, social* and *cultural*.

Thus, for example, when considering the forms of buildings they may be hypothesised to reflect either a concern with individual comfort, or with opportunities for social contact, or with the cultural significance of the building. Of course, because these are all co-occurring aspects of the same system it is expected that they are all operative at the same time. The hypothesis is therefore that different emphases will be given to them for different buildings. It is these differences in emphasis that are hypothesised to underly, for example, different building forms.

Just as there were possible gradations between central and peripheral elements of the first facet, so gradations may be identified between these three elements. Psycho-social and socio-cultural emphases for example each combine two elements. The third possibility of psycho-cultural objectives in places illustrates an important aspect of this and all facets. If such a third possibility had a logical and empirical existence it would mean that this was not a simply ordered, essentially quantitative facet. If elements could be found that had a logical location between psychological issues and cultural issues then the simple sequence from the individual to the social and then on to the culture would be untenable. In a sense the sequence would have to double back on itself to provide a position for an element between the supposed two extremes.

The question about whether psycho-cultural aspects of places do exist helps to demonstrate that the logic of the facet approach implies hypotheses not only about the existence of facets but also about the structure of the elements within those facets.

To clarify this crucial idea further, it may be hypothesised that there are aspects of people's personal experience of places which are more directly related to their cultural context than to their social, interpersonal context. Any data dealing with such psycho-cultural matters, as for instance personal identity, would therefore be expected to relate more closely to psychological and cultural data than to social, interpersonal data. A simple order of relationships from psychological through social to cultural would not be found in such a case. This contrasts with the logic of the first, functional differentiation, facet. What elements could logically exist part way between highly differentiated and low on differentiation except those that were between low and high differentiation? In other words the very logic of the differentiation facet leads to hypotheses of it being simply ordered, i.e., being essentially quantitative.

But what of the relationship between these two facets? A system is being described so all the component parts must have distinct inter-relationships. The logic would seem to be that the degree of differentiation must interact with the objectives facet. The more differentiated the aspects of a place are the more clearly that they should reveal particular objectives. A simple example would be that if the possibilities of certain levels of comfort was a crucial differentiator between the qualities of rooms, but the options it provides for social interaction had less of an impact, then satisfaction with the space in a kitchen would be predicted to have less relationship to satisfaction with space in a bedroom of any given house than would the comfort (satisfaction) levels of heating and lighting levels. But the general mood of a house would be hypothesised to reflect the space for social contact rather than lighting and heating provision. In other words facets A and B are not expected to operate like either two independent dimensions or distinct clusters.They are hypothesised to be part of a set of related processes. Indeed, the second main facet gives content (e.g., focus on individual comfort, social contact, or culturally related meanings) to the place differentiation of the first, by interacting with it.

Facet C: scale of interaction. The third facet is so fundamental that it is often ignored in theory building, although typically used in organising the contents of text books. Put simply this is the issue of environmental scale. It is generally accepted that there is a difference between use of space in the home and in the city. The experience of rooms is usually discussed very differently from the experience of buildings, or neighbourhoods, or regions of a city. Researchers usually decide to ask different questions, or record different behaviour when considering a playground in contrast, say, to a national park. But it is rare to question what the fundamental psychological differences are between these different scales and whether there are any parallels from one scale to the other, or even how these different scales, which are elements of a common facet, relate to one another.

This facet is an ordered facet like facet A, place differentiation. Places can be categorised from the smallest to the largest in a quantitative sequence of scales. However, it differs from facet A in that there is an empirical question as to how facet C relates to the other two facets. As has been argued, it is logically necessary for place differentiation to interact with place objectives, but how might it be expected that the scale of a place interacts with facets A and B ? There are at least two hypotheses that can be developed for the possible relationships between different facets.

One hypothesis for example, would be that the experience of the large scale, a town or an area of countryside, is a direct combination of the experiences of smaller scale constituents, streets, buildings, fields, streams. This hypothesis would predict that it was possible to predict the satisfaction an area of countryside from knowledge of satisfaction with each of its constituents, the trees, streams and so on. Another example would be that it would be possible to build up models of the significance of a building from analysis of each of its components isolation. A contrasting hypothesis would be that people experience a place in a more holistic, molar way, whatever its scale. This would mean that it would be more difficult to predict the qualities of that experience from knowledge of the experience of the sub places it contains, say predicting the overall use of a building from the use of individual rooms. However, it would imply that no matter what the scale of the place the personal, social and cultural elements would be identifiable in much the same way.

The two contrasting hypotheses about the relationships between the experience of one scale of place to larger or smaller scales are, in facet terms, actually hypotheses about the interpendence of the scale facet with the others. The first hypotheses proposes that facet C will interact with Facets A and B. It suggests that experience at any scale, i.e., the quality of places and how differentiated they are, will interact with experiences of the smaller scale components. The second hypothesis suggests that facet C will be independent of the other two facets. The same relationships between the components of place experience will be found at each scale. As will be shown, it is possible to carry out direct empirical tests to establish which of these two structural hypotheses has the most support.

Facet D: aspects of design. Markus' three-fold constituents of design; function, form and space are also a major facet of places. This facet draws attention to the different aspects of the design of places that need to be considered when exploring the other three facets. Facet D therefore gives rise to a whole basket of hypotheses about how the structure of place experience may take on different forms in relation to the aspects of design that are being considered. For example personal comfort at the immediate scale, say in a room, may be most clearly revealed by examining the functions of a particular space and how readily these are achieved. This is probably what most building *evaluations* seek to do. To take another example, the form (or style) of a place may be examined to see whether it reveals emphases at the personal, social or cultural level of differentiation.

This complex range of hypotheses will take considerable elaboration. Given the limits of the present chapter a few examples will be given, in the presentation of example studies, of some of these hypotheses being tested. A more detailed review of all the hypotheses and their relationship to each other will have to await a lengthier publication. However, it is worth noting that the combinations of elements from facet D with those of other facets do appear to provide a framework that might well incorporate most types of environment and behaviour study. Building evaluations, studies of environmental cognition, explorations of personal space use, and so on, may all be analysed as focusing on particular combinations of the elements of facet D and the other facets.

A general mapping sentence

The network of facets that have been summarised is quite complex. Four have been presented above, but many others could be proposed. This is typical of most facet theories. Guttman (see Shye, 1978, for details), who formulated the facet approach, therefore proposed a summarising device for presenting the main points in any facet theory. The essence of this device has three constituents.

a)   To identify what it is that all the facets have in common.This will be another superordinate facet that indicates the range over which the observations can vary. This *common range* is typically frequency, accuracy or value.

b)   To specify the population to which the facets are seen to apply, with any facets that might describe that population. This may be the population from which the people whose views are being solicited is drawn, or the types of places that the places being studied are taken to represent.

c)   To summarise in ordinary language the relationships between the facets.

This summarising device, then, shows how the facets map together into the common range facet, encapsulating all the possible descriptions of the variables being mapped. For this reason it is known as a *mapping sentence*. It has the distinct advantage of making explicit many of the aspects of a theory that are often kept implicit. The algebraic ideas behind it are discussed most fully in Borg (1978).

For the Theory of Place a preliminary mapping sentence is proposed, in *Table 1*, summarising the key points of the earlier discussion.

The major hypothesis that is encapsulated in the mapping sentence in Table 1 is that there will be distinctions between the individual, social and cultural effectiveness of any place when that effectiveness is examined in terms of the functions of the place, its spatial qualities or its form. The mapping sentence, as such, does not propose details of the relationships between the hypothesised facets, although their interconnections are indicated by connecting words. Logical discussion and presentation, as in all scientific discourse, is required to elaborate the details of the facet structure. A number of hypotheses about the relationships between the elements of a facet and the relationships between facets, all of which are more detailed hypotheses about the facet structure, were summarised in the earlier presentation of the facets.

As has been mentioned, the purpose of the mapping sentence is to summarise a variety of hypotheses, all of which are open to empirical test, as will be illustrated in the following sections. The range of types of hypothesis are so many, though, that it is useful to list the *types* of hypothesis that are inherent in any mapping sentence. There are three broad types of hypothesis.

1.   Existence of the facets.
        These are hypotheses that the elements indicated in the facets will be empirically distinct within the domain under study.

2.   Internal structure of the facets.
        If the facets do exist then the structure of each facet, i.e. the relationships between its elements, is open to consideration. Whether it is ordered or not. If it is ordered what the actual order is.

3.   Relationships between the facets
     Once facets can be seen to have a structure to them it is possible to
     hypothesise relationships between them. The consideration of these
     relationships reveal the processes that underly the system being examined.

Table 1   A summary mapping sentence for the theory of place
facet D

The extent to which Aspects of Design of Place (p) achieves
                    [1.Function]
                    [2.Space   ]
                    [3.Form   ]

facet A	*facet B*	*facet C*
Differentiated	Place	Scale of
	Objectives at	Interaction
[1.Central]	[1.Personal]	[1.Immediate]
[2.Peripheral]	[2.Social]	[2.Local]
	[3.Cultural]	[3.Distant]

                      common range
                      [Effective]
will be   to   achievement of objectives
                      [Ineffective]   through design aspects

Where place (p) is one of a Population (P) of places that are experienced
by people and open to empirical study.

The facet approach is therefore also fruitful in providing a strategic structure for
considering many different types of environment and behaviour study. Three
examples of this will be presented and empirical study of them reviewed later in the
chapter:

1.   The consideration at the immediate level (element 1 of facet C) of social
     aspects (element 2 of facet B) of space (element 3 of facet D) can be
     regarded the study of 'territorial' and related uses of space, as for example
     reviewed by Altman (1975).
2.   Personal objectives (element 1 of facet B) at the immediate scale (element
     1 of facet C) may be most clearly revealed by examining the functions
     (element 1 of facet D) of a particular space and how readily these are
     achieved. This is probably what most building *evaluations* seek to do (e.g.,
     Marans and Spreckelmeyer, 1981).
3.   Studies of environmental meaning can be seen as explorations of how the

form (or style) of a place reveals personal, social or cultural significations (Rapoport, 1982). Typically such studies are at the immediate or local level of interaction. Lynch's great contribution (shown so fully in Banerjee and Southworth, 1990) was to point out that such studies are also very valuable if conducted at the distant level of interaction.

Testing facet models of place experience

In order to elaborate the research implications of the facet theory of place, summaries of three sets of empirical studies will be presented. Each illustrated the application of different aspects of the theory to the consideration of a number of studies. The three areas of research have been chosen to provide one example for each of the elements of facet D, aspects of design. The first example deals with space use (element 2) and the second with functional matters as revealed through evaluations (element 1). The third facet considers a study of architectural form (element 3). It will be argued that all three studies reveal analogous empirical structures, thereby supporting some of the key hypotheses of the general mapping sentence of the theory of place.

Actions and space

One starting point for the theory of place is the hypothesis that particular patterns of activity are associated with particular places. This is an hypothesis that has been accepted by many architectural theorists, most notably Alexander (1964 and subsequently Alexander et al, 1977). However, few of these theorists have explored the processes that may generate such patterns or the empirical evidence for the system of interrelationships which maintains them. A development of these ideas can be derived from the facet framework above. Facets A and B and C would be hypothesised to be reflected in all three of the facet D elements. Here, however we are concentrating on facet D, the spatial environment, at the immediate level of space use.

In other words, the facet model of place use leads to three hypotheses. The first is that there will be differentiation of places in terms of the uses to which they are put, as discussed earlier when describing facet A. The second is that there will be three distinguishable types of place use. One, linking to element 1 of facet B, (Saegert and Winkel's first paradigm), would be hypothesised to emphasise the physical adaptations that are necessary for the actions associated with the places. Another, derived from element 2 of facet B, would be hypothesised that emphasise relationships between people. The third (B3) would deal with the socio-cultural structure, reflecting connections with the broader culture and, for example, power and status.

The third hypothesis, discussed earlier, is that the two facets of place use will interact with each other.

This three-fold framework can be seen as an hypothesis that there are three broad classes of behavioural setting (Barker 1968). These three classes, however, are expected to interrelate to form a system of space uses for any given type of place. Somewhat paradoxically, then, this set of hypotheses is more 'ecological' than Barker's original (1986) behaviour setting theory. Barker wrote little about how one setting influenced the existence of others. His primary task was to identify distinct settings. The present model, however, presupposes a set of interrelationships between settings. They form a system, each defining the other.

Physical layout is seen, in this regard, as a manifestation of the rule structures that exist across a set of social processes. These rules are a product of the co-existence of a number of related activity expectations, shaped by processes of social control, such as privacy (Altman, 1977). Facet analysis leads to the hypothesis that there will be underlying structures for activities associated with places.

A number of studies have been carried out in which the actions typical of particular locations are recorded, usually through an interview, e.g., studies of the use of different rooms in the home (Canter, 1983). Studies of societies in which space use is not obviously fixed, or difficult for a foreign observer to take for granted, are particularly helpful in revealing patterns which might otherwise be obscure. An early study of Japanese apartments (Canter and Lee, 1975) or more recent studies of Polygynous households (Omotayo, 1987) are interesting examples of these type of study.

In these studies a matrix is derived in which the columns are different activities and each row is a different room. In studies of space in the home a number of different homes are studied and the activity that takes place in each room noted in the appropriate cell of the row and column. By adding up the frequencies across all the homes studied and putting those values into the cells of the matrix a summary matrix is created that indicates the frequency with which each room is used for each particular activity. Other aspects of the rule structure, such as who is responsible for the room or has control over it can also be incorporated. This matrix therefore encapsulates the similarities and differences between the rooms in a house in terms of the uses to which they are put.

The theory of place predicts that there will be a facet structure underlying the co-occurrence of activities. Activities that have similar defining facets, for example being highly functionally differentiated (element 2 of facet A), and also social in orientation (element 2 of facet B), e.g., having a formal meal, would be hypothesised to be more likely to occur in the same range of places as other similar activities e.g., holding an important family meeting, and not to occur in other locations that typically housed activities with very different facet profiles. In other words, an empirical correspondence between the facet definitional structure and the empirical structure is taken as support for the original facet hypotheses.

This is known as the facet *principle of correspondence*. Conceptual, *theoretical* relationships, implied by a similar combination of facet elements, are tested by looking for corresponding relationships in the observations. In other words, each activity that might occur in the home (e.g., sleeping, eating, studying etc) is classified in terms of the two facets of interest here (facets A and B). This means that a number of activities will have a similar *facet profile*. For example, having a meal together 'dining', would be classified as similar to having a casual snack with other 'snacking'. Similarly, studying and practising a musical instrument would be deemed to have the same facet profile and therefore be hypothesised to take place in the same locations.

The facet framework is essentially multivariate. All possible relationships between variables are of potential relevance to the hypotheses because every observation (variable) can be classified on every facet. However, no assumptions have been made about the statistical structure underlying these relationships, furthermore because a system of relationships is being explored it is to be expected that some facets will relate to each other. Orthogonal, distinct linear dimensions can therefore not be assumed. Indeed, as discussed earlier, some of the facets are theoretically posited to be non-ordered, so that a linear dimension may be a very inappropriate model around which to search for any evidence to support or challenge facet hypotheses.

These considerations of the importance of not using models that make strong statistical assumptions has taken the people who use the facet perspective away from the use of multiple regression and factor analytic approaches and encouraged them to use multi-dimensional scaling (MDS) procedures, especially non-metric procedures (Shye, 1982, 1989; Canter, 1985). These procedures represent relationships between variables as distances in an abstract 'Euclidian' space, i.e., an area or volume that has no predetermined axes. Typically each variable is represented as a point such that the further apart any two point are the lower the relationships between them. Points can represent people, places, actions, drawings or any of the possible populations of entities that may be studied.

MDS procedures, then, typically start with an association matrix. In the example of place use this would be a matrix that is derived from the original summary matrix of the frequency of room use. It is derived by correlating the frequencies of every activity with every other across the rooms. Put simply, the more likely any two activities are to occur in the same rooms the more highly correlated they will be. One of a number of possible algorithms is then used to produce a spatial configuration of activities that represents the correlations as closely as possible. So, the closer together any two points in the space, representing two activities, the more likely are those activities to occur in the same rooms.

The interpretation of these MDS configurations is not limited to the search for dimensions or any other particular structure. Instead a *regional hypothesis* is used. This is the hypothesis that the elements of a facet will be reflected in distinct regions of the MDS space. If no regions can be identified that relate to the elements then there is no support in that analysis for the particular facet. As illustrated in *Figure 1*, the relationships between elements, whether they are ordered or non-ordered, and between facets are tested by examining the topographical relationship between the regions.

Of course, the MDS procedures can be used to generate hypotheses about facets and their relationships as well as testing such hypotheses. As in all science the replication of results is the key to establishing the robustness of hypotheses.

For the study of space use in the home, the facet approach leads to the examination of the relationship that every activity has to every other activity. The activities are represented as points in a space, the nearness of the points to each other representing the similarity in their patterns of occurrence across rooms. A summary of such analyses is given by Canter (1983) and reproduced in Figure 1.

This configuration provides some interesting perspectives on the theory of place framework. First, the overall structure does point to a system of interrelating places within the home. Strongly distinct places, or those ordered say along one continuum

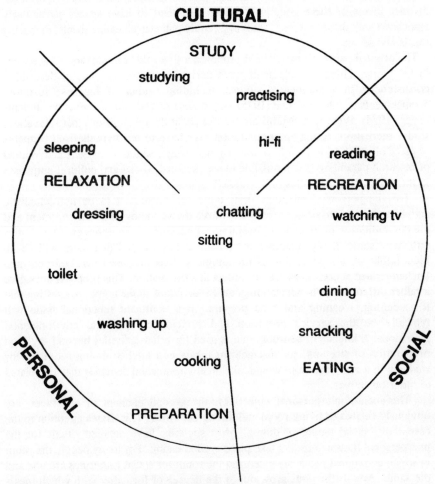

Figure 1 Schematic representation of domestic activities.

from public to private, are not demonstrated by this analysis, although for some households there may be clear discontinuities, e.g., where a husband has a number of wives living with him in the same compound (Omotayo, 1989). In general, then, Figure 1 shows a picture of some activities being more central to the plot and therefore likely to occur in most rooms. Others activities are much more differentiated. This is taken as support for the existence of facet A, place differentiation.

With concrete instantiation it is possible to say something about the nature of this place differentiation in the home. The general activities are those that are the essence of domestic existence having some of the qualities of the more differentiated activities, brief moments of relaxation, casual reading, chatting to others, eating snacks. The analysis also reveals that there are more developed, distinct forms of these general activities that tend to have spaces particularly associated with them, sleeping, studying, family gatherings, eating meals, preparing meals and so on.

The original paper (Canter, 1983) proposed a five-fold segmentation of activities in the home. These five elements were derived post-hoc as ways of describing consistencies in a number of studies, including studies of Japanese furniture arrangements (Canter and Lee, 1975) and the use of bed-sitting rooms by students (Tagg, 1974). What speculations are fruitful about the relationships that relaxation, study, recreation, eating and preparation may have to our hypothesised elements of place objectives (derived from the original categorisation by Saegert and Winkel of research paradigms)? Is it possible to see personal, social and cultural emphases in the structure of activities in the home?

To take personal objectives first, these are postulated to be individualistic activities that are physically oriented towards the servicing of an environment and the possibilities in particular of physiological adaptation. So although all activities will have some of this adaptive component it is proposed that there will be an identifiable set for which this is predominant. It is proposed that bedroom and kitchen related actions most readily reflect this orientation. This proposal does give a rather different bias to adaptation goals for activities in the home, suggesting that for sleeping, cleaning and food preparation a dominant functional issue will typically be the service provision and fundamental physical environmental provisions. A kitchen or bedroom that is used for other activities beyond say food preparation or sleeping, for instance for meals in a kitchen dining room, or for studying in a study bedroom would take on environmental demands that are related to other objectives.

The social, interpersonal objectives, the second element of our facet, are obviously related to living room and dining activities. This draws attention to the essentially social nature of dining. Most societies have detailed rituals for the interpersonal transactions that take place around eating. For many people the room in which communal meals are eaten and the room for social gatherings are one and the same. Any distinctions grow out of the degree of formality with which meals are eaten. Regarding eating and lounge areas of a home as the ones that make possible various social opportunities, does help in understanding the significance that is typically given to these places in many households. The detailed studies of how the use and décor of these rooms carry social significance (Giuliani et al, 1988) is one important way of developing the exploration of these issues.

If the two elements are interpreted as indicated, the resulting hypothesis is that the cultural identity objectives (the third element of facet B, derived from Saegert and Winkel's socio-cultural paradigm) are most dominant in what was called the 'study' activities of the 'workroom/den'. Clearly, as with both the other elements, there is an aspect of achieving some culturally related meaning with all the activities. Even sleeping is done in different ways in Japan, for instance, when compared with Western countries. Yet it does not seem so plausible that the location chosen to sleep has major implications for cultural identity. By contrast, it might be expected that it is in the social and recreational activities that significance as a member of a society is most emphasised. For example, the music people listen to often appears to define the particular sub-group to which they belong. However, to define an activity as strongly cultural in its emphasis it is necessary to be clear as to whether this is seen as at the far extreme from it being a personal activity, with social activities sitting somewhere between the two. Empirically no analyses have revealed such a linear ordering from the most individualistic, through the social and on to the cultural. Instead, the results suggest that cultural emphases sit *between* the individual and the social. This raises the question of what an extreme, *purely* cultural activity could be? An example that comes to mind is of religious actions, like praying. But are these not also personal as well and often conducted in groups? Their emphasis may be to strengthen an individual's identity within a particular cultural context but this does not put them at the end of a continuum.

In daily usage, as non-technical term, 'cultural' activities would be taken to include listening to music or other forms of participation in the arts. Most commentators argue that in the modern home the television provides the focus for such cultural activities and that in a more anthropological sense the mass media are the culture of our age. But this view reveals that the contact which a person has with their culture often takes place at a personal, individual level. The objectives facet should not be taken to imply, necessarily, that they will be reflected in increasing sizes of group contact. In fact since at least the early writings of G.H. Mead it has been clear that one of the most culturally determined aspects of experience is a person's concept of self. Is it far-fetched to suggest, therefore, that the activities that coalesce around recreation, study and relaxation may be usefully thought of as having a dominant objective of enhancing a person's own identity through socio-cultural transactions?

More detailed hypotheses for future test emerge from these considerations. For example the design qualities that are important for the study/recreation areas would be hypothesised to carry considerable symbolic significance especially in regard to how they reflect the user's view of themselves as portrayed through known cultural artifacts. By contrast the design qualities of a kitchen or bedroom would be expected to have roots in the services it is wished to reveal that they supply.

Purposive evaluation

The studies to be summarised in this section deal with the effectiveness of the functioning of a place (element 1 of facet D). In essence studies of the strengths and weaknesses of a particular design are dealt with under the heading of 'evaluation'.

Evaluations of places are the products of assessing how the components of places combine to help people achieve a variety of objectives. This perspective puts environmental evaluations centre stage. They enable us to examine the satisfactions that reveal how effectively a place supports a person's objectives. Evaluations are seen as an important part of the experience of places, of value to study in their own right.

The 'purposive evaluation' approach complements other approaches to evaluation such as that of Marans and Spreckelmeyer (1981) in that it hypothesises that evaluations will consist of a system of interrelated components that centre on dominant purposes for any given place. Part of the task of research, then, is to establish whether the core of purposes is identifiable for classes of place.

If a place has some sort of 'core' it would be expected that a place evaluation would reveal some common theme in any particular setting. This theme would be an aspect of the place that was crucial to its evaluation. For example, the acoustics of a concert hall might be hypothesised as being the best predictor of the evaluation of most other aspects of the place. The physical comfort of a bedroom, or the spiritual mood of a church, are other examples that come to mind. What the theme was would depend on the type of setting. It would be identifiable from an empirical structure that revealed variables which had high average correlations with all the other variables. The fundamental hypothesis here is that there will actually be variables that have a high average correlation with many other aspects of evaluation, rather than there being a lot of separate groupings of inter-correlations. In MDS terms these variables are likely to be central to the configuration as well as having a conceptual centrality to the experience of that place.

Donald (1985) reviewed a number evaluation studies carried out within the facet framework, finding strong evidence for the differentiation facet A, and consequently specific foci for different types of place. For example, in hospitals it is the care and attention at the bedside, and the way in which the design facilitates that, which is crucial to the whole evaluation (Kenny and Canter, 1981). In contrast, satisfaction with the space and servicing of the living room has been proposed as the core of housing satisfaction (Canter and Rees, 1982).

In some settings the reported research expresses more difficulty in identifying what is at the heart of satisfaction with that particular place. In offices, for example, the ability to communicate with other people within the organisation emerges as central but may not be tapped by any particular question dealing with place evaluation in an office (Donald, 1983). This raises the possibility that there may be places that are conceptually encapsulated by what *happens* within them almost to the exclusion of spatial or stylistic issues. An alternative hypothesis is that these settings do not form a coherent system of related aspects but are separate clusters of places. Support for such an hypothesis would be very important because, within the framework presented here it would be predicted to be an inherently unstable type of place. Such places could therefore be of great theoretical value in testing the limits of the theory of place. This is clearly an area in which future research would be very productive.

If there is a core to place evaluation then the other aspects of the evaluation are likely to have degrees of differentiation that enable the distinct aspects to be identified. It is thus hypothesised that any aspect of evaluation has a number of constituents that interrelate, rather than a set of orthogonal dimensions. Following the discussion above it is hypothesised that the key constituents should reflect the aspects of place experience of facet B, i.e., adaptation that relates to the servicing of the environment, assessment of the action opportunities that are achievable and thirdly, the self-identity enhancing socio-cultural implications of the setting. In effect, these constituents would be hypothesised to radiate out from this core as illustrated in *Figure 2*.

Figure 2 is derived from the analysis of questionnaire based post-occupancy evaluations of buildings. It summarises the results of a number of studies as reviewed by Donald (1985). For each of these studies a large number of building users evaluated their places of work or residence by answering a set of Likert type questions. The questions were then inter-correlated and MDS analyses carried out in which each question is represented as a point in space. The closer together the questions the more highly correlated they are. By looking at the meaning of the questions it is possible to identify the theme that describes the region of the space in which the questions are found. Figure 2 is a schematic representation of that regional structure. The full technical details are given by Donald (1985) or in the papers he cites.

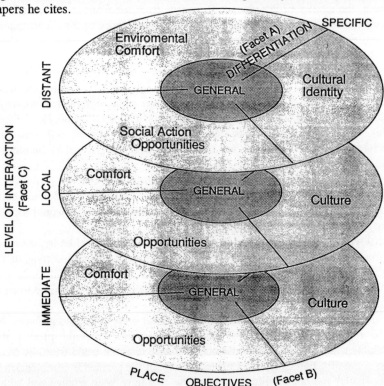

Figure 2 Schematic model of the structure of place evaluations

As will be seen in Figure 2 the elements of the place objectives do not produce some simple order. As with the activities in Figure 1 they have a circular sequence to them. This implies that all place evaluations share the different aspects to various degrees. What is of a special note is that the different elements do indeed group together. So that it is typically the case that heating, lighting and acoustic aspects of an environment highly correlate with each other. These were assumed to be the individual aspects of evaluation relating to element 1 of facet B.

Similarly, the different spatial aspects relate to each other. It is proposed that when considering spatial evaluation the main implication is for social contact. Therefore this region is seen as evidence in support of element 2 of facet B. These questions about satisfaction with spatial equations are also distinct from those aspects that link to the sort of people who are found in a place and the symbolic meanings that a place has. These are all aspects to do with what we have called cultural processes, i.e., element 3 of facet B.

The scale of transaction with the physical surroundings (facet C) also appears to operate as a separate facet. It can be found in a dimension quite independently of the other two facets. It implies that the transactions with a place that a person has, have the same basic psychological structure to it whether that place be conceived as an area of a town or a particular room. Whether it be an urban park or a restaurant, the quality of the place will emerge from the interaction between the three constituents that have been identified. The significance of these constituents will be directly related to the central objectives or purposes that characterise a place.

A further hypothesis that emerges from the model of evaluations in Figure 2 is that different classes of place will give differing emphases to the major elements. For example, buildings which have a great deal of ritual significance would be expected to be evaluated with special weight given to their symbolic, cultural qualities. Most architecture regarded as significant would fall into this categorisation. Here are the churches and parliament buildings, and in the modern city the banks and the insurance companies.

Buildings which are aimed at providing opportunities, and the provision of particular types of social transaction, are predicted to be built around their spatial components. Theatres and airports would fall into this scheme, as would football grounds.

A third type of emphasis, on the services and provision, would be hypothesised to be characteristic of those places in which the adaptation and coping of the individual was a central focus. Or in which there were activities that made very special demands on the users. Hospitals and schools may be hypothesised to be of this type.

This outline of ways in which buildings may differ emphasises those places that may be regarded as pure types. However, the model would predict that recognisable combinations would also occur. Future research could fruitfully move towards a classification of types of place in terms of the particular combination of service, spatial and socio-cultural components that have been emphasised within them.

One further advantage of such a multivariate typology would be that the effectiveness of a building could be examined in relation to what was considered a typical profile for places of that type. This would go beyond explorations of the meaning of places and their symbolic functions or the ad hoc attempt to identify the characteristic purposes. It would provide a cumulative framework within which to consider the different approaches taken to a variety of designs.

Place form and meaning

The final study to be considered draws upon the formal element 3 of facet D. It looks at the way in which the designs and styles of famous buildings may reflect the same psychological distinctions as do the functional and spatial aspects.

The theory of place draws attention to the ways in which forms of building may be hypothesised to reflect different approaches to modes of transaction with places. It is hypothesised that these variations would be analogous to those found for activities and building evaluations. Here the hypotheses derive from consideration of the ways in which the form or style of a building, mainly reflecting visual aspects of its design, may emphasise different approaches to place objectives. Is there any evidence for personal, social or cultural elements in the style of buildings? If there are, how do they overlap? What is the core of architectural style?

In order to develop further an understanding of how architectural styles may be considered, within a theory of place perspective, it is useful to review briefly the central discussions of differences in style that have been characteristic of aesthetic criticism. Historians of Art and Architecture have always pointed to a clear distinction between the classical and the romantic approaches to the creation of art forms in all media, including architecture. In the classical styles there are pure abstract rules that are seen as being free of culture and related to effects that are immediate and personal. Collins dictionary defines classical as 'marked by stability of form, intellectualism and restraint'. The romantic style by contrast is more local, it does not espouse abstract principles that define what is good and bad. The Collins definition is 'an emphasis on feeling and content rather than order and form .... the free expression of the passions and individuality'. In his extensive review of the history of art Gombrich (1950) showed in considerable detail how these broad movements in art touched every aspect of their activities, so that the terms 'romantic' and 'classical' could be taken as summaries of a conglomeration of objectives that the designers themselves were espousing.

Is the individual adaptation perspective, when seen as style, essentially classical; the social and cultural, aspects of a romantic style of architecture? A precursor to these questions is whether even architects can recognise relationships between different building styles that has any structure to it. If they can then their judgement could reflect these hypothesised architectural movements. One series of studies (Wilson and Canter, 1990) does lend some intriguing support to these hypotheses.

In the Wilson and Canter studies architecture students were given 26 examples of contemporary architecture in the form of colour photographs. Using the multiple sorting procedure (Canter et al, 1985) students of different years in two schools of architecture freely assigned the building to categories of their own choosing. A particular type of MDS procedure, multidimensional scalogram analysis (MSA), that is especially suitable to this type of data was then used to examine the underlying structure of their judgements. For the present discussion the judgements made by final year students are of most relevance. These respondents had all spent a year in professional practice and were therefore acting from a basis of some considerable experience. *Figure 3* summarises the results of the MSA for the 15 final year architecture students.

In Figure 3 each of the buildings that was judged is represented by a small line drawing. The closer together these drawings the more likely were the buildings to have been assigned to the same groupings in the sortings that the students made. So, just as with activities and evaluation questions, it is possible to look at the configuration of buildings and consider what underlying structure it might reveal. A schematic summary of one proposed structure is drawn onto Figure 3. (A full list of the actual buildings used is given in Wilson and Canter, 1990.)

In the top half of Figure 3 are buildings that are undoubtedly modernist in their form, perhaps most obviously building 21, Mies Van der Rohe's Seagram building, and building 23, Eisenman's House VI. The other buildings in the top half all have an essentially simple, almost cubist form to them that is apparently driven by abstract concepts typical of classical 'intellectualism and restraint'. By contrast the lower half of the configuration contains buildings that are more complex in form and make more obvious reference to local, social and cultural issues. They exhibit much more directly than the top group romantic 'free expression of the passions and individuality', typically being drawn from styles described by Jencks (1972) as clearly 'post-modern', e.g., building 22, Moore's Piazza d'Italia, or building 24, Turner Brooks' Butterworth House.

It is therefore suggested that 'modernism', with its abstract, classical forms, creates places in which the individual's reactions to the building, independently of any social or cultural processes is the essence of the design approach. As such, a simple, pragmatic view that the form relates directly to the functions of the building would be consistent with the aesthetic stand. By contrast, the major developments of post-modernist thinking are to accept the relevance of the social and cultural significance of a design.

Within the theory of place, then, Figure 3 is seen as evidence for a general approach to architectural style being influenced by either the notions of individual adaptation, or by the opportunity and socio-cultural objectives that form other paradigms of person-place transactions. Indeed, a close examination of Figure 3 does indicate two distinct sub-regions in the 'post-modern' region. To the left are buildings that draw upon broad references to cultural meanings, including what Jencks (1972) called 'post-modern classical', whereas to the right are buildings, that Jencks called 'post-modern vernacular'. These latter have a much closer reference to local, social and sub-cultural design issues. It is therefore hypothesised that the distinctions between the cultural identity place objectives and the social place opportunity objectives are reflected in these two different approaches to architectural styles.

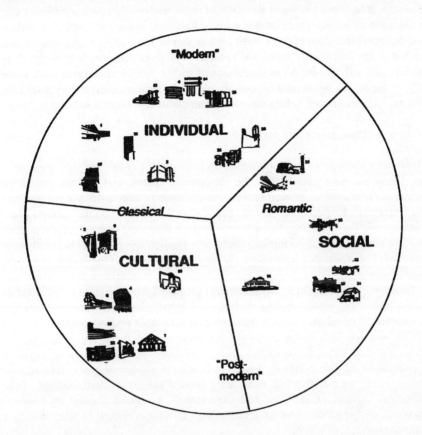

Figure 3 Schematic model of architectural style.

Is there a core to architectural place styles? The centre of Figure 3 is empty. There therefore does not appear to be any archetypal place within these contemporary buildings that could find an association with most of the other buildings. The idea of the evolution of places would predict this, arguing that by focusing on contemporary buildings a later stage in differentiation is being illustrated. This leads to the hypothesis that the central region would be filled by older buildings such as the early work of Frank Lloyd Wright. This is an hypothesis relatively easy to test.

Implications for future theory, research, and utilisation

This chapter has provide a broad sketch of a theory of place. Patterns of place use, building evaluations and explorations of architectural style have been discussed as distinct but related examples of issues that all have a place within our experience of places. It has been proposed that each of these studies illustrates a different one of the three major aspects of design, namely function, space and form. The theory also predicted that each of these three aspects would show similar constituents that related to the individual, social and cultural objectives that people have for their transactions with places. A re-examination of earlier published research gave some general support to this central hypothesis, although there is clearly a very great deal of research still needed before the theory can claim any general validity.

Linking function, space and form

The results summarised and illustrated do indicate that consistent facet structures are likely to be found within the functional, spatial and formal realms of architectural discourse. In each of these realms there is some evidence for distinct, but interrelated, personal, social and cultural aspects of the person-place transactions. These findings throw a new light on the nature of evaluations, studies of place use and of architectural meaning. The possibilities for links between these three areas of research are also strongly suggested by some of the common aspects of their structure.

However, the complexity of the models proposed here presents a challenge to future research. How can the richness of possibilities that derive from the combinations of all the facets be reduced to manageable proportions?

One answer lies in the comment by Markus that there are basic, typical conjunction of form, function and space. Are there, at least by analogy, typical conjunctions of the personal, social and cultural modes of place transaction? Indeed, is it not possible that there are a limited sub-set of combinations of the particular aspects of building and experience? A sub-set limited by custom, tradition, design process and the requirements of human beings; in other words, a faceted typology of places?

This is a topic directly open to study using procedures like those described above. The hypothesis would be that identifiable structures would be found that have characteristic profiles across the facet elements discussed. Preliminary pilot studies following up these ideas have produced encouraging results.

Exploring the development and decay of places

If such characteristic places profiles can be identified then the question immediately arises as to how they came about. To answer this there is a need to address more closely the issue of the inherent processes of change in places. The general theory of place evolution argues that the major changes will be towards increasing differentiation of places, although the mechanics of this have hardly been touched upon. Does this mean that there are no conditions under which places will become less differentiated? These would be situations in which a number of separate places, housing distinct functions, were amalgamated whilst still supporting the different uses. My own view at present is that such a reduction in differentiation is inevitably decadent in the sense of implying a deterioration of social and psychological processes. Examples of this are therefore likely to be found in destructive contexts such as war or famine. However, this is a matter of importance for future research.

A further range of research possibilities within this framework derives from new ways of looking at the physical forms of places. For example some of the meanings of physical forms derive from the opportunities that those forms offer. Size of a space, for instance carries limitations on what can happen in that space. Other meanings are more arbitrary, relating to historical accident or the availability of materials, such as the use of bricks in English houses. Studies to establish the universality of the association of meanings with forms could help to demonstrate whether functionally based meanings, such as space and status, are any less manipulable than those that are arbitrary, such as brick and domesticity.

Another related area of research would be to study, say, the evaluation of contrasting building forms that offer the same function but have quite different social connotations. Pilot work in which I have been involved does indicate that the evaluation of any given physical form will change enormously if the perceived function of the building is changed, even when only visual aspects are considered.

Developing place programming

Even a general acceptance of the theory of place outlined above has profound implications for the approach to design. Consideration needs to be given to the different modes of transaction that the building will facilitate, at the personal, social and cultural levels, as well as the functional, spatial and formal qualities of the building. The various interactions between these different components also need to be considered. The way the interactions will vary with the type of place that is being produced, and how they might evolve over time, add a further complexity to the processes that could be studied. A tall order indeed, and one that is only feasible if more research is carried out to reduce the implicit complexities of the processes involved, creating a distilled framework of the facets of place.

Acknowledgments

Gary Moore and Bob Marans went far beyond the call of editorial duty in helping me to revise this chapter. I am very grateful to them and to their specialist advisor, Linda Groat, for their assistance.

Note

1. I am especially grateful to Linda Groat for sharing with me her unpublished lectures that clarified the ways in which styles may reflect different psychological emphases.

References

Alexander, C. (1964), *Notes on the Synthesis of Form*, Harvard University Press, Mass.

Alexander, C., Ishikawa S. & Silverstein. M. (1977), *A Pattern Language*, Oxford University Press, New York.

Banerjee, T. & Southworth M. (1990) (eds), *City Sense and City Design: Writings and Projects of Kevin Lynch*, MIT Press, Cambridge Mass.

Barker, R. (1968), *Ecological Psychology: Concepts and Methods for Studying the Environment of Human Behavior*, Stanford University Press, Stanford.

Borg, I. (1978), 'Some Basic Concepts in Facet Theory', in J.Lingoes (ed.), *Geometric Representation of Relational Data*, in Ann Arbor, Mathesis Press.

Canter, D. (1977), *The Psychology of Place*, Architectural Press, London.

Canter, D. (1983), 'The Purposive Evaluation of Places', *Environment and Behavior*, Vol. 15 (6), pp. 659-698.

Canter, D. (1985) (ed.), *Facet Theory: Approaches to Social Research*, Springer-Verlag, New York.

Canter, D. (1986), 'Putting Situations in Their Place' in A.Furnham (ed.) *Social Behaviour in Context*, pp. 208-239, Allyn and Bacon, 208-239, Boston.

Canter, D., Brown, J. & Groat, L. (1985), 'A Multiple Sorting Procedure for Studying Conceptual Systems' in M. Brenner, J. Brown and D. Canter (eds), *The Research Interview*, Academic Press, London.

Canter, D. & Lee, K.H. (1975), 'A Non-Reactive Study of Room Usage in Modern Japanese Apartments', in D. Canter and T. Lee (eds), *Psychology and the Built Environment*, Architectural Press, pp. 48-55.

Canter, D. & Rees, K. (1982), 'A Multivariate Model of Housing Satisfaction', *International Review of Applied Psychology*, Vol. 31, pp. 185-208.

Donald, I. (1983), *The Multivariate Structure of Office Evaluations*, MSc Thesis, University of Surrey, unpublished.

Donald, I. (1985), 'The Cylindrex of Place Evaluation', in D. Canter (ed.), *Facet Theory: Approaches to Social Research*, Springer-Verlag, New York.

Fishwick, L. & Vining, J. (1992), 'Towards a Phenomenology of Recreation Place', *Journal of Environmental Psychology*, Vol. 12, pp. 57-63.

Girouard, M. (1978), *Life in the English Country House: A Social and Architectural History*, Yale University Press, New Haven.

Girouard, M. (1985), *Cities and People*, Yale University Press, New Haven.

Girouard, M. (1990), *The English Town*, Yale University Press, New Haven.

Gombrich, E.H. (1950), *The Story of Art*, The Phaidon Press, London.

Jencks, C. (1982), *Current Architecture*, Academy Editions, London.

Kenny, C. & Canter, D. (1981), 'A facet structure for nurses' evaluations of ward designs', *Journal of Occupational Psychology*, Vol. 54, pp. 93-108.

Marans, R.W. & Spreckelmeyer, K. (1981), *Evaluating Built Environments: A Behavioural Approach*, Ann Arbor: University of Michigan, Institute for Social Research and Architectural Research Laboratory.

Markus, T.A. (1982) (ed.), *Order in Space and Society: Architectural Form and Its Context in the Scottish Enlightenment,* Mainstrean Publishing, Edinburgh.

Markus, T.A. (1987), 'Buildings as classifying devices', *Environment and Planning B: Planning and Design,* Vol. 14, pp. 67-484.

Moore, G.T. (1987), 'Environment and Behavior Research in North America: History, Developments, and Unresolved Issues', in D. Stokols and I. Altman (eds), *Handbook of Environmental Psychology,* pp. 1359-1410.

Omotayo, F.B. (1988), 'A Cross-Cultural Comparison of Space Use in Hausa, Ibo and Yoruba families of Nigeria', PhD Thesis, University of Surrey, Unpublished.

Proshansky, H.M., Fabian, A.K. & Kaminoff, R. (1983), 'Place Identity: Physical world socialization of the self', *Journal of Environmental Psychology,* Vol. 3, pp. 57-83.

Rapoport, A. (1982), *The Meaning of the Built Environment: A Nonverbal Communication Approach,* Sage, Beverley Hills.

Relph, E. (1976), *Place and Placelessness,* Pion, London.

Saegert, S. & Winkel, G.H. (1990) 'Environmental Psychology', *Annual Review of Psychology,* Vol. 41, pp. 441-477.

Seamon, D. (1987), 'Phenomenology and Environment-Behavior Research', in E.H. Zube and G.T. Moore (eds), *Advances in Environment, Behavior, and a Design,* Vol. 1, pp. 3-29, Plenum, London.

Seamon, D. & Mugerauer, R. (1985), *Dwelling, Place and Environment: Towards a Phenomenology of Person and World,* Nijhoff, Dordrecht.

Shields, R. (1991), *Places on the Margin: Alternative Geographies of Modernity,* Routledge, London.

Shye, S. (1978) (ed.), *Theory Construction and Data Analysis in the Behavioral Sciences,* Jossey-Bass, San Fransisco.

Shye, S. (1985), *Multiple Scaling : The Theory and Application of Partial Order Scalogram Analysis,* North-Holland, Amsterdam.

Sixsmith, J. (1983), 'Comment on the Phenomenological Contribution to Environmental Psychology', *Journal of Environmental Psychology,* Vol. 3, pp. 109-111.

Stea, D. & Turan, M. (1990), 'A Statement on Placemaking', in M.Turan (ed.), *Vernacular Architecture,* Avebury, Aldershot, pp.101-121.

Tagg, S. (1974), 'The Subjective Meaning of Rooms' in D. Canter and T.R. Lee (eds), *Psychology and the Built Environment,* Architectural Press, London.

Wilson, M.A. & Canter, D.V. (1990), 'The Development of Central Concepts during Professional Education: An Example of a Multivariate Model of the Concept of Architectural Style', *Applied Psychology: An International Review,* Vol. 39(4), pp. 431-455.

Wineman, (1985) (ed.), *Behavioral Issues in Office Design,* New York: Van Nostrand Reinhold.

Winett, R.A. (1987), 'Empiricist-Positivist Theories of Environment and Behavior:

New Directions for Multilevel Frameworks', in E.H. Zube and G.T. Moore (eds), *Advances in Environment, Behavior, and Design*, Vol. 1, pp. 30-58, Plenum, London.

6 Way-Finding and Signposting: Penance or Prosthesis?

A 70 year old woman up from the country spent three days trying to get out of a hypermarket in Utrecht. She told police who rescued her she was afraid to ask other shoppers how to get out (*Glasgow Herald*, April 1979).

All form of public information and direction finding systems, whether they are maps, signposts, guides, display boards or whatever, exist within the context of the human use of the built or natural environment. The use and purpose of these communication systems is therefore of interest to people, from a variety of disciplines, who also have a concern for the human use of the physical environment, human geographers, architects, planners and environmental psychologists. Furthermore, in order to understand fully the psychological significance of signposting and the like, and thus be able to produce systems which can be more effectively utilised, it is necessary to understand the relevance of the normal use of the physical surroundings. This chapter summarises some of the research into the ways people navigate within, and make sense of, their physical surroundings, of such relevance to the creation and study of public information and direction-finding systems.

Penance or prosthesis?

In many cases signposting is an admission of design failure. It reflects the fact that there are many situations in which the designer cannot rely upon the knowledge or experience of the user for finding the way. Many modern building complexes, notably universities, hospitals, civic centres and shopping precincts, seem to make demands upon orientation skills and way-finding abilities which few people have. These provide situations in which people need to know where something is, but the nature of the design makes it virtually impossible for them to readily gain that knowledge without some form of help. An attempt at signposting, or direction-giving, is therefore made in order to provide prosthesis for a disability, which, we can argue, was created by the design itself. We are in a great danger of studying the design of crutches, on the assumption that somehow or other they can replace our normal means of navigation. We should be spending some time finding out how the incapacity has come about in the first place. Nonetheless, some prosthetic devices can be very effective. It also cannot be denied that there are many design problems relating to site, or to cost, or to the sheer complexity of what has to be housed, which may conspire to make it impossible for people to rely on their normal day-to-day abilities in order to find their way around. However, even in these situations we should be designing our crutches to make use of the natural processes which occur when those crutches are not necessary, rather than working from the starting point of what is a good design for a crutch. We need to identify what it is about the particular situation which has deprived people of the intellectual resources to find their way without signposting and to identify what resources they do have upon which we can build. If this approach is not taken, then there is a strong risk that signposting systems do not even work effectively as prosthesic devices. Instead they become a public penance, a declaration of the aspects of' the design which are incomprehensible.

It should be noted that it is only in the minority of cases that signposting is necessary. The great majority of our orienting, way-finding and location-identifying behaviour is done completely independently of public information and direction finding systems. We do not normally rely upon signposting to find our way home from the office. The cues we make use of to visit a friend in an area we know may often be informal ones. Indeed, there may well be a variety of relatively sophisticated natural processes upon which we draw, but of which we are not aware.

In examining these processes there are four separate topics we should consider. First of all we need to explore what it is that people already know that can be built upon. Having done this we can move on to the problem of representing new information through signs and symbols. This includes exploring both the representation of location and the representation of the relationships between locations. These explorations derive from an implicit theoretical model which it is valuable to make overt. Having done this we are in a position, finally, to examine the various uses which can be made of public information systems, i.e., (a) for emergencies, (b) in order to reach goals and (c) to facilitate the formation of plans.

Existing user knowledge

Where I am

Probably the most fundamental starting point for way-finding is the knowledge which the individual has about his present location. Any future navigation is probably built upon knowledge of present location. From the earliest discussions of people's orienting behaviour it has been recognised that there are different degrees of sophistication in terms of the knowledge a person can draw upon in identifying where he is. Trowbridge (1913) made one of the strongest early statements on this. He argued that there was a difference between civilised minds and the minds of others, in which he included 'birds, beasts, fish, insects etc but also, in all probability, young children' and a large proportion of mankind living in an 'uncivilised state'. He suggested that these primitive groups could only understand their present location in relation to the whole history of their previous locations, starting with the place of their birth. The civilised mind by contrast could identify its location by reference to some abstract external coordinates, which Trowbridge insisted were the four points of the compass.

It is important to recognise, however, that just as people will differ in their degree of disorientation for any given location. *Places* vary in the amount of 'lostness' they engender. Whilst we are all aware of the individual differences between people, any signposting system should also take into account the variations between places. In one study we carried out in Surrey we explored the possibility of measuring the differences between buildings in order to see what variation in measured lostness could be shown to exist for the different buildings on the university campus. Some of our post-graduate students on the Master's course in Environmental Psychology at the University of Surrey (Agabani and Weaver, 1974) carried out the study. Using the conventional device of a questionnaire which dealt with as many aspects of lostness as could be thought of, these students went round a number of university buildings and questioned people in the corridors about their perceived lostness. A factor analysis of this twenty-one-item questionnaire completed by one hundred and seventy eight people demonstrated that there was a major dimension accounting for 40% of the common variance. This dimension brought together questions dealing with how confusing the building was felt to be, how well oriented the individual felt within it, how easy they found it was to get lost within that building and the amount of time they wasted looking for the way within the building. Items dealing with asking for and giving directions within the building also came up highly loaded on this dimension. Of note was the finding that there were large variations between different buildings on the University of Surrey campus in terms of their mean scores on the derived 'lostness inducingness' scale. The significance of this study is to demonstrate that there are systematic differences between different buildings in terms of how easily the users know where they are in those buildings. In the Surrey study, the aspects of building form which could be most readily related to degree of lostness were how open they were in plan and how simple the overall structure was. Those buildings with many short, winding corridors came out worst, whereas the Students' Union building which consists essentially of a large open, partly differentiated space came out the best. More detailed explorations of this kind would be necessary to identify the particular building properties which seem to induce a feeling of lostness, but this student project certainly served to indicate that such a study would be directly rewarded with design recommendations.

In considering the processes involved in knowing where you are it is worth emphasising that this knowledge would appear to be built up upon knowledge of where you have been. The knowledge of earlier location will then be linked to knowledge of present location by the person's understanding of how he travelled in between. This is a rather complex process. If it is made further sophisticated by the type of external referents to which Trowbridge paid attention, then it is apparent that there is considerable possibility both (a) for errors in this process to occur which can give rise to later difficulties, and (b) for the knowledge, when it is clearly established, to be so efficient that it will overrule any other information sources which might be available. In the former situation, the example of putting a 'you are here' point on a plan may be quite useless because the individual is not all clear exactly where 'here' is, either in his own cognitive system or in that represented on the map. In the latter circumstances the individual's knowledge that he has reached a particular location by a particular route may counteract any attempt by the signposting system to indicate the nature of his current location in relation to other routes.

Where there is

If we accept the metaphor of the 'mental map' which is used for identifying our current location then a design which ignores the way in which people store and draw upon their internal representations is likely to be more difficult to use. As a consequence, it is much more likely to rely upon the prosthetics of signposting than a design which has a psychologically acceptable structure to it.

The idea that we have an internal representation of an area, which has a map-like form, drew its major impetus from the work of Lynch (1960). By asking people to draw maps of Boston and finding that their maps had certain regular errors to them Lynch pointed the way to the exploration of the type of geographical representation people have available to them for helping orientation and navigation. In fact the value of identifying people's psychological geography was highlighted at least fifteen years earlier by a president of the American Geographical Association (Wright, 1947). But it took Lynch's approach of asking people to draw maps to set research in motion. Since his book *The Image of the City,* a variety of studies have been carried out in an attempt to identify what aspects of the built surroundings people draw upon in forming their internal representations. In a later book by Lynch (1976) a number of examples are given of the use of this approach in relation to detailed planning proposals. Lynch's identification of features such as landmarks and boundaries, as important orienting points, is all too readily forgotten. However, it has been argued at length in another context (Canter, 1977) that an approach which relies *entirely* upon the physical features that people will identify may often miss the socio-emotional processes which are part and parcel of our conceptual systems of places. A simple example of the power of the nature of our interactions with the environment to influence our consequent ability to remember locations is demonstrated by another study carried out by one of our MSc students (Rawlinson, 1976). She carried out a study of children finding their way about London Zoo. She found that the only place that they could all remember, without exception, and which most of them were able to locate on a map was the Zoo shop. This was the only place where they themselves had some active interaction with their surroundings and in which they were not under the direct perceptual control of their teacher. Many other aspects of the Zoo which, from a Lynchian perspective, may have been thought of as dominant features were insignificant when compared with that location where it was possible to buy something to take home.

Part of the conceptual system we build up for dealing with our surroundings does contain physical or geographical information about the location of places and their relationships to each other. However, this is only part of the information we need to store. There is for example, a research literature to suggest that, in some cases at least, estimates of distance are distorted by whether the distance is to some location which is preferred or a location which is disliked. (See Canter, 1977 for a review of this material.) There are also studies to demonstrate that certain properties of buildings make them more memorable (Appleyard, 1969). However, it is important to recognise that we are dealing with processes which relate to people's interaction with their surroundings, not folded Ordnance Survey maps which happen to be stored in memory.

A number of the recurring findings from studies of how we store physical information are of value to the designer. There is evidence that we store our knowledge of the physical surroundings by converting our experience into relatively simple geometric forms. An elliptical railway system may well be thought of as a circular one (Canter and Tagg, 1975). Although two crossroads may meet each other at oblique angles, they may well be thought of as having the neater, right-angle cruciform arrangement (Pocock, 1973). Rivers such as the Thames and the Seine which wind their way through the centre of large cities are likely to be thought of as simple curves, rather than the convoluted configurations which they have in actuality (Milgram, 1976; Canter, 1977). It therefore seems likely that any design which makes this type of simple storage more difficult will be more likely to lead to user confusion. Given the knowledge we now have about these relatively consistent processes, it is surprising to find recently completed buildings which still manage to break many of the rules of practice which may be derived from these principles, in some cases with direct commercial loss as a consequence.

How places are organised

Besides developing an internal representation of the geography of any place, in order to make use of it we develop more complex *process* knowledge of the typical logical (or psychological) structure of places. A simple example can be given for entertainment buildings which require a ticket from members of the audience. It is usually accepted that people buy or present a ticket before entering a building, rather than in the middle of it.

Indeed, research by Peled (1975) has demonstrated that people may well think of building complexes either as those that house a sequential process through which they proceed more or less as linear in structure leading to a variety of routes and peripheral pockets of activity. It is quite likely that these different types of process have associated with them different strategies for making use of them. Thus, if an airport terminal is thought of as essentially linear, processing people through it, any attempt to provide welcoming corners scattered around the periphery may be very confusing. On the other hand, if a students' union is conceived of as essentially centrifugal in organisation, enabling students to find semi-private nooks and crannies for a variety of activities, then it will be found uncomfortable, and possibly difficult to orient within, if it is laid out in a form that implies a linear processing through it. This is one area of research in which designers and academics could fruitfully collaborate. The tools for the research have been developed so that it no longer needs to be a massive pilot exercise before we get any usable results. The likely pay-off in terms of more manageable and comprehensible environments give indications of being very great indeed. Furthermore, it is precisely when a design is contrary to popular expectations, or when it is difficult for users to comprehend its organisation, that sign systems are both so important and difficult to provide.

One more aspect of our knowledge of the way in which places are organised bears comment. This is the fact than an important aspect of this knowledge is an understanding of where *further* information about the organisation of the place can be found. For example, one of our students (Nash, 1977) carrying out a study in Euston Station found that railway officials in uniform who happened to be near the notice board, or signpost, were very likely to be asked for details of trains or location of facilities which were written up, supposedly for all to see. No-one has really explored the difference between obtaining information from a person and obtaining information from a notice board or signpost. However, it may be suggested that there are some differences between these two sources of information which are not normally considered.

(1)   A person can give you some indication as to how confident he is of the information he is presenting, whereas a noticeboard always seems to imply that it is 100% correct.

(2)   A person can indicate how up to date his information is, whereas a notice board seems to have been there for all time, and does not normally give any indication as to when it was last brought up-to-date.

(3)   A person can interact with queries and so restructure his information in response to the particular requirements of the questioner.

(4)   Typically, one notice board cannot be checked against another. They are usually monolithic in the information they carry. Two or three different people in uniform can be asked separately. (In some countries this pooling of information from different human sources is often essential if a reasonable accurate picture is to be obtained!)

These are all reasons why in some countries, no matter how clearly a notice is displayed, an official in uniform, or a seemingly knowledgeable member of the public, will be utilised in preference. It is likely that the countries in which this pattern occurs are ones in which mechanical sign systems of other forms of centralised public display have been found to be unreliable in the past. If the system is known to be reliable, then individuals are less likely to be drawn upon for information. However, given the fact that the signposting system does not indicate its reliability very clearly, it will only take some confusion or hesitation in that system for a reversion to the use of people as information sources.

It can be appreciated, as a consequence, that the use of information systems is part of our utilisation of the knowledge we have of the way in which the environment operates. This in turn is an aspect of the conceptual system we employ to enable us to navigate and orient ourselves. The structural information we have about how the physical world is organised and the process information we have about how any particular facility is used, or how knowledge of that facility is to be gained, are both built upon and provide us with an understanding of where we are at the present time. All this information, therefore, needs to be understood and made use of by the designer, both in creating a particular design, and then in trying to remove the weaknesses in that design by the provision of information and direction-finding systems. Let us now turn to a consideration of the properties of these systems which are necessary to enable people to make effective use of them.

Representing the world through signs and simulations

Once it is accepted that there are weaknesses in the design itself which do not enable individuals to find their way simply by their knowledge of the actual building, then it is necessary to, in effect, provide a comment upon the environment which will enable people to use it. It is fruitful to think of this process as one of simulation. In other words, what is necessary is to represent the environment in such a way that people can relate that representation to their own objectives and draw from it the information they require. There have been a number of studies of environmental simulation which are possibly of much more direct relevance to these issues than has been appreciated in the past. Canter et al (1975) provide a brief review of these studies.

One consistent finding of the studies, which is encouraging, is that it is possible to provide simulations of environments which generate the same responses as do the environments themselves. Typically, the researchers carrying out these simulation studies are more directly concerned with the evaluative or emotive aspects of the environment than with their use. There is therefore considerable work to be done to establish links between making decisions based upon some representation of an environment and making decisions based upon detailed and familiar knowledge of that environment. However, these studies do demonstrate that there are distinct advantages and disadvantages associated with the major forms of simulation which are available; whether they be photographs, line drawings, plans or even verbal description. There is thus a wealth of material available to indicate the types of representation which may be fruitful for particular situations. Indeed, it has been found (BPRU, 1972) that verbal representation of environments can be just as effective as drawings.

Against this background of the optimistic results of this research it is possible to identify two aspects of the environment which need to be simulated in most sign systems. One is the identification of particular locations. The other is an indication of the relationships which locations have to each other and, associated with that, the distances between them.

Locations

In identifying a location the task is to represent what the location is by reference to some knowledge which the individual can already be assumed to have. The notion frequently used here is that of 'labeling'. However, it must be appreciated that the label is only another form of simulation with all the associated problems of' 'validating' that simulation. Some forms of representation may be less effective than others because they fit less readily into people's understanding of the place in question. Simple, relatively ambiguous labels for male and female toilet facilities, for example, may work very well because most people expect such facilities will be provided. If, for example, a decision were to be made to provide toilet facilities common to both men and women, then much less ambiguous signposting would be necessary.

Agabani (1975), for example, developing the study of 'lostness' to compare four university campuses found that the one which was most disorienting (our own at Surrey) was the one for which there were most complaints about the 'confusing changes in level'.

The simulation strategy which would find psychological support would therefore deal with only two dimensions at a time. In other words, items would be designated by floor, but no indication would be given as to their location on a floor until the individual concerned is on that particular floor. Then a further two-dimensional plan or other form of signposting system can be made available.

This proposed strategy is derived in part from a study published in 1970 by Best. He studied people getting lost in one of Britain's larger town halls. He related the degree to which they got lost to the number of choice points in their journey. Best argued that if people could be given some indication as to what choices were coming up, and each choice could be made as simple as possible, the amount of 'lostness' would be reduced. He therefore developed a signposting system which presented people with information from which to make a journey choice, together with advance warning as to when the next choice was coming. Best was able to demonstrate quite clearly that his new system reduced the number of people getting lost. The fluency with which a person would find a route could be reduced if all the minor choices were laid before him. However, it seems quite feasible to identify a hierarchical series of choices whereby people only need to be concerned with major choices of direction until they get quite close to their target, in which case they would draw upon more detailed information available. This may seem a ponderous procedure to go through, and certainly would put great demands upon the graphic ability of those creating it. However, there may well be cases in which such labour is justified. It is also worth noting in passing that the utilisation of 'supergraphics', whereby the graphic symbols become a decoration in their own right, is a solution to the aesthetic problems posed by these ideas which has not been utilised as widely as would seem justified.

Simulating distances

We rely upon a great variety of distance information in our day to-day movement around the environment. We frequently know how long, how far and how much effort is involved in moving between two points. Furthermore, it has been found in a detailed study on London (Canter, 1975) that people are, on average, surprisingly accurate in the estimates they make of distances between places. There are consistent errors built in to this overall response which have not yet been explored in relation to their implications for signposting. But, to give one example from the study of distance estimation in London, it was found that distances were underestimated below six miles whereas they were overestimated above this point. For some reason, in London at least, people are reasonably accurate when they estimate a distance to be about six miles. This raises the question as to whether there are units of distance with which people can operate and be very accurate, and therefore distances should be provided between points which have this relationship to each other. Certainly it is clear from the research that distance figures could be more fruitfully used to help people navigate. It may well be that for particular situations certain types of distance information are useful. For example, if people are queuing it may be more important for them to know the length of time they will be kept waiting than any absolute value of the length of the queue. If they are walking, it might be of more significance for them to know what proportion of the distance is downhill, and if they are carrying parcels, they may like to find out something of the obstacles to be negotiated along the way. Thus, identifying the appropriate type of distance metric to be provided in any situation as an aid for people in their use of the facilities is an important goal for future studies.

All in all, then, it would appear that if it is necessary to provide the prosthetic devices to enable people to find their way in our modern environment that there are available a great variety of forms of simulation upon which to draw. Furthermore, it would appear to be possible to identify which simulation is most appropriate for which particular setting. In doing this, it is necessary to draw upon the conceptual systems which people employ for making sense of the particular environment in question.

Indeed the converse of this issue, the *power* of the label, also needs to be considered. A number of researchers studying the use of space in buildings (e.g., BPRU, 1972) have reported that the labels assigned to rooms can have a big impact on how readily those rooms are used. People will refuse to give a lecture in a room labelled 'laboratory' even though it might serve the purpose quite well. Indeed, a television crew who put labels on telephone kiosks, indicating that some of the telephones were for men and others for women, was able to produce some very amusing film of' women queuing up outside a telephone kiosk labelled 'women' even though those telephone kiosks labelled 'men' were empty.

The theoretical point here is that a label is the representation of a location. It may be simply a map reference with which no association on the part of the user is expected. Such labels seem to be only of value to the expert who can relate them to a complex system of conceptualisations. For most other individuals, it is not necessary to know only where the location is, but *what* the location is. The particular local label assigned to that location may be of little value if the person has to come in search of a *particular* use. Terms like 'services', designations of 'levels' in a building, drawings of standing men and a whole host of other symbols which may be perfectly meaningful to one group, yet which do not necessarily carry any implications for people who have another cognitive system to draw upon, frequently only serve to cause confusion.

Descriptive information can be given about locations in order to facilitate understanding of their use. In a conference complex, for example, the sizes of lecture theatres may well help people to gauge their relevance. In other cases, knowing the age of the participants may be of value. Unfortunately the demands of typographical elegance may often reduce the information which people may call upon. Certainly the power of visual representations seems often to be neglected because of the graphic problems of incorporating them. Our visual powers of recognition are very considerable indeed, and visual information provides an important component of our conceptual systems of places. Work on maps for the blind (Armstrong, undated) has demonstrated that, even for those groups, the spatial arrangement of material and the use of textures can greatly aid identification and navigation.

By thinking of the identification of locations as a problem in simulation that is, a problem of representing the physical environment in a way which bears a direct and popularly accepted relation to the actual environment - we may be able to move towards a more systematic set of ways of representing locations.

Relationships between locations

There are two aspects of representing the relationship which locations have between each other in space. One is an indication of direction and the other is an indication of distance.

With regard to both of these aspects of relationships we have similar problems of simulation. Simulating direction seems to be particularly difficult because it inevitably involves some form of geographic *projection* whereby the individual 'reading' the simulation is required to convert the actual geographic direction into some other represented direction. This is a manipulation which requires some sophistication; whether it be through the use of plans, involving the conversion of what is essentially a vertical experience into a horizontal viewpoint (in other words, from the experience of moving through a space to the experience of looking down on it), or more simply the use of arrows or other pointing devices which will invariably be at right-angles to some of the relevant lines of movement.

The difficulty in signposting through both arrows and maps relates to the problem of unravelling three-dimensional instructions. There is some research evidence to suggest that performing manipulations upon our internal representational processes is one of the more difficult actions for us to carry out (cf. Canter, 1977, Ch. 4). A simulation, therefore, which not only implies the conversion of symbols into actual places but also involves a change in the geometric projection employed would thus appear to have within it great potential for confusion. This confusion is magnified when the representations have to cope in a two-dimensional mode with what is essentially a three-dimensional environment. Thus the shopping precinct or a central city development which contains pedestrian pathways crossing over vehicular roads, in which both transport routes change levels, presents particular difficulties, either in forming a representation or for an individual to formulate an effective conceptual system.

Environmental roles and conceptual systems

Before turning finally to the various uses which can be made of public information systems it is necessary to pause to consider in a little more detail the theoretical model from which much of the ideas presented above have been drawn. This theory is derived from *The Psychology of Place* (Canter, 1977). In this book the theory is propounded that people build up complex, robust conceptual systems of those places with which they interact. As has been illustrated above, it is argued that these conceptual systems include information about physical locations and likely activities, as well as evaluations of those places which compose a conceptual system.

The conceptual system will be built upon whatever information is available, so that even a new, unfamiliar place will give rise to some attempt at conceptualising it, even if it is only based on the building facade, or the first view on entering it. There is a great deal of research to support the argument that people can build up rich and complex conceptual systems of environments for which they have relatively little information. What information is missing will be supplied by expectations drawn up from previous experience. Any information system which ignores the well-developed skills which people need to have will operate more like a badly fitted artificial leg, always acting as a handicap, rather than as a crutch that can be thrown away once the individual has recovered.

There is a further important point about the theory of place which is being presented here. It is argued that the conceptual systems which people have are derived from their interactions with their environments. As a consequence, people who have different roles within an environment, leading to them interacting with it in different ways, will form different conceptual systems of those environments. One very important implication of this is that those people whose essential interaction with an environment is to create it will almost inevitably have an understanding and conceptualisation of it which is different from those whose major interaction with it is to use it. This distinction between user and provider of an ·

environment, and the consequent differences in ways of understanding that environment, have implications in a wide range of environmental considerations. We have talked about these information systems as consisting of simulations of environments. Indeed the whole notion of information implies that there will be some individuals performing interpretations of stimuli provided by others. If we accept that the users and the providers will very likely need to draw upon different processes for interpreting this information then it is clear how necessary it is for the providers to explore with the potential users the interpretations that they are likely to make.

This exploration with potential *future* users of environments which do not exist at the present time has frequently been heralded as the stumbling-block for systematic scientific research in relation to people's reactions to settings being designed. However, here the possibility of simulating an environment is very positive indeed, for it enables the design team to provide representations and explore the reactions and uses which are made in relation to those representations. By careful sampling procedures and the appropriate use of scientific processes it is now clear that such research activity can take place in parallel to other design processes so that it does not add any considerable time element, or indeed any considerable cost elements, to the creation of the new setting.

It is said that the Japanese built their cities in a complex and maze-like fashion so that any marauding armies or foreign enemies would get lost on their way to attacking the palace. It is now feasible for any group to create an environment which is comprehensible to them but which is an incomprehensible maze to some other group. As our technological systems become more sophisticated and the scale of development of our environments become more complex, so does the possibility increase of our producing environments which are only comprehensible to those who have produced them. The way out of this impasse is through systematic pre-design research on the lines that have been indicated above.

Evaluation and use

No matter how it is generated, it is necessary to evaluate any information/sign system in order to learn from its strengths and weaknesses. Indeed, if this evaluation can be carried out prior to the completion of the design, then such evaluation can have a substantial effect on the development and modification of that design. There is in fact now a substantial literature on environmental evaluation (cf. Canter et al, 1975) but little of it seems to have been directed to the evaluation of public information systems. One reason for this may well be that no detailed attention has been paid to the criteria against which it is necessary to evaluate such systems. I would like to suggest that the evaluation of these systems depends very much upon the uses to which the system is to be put. There are at least three different classes of use which impose different degrees of intensity upon the system and which therefore may well lead to different types of evaluation. These are:

uses in emergency,
uses in order to obtain specific goals and
uses to facilitate the formation of general plans.

Emergency use

Recent research which we have carried out (Canter, 1980) has looked at human behaviour in fires in buildings. This is only one type of emergency situation which is found in present-day buildings. It does serve, nonetheless, to illustrate the general issues involved in the use of information systems for emergencies. Many of the information systems available, whether they be fire alarms, emergency signs or indications of the equipment available, seem to ignore many of the issues identified above. They are typically superimposed upon the environment by a cautious fire officer, with little attempt to understand the details of the context into which they are placed, or the conceptualisations of those who will be using them. As a consequence, it is not uncommon to find alarm bells which are ignored, egress routes which are not effectively utilised or fire fighting equipment which is either not used or is found inoperable when attempts are made to use it.

Considerable costs are involved in the provision of these fire and emergency facilities. Yet it has been found, in a number of fires, that people frequently expose themselves to danger rather than respond to the information presented to them through the alarm signals or in other ways.

In an emergency an individual has to act upon limited information as quickly as possible. In a fire, and probably many other emergencies, the early stages are very ambiguous. Furthermore, the threatening situation is liable to be changing very rapidly, so that up-dating of the state of the emergency may be necessary for effective action. An existing organisational structure is also present which will be utilised in dealing with the emergency. Information systems which ignore the current organisation are liable to add further confusion.

In order to evaluate the provision of public information systems for emergency, then, it is necessary to demonstrate their relationship to existing organisational structures and to the expectations and comprehension of those who will need to make use of the system. Such explorations may well be of more value than the 'dry run drill'. Such a fire 'practice' may serve solely to emphasise the fact that this is a separate system which has nothing to do with the day-to-day activities, with its consequent failure in emergencies.

Goal-directed use

In order to evaluate systems for people who have particular goals to achieve it is necessary to identify what those characteristics are which lead to people needing to rely upon the system provided. It is then necessary to identify what are the family of goals and sub-goals which these users are likely to have. Many assumptions are frequently made in shopping centres, for example, that major goals will be to locate departmental stores, sometimes referred to as 'magnets', whereas smaller shops will be 'taken in' on the journey. Watts (1978) explored people's shopping behaviour to see how much evidence there was for this belief, and found very little indeed. This serves to demonstrate further that the popular concepts of management, or marketing directors, may well be at variance with what is actually the case.

One significant point to note is that if people are relying directly upon signposting systems in order to achieve specific goals then any direct breakdown in the signposting system can lead to great confusion. For example, a series of direction signs that are relied upon quite heavily, but which then cease, are likely to cause more confusion than some general indication of direction which right from the start is general and intermittent. Another important point is that the pattern of behaviour observed in many situations may well be a function of the information system available. Thus it is necessary for the designers to consider the information system in relation to the pattern of activities which it is wished to generate, or which it is wished to avoid. Placing detailed signposting in a location where it is not wished to encourage people to stop for any length of time can be counter-productive, for instance. However, it might not be apparent that there are many situations in which the source of information and its organisation can have far reaching effects on the pattern of behaviour of people in that place. One example of this is the use of centrally located notice boards in railway and airport terminals. If there is widespread anxiety about missing an important piece of information, then such a location may well generate uneven dispersal of people around the facility.

One further, more surprising, example of this influence of the information system was found by one of our students who carried out a study of dentists' waiting rooms (Ottar, 1974). Another found a similar pattern when looking at doctors' waiting rooms (Reid, 1977). In both cases it was clear that the seats selected by patients were a function of both the location of the receptionist's desk and the nature of the patient call system. It was further possible to demonstrate that the anxiety level of the patients influenced their selection of seats. More anxious patients take seats nearer to the receptionist than the less anxious patients. As a consequence, in these waiting rooms an ecology of seating behaviour was generated by the location and type of information source. Using different types of information systems, whether they be public address systems, notice boards, flashing lights or the assignment of numbers to customers, are all likely to generate different patterns of space usage.

Finally, in considering the use of signposting systems for specific goals it is worth briefly mentioning their use in libraries and museums. A full review of the current theory and practice in this area is provided by Spencer and Reynolds (1977). From that review it is clear that this is a particular case in which directional signing and labelling is of paramount importance for use of the building. These systems may be thought of more as tools for the appropriate use of the facility rather than crutches to help the disabled. Nonetheless, the development and design of these tools would still seem to require acknowledgement of the principles we have discussed above. It will still be necessary to evaluate these systems in terms of the goals which people have and the abilities they have available for the use of the displays provided.

Plan formulation

One final way in which information systems may be used is as an aid to the development of a plan of action, or to enrich conceptualisations and thus the development of future plans. In this case the signs and information provided can be drawn upon to help the individual elaborate any existing conceptual system. One recent experiment we carried out serves to illustrate the potential implications here. Students (Young et al, 1978) showed slides of buildings whose functions were ambiguous to groups of subjects and asked them to evaluate these buildings. In some cases 'plausible' labels were assigned to the buildings as determined by previous research. In other cases, 'implausible' labels were assigned to the buildings. It was found that the plausibility of the labels had a direct impact upon the evaluation of the buildings. The study served to demonstrate that inappropriate or ambiguous use of signs or symbols, whether they be labels or physical forms, can have far-reaching effects on users' conceptualisations.

In order to evaluate signs and direction systems for the purpose of plan formulation it is necessary to consider their organisational structure. This structure helps or hinders people in building up an accurate conceptual system of the places involved and the relationship those places have to each other. Facilitating this overall conceptualisation may be more important in the case of plan formulation, than in remembering specific details. Hence, clear locations which can easily be remembered and associated with broad patterns of activity may be more fruitful than providing precise and detailed symbols.

An example of this process which comes to mind is the possibility of using, say, large brightly coloured plastic animals instead of the more mundane and clinical building code numbers. The use of sculpture as landmarks is not unknown, but it is rare to use this procedure in a consciously organised way to enable people to build up an accurate conceptual system of any particular facility. A careful arrangement of brightly coloured plastic animals could, for example, enable people to plan in the knowledge that, once they have found the green giraffe, then it is very easy to get to the pink elephant. (The use of English pub signs as landmarks has some relevance here!) In effect, it is being suggested that if the design itself fails to provide an articulated conceptual system then it must be accepted that any sign or symbol system is an attempt to impose upon the building complex an articulated and comprehensible conceptual structure. It is my belief that if we can be successful at this level, and thus enable people to plan effectively their use of a facility, then all the other uses we have indicated will be accomplished.

References

Agabani, F. (1975), Way-Finding Behaviour, Unpublished MSc thesis, University of Surrey.

Agabani, F. & Weaver, M. (1974), *Lostness in Buildings*, Mimeo, University of Surrey.

Appleyard, D. (1969), 'Why Buildings are Known', *Environment and Behaviour*, Vol. 1, pp. 131-136.

Armstrong, J.D. (undated), *The Design and Production of Maps for the Visually Handicapped*, Blind Mobility Research Unit, Mimeo.

Best, G. (1970), 'Direction Finding in Large Buildings', D. Canter (ed.), (1972), *Architectural Psychology*, RIBA Publications, London Building Performance Research Unit.

Canter, D. (1975), *Fires and Human Behaviour*, Wiley, Chichester.

Canter, D. et al (1975), *Environmental Interaction*, Surrey University Press, London.

Canter, D. & Tagg, S.K. (1975), 'Distance estimation in cities', *Environment and Behaviour*, Vol. 7(1), pp. 59-80.

Lynch, K. (1960), *The Image of the City*, Mass MIT Press, Cambridge.

Lynch, K. (1976), *Manating the Sense of Region*, Mass MIT Press, Cambridge.

Milgram, S. (1976), 'Psychological Maps of Paris', Proshanky et al (eds), *Environmental Psychology*, Illolt, New York.

Rinehart, A. & Winston Nash, J. (1977), *Observations in Euston Station*, unpublished report, University of Surrey.

Ottar, T. (1974), *Seat Selection in Dental Waiting Rooms*, unpublished MSc thesis, University of Surrey.

Peled, A. (1975), *The Spatiality of Situations*, unpublished PhD thesis, University of Strathclyde.

Pocock, D. (1973), *Urban Environmental Perception and Behaviour*, Social Geography, Vol. 62.

Rawlinson, A. (1976), *Children's Cognitive Maps of London Zoo*, unpublished MSc thesis, University of Surrey.

Reid, P. (1977), *A Study of Health Centre Environment and Patient State Anxiety*, unpublished MSc thesis, University of Surrey.

Spencer, H. & Reynolds, L. (1977), *Directional Signing and Labelling in Libraries and Museums: A Review of Current Theories and Practice*, Readability of Print Research Unit, Royal College of Art, London.

Trowbridge, C.C. (1913), 'On Fundamental Methods of Orientations and Imagining Maps', *Science*, Vol. 38, pp. 888-897.

Watts, S. (1978), *Shopping Behaviour*, unpublished MSc thesis, University of Surrey.

Wright, K. (1947), 'Unrecognised Territory: The Place of Imagination in Geography', *Analysis of the Association of American Geographers*, Vol. 37(1), pp. 1-15.

Young, D., McIntosh, S. & Boylan, B. (1978), *The Effects of Labels on Building Evaluation*, University of Surrey, Mimeo.

FIRES AND HUMAN BEHAVIOUR

7 An Overview of Behaviour in Fires

The major differences between fires in the patterns of behaviour that are associated with them are not due to variations between the personalities of the people present or to particular physical details of the design of the buildings involved. Rather they relate to the type of 'place' in which the fires occur. The term 'place' here is used in the sense discussed by Canter (1977), implying a combination of social and physical processes that give any setting its particular qualities. In the parlance of the fire brigades a place is very similar in meaning to a 'building occupancy', because each occupancy has its own characteristic physical structure as well as its own type of organisation and associated fire risk. The following summaries will therefore consider fires in relation to the type of setting in which they occur.

In order to clarify and elaborate these aspects, details of behaviour in various types of buildings are worthy of closer consideration.

Fires in the home

In domestic fires people frequently rely on others for information and check the information they are given. It is also apparent that people frequently have to cope with smoke and other environmental difficulties in fire events. Furthermore, even though they often come into contact with smoke and other fire cues there is a tendency to ignore or misinterpret this as being an indicator of a serious event.

Sequence of events

Detailed analyses of the sequence of events in domestic fires can be summarised as follows.

1. In the very early stages people report noticing cues but finding them ambiguous, often hearing noises, misinterpreting or ignoring these, or discussing them with anyone present. If the cues persist, investigation will take place to find the source of the noise or smell. The only variation from this initial group of actions is if smoke or the fire is encountered directly.
2. If investigation follows the early ambiguous cues, then it inevitably leads to encountering smoke, either within the room of fire origin or outside

---

This is a version of the chapter edited to make sense independently of the rest of the book.

this room if the smoke is spreading. If the latter people are still likely to enter the room where the fire is.

3.   A direct encounter with the smoke or fire generates variability in the likely response sequence. This variability is a function of the stage of fire growth and location of the fire at the time when it is encountered. Much of the variability present can be accounted for by differences between men and women, occupants and neighbours. In other words, it is the difference in the roles which people have in the setting which underlies their different behaviour.

4.   The main differences exist at the initial interpretation stage and the behaviour following investigation and encountering the smoke. While both males and females tend to misinterpret ambiguous cues, males are more likely to do so and delay investigation. The response of a female may be delayed by interaction with a male if present. Eventually one of them initiates investigative activity. Both males and females are likely to investigate.

5.   If informed by someone who has returned to say there is a fire, the tendency is to check this information for oneself. The indications are that this may be more likely if males initially receive a warning from females than vice versa. This tendency to continue investigation after being informed, is particularly characteristic of domestic as opposed to other building/occupancy types. It is apparently related to the role of the individual in his or her own home as well as the proximity of a fire. More responsibility may be felt for the safety of others who are likely to be present and for the prevention of damage.

6.   The variability of the actions which follow the encounter with the smoke and fire itself is explained by male/female differences. Females are more likely to warn others and wait for further instruction (for example, if husband and wife are both present). Alternatively they will close the door to the room of fire origin and leave the house.

7.   In both cases females are more likely to seek assistance from neighbours. Male occupants are most likely to attempt to fight the fire. Male neighbours are more likely to search for people in smoke and attempt a rescue.

Fires in hospitals

Act frequencies

In domestic fires the very high frequency of acts involving the search for information and of ambiguous behaviour seems to be characteristic of an essentially informal, unstructured situation. In hospital fires however there is an organised disciplined staff present throughout the 24 hours of the day. Therefore the role of the nurse in helping others to safety is to be expected and is reflected in the high frequency of acts of assistance. The more responsive role of nurses in receiving instructions can also be seen.

A number of patterns of action sequences are revealed by the examination of the order of behaviours of those involved. These sequences are more complex than in most domestic fires, in part because of the larger number of people involved. However, some general event sequences can be summarised.

Sequences of actions

Detection and investigation of the fire takes place relatively early in fire development as compared with other occupancies. This is likely to be due to the more general spread of people throughout the building and the fact that there is always somebody awake, on duty. Once detected, the transfer of information concerning the fire is highly specified, with senior nursing officers tending to be initial recipients. Thus investigation is typically first carried out by these people. Shortly thereafter they relay information to their junior colleagues, although junior staff are likely to receive early warning that there is a fire. There is a great demand on their part for information concerning location and intensity which they will subsequently need to know in planning patient evacuation. Interviews suggest that from their point of view this information is often late in arriving.

Ultimately destinations and routes are usually specified by senior staff. Action by junior staff (except for preparing patients) is guided by prior instructions, both through previous training and orders received during the incident. The act of evacuating patients is often related to several other actions and processes which when viewed in toto reflect great behavioural complexity. However, due to greater organisational sophistication this higher action complexity does not appear to be strongly related to increased threat.

Evacuation and movement through smoke does occur. It would seem to be due to inadequacies in the building structure (exits not wide enough to accept beds leading to slower or delayed movement; ventilation systems contributing to smoke spread) or delays in information reaching junior staff.

Multiple occupancies

High rise apartment blocks and hotels known as 'multiple occupancies' provide a particularly interesting combination of the domestic setting in which some overall, large scale organisation exists, although it is very informal. In a fire the effectiveness of the communications within this organisation becomes critical. Seeking information is therefore, not surprisingly, the most frequent act in multiple occupancy fires. However, the more passive position people can find themselves in is reflected in the high frequency of noting the fire cues. Nonetheless there are still a large number of instances of the passive reception of ambiguous information. It should also be noted that behaviour in multiple occupancy fires does involve quite a lot of contact with other people, giving and receiving assistance. Acts are thus not the isolated events which might be anticipated in single occupancy dwellings.

Act sequences

As with domestic fires, the awareness that something unusual is happening commences with the hearing of strange noises which are usually misinterpreted or ignored. However, in this case, if the cues persist investigation normally follows. Typically this gives rise to direct contact with fire or smoke and consequent return of the person to where he/she was.

The characteristic sequence which follows from this then relates to the individual going to the window, shouting for help and being rescued. Clearly the multiple occupancy case, especially that occurring in hotels, produces a pattern much more complex than that for domestic fires. This complexity is most apparent in the number of possible outcomes of any given act and the number of sequences of act which are found to occur. The increased complexity appears to be a function of the range of potential sources of information about the fire and about appropriate actions.

Where actions in the domestic situation could be related to the roles of husband, wife or neighbour, in the multiple occupancy setting a person can be at a loss as to whether he is the prime discoverer of the fire or one of many individuals with similar experience. This added complexity can be highlighted by the emergence of the action cycle associated with receiving a warning, receiving instructions, seeking assistance and making attempts to cope with the increasingly dangerous situation before again interacting with others who can possibly help.

The fact that people are aware of the likelihood of meeting others is demonstrated most directly by the way in which their assessment of the fire is typically followed by their dressing and gathering valuables. Surely these acts, which waste time, would feature less if the individual did not anticipate that there were others in the immediate vicinity? There is no clear indication of any parallel acts in the domestic situation.

Returning to the opening acts, these are associated with the reception of ambiguous cues, usually odd noises, followed by a process of misinterpretations. The misinterpretation seems to be of more danger in the multiple occupancy fires studied than in the domestic fires. In the multiple occupancy situation the options for leaving the building appear to reduce more rapidly because the initial time loss militates against later unassisted escape.

It is also of interest that the early cues to the fire in domestic settings may more often be olfactory and/or auditory as opposed to just the auditory cues of the multiple occupancy fires. A further distinction from the domestic settings is the absence of any attempt to fight the fire in multiple occupancies. Indeed, people rarely get to know where the room of origin of the fire is as they do in a domestic setting. People become vaguely aware of something happening at some distance from where they are, realise there is danger, then draw upon whatever information they can obtain from others in order to get away from the danger. It is worth noting that many individuals return to their rooms in multiple occupancies, particularly hotels during a fire.

Public buildings

Another occupancy for which there is concern regarding the potential fire hazard to occupants is that of buildings open to the public, such as department stores and recreation complexes. The scale and complexity of the few fires which do occur in this building type are such that a detailed consideration of them has not been possible in earlier chapters. Furthermore, because of the resources required to collect and analyse information on human behaviour in such fires there is very little information available on the major incidents which have happened.

There are, nonetheless, four fires for which interviews have been collected either by social scientists or by the police in the form of witness statements. Here, these are used as the basis for considering human behaviour in these events. Information on a further eight fires, on which less detail was available, was also examined to establish whether there were any indications that the conclusions from the detailed studies were atypical. Indeed, the general patterns found appear to be similar to those found in other types of fires, with some notable differences.

Because of the complexity of fire incidents in public buildings it is appropriate to focus on limited aspects of human behaviour, the early stages of fire recognition and the decision to leave the building being of special interest, dealing, in particular, with the effectiveness of the behaviour which the public display. This can done by considering all the actions which occurred prior to a given individual deciding to leave the building. A simple classification of these actions is given in *Table 1* and their frequency is summarised in *Table 2*. This shows that although the majority of people perform effectively, early on in the fire growth, there are still a large minority carrying out ineffective acts, most notably delay in responding to the early warnings.

Table 1 Examples of actions in fires in public buildings

Examples taken from transcripts, of the main classes of action identified in the fire. (Table 2 gives the frequencies of each class of action occurring in each fire.)

Effective actions

Getting a fire extinguisher (or hose reel):
General Manager of Henderson's '... and saw flames of a minor nature coming through the ceiling tiles ... I ran to the Church Street end of the floor for a fire extinguisher ...'

Activating the fire alarm:
Security Guard 'Up to this point when I turned off the escalator there was no alarm bell ringing in the store. I activated it on the first floor ...'

Evacuating the area:
Security Guard '... I also checked the first floor to see that it was evacuated'.

Telephoning for the fire brigade:
Telephone operator at Henderson's 'The first time I knew that there was a fire in the Store was when I received a call from Mr Cannon (the General Manager). He said to me: Fire Brigade, second and third floor. I immediately dialled 999 and told the Fire Brigade ...'

Raising alarm/warning others:
Shopper in Woolworth's, having lunch with her brother '... we were having a laugh,... all of a sudden I looked up and saw all this smoke coming ... I just shouted 'FIRE' because I saw a lot of people'.

Ineffective actions

Repetitive/pointless. Bartender in the Empire Room at Beverly Hills: '... my first instinct was to go back to the Empire Room. So, that's where I went'.
Buyer at Hendersons's: (having lunch in restaurant, 4th floor): As soon as he saw the smoke he got up and went to speak to Mrs Summer and asked her if she had phoned for Mr Terry. Then 'I went to the escalator ... and I turned back, (to see if all the customers and staff were out)'.

Ignoring or delaying actions. Holidaymaker at Summerland, in Terrace Bar: '... I heard some commotion and on looking towards the Amusement Arcade I saw a small amount of black smoke ... I then left the Terrace Bar and went into the restaurant'.
Waitress at Beverly Hills:
'I saw some smoke in the front bar and thought it was peculiar, but I went on to the Zebra room anyway ...'
Shopper in snack bar at Henderson's:
'... as soon as I entered the restaurant I noticed smoke hanging about but nothing very much and it didn't appear to be causing any concern; I had started to eat a sandwich ...'

Misinterpreting situations. Casual relief telephone operator at Woolworth's: 'He came in and the door didn't shut behind him and he shouted something and then went back out again. I thought he said "There's a fight on the 2nd floor" ... I just continued working on the phone. I wasn't aware of anything untoward'.
Shopper having lunch with mother in Woolworth's restaurant: 'Then I saw some smoke. It seemed to be coming from the kitchen. There was a small flame. I thought it was the chip pan. I just continued chatting to my mother'.
Model at Beverly Hills: Asked if she noticed any change in the temperature of the room: 'I didn't because well because they turned up the air conditioning because they said it was hot in there ...'
Incautious actions. Waitress in restaurant at Henderson's: 'I waited to see what their reactions was when I told them there was a fire and we had better get out. One went back to get her handbag. I waited for her to come back'.

Waitress in restaurant at Henderson's: On telling a customer in the restaurant that the place was on fire and would she please leave quickly: '… she started banging the floor with her stick. She said "I want to see the Manager". I said "You can't see him. He's rather occupied at the moment". She said "This is disgusting!" The customer still wouldn't leave. She went over to the cash desk and more thick smoke entered the restaurant'.

Cashier in restaurant at Henderson's: 'Miss F … the supervisor of the Jiffy Bar, told me to collect the money out of my cash desk and get out of the building. … Just before Miss F told me to get the money from the till all the lights went out. At the time there was a queue of people at my cash desk waiting to pay their bills'.

The four fires listed in Table 2 are:

(a)   Andersons department store in Liverpool, 22nd June, 1960.
(b)   Beverly Hills Supper Club, Kentucky, 28th May, 1977.
(c)   Woolworths department store in Manchester, 8th May, 1979.
(d)   Summerland recreation complex, Isle of Man, 2nd August, 1973.

The initial stages of the fire appear again, in these fires to be characterised by ambiguity and misinterpreted cues. But in public buildings the context is of great significance. For example, in a restaurant area smoke is frequently assumed to be from the kitchen and non-threatening. Other cues, such as smells are often also interpreted as non-serious. Once people have recognised that there is something untoward happening there is a tendency for investigation and thus a movement towards the fire area.

Delay in response to a fire in public buildings is likely to depend on the nature of the present activities in which the individual is engaged. For example a delay is probably more likely when the activities have a clear, expected sequence of events each of which lasts for a few minutes, such as having a meal. The sequence of ordering, eating, paying, for instance, is rarely broken in a conventional restaurant and so people anticipate completing this sequence before they move on to other activities.

Of the ineffective actions more are to do with a misinterpretation of what is going on, rather than directly incautious actions such as going into smoke. This misinterpretation, on occasions, is clearly supported by the social situation. People in a group look to each other to confirm or deny the presence of danger. Within this group context there is often a tendency to play down the risks involved, relating in part to the possible desire not to 'lose face' when there may be no danger. Importantly, families that have a clear 'head' such as the mother or father may not operate in this way, but take their lead directly from the person in their group who they all see as the most responsible figure.

Furthermore, there is a reliance by the public on people in authority (usually

Table 2 *Frequency of actions prior to deciding to leave in four fires in public buildings*

FIRE (Total No. Actions)	ACTIONS							
	Effective		Ineffective					
	Freq	%	Total Freq	%	Pointless	Delay	Misinterpret	Incautious
Andersons Liverpool (89)	43	(48)	46	(52)	2	14(30)	14(30)	16(35)
Beverly Hills (65)	33	(51)	32	(49)	2	17(53)	11(34)	2(6)
Woolworths Manchester (75)	51	(68)	24	(32)	1	11(46)	4(17)	8(33)
Summerland I.O.M. (404) (633)	217	(54)	187	(46)	1	62(34)	90(49)	29(16)
Total Frequency	344		289					
Average % :	55		45					
Average percentage of ineffective actions:					<1%	41%	33%	23%

staff) for information, also on senior staff by juniors. If the staff do not realise this and do not give the necessary leadership this can create a situation of great danger as in all four cases in Table 2. However, even when staff recognise their role in helping people to evacuate the building they sometimes feel the need to inspect the fire or try to do something about it even when evacuation would be the most effective action. The reliance on senior staff to define the situation as a 'fire emergency' can lead to serious delay. Yet, when appropriate information is given evacuation is frequently rapid.

Relationship to other studies

A few researchers in North America have also carried out detailed case studies of fire incidents (Lerup, 1980; Haber, 1980; Edelman et al, 1980; Bryan, 1983; 1983a). With the exception of Bryan's study (1983a), of the Westchase Hilton Hotel fire, these studies tend to be of domestic fires or fires in institutions such as prisons or nursing homes.

All of these studies support the trends described from the British cases cited above. For example Bryan 1983, reviewing behaviour of 580 people in fires which were mainly in dwellings, showed that the first action of 15% was to notify others, and for a further 10% it was to search for the fire. Nine percent called the fire department as their first action and 8% got dressed. In a second study also reported by Bryan (1983), which focused on nursing homes and other therapeutic institutions, of the 149 people questioned the first action of 45% of them was to investigate the initial cues.

The consistency found across case studies conducted independently by five different research teams in Britain and North America are remarkable, given the popular view of the unpredictable irrational behaviour which is supposed to characterise fires. A general agreement amongst researchers does provide the basis for proposing a general model of behaviour in fires. But before discussing this model further it is of value to consider the results of questionnaire studies which provide a further statistical basis, whilst not providing the detail of the case studies considered so far.

Corroboration for a questionnaire survey

Each approach to studying behaviour in fires has its biases and difficulties. Questionnaire surveys have the advantage of larger data sets, but they are especially difficult to carry out. The first major survey of fire victims was carried out by Wood (1972). Bryan (1983) developed this survey further with similar results. The Fire Research Unit at the University of Surrey completed a further survey, the results of which have not been widely disseminated. There, therefore, follows a summary of the conduct of this survey and its main results. Brief comparison is made with the results from the case studies.

The main purpose of the questionnaire survey was to extend the sample of fires and people covered beyond those of earlier studies. Furthermore, as the case studies had revealed some interesting details about certain events which were apparently common in fires it was decided to obtain more information on these events. In particular, the survey to be reported focused on:

(i)   early stages of behaviour in a fire
(ii)   actions during the fire in a building
(iii) escape from a building on fire

Questionnaire development

On the basis of material collected from the case studies and earlier published questionnaire surveys of behaviour in fires (Wood 1972, Bryan 1978), a questionnaire was developed and then posted to addresses of recent fires in London. On the basis of these responses and discussions with the fire brigades a revised questionnaire was developed. This was designed for distribution by the fire brigade to the victims of fires they attended. The following fire brigades were approached and agreed to cooperate: 1. London 2. West Midlands 3. West Yorkshire 4. Greater Manchester and 5. Merseyside. This range of brigades provided a suitable geographical spread and included areas which would be associated with a large, varied sample of building types.

Senior staff of the brigades were visited by members of the Fire Research Unit and briefed as to the nature of the study and the reasons for conducting it. A set of consultative notes concerning the method of distribution were also provided for the senior liaison officers.

Each brigade was to give out the questionnaires at fires they attended. Together with the questionnaire was a freepost envelope for returning the completed questionnaire to the Fire Research Unit at the University of Surrey, and a letter explaining the nature of the survey and instructions.

578 questionnaires were returned during the period of the survey,December 1977 to March 1980 (some returns contained incomplete information).

Description of the sample

There were 29 cases of injury, three cases of serious injury and, 40 people required help in leaving the building. The lack of fatal fires in this sample is due to their general rarity and the social and legal difficulties inherent in obtaining completed questionnaires from such a tragedy

From the figures in *Table 3* it is apparent that although there was a range of building types and fires in the sample the majority were domestic fires occurring in the daytime, of relatively little severity. The fire brigades' assessment of damage also indicated that, in general, the fires surveyed here did not have a large amount of damage associated with them.

Table 3 Summarises the main characteristics of the sample

	Numbers
Number responding	
Women	310
Men	268
Total	578
Time of fire	
2200 - 0800	118
0800 - 1700	285
1700 - 2200	141
Building type	
House	297
Hospital	21
Hotel	14
Factory	53
Office	23
Flats	167
Age of respondents	
< 15	8
16 - 35	273
36 - 55	156
> 55	128

Results of questionnaire survey

Early stages of behaviour in a fire

Recognition. As can be seen from *Table 4* the early stages of fires are clearly characterised by the awareness of something unusual, often smells or noises rather than direct contact with the fire. There is a common tendency for these to be treated as insignificant but on their persistence the most dominant response is to investigate the suspected source. It is this investigation, or a report from someone else who has made such an investigation which leads, most often, to an individual becoming definitely aware of a fire.

The figures in Table 4 are very sparse, with a great deal of missing information. This does mean that on their own these figures would need to be treated with caution. However, when they are compared with the sequences established in the case studies and data from other investigations it is plausible to assume that the sparse data here are a direct product of the ambiguity and confusion present in the early stages of a fire. It is likely that many respondents were not sure what to put in answer to these questions because they were not really sure what was happening at these very early stages.

Table 4 Early stages of behaviour in a fire as indicated from questionnaire responses

A *Cue to fire presence*

	Frequency
No cue	160
Smell	144
Noise	99
See something unusual	76
Hear alarm	22
See brigade	5
Feel temperature change	4
No answer	18

B *Interpretation of cue*

	Frequency
Event	
Not significant	138
Don't know	126
Fire	29
Significant event	11
No answer [or no cue]	202

C *Response to cue*

	Frequency
Investigate	171
Have a look (curious)	79
Other	28
Continue previous activity	22
Ask someone to look	8
No response	268

D *Became definitely aware of fire due to*

	Frequency
Investigation	240
Was told	146
Interrupted by smoke and flames	56
Present when fire started	40
Accidentally noticed fire	34
Other	47
No answer	15

Communication. In more serious fires it has been suggested that access to a telephone might have played a crucial role. Therefore it is valuable to consider in the present, less serious fires whether there was any evidence of ready use of the telephone. *Table 5* provides a summary of telephone use. 490 respondents reported having a telephone available. 336 of these people did use it, in the great majority of cases to call the brigade.

Thus the relevance of telephone use in these fires is clearly established. It is also of interest to note that of the 154 people who said they did not use the telephone 78 said that this was because they knew someone else had called, showing the importance of social contacts with others in these fires. This is further supported by the direct answer to the question of who else called the brigade besides the respondent:

Who else called the brigade?

Neighbour	86
Staff	70
Relation	47
Friend	17
Stranger	9

Table 5 Telephone use in fires

Total Sample (578)

Telephone not available (53)	Telephone available (490)
No response (30)	
Do not know (5)	

Did not use telephone (154)	Used telephone (336)
Because:	to call:
Knew someone else had called (78)	Brigade (313)
Could not reach it (17)	Switchboard (14)
Too pre-occupied (16)	Warn others (4)
No urgency (11)	Get advice (5)
Location unknown (1)	
Forgot (1)	
Other (30)	

Actions during the fire

Sequence. Table 6 gives the most frequent first four acts for all respondents at each of five positions in the act sequence. These figures support the earlier findings that investigation is often the first conscious action. Thereafter the likely sequence is not as clear cut, presumably depending on what is discovered. There is a slight tendency for those who do not call the brigade as a first action to call it as a second action, but quite a high proportion of people will tackle the fire in these early actions while those who do not will tend to warn others. Overall 268 people did attempt to fight the fire and 273 did not.

Table 6 Four most endorsed acts over five positions (all applicable respondents)

Act Position		Frequency
1st	Have a closer look	149
	Combination/contain fire	103
	Warn others	86
	Call brigade	50
2nd	Call brigade	103
	Warn others	82
	Combat/contain	73
	Secure immediate area	52
3rd	Call brigade	78
	Combat/contain	73
	Secure immediate area	50
	Organise others ·	36
4th	Call brigade	55
	Secure immediate area	46
	Combat/contain	41
	Attempt to bring others to safety	36
5th	Organise others	30
	Call brigade	30
	Combat/contain	29
	Attempt to bring others to safety	26

Fire Fighting. In answer to the question of how the fire was fought the following frequencies of answers were given:

Various (not listed below)	88
Bucket of water	68
Extinguisher	65
Blanket	20
Hose-reel	17
Unknown	10

The frequency of extinguisher use here is higher than reported for the detailed case studies of more severe fires (Sime et al 1981) and could have been a contributor to the low amount of damage reported in these fires. Of interest also is the use of extinguishers in relation to knowledge of their presence. 268 people were aware of an extinguisher being present nearby. Of these 135 made some attempt to combat the fire but only 61 actually used the extinguisher to tackle the fire. Of the people who had not been previously aware of an extinguisher being present, 85 in all, only 7 found and used an extinguisher in the fire. Of 82 people reporting an attempt to use an extinguisher 9 were unable to get it to work. These figures accord well with Chandler's (1978) study which showed that people were less likely to use fire extinguishers on small fires. It also supports the findings of Ramachandran et al (1972) that people are 'less successful with extinguishers than with other first aid methods'. Although when a fire is attacked by people before the brigade arrives Ramachandran et al found that the severity of the fire is reduced.

Thus, although fire extinguishers can clearly make an important contribution to fire fighting, as previous research has shown, this contribution is subject to many constraints in an actual fire.

Escape. The generally 'benign' quality of the fires in this sample is revealed by the escape routes available to and used by the respondents. In general, where people did leave the building they left by the exit stairs they normally used. As *Table 7* also shows 10 out of 77 people also used lifts to escape from the fire, a potentially dangerous route, but apparently causing no injury in the present sample. 6 out of 85 people did not use the emergency stairs because they could not gain access to them, the route being too dangerous. Thus once again, as with fire extinguishers, the significance of special escape routes is shown to require further examination. Even in such a sample an identifiable proportion find these routes unusable, thus it is clearly important to establish the conditions under which they are likely to be of especial value.

Smoke and egress. One question on the survey explored the conditions under which people left the building, asking about smoke, injury and assistance. On the basis of this question the difficulties of egress can be examined. In effect, each individual can be classified in accordance with the difficulty he/she found in escaping. Using a (i) to indicate no problem and higher values to indicate degrees of problem, so a person with least difficulty would be one who did not encounter smoke (i), left by the normal exit route (ii) and experienced no difficulty in leaving the building (i). Such an individual is represented in *Table 8* by the profile 111, there being 86 such individuals in the survey sample. By contrast there were two individuals who experienced very thick smoke (a value of 4), had much difficulty in leaving (3), and had slight injury (2). The profile of these two individuals is thus, 432, in Table 8.

If the profile values for each person are added then this total 'joint score' provides a basis for ordering people in terms of the difficulty of their egress. In some cases, it is found that people with the same 'joint score' have different profiles. For example there are three individuals who were slightly injured (2), experienced no difficulty in leaving (1), but experienced thick smoke (3); a profile of 312 giving a joint score of '6'. This is the same value as the six individuals with a profile of 411 and the 22 individuals with a profile of 321.The profiles with identical joint scores are qualitatively different although quantitatively similar. They thus indicate different *kinds* of fire event, of similar severity.

The reason for carrying out the analysis illustrated in Table 8 is to establish if the severity of a fire can be related clearly to particular types of experience or to see if there are so many qualitative differences that no generalisations about severity can be made. To answer this question Table 8 lists all the profiles for people who left the building without anyone's help and by an often used entrance or exit. What it shows clearly is that there is indeed a strong quantitative trend throughout these fires. This is revealed by the fact that the central column of the table accounts for 234 out of the 252 cases. In other words, 93% of the cases fit a single order relating to the experienced severity of the incident. A closer examination of this order also indicates some interesting trends.

Table 7 Means of escape

Was a lift available?
    No   452
    Yes   77   Did you use it?   No 67
                                                                                                       Yes 10

Were emergency stairs available?
    No 311
    Yes 148 Did you use stairs? Yes 63
                                             No 85 Why Not?
                                                     No urgency   40
                                                     Used different exit   21
                                                   Remaining in building 17
                                                   Route too dangerous   5
                                                   Location unknown   1
                                                   Was trapped   1

Was the exit you used the one you normally use?
    Yes   302
    No   38
    Did not leave 156

The overall benign nature of the fires from which these people escaped is shown by the fact that the great majority of the profiles have low joint scores. Nonetheless the profiles do show the important role of smoke spread even in these fires. It is only when there is some smoke (2) that anyone admits to some difficulty in leaving (2), but the frequency of the 221 profile is still considerably less than the 311 profile. So moderate smoke is more likely to be associated with no difficulty. However, once the smoke is classified by people as 'thick' then the great majority of people are likely to describe egress as being with 'some difficulty'. No-one who experienced 'very thick smoke' described their egress as having 'no difficulty'. Thus smoke is usually present when people find themselves in difficulty, but even thick smoke does not necessarily cause difficulty in egress (cf Bryan, 1977).

One further point worth noting from Table 8. Consider all those who were slightly injured, the two profiles in 312, 322, and the one at the bottom of the central column 432. These people did not necessarily describe their exit as difficult (although some did) but they all experienced thick smoke.

Once again this reveals the significance of smoke in hindering some people from making a safe escape from a fire.

Comparison with case studies

In the case studies of fires it was possible to deal with a few major, serious incidents. In contrast the questionnaire survey allowed the study of many more fires of a less serious nature. In effect, the questionnaire survey examined fires which were effectively dealt with before they became very serious, whereas the case study fires had all developed into extremely dangerous conflagrations. Thus the two sets of studies complement each other. The case studies emphasise what can go wrong in a fire which results in it becoming dangerous. The survey emphasises what people do which is effective in reducing the danger of a fire.

From the questionnaires it can be seen that when the early stages of investigation and clarification of ambiguous cues lead to early recognition of the presence of a fire, then people are able to cope effectively with that fire. This effective coping includes a high proportion of people attempting to fight the fire. Furthermore, from the case studies it would be expected that less dangerous fires would be characterised by ready access to a telephone in calling for help and productive use of fire extinguishers and fire escapes. These expectations are substantiated from the questionnaire results.

American studies of behaviour in fires

The studies considered so far in this chapter were conducted by the Fire Research Unit at the University of Surrey, under the aegis of the UK Fire Research Station.

In the United States the National Bureau of Standards and the National Fire Protection Agency have commissioned a number of studies of human behaviour in specific fire events. These studies have usually combined detailed interviews with questionnaire surveys. They provide useful additional information on the many issues considered so far, more especially because the studies were carried out in a country where fire regulations and fire fighting procedures are different from those in Great Britain.

Studies of single fires

A nursing home fire

Haber (1980) describes a fire that occurred on the 3rd floor of a nursing home in which there were 21 deaths. The fire had been discovered by a nurse accidentally, through noticing unusual smoke and heat. Her initial reactions had been to call for assistance. The fire alarm was then sounded by a second nurse who had been alerted. Other members of staff came to assist. Most notably a senior administrator, who gave instructions to organise others, whilst nurses evacuated patients. Some of this evacuation was delayed whilst nurses and administrators discussed what might be done, especially to clear smoke. The director also took an extinguisher from a nurse to fight the fire.

The janitor of the building heard the alarm, but assumed it was a false alarm until personally told it was not. He then attempted to fight the fire, with the help of the administrators, until the heat became too intense. At this point he found that the heat was so intense that he could not shut the door to the room in which the fire was. This appears to have been the most direct cause of the deaths, as all deaths were caused by asphyxiation from smoke on the floor of the fire origin.

Table 8 Ordering of severity of incidents in relation to exit behaviour

Key to profiles:

Experience of Smoke	Ease of Exit	Amount of Injury
1 No smoke	1 No difficulty	1 No injury
2 Some smoke	2 Some difficulty	2 Slight injury
3 Thick smoke	3 Much difficulty	
4 Very thick smoke		

Overall frequencies in parenthesis next to profiles

			joint score
	1 1 1 (86)		3
	2 1 1 (87)		4
	3 1 1 (24)	2 2 1 (7)	5
3 1 2 (3)	3 2 1 (22)	4 1 1 (6)	6
3 2 2 (2)	4 2 1 (8)		7
	4 3 1 (5)		8
	4 3 2 (2)		9

A prison fire in a women's prison

Haber also describes a fire in a prison. The fire was started by a prisoner, who then shouted that there was a fire. The matron in charge then went to investigate and, seeing the fire, got wet towels to give to the prisoner in the fire cell and told other inmates to lie on the floor. She then went to get keys to the cell and finally told other staff to sound the alarm. It took the matron two minutes to seek assistance and tell someone to sound the alarm.

When the others heard the alarm they assumed that it was a small fire because this had been a frequent occurrence. The men who came to help brought no equipment, having been given no clear information as to the extent of the fire. They eventually obtained fire fighting equipment and put out the fire before evacuating prisoners.

No one was killed in this fire, possibly because one wall of the cell in which the fire started was all bars, allowing the smoke to escape. The rapid response of the staff who came to assist once they knew of the seriousness of the situation possibly also helped save lives.

A fire in a home for 'retired aged'

The third incident described by Haber was started deliberately, at 3.15 a.m. by an ex-employee of a nursing home with petrol bombs. The nurse on duty heard breaking glass and went to investigate. She followed the intruder as he threw petrol bombs, closing doors as she went. She also tried to telephone for help but the telephone had been cut off by the intruder. She then pulled the alarm and told other nurses, after which she went to a public pay-phone in the building, but gave up half-way through the call because she thought that the telephone operator was being obstructive.

Eventually others called the fire department and a nearby policeman was brought in to help. Throughout, nurses closed doors to contain the fire and smoke. One nurse on hearing the alarm and breaking glass immediately switched off the oxygen supply. The engineer, located in the basement was the only one to attempt to extinguish the fires.

In general this potentially, extremely dangerous incident passed without loss of life because the nurses acted as a team in accordance with their nursing training. There was also only one chain of command present, unlike in the nursing home fire above, and so people knew who to communicate with and from whom to take instructions.

Survey of a nursing home fire

Edelman et al (1980) carried out a survey of 22 people involved in a nursing home fire, involving approximately 250 people, which occurred one evening and as a direct result of which two patients died. The people in the nursing home were, in the main, reasonably fit and able to move about on their own. The fire lasted 16 minutes, the fire brigade arriving after eight minutes. Five members of staff assisted the evacuation of the patients but no patient aided evacuation.

Edelman and his colleagues report that some people took the alarm bell being sounded as an initial indication of some 'trouble'. Six people did not interpret it as a fire and took no action. One person closed his door to stop the noise. Of two people who were told by staff, one person was convinced and left the room. Three people heard screaming and went to investigate. Of the twelve people who heard others shouting 'fire' six took no action. Of the 22 people questioned, 14 were not convinced that there was a fire, even having heard noises suggestive of one.

In leaving the building, 16 people used the centre stairway taking them closer to the fire rather than emergency exit routes away from the fire source. The remaining six received assistance from the fire brigade. In all 85 residents were evacuated via the centre stairway. Some respondents had to pass the room in which the fire was contained, which meant that they had to pass through smoke. They ignored emergency exits within feet of their own room for a number of reasons.

1. They were told to leave by staff. This usually meant via the centre stairs, it was assumed that this was the appropriate action in this event.
2. Use of any other stairway normally resulted in an alarm sounding and a severe reprimand for the resident by the staff.
3. Residents saw others leaving by this exist and simply followed.

This led to even greater problems as the fire brigade used the centre stairway to gain access to the fire.

Studies of hotel fires

As mentioned earlier Bryan (1981, 1983) has carried out a number of detailed questionnaire surveys of behaviour in fires. Of particular note here are his studies of people who were guests in large hotels when a fire started. His detailed analyses are best summarised, for the present purposes as follows.

1. The fire alarm evacuation signalling system was not effectively utilised in either hotel fire, guests becoming aware of the fire by a variety of means over an extended period of time.
2. Guests did tend to help each other, by such actions as knocking on doors admitting others to safer rooms and rescuing people.
3. No nonadaptive behaviour ('panic') was observed.
4. The early actions of the guests on discovering an unexpected event were the seeking of information and making contact with others. Packing and dressing prior to leaving were also not uncommon.
5. Instructions obtained from hotel staff, primarily from telephoning to the hotel reception, were instrumental in many cases in influencing the actions of the guests.
6. Those people who left the buildings, did tend to leave by the available stairs, although smoke sometimes cut-off this escape route. However, a number of people did move through smoke under conditions they described as zero visibility.

7. No guests re-entered the building once they had left and only one guest attempted to fight the fire.

The project people studies

In two major questionnaire surveys of fires carried out by Bryan for the National Bureau of Standards (summarised in Bryan, 1977), a procedure was used based on that first established by Wood (1972) and elaborated by the Fire Research Unit, as reported above. This involves fire officers giving out questionnaires to fire victims. In the first major study by Bryan (Project People) 584 individuals returned completed questionnaires from 335 fire incidents. In the second study, focusing on health care occupancies (Project People II) interviews as well as questionnaires were used to obtain information from 159 people involved in 59 incidents.

This extensive data base was analysed, in the main, to look at the frequency of events and actions. Unlike the case study material, the details of the actual sequence of events or the organisational aspects of individual fires were not established, but some valuable general trends were drawn out of the data and presented in 81 tables. Bryan uses this data to test a variety of proposed models of behaviour in fires, and in order to comment on fire regulations.

Bryan summaries the behaviour response pattern observed across all fires as follows:

A. Investigation
1. Investigated cues
2. Discovered fire
3. Searched for fire

B. Alerting
1. Pulled manual fire alarm
2. Called operator
3. Called fire department
4. Alerted other staff
5. Notified others
6. Had others call fire department
7. Enter building
8. Went to fire alarm
9. Telephoned others/relatives
10. Woke up

C. Fire Fighting
1. Got extinguisher
2. Attempt extinguishment
3. Fought fire
4. Went to fire area
5. Removed fuel

D. Evacuation
1. Rescued threatened patients

       2.   Evacuated patients
       3.   Attempted rescue
       4.   Got dressed
       5.   Left building
       6.   Got family
       7.   Left area
       8.   Got personal property
       9.   Tried to exit
     10.   Went to balcony

E. Protective Procedures

       1.   Closed doors
       2.   Directed operations
       3.   Stood by
       4.   Ventilated
       5.   Performed first aid
       6.   Turned off appliances
       7.   Nothing
       8.   Check on pets
       9.   Await fire department arrival
     10.   Removed by fire department

Summary of findings from USA studies

The particular cases examined by North American researchers cannot be regarded as representative of any known population of fires. Rather they are best regarded as illustrative examples of serious incidents to which public attention was drawn. They differ from the cases studied in Great Britain in being, in general, more severe with a greater loss of life involved. One reason for this is that the legal procedures and police activities in regard to fatal fires allows ready access to potential witnesses in the United States, but in Great Britain it is only after all legal proceedings have been completed that researchers are enabled to gain access to witnesses.

Nonetheless, despite the different context of the fires studied and their different nature, their details serve to complement the trends found in British fires rather than casting any doubt on the generality of these trends. In all the fires the confusions and ambiguities of the early stages are apparent, with the subsequent search for further information. This is followed by fire fighting or flight, depending on the particular circumstances. The part played by the existing communication pattern within the organisation in either helping or hindering coping with the fire is also clear in all incidents. Escape then appears to take place directly in relation to normal modes of entry and exit from the building. In this smoke plays a role of hindering egress but not necessarily preventing it, some people moving long distances through quite dense smoke. Furthermore, sensible actions are frequently found whereas irrational nonadaptive responses are never recorded. Where fires lead to loss of life there is frequently not only a slow response to early cues but also administrative confusion in terms of who should take what actions.

Recent examples

This summary of what happens in fires is derived in the main from studies of fires that took place in the 1970s, yet it is distressing to see how accurately it describes incidents that have continued to occur since then. The most tragic example is the fire at Kings Cross underground station. Here a small fire under a moving escalator was allowed to develop to the extent that it flashed over into an entrance hall killing 31 people. There appears to have been no stage at which the entrance hall was evacuated and isolated and there were a number of stages in the development of the fire at which time was lost in seeking further information and deciding what actions were to be taken.

At Kings Cross the routes people took out of the fire also appear to have related very closely to the routes that were normally taken by people. The position of the bodies found seemed to relate directly to where people were intending to go. Members of the public, further, responded without demure to the authority of the police officers present, although in a number of cases this lead people to their death.

The role of authority figures was also apparent at the Bradford City football ground fire in 1985 (discussed in Canter et al, 1989). There an initial reluctance to climb from the stands onto the pitch and the use of the normal route out, up along a passage behind the stands, probably both contributed to the loss of life in the very rapid development of the fire. Here again the authority of the police, in stopping the game and calling spectators onto the pitch, was crucial.

The Bradford disaster may be contrasted with the one that occurred at Hillsborough football ground in 1989. For although there was no fire the need to manage the emergency and deal with sudden crowd flows had many parallels to dealing with similar problems in a fire. As the official enquiry made clear, it was the inept policing of this incident that was a major contribution to the loss of life.

A general model of human behaviour in fires

The Bradford loss of life. The inquiry that followed the Hillsborough Stadium Disaster (HMSO, 1990) did lead to questioning of the fundamental issue of why a major recreational activity should rely so heavily on police management (Canter et al, 1989). The result of this was a major rethink of the design and management of sporting facilities which has had marked benefits in turning football grounds from fortresses into places of entertainment.

In his extensive comparisons of the various models available of human behaviour in fires and the checking of their validity against his own Project People data, summarised above, Bryan (1983a) states:

'The behavioural models of Withey and the heuristic systems model of Canter appear to have the most validity in the understanding and organisation of human behaviour in fire incidents' (p. 195).

Withey's work (1962) is concerned, in the main, with modelling the processes internal to the individual in an emergency situation without drawing on quantitative data. Canter's model does attempt also to incorporate the action sequences as they relate directly to behaviour in fires, which is why Bryan refers to it as 'systems' model.

Furthermore, the model in Canter, 1990 (chapter 8) does derive directly from the transitional probabilities found from case studies. It is this extrapolation from existing records which gives their model its 'heuristic' qualities. In the present summary, then, that model will form the basis for the general account of human behaviour in fires.

This account sees human behaviour passing through a number of identifiable stages, with the possibility of various routes from one stage to the next. In summary the fire is seen as having three broad stages:

i.   the individual receives initial cues and investigates or misinterprets these initial cues,

ii.   once the fire is apparent the individual will try to obtain further information, contacts others or leave

iii.   thereafter the individual will deal with the fire, interact with others or escape.

To develop these stages in more detail, each will be considered separately.

1. Pre-fire activity. It seems that pre fire activity is an important factor in predicting subsequent actions. If a person is engaged in an activity with a well known preset/prescribed 'script' e.g., eating a meal in a restaurant, the implications for subsequent behaviour are considerable.

Additionally, from research, the pre-fire activity can be seen to influence the type of cue received and readiness with which people react. For example noise and smells are more likely to be the initial cues for a waking/alert population. This may lead to earlier recognition and so to a less severe fire.

2. Cue reception. Cue reception may be a function of pre-fire activity. There may be a tendency for sex differences with females more likely to be recipient of noises and odours, though the effect is only slight and may be a result of an over sampling of domestic fires with an alert population. In larger establishments the cue may be an alarm warning.

There are role differences in initial response to the cue. If it is in an environment with an organisational hierarchy or structure there will be an alerting of senior members of staff after an investigation by the recipient. In domestic fires if the female receives the cue and investigates, the male when told is likely to 'have a look' and delay further actions.

Initial cues are usually ambiguous. To resolve ambiguity investigation takes place. This helps establish the nature of the situation and provide more detailed information on which to act.

Information may come from others and has been found in fires that prove to be dangerous to be frequently inadequate for effective behaviour (cf. USA hospital case studies).

3. Interpretation: definition of the situation. Individuals may or may not have realised there is a fire. An understanding of their behaviour must take account of whether or not they have defined their situation correctly. Because people act on *their* definition of a situation the clues and information that lead to this must be taken into account, with due consideration of the influence of both the place and roles of the people concerned.

A person may assume that staff in a public building are in control or that cues perceived are indications of something already under control e.g., burned toast in a restaurant which poses no threat and so will not be interpreted as indicating a dangerous situation. If staff do not inform the people present appropriately, ineffective behaviour on the part of the public will ensue.

In a domestic fire the presence of smoke is a clear indicator of the need for 'fire related' activity which is more likely to follow as there is no reliance on others for action. In an organisation a fire will be correctly interpreted if a strict hierarchy is already in existence, with a senior member clearly responsible for defining the actions of his/her juniors.

4. Prepare. Once the fire has been defined the 'prepare' stage occurs which includes 'instruct', 'explore', 'withdraw'. The particular type of occupancy is likely to have a great influence on exactly how this stage develops.
'Instruct' Who does the instructing depends almost entirely on their existing role in an organisation.
'Explore' consists of a variety of activities associated with establishing exactly what is happening. It frequently consists of going to the room of fire origin and trying to see the fire directly, being a development of other less intrusive investigations.
'Withdraw' The phenomenon of withdraw/wait is most typical in the context of hotels where the privacy and self-reliance associated with being a hotel guest seems crucial.

5. Act. The final stage depends considerably upon role, occupancy and earlier behaviour and experience. With early definition it may be possible for early evacuation or effective fire fighting to occur. Both males and females will fight the fire but a more dynamic role is apparent for males.

'Wait' may be confined to hotels and guests, however in other circumstances people may wait after giving instructions.

Instruction leading to fire-fighting/evacuation are dependent on hierarchy in organisations where staff members will be told whether to evacuate or fight the fire.

The increasing complexity of the fire as it develops is best seen from the spatial representation in *Figure 1* of the major sequence of events.

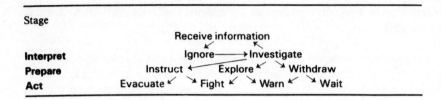

Stage					
		Receive information			
Interpret		Ignore ─────→ Investigate			
Prepare		Instruct ← Explore ↙ ↘ Withdraw			
Act	Evacuate ↙ ↘ Fight ↙ ↘ Warn ↙ ↘ Wait				

Figure1 Model of human behaviour in fire

A number of points about this model are worth emphasising.

1. The triangular shape of this diagram is symptomatic of the fact that the potential actions increase in variety as the experience of fire event develops. Thus the later the stage of the fire the more difficult it is to predict the individual's behaviour, and the more likely are the experience and behaviour to be specific to a particular occupancy.

2. Influences on the sequence should be examined in relation to the three stages, i.e., whether they are derived from the building and its fire protection system or from the people and their previous training, or the organisational influences.

3. Regarding the 'Prepare' stage, the particular occupancy is likely to have a great influence. The roles and associated rules which people regard as relevant to their situation have an influence on the particular outcome and experience of this stage in the sequence.

Role/rule model

People can best be understood as being goal-oriented. The goals provide the motivation and explanation for behaviour.

It is the nature of the social quality of human activities that the goals which people have at any point in time are a function of their role in the setting. Moreover roles have certain expectations associated with them, notably expected actions. These role or situation related expectations may be referred to as 'rules'. These are the principles of action which typically underlie behaviour in any given situation.

As a consequence, the roles and their associated rules, provide an important guide to understanding and prediction of their actions.

From case studies it can be seen that commonly occurring rules can be established for different classes of occupancy and fire.

Conclusions

From case studies a full and coherent account can be given for the sequence of actions without recourse to 'panic' as any form of explanation. Though fire is a complex process, a valid summary of types of fire can be made. Behaviour sequences appear to be a product of attempts to cope with ambiguous, rapidly changing information. Much of the observed variation in behaviour can be accounted for by considering the role of the person carrying out the acts and attempting to postulate rules which may be associated with those roles.

References

Bryan, J. (1977), *People Project*, University of Maryland.

Bryan, J.L. (1977), *Smoke as a Determinant of Human Behaviour in Fire Situations (Project people)*, University of Maryland, College of Engineering.

Bryan, J.L. (1981), *An Examination and Analysis of the Dynamics of the Human Behaviour in the MGM Grand Hotel Fire*, NFP, Mass, Mimeo.

Bryan, J.L. (1983), 'An Examination and Analysis of the Dynamics of the Human Behaviour in the Westchase Hilton Hotel Fire', Mass: NFPA (Mimeo).

Bryan, J.L. (1983a), 'Implications for Codes and Behaviour Models from the Analysis of Behaviour Response Patterns in Fire Situations as Selected from the Project People and Project II Study Programs', College of Engineering, Maryland.

Canter, D. (1977), *Psychology of Place*, Architectural Press, London.

Canter, D., Comber, M. & Uzzell, D. (1989), *Football in its Place: An Environmental Psychology of Football Grounds*, Methuen, London.

Chandler, S.E. (1978), *Some Trends in Hospital Fire Statistics*, Building Research Establishment, Current paper CP 67/68, Borehamwood.

Edelman, P., Herz, E. & Bickman, L. (1980), 'A Model of Behaviour in Fires Applied to a Nursing Home' in Canter, D. (ed.), *Fires and Human Behaviour*, Wiley, Chichester, pp. 181-204.

Haber, G.M. (1980), 'Human Behaviour in Fires in Total Institutions' in Canter, D. (ed.), *Fires and Human Behaviour*, Wiley, Chichester, pp. 137-154.

Lerup, L., Conrath, D. & Liu, J. (1980), 'Fires in Nursing Facilities' in Canter, D. (ed.), *Fires and Human Behaviour*, Wiley, Chichester, pp. 137-154.

Ramachandran, G., Nash, P. & Benson, S.P. (1972), 'The Use of Fire Extinguishers in Dwellings', *Fire Research Note 915*, Building Research Establishment, FRS, Borehamwood.

Sime, J., Canter, D. & Breaux, J. (1981), 'University Team Studies Use and Success of Extinguishers, *Fire*, March.

Withey, S.B. (1962), 'Reaction to Uncertain Threat', *Man and Society in Disaster*, G.W. Baker, D. Wight & W. Chapman (eds.), Basic Books, New York.

Wood, P.G. (1972), 'The Behaviour of People in Fires', *Fire Research Note* 953, Building Research Establishment, FRS, Borehamwood.

CRIMINAL BEHAVIOUR

8 A Multivariate Model of Sexual Offence Behaviour: Developments in 'Offender Profiling'

Abstract

The extrapolation of characteristics of criminals from information about their crimes, as an aid to police investigation, is the essence of 'profiling'. This paper proposes that for such extrapolations to be more than educated guesses they must be based upon knowledge of a) coherent consistencies in criminal behaviour and b) the relationship those behavioural consistencies have to aspects of an offender available to the police in an investigation. Hypotheses concerning behavioural consistencies are drawn from the diverse literature on sexual offences and a study is described of 66 sexual assaults committed by 27 offenders against strangers. Multivariate statistical analyses of these assaults support a five component system of rapist behaviour, reflecting modes of interaction with the victim as a sexual object. The potential this provides for an eclectic theoretical basis to offender profiling is discussed.

'Offender profiling'

Over the last decade a variety of 'profiles' have been created by behavioural scientists to assist police investigations. Although most have been produced by the FBI Behavioural Science Unit (Hazelwood, 1983), there have been some notable successes in the United Kingdom (Canter, 1988). Indeed Hazelwood (1983) claims an accuracy rate in excess of 80%, and in a more detailed review Pinizzotto (1984) proposes that suspects were identified with the help of profiling in 46% of the 192 cases he examined.

Holmes and DeBurger (1988) describe a psychological profile as a report on a violent crime, utilising information and approaches from various social and behavioural sciences, intended to assist law enforcement personnel in their investigations. Other authors are even more vague, writing of a combination of brainstorming, intuition, and educated guesswork (Geberth, 1983) or a collection of leads (Rossi, 1982) about an offender. Vorpogel (1982) simply describes a profile as a biographical sketch of a criminal's behavioural patterns, trends, and tendencies. The question of how such profiles are produced and what the underlying psychological principles are that enable them to be created is given less emphasis in the existing publications than descriptive accounts of what profiles may contain.

No profile is all inclusive, nor is the same information provided from one profile to another, being based on what was or was not left at the crime scene and on any other information that might be available from victim or witness statements, since the nature and amount of information varies, the profile may also vary. Ault and Reese (1980), for example, provide the following list of what may be included in a profile:

(1)   the perpetrator's race
(2)   sex
(3)   age range
(4)   marital status
(5)   general employment
(6)   reaction to questioning by police
(7)   degree of sexual maturity
(8)   whether the individual might strike again
(9)   the possibility that he has committed a similar offence previously
(10)   possible police record.

But this list omits aspects such as likely style of social interaction, general personality characteristics, possibility of associated undetected crimes and the very important matter of possible area of residential location, all of which are aspects that have been successfully included in University of Surrey profiles (Canter 1988, 1989).

The derivation of an account of the perpetrator of a crime from knowledge of the events associated with a crime is a process open to scientific development. As pointed out by Canter (1989) it reflects the central psychological questions of how characteristics of individuals are reflected in their behaviour. In this case the characteristics are those of value to the police in identifying suspects and the behaviour is that associated with the crime.

Present focus on sexual offences against strangers

Profiles as an aid to criminal investigation have been produced for a variety of offences covering homicide, rape and arson (Pinizzotto, 1984). As a starting point for empirical research, though, serious sexual offences are particularly suitable. They are crimes in which there is information about a great many of the perpetrator's actions. These actions in themselves, focusing as they do around interpersonal sexual aggression, are likely to be revealing of the individual who commits them.

The investigation of sexual assaults committed by a person unknown to the victim are also particularly difficult for criminal investigators to solve. Yet they do account for a high proportion of sexual assaults. Mulvihill et al (1969) found 53% of victims reported being raped by a stranger. There may well be important cultural differences in these figures, because Kocis (1982) reports for Eastern Europe that 55% of the victims are known to the offender and a further 40% of the victims come into contact with the offender before the crime is committed; only a small minority of the victims appear to be absolute strangers. In Britain the figures available are rather closer to those for the U.S.A. Lloyd and Walmsley (1989) report that in 1973, 49% of rape victims were attacked by strangers. In 1985 the figure was 40%.

The studies reported here therefore focus on sexual assaults in which the victim had no prior knowledge of the offender. Some of these offenders also committed murders, usually with sexually related aspects. Sexual homicide is therefore included in the crimes examined.

The need for an eclectic model of offender behaviour

The central hypotheses of profiling, open to direct empirical test, relate to the idea that offenders differ in their actions when committing a crime and that these differences reflect (and therefore correlate with) overtly available features of the offender. However, most published conceptualisations of variations in offender behaviour have tended to combine accounts of actions in an offence with explanations of the intentions, motivations and inferred offender characteristics. For example, a commonly cited approach to rapist typology, Groth's (1979), is premised on the assumption that rape is not an expression of sexual desire but the use of sexuality to express power and anger. The typology that is derived from this perspective, as a consequence, emphasises the various psychological functions that rape has for the offender not what varieties of action rape actually consists of. A further example is given by the work of Prentky et al (1985). Their attempts to characterise and classify rapists makes little distinction between the overt behaviour as it occurs in the sexual assault and the psychodynamic processes that are taken to account for or produce that behaviour. There is little attempt to distinguish aspects of the offender's motivations and life-style from his offending behaviour. Yet any attempt to understand the actions that occur in the offence requires the classification of offence behaviour as distinct from classifications of the person in either psychological or social terms. So although each approach to classification is guided by a particular explanatory framework any composite modelling of offence behaviour for use in 'profiling' will have to draw upon all those approaches that are supported by scientific evidence.

This confusion of action and person is less problematic in the clinical context, in which earlier theoretical formulations were derived. After all, unlike a police detective, Groth had actual patients present in interviews when carrying out his research and his therapeutic mission requires him to enable the offending person to deal with his actions. Such typologies undoubtedly contribute to the understanding of the motivations of rapists and this can help to indicate why certain sorts of rapist will perform certain types of offence. Yet there remains the primary question of what variations in offence behaviour can be reliably identified without any knowledge of the person who committed them. The exploration of how any empirically validated variations relate to offender characteristics is an important issue for subsequent examination.

The focus on the perpetrator's actions is not a purely pragmatic requirement shaped by the limitations of criminal investigation, nor is it naïvely behaviourist, assuming that it is only behaviour that is open to scientific investigation. Rather the emphasis points to the social/interpersonal nature of criminal behaviour, especially in crimes against the person. It is the variety of actions that happen in sexual attacks that indicate the different modes of relationship that offenders have with their victims. Any empirical model of offence behaviour must therefore encapsulate and explicate these variations in mode of interaction with the victim.

The literature points to a number of aspects of the relationship that a rapist has with his victim. The most obvious of these are sexuality, and aggressiveness, the behaviour on which Groth (1979) bases his typology. But other writers, notably Rada (1978) and Scully and Marolla (1983) point to the fact that many rapes of strangers are carried out by men who carry out other criminal acts and for whom rape is one such mode of criminal activity. This perspective indicates that, besides the sexual acts and the violence, attention also needs to be paid to those aspects of the offence that relate to its fundamentally criminal nature.

In contrast to the issues of sexuality, aggressiveness and criminality emphasis has also been given recently to the argument that it is the desire for social contact, or intimacy that is a primary motivation in rape (Marshall, 1989). Yet it is the difficulty the offender has in achieving intimacy that leads to an assault. This perspective may be contrasted with the others, from the viewpoint of profiling research, in the attention it draws to behaviour that goes beyond physical contact to attempt some sort of personal relationship with the victim.

The contrast of Marshall's (1989) emphasis on intimacy with Groth's (1979) focus on power and aggression serves to show that, as logical as each one is, there is some potential for inherent contradictions between them. At the very least they raise questions about how a quest for intimacy and the desire for power or aggression are combined in actual behaviour in actual offences, if at all. Such possible contradictions, although not as strong, may also be seen in the difference between the emphasis on the essentially psychopathological nature of sexual assaults, as argued by those with a clinical perspective (e.g., Groth 1979, Prentky et al, 1985), compared with the views of sociologists such as Scully and Marolla (1983) who see these offenders as essentially normal males operating within criminal mores.

A further contradiction of perspective can also be seen between those such as Marshall and Groth who emphasise the fact that the attack is based upon psychological contact with a person, whether for aggressive or intimacy reasons, and those who argue that rape is fundamentally impersonal (notably Scully and Marolla 1983). From the latter perspective the victim is an object used to satisfy a physical craving with whom the offender wishes to have completely 'impersonal sex'. A view expressed strongly by Symons (1979: 284) is that 'males tend to desire no-cost, impersonal copulations'.

Broadly, then, at least five modes of interaction with the victim are suggested by these different perspective. Each of these would be expected to have an observable counterpart in the actions that happened during an offence. Some of these actions would be hypothesised as unlikely to co-occur in the same offence, being contradictory.

In summary they refer to the following elements of sexual offence behaviour:

(1)   sexuality
(2)   violence and aggression
(3)   impersonal, sexual gratification
(4)   criminality, and
(5)   interpersonal intimacy.

A number of hypotheses can be derived from this fivefold framework about the likely co-occurrences of specific behaviour in sexual assaults, given that all of these types of behaviour may potentially occur in any sexual assault.

One hypothesis is that they all occur with each other in any combination across a range of assaults. This would suggest that none of the explanations provides a basis for distinguishing between offences. A completely random combination of any behaviour with any other would also suggest that there is no consistently coherent distinction to support empirically the concepts used by each author. This is, in effect, a null hypothesis that no interpretable relationships will be found between the actions that occur in offences.

A second hypothesis is that a sub-set of conceptually related actions, (e.g., physical and verbal aggression) will consistently happen together. Any such grouping would support the perspective related to that behaviour. If, for example, different forms of aggressive behaviour co-occurred but various attempts at intimacy were quite independent of each other, then there would be support for aggressiveness as a coherent salient aspect of sexual assault, but not for intimacy. In effect, such a result would reduce the number of explanations that are empirically distinct.

A third hypothesis is that all of these aspects of offence behaviour can be identified in details of actual events and that they therefore combine together to provide a composite model of offence behaviour. Such an eclectic model would be expected to have an interpretable structure to it. For instance, those types of behaviour that are associated in the literature, such as the sexual nature of the offence and its violence (cf. Groth, 1979) would be expected to have some empirical relationship distinct, say, from the relationship between the criminal actions and those dealing with the victim as an impersonal sex object (cf. Scully and Marolla, 1983).

Empirical evidence for either the second or third hypothesis would contribute to scientific support for the possibility of offender profiling because it would indicate that there are indeed structured variations between offenders, revealed in what they did when they committed a crime. Furthermore, such a structure, or system of behaviours, could be used as the basis for specific hypotheses about the aspects of behaviour that would be associated with differences between offenders.

This proposal, then, hypothesises that an examination of the behaviours as they occur in actual sexual offences will reveal a structure that reflects the variety of modes of interpersonal interactions that underlie those offences. The study reported here describes an empirical test of that hypothesis.

Relationships between offence and offender characteristics

The study to be reported is part of a series of studies being carried out at the University of Surrey. The central quest throughout this research is to identify associations between aspects of the offender's characteristics and offence behaviour. There are a number of ways in which such associations can be established, but whatever methods are used they will be more powerful in their application if they are part of a logical explanatory framework. The framework (or theoretical stance) adopted in the present paper (first outlined in Canter, 1989) may be characterised as a cognitive social one, in which the offender's interactions with others, on a daily basis, is seen as the key to his criminal behaviour.

This is a generalisation of the hypotheses underlying the study by Silverman et al (1988). They analysed the case records of 1,000 consecutive rape victims seen at a crisis centre. They found that broad differences in the approach to the victim were related to many other aspects of the offender and the offence. They showed that crimes in which an offender used a sudden attack (blitz) and those in which he used a confidence trick form of access (con) were distinct in a number of ways; the victims' characteristics, the rape settings, the victims' activities before they were raped, the assailants' characteristics, and the victims' immediate responses to the assault. The present study is the first step in elaborating a more detailed conceptualisation of sexual assaults and their perpetrators.

A study of the structure of offence behaviour

As discussed, the scientific basis to profiling requires an identification of what the main variations in the actions of offenders in relation to a given offence are. There are many possible aspects of an offence that may be considered as significant, especially if there is a victim's account to consider. The present study was an initial exploration of a range of crimes on which full information was available. It is therefore of interest as an indication whether future research following this approach is likely to be worthwhile.

Sample selection and features considered

A total of 33 offence variables were identified through data available such as victim statements and other police reports, in order to provide a list of categorical descriptions of the behaviour across all the offences. Behavioural variables with very low frequencies across the sample were not included since little would be gained from their inclusion at this feasibility phase of the analysis. Indeed the rare characteristics may be important for linking offences to one individual, but are likely to be unique to particular individuals and therefore of less value in developing general principles. Care was taken to define variables so as to allow an easy decision to be made as to the category of behaviour. All variables were treated as dichotomous with no/yes values based on presence/absence of each behaviour in any one offence.

The full list of variables, with explanatory elaborations, used to describe offence behaviour is given in Appendix I in relation to the five modes of interpersonal interaction discussed above.

Data were collected across 66 offences, made available by a number of English police forces in response to a request for details of sexual assaults against victims unknown to the offender. These offences were committed by 27 offenders. The 33 dichotomous variables across the 66 offences provided the data matrix on which subsequent analysis was conducted.

Smallest space analysis (SSA) of behaviour matrix

These data were subjected to an SSA-I (Lingoes, 1973). In essence, the null hypothesis is that the variables have no comprehensible relationship to each other. In other words, it is possible that those offenders who change their actions in response to the reactions of the victim are not the same as those who talk to the victim and encourage her to indicate her reactions to the attack. It may be a common sense assumption that these two variables will relate to each other because they both indicate a desire to indicate some relationship with the victim, but the SSA allows a test of this assumption and all the other possibilities suggested by the relationship every one of the 33 variables has to every other variable.

Although the literature, reviewed above, does suggest a fivefold way of classifying the variables and this provides a set of hypotheses for the interpretation of the SSA, the use of SSA also allows the generation of hypotheses both about the components of the behaviour under study and about the relationships between those components, the system of behaviour that exists. In other words, the analysis to be presented may best be regarded as both hypothesis testing and also of heuristic value in helping to indicate if there are any directions from the results that can be used to focus future studies aimed at developing profiling.

Smallest Space Analysis (Lingoes, 1973) is a non-metric multidimensional scaling procedure, based upon the assumption that the underlying structure, or system of behaviour, will most readily be appreciated if the relationship between every variable and every other variable is examined. However, an examination of the raw mathematical relationships between all the variables would be difficult to interpret so a geometric (visual) representation of the relationships is produced.

SSA, then, is one of a large number of procedures that represent the correlations between variables as distances in a statistically derived geometric space. Although it was first used a number of years ago (Guttman, 1954) only recently have developments in computers made it readily available for general use. As described by Guttman (1968), Smallest Space Analysis (SSA) was so called because, when compared with other approaches to multidimensional scaling, it produces a solution of smallest dimensionality. This is primarily because it operates on the rank order of the original correlations rather than their absolute values.

The SSA program computes correlation coefficients between all variables, then rank orders these correlations. In this case transforming an original rectangular data matrix into a triangular matrix consisting of correlation coefficients for each variable as correlated with all other variables. It is these correlation coefficients that are used to form a spatial representation of items with points representing variables, the rank order of the distances between points being inversely related to the rank order of the correlations. Iterations are performed comparing the rank order assigned to the correlations with the rank order of the distance while adjustments are made to the geometric representation. The closer the two rank orders the better the 'fit' between the geometric representation and the original correlation matrix, or as it is called technically the lower the 'stress'. The iterations continue until the minimal 'stress' possible is achieved, within the predesignated number of dimensions. A measure of stress called the coefficient of alienation (see Borg and Lingoes, 1987 for details) is used within the computing algorithm as the criterion to use in bringing the iterative procedure to an end. It can therefore be used as a general indication of the degree to which the variables' intercorrelations are represented by their corresponding spatial distances. The smaller the coefficient of alienation, the better is the fit, i.e., the fit of the plot to the original correlation matrix. However, as Borg and Lingoes (1987) emphasise, there is no simple answer to the question of how 'good' or 'bad' the representation is. This will depend upon a complex combination of the number of variables, the amount of error in the data and the logical strength of the interpretation framework.

In the present case the data is mainly derived from statements taken by the police from victims. As such they were not collected for research purposes, nor was the information recorded against a detailed protocol and careful training. Furthermore, the content analysis of this material was an initial exploratory attempt of the possibilities for drawing out clear, descriptive variables from this data. It would therefore be expected that the data was not error free and would contain considerable 'noise' that would reduce the possibility of interpreting the results. On the other hand, the published literature is quite rich in suggestions about the behaviour under study and, as presented above, a reasonably clear set of distinguishing concepts can be derived. A reasonable fit to the conceptual system presented would therefore be acceptable, as of heuristic value for future research, even with a high 'stress' value in the SSA results.

In the SSA configuration, then, in broad terms, the more highly correlated two variables are, the closer will be the points representing those variables in the SSA space. Since the configuration is developed in respect to the relationships among variables and not from their relationship to some given 'dimension', or axis, the orientation in space of the axes of the resulting geometric representation are arbitrary, even though the relationships between the points are replicably determined. Therefore, the pattern of points (regions) can be examined directly without the need to assume underlying orthogonal dimensions.

The testing of the evidence for ways of classifying variables by examination of the regional structure of an SSA is part of an approach to research known as Facet Theory (Canter, 1985). The 'facets' are the overall classification of the types of variables. The spatial contiguity of the points representing them provides a test of the major underlying differences amongst these variables as revealed through their co-occurrence in actual incidents, and is therefore a test as to whether the 'facets' are empirically supported. The SSA representation therefore offers a basis for testing and developing hypotheses about the structure of relationships between offence behaviours. Contiguous behavioural variables, forming an element of an interpretable facet, provide a productive basis for future research to distinguish between offenders.

The postulation of facets goes beyond the rather arbitrary proposals of 'grouping', by using the principle of contiguity (Foa, 1958; Guttman, 1965; and Shye, 1978), which states that because elements in a facet will be functionally related their existence will be reflected in a corresponding empirical structure. In other words, variables that share the same facet elements would be more highly correlated and thus should appear closer together in the multidimensional space than variables not sharing the same element.

This idea of contiguity can be extended as a general, regional hypothesis. Items that have facet elements in common will be found in the same region of space. Likewise, variables which have very low intercorrelations will appear in different regions of the plot, indicating dissimilarity, and no membership of the same facet element. Contiguous regionality in a multidimensional space is a quite specific identification of a facet element, provided a clear statement can be made of what the variables in that region have in common. Of course, once the exploratory phase of hypothesis generation has led to the establishment of facets, or when a literature suggests facets, then the existence of contiguous regions can be used as a strong, precise test of the hypothesised facets. The usual processes of scientific replication can also be carried out.

Areas of the SSA plot which contain few or no points are also of interest. Cases such as this, may indicate weak areas in the data or in fact missing facet elements. Subsequent studies may then be carried out with new data sets to test for the existence of these missing elements. In this way the interplay between the formal theory, as specified in the facets, and the empirical structure, as revealed in the regional contiguity, can lead to the identification of issues not within the original set of data.

The approach taken to hypothesis test and generation, then, is to establish whether the SSA plot, shown in *Figure 1*, has any interpretable regional structure to it. The general hypothesis (null) being tested here is that the variations amongst offenders as discussed above are so diffuse that no coherent interpretation of the SSA plot is possible.

Results of SSA

The SSA-I was carried out on an association matrix of Jaccard coefficients, these being the most appropriate measures of association for this type of binary data. The 3-dimensional solution has a Guttman-Lingoes' coefficient of alienation $= 0.22$

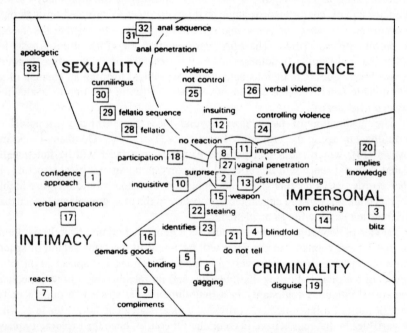

Figure 1 SSA of behaviour in 66 sexual assaults with regional interpretations. (Numbers refer to variables in Appendix I. Labels are brief summaries of content analysis categories.)

with 22 iterations, indicating a reasonable fit for this type of data. However, the interpretation of this configuration turns out to be very close to the regional structure of the 2-dimensional solution (which has a coefficient of alienation of 0.30 in 11 iterations) so for simplicity the 2-dimensional structure will be presented. Figure 1 shows this projection of the resulting configuration.

For clarity it should be reiterated, each point is a variable describing offence behaviour. The numbers refer to the variables as listed in Appendix I, although for simplicity a brief title for the variable has also been placed on the plot. The closer any two points the more likely are the actions they represent to co-occur in offences, in comparison with points that are farther apart.

Focal aspects of rapes

A first stage in the interpretation of Figure 1, to test the hypotheses and explore the structure of offence behaviour, in the present case, is to consider the frequency of occurrence of each of the variables. Because they are all binary indications of the occurrence of actions each variable has an associated frequency in the whole sample. The SSA is derived from the associations between the variables and so has no inevitable link to their overall frequency. However, with dichotomous variables

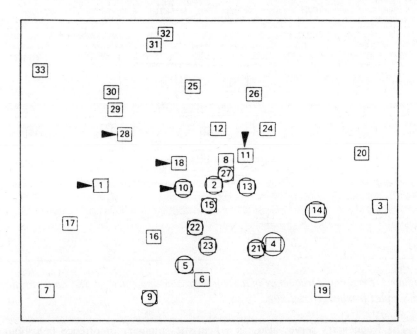

Figure 2 SSA of 66 assaults illustrating one offence as circles, one as arrows. (Numbers refer to variables in Appendix I.)

it is possible for those variables that are frequent to have higher associations with each other, unless there is one or more subsets of variables with lower frequencies that co-occur with high probability. The relationship, then, between the frequencies of the actions and the SSA structure is not artifactual. It is an empirical one open to some substantive meaning. *Figure 3* presents the frequencies of occurrence of every offence action.

As can be seen it is possible to draw very clear contours on this diagram to cover variables that occur in more than 65% of cases, 40% to 60%, 25% to 35%, 20%

to 25% and less than 15% of cases (Figure 3). This polar sequence lends strong support to the focal (polarising) nature of the high frequency variables. It also indicates those actions that differentiate between offences, being at the edge of the plot. As discussed later, the identification of a high frequency core and a polarising sequence from it also opens up the possibility that the activities around this circular structure coalesce along radii, creating wedges of modes of interaction, relating directly to the decreasing frequency of those particular sets of variables.

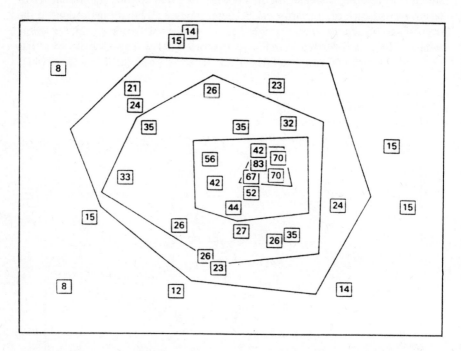

Figure 3 Percentage frequency of assault behaviour indicated on SSA configuration with equal frequency contours.

The frequencies serve, also, as a heuristic summary of offence behaviour, showing that those behaviours further out from the core are the ones that are most distinct, giving any particular offence its specific characteristics.

The hierarchy of frequencies indicate that there are certain activities that are conceptually central to rape, in other words, at the core of sexual assault. The activities at the outer rim reflect different aspects of the same overall phenomena, differing in their reference to some common focus.

This focus and the referents that make it up can be given a clearer meaning by considering those items at the centre of the plot. Such items share most with all the others around them and so are both literally and metaphorically central to the issues being examined. In Figures 1, 2 and 3 the following variables are central:

vaginal intercourse (27)
no reaction to the victim (8)
impersonal language (11)
surprise attack (2)
victim's clothing disturbed (13)

This core is not the overtly aggressive set of actions that Groth's (1979) typology would emphasise. It includes sexual intercourse, but not the variety of sexual activity that might have been expected if sexual desire was a totally dominating aspect of the offence. Nor are those variables central that indicate a desire to relate to the victim as might be indicated from Marshall's (1989) considerations. The discussion that best fits these variables is that of Scully and Marolla (1983), indicating an impersonal, surprise attack in which the victim's response is irrelevant to the offender. The five variables here could be regarded as the *sine qua non* of a sexual assault; dealing with the victim impersonally with a surprise attack disturbing her clothes and having vaginal intercourse. Their position at the centre of the plot, therefore, does add credibility to the whole structure and shows that the use of a woman as a sexual object is at the core of sexual assault.

Modes of interaction with the victim

The results allow a further development of the idea of sexual assault being essentially an interaction with a woman as an object, by the identification of the other related regions in the plot. Because there is an interpretable core to this plot it is appropriate to consider the various emphases that can be given to this focus by examining the variables around the plot. This allows a further test of the hypotheses derived from the published literature, by exploring whether any of the emphases in the literature have empirical support and, if they do, how they may relate to each other.

Attempted intimacy with the victim

As noted earlier, some discussions of rape suggest that it is the lack of ability to form intimate relationships with women that is an important aspect of the motivation to rape (Marshall, 1989). If this were ever dominant in rape then it would be expected that those actions that would indicate an attempt at intimacy, or at least some preparedness to relate to the victim as a person rather than an object, would co-occur in some rapes. Five variables, particularly, indicate that the offender is attempting to, or at least not deterred from, entering into some sort of personal relationship with the victim:

the victim's reaction influences/deters the offender (variable 7)
the offender requires the victim to participate verbally during the assault (17)
the offender requires the victim to participate physically during the assault (18)

the approach is one of a confidence trick (1)
the offender is inquisitive about the victim (10)
offender compliments the victim (9)
the offender apologises to the victim (33)

These seven variables can be found in the lower left quadrant of the plot. There is therefore some support for this interpersonal aspect of the offence being a coherent and possibly significant feature of offence behaviour.

This distinct aspect of offence behaviour provides an initial heuristic for generating hypotheses of associations between offender and offence. Those offences in which most of these five actions happen, especially those actions which are less frequent in the present sample, would be hypothesised to be correlated with significant aspects of an offender's interpersonal background. For example, following Marshall's (1989) arguments, it would be hypothesised that these offenders would have had difficulty in formulating intimate relationships with women, but that they may well have attempted this. For example, marriage to a younger woman with a very short courtship and subsequent distancing in their relationship would be predicted. Considerably more research, however, is needed both to replicate this facet element and to establish the hypothesised correlations.

Sexual behaviour

Although it is often underemphasised in clinical accounts of rape, there can be little debate about the fact that sexual activity is a crucial component of the attack. There is therefore an important question about whether the different types of sexual behaviour are related and form distinct constituents of an attack or whether they are diffuse, related more to other aspects of the offender's behaviour.

Six variables dealt specifically with the sexual behaviour:

vaginal intercourse (27)
fellatio initially (28)
fellatio as part of the attack sequence (29)
cunnilingus (30)
initial anal intercourse (31)
anal intercourse as part of the offence sequence (32)

The top left quadrant of the plot contains all these variables.

It is interesting to note that vaginal intercourse is central to the whole plot, so that the upper left quadrant is defined by the other sexual activities.

The sexual variables, then, do form a region indicating that together they provide an aspect of offence behaviour that needs to be considered further. This accords with the arguments of Scully and Marolla (1983) that the desire for certain sorts of sexual experience is a significant facet of rape, leading to hypotheses that when a variety of sexual activities take place the offender may have be found to have either considerable earlier sexual experience or a great interest in such experience as revealed through a collection of pornographic material. In general, however, the existence of a distinct region in the SSA configuration indicates that the actual sexual aspects of a sexual assault should not be undervalued, as some authorities have tended to do.

Overt violence and aggression

The clinical literature on sexual offences usually places most emphasis on the fact that these are aggressive violent attacks. Violence therefore seems to be a salient issue for consideration. Groth (1979), in particular, as discussed above, argues that aggression is a primary motivation in sexual assault. The following four variables dealt directly with overt violence and aggression:

violence used as means of controlling the victim (24)
violence used, but not as a means of control (25)
aggressive verbal behaviour (26)
insulting language (12)

All four variables are to be found in the top right quadrant of Figure 1. These therefore appear to be coherent aspects of the offence behaviour. For some offenders, then, this is a distinct aspect of their offending. However, it is a distinct aspect which is not overtly apparent in many offences. Their relationship to prior history of aggressiveness is worthy of exploration.

The adjacency of these aggression variables to the sexual variables is of interest, showing that they are quite likely to be linked, as the clinical literature suggests. In particular the closeness of the violence not used as control variable (25) and the anal intercourse variables (31 and 32) does indicate that this particular form of sexual act is likely to be associated with violence and may indeed be motivated by similar psychological processes.

Impersonal interaction

The antithesis of the actions that indicate the offender is trying to relate to a person (as presented in (1) above) are the actions that treat the victim very much as an object, dealing with her as an entity entirely for the criminal's use. Six variables relate to these aspects of the offence:

'blitz' attack (3)
impersonal language (11)
no response to the victim's reactions (8)
surprise attack (2)
tearing of victim's clothing (14)
victim's clothing disturbed by offender (13)

These six variables are all to be found in the middle right segment of the plot. They therefore provide a graphic combination of quite wide ranging behaviours indicating the offender's callous disinterest in his victim. They do, however, include a number of variables that were identified as having a high frequency and at the core of sexual assaults. The existence of a distinct region indicates that for some offenders this may be the dominant characteristic of their offending even though overall offender behaviour is somewhat biased to this aspect of assaulting, as reflected in the off-centre position of the 'core' actions.

The variable recording that the offender implies knowledge of the victim (20) is also at the edge of this region. This is difficult to interpret at this stage but possibly implies that the offender had prior knowledge of the victim, having identified her as a desirable object.

The distant, impersonal contact with the victim, indicated by this sub-set of variables is hypothesised to be a reflection of a general approach to women that would be apparent in the offender's daily life. He would be predicted to be known as someone who does not regard women as experiencing the world in the same way he does, seeing them as vessels for men's desires. Clearly, such a perspective on an offender has implications for approaches to therapy as well as for assisting criminal investigations.

Criminal behaviour and intent

Rapists often also operate as criminals committing crimes not obviously sexually motivated. There are also a number of aspects of their sexual crimes that have non-sexual but still distinctly criminal components, such as the wearing of a mask to hide the offender's identity, or the carrying of a weapon to the crime scene. The question therefore arises as to whether these actions have some relationship and coherence.

There are seven variables that can be interpreted as reflecting criminality:

the use of bindings (5)
the use of gagging (6)
stealing from the victim (22)
the use of some form of disguise (19)
blindfolding the victim (4)
demanding goods (16)
controlling the victim with a weapon (15)

Some of these actions may be considered as more directly related to sexual sadism, notably binding and gagging, with the implication that the offender obtained some sexual gratification from these actions. That, of course, may be true in some offences, but the position of these actions in the SSA configuration near to wearing a disguise and carrying a weapon indicate that in the present sample the behaviour of binding and gagging is more readily associated with criminality of the actions. The position of these variables on the opposite side of the plot from the sexuality and violence variables also supports the proposal that, within these offences at least, the behaviours do not indicate sexual sadism.

All seven of these criminality variables, then, are in the same regional segment of the plot at the bottom right. Interestingly two other variables are clearly within the same region; the threat to the victim not to tell anyone about the offence (21), and the informing of the victim that she is known by the offender (23). It is not difficult to conceptualise these actions as part of the criminal repertoire.

Taken together these nine variables indicate an emphasis to a criminal's behaviour that, if present to any degree, would be hypothesised to correlate with aspects of his previous criminal offences. In particular, it is hypothesised that offenders who commit many of these actions are likely to have extensive history of non-sexual crimes.

Summary and conclusions

In order to establish whether it is possible to derive the characteristics of a criminal from his actions when offending ('offender profiling') it was proposed that it was first necessary to demonstrate that the behaviour of offenders during a crime had some comprehensible coherence to them. Focusing on sexual assaults against strangers, theoretical accounts of variations between offenders were reviewed in order to establish the range of offence behaviours that should be examined. This review revealed that there were a variety of proposals as to the differences between sexual assaulters, some of these being contradictory.

From these considerations five aspects of a sexual assault were identified. These aspects provided a set of hypotheses about the behaviours that would co-occur during an assault. To test these hypotheses 66 offences, committed by 27 offenders were content analysed into 33 behavioural categories. The occurrence of these categories of behaviour across all offences was examined using SSA-I.

The results of the SSA indicate that sexual assault can be understood as various ways of carrying out sexual acts in an impersonal fashion, treating the unwilling victim as an object. The results, further, lend support to all five different aspects identified from the published literature. They show that the various explanations given may be construed as different emphases of an assault, different ways of engaging in rape, any offence drawing on one or more aspect.

This set of aspects of elements that make up a rape attack form a circular order in the SSA space. This implies that those regions which are closer together are more likely to contain actions that occur in the same offence. The sequence around the plot is therefore of some substantive, theoretical interest.

Broadly, the actions on the top half of the SSA deal with actions of interest, and often noted by those with a psychopathological perspective on rape such as Groth (1979). They cover the variety of sexual activities and the aggressive acts. As such they cover actions that may be akin to the expressive aggression to which Prentky et al (1985) draw attention. Their concept of 'instrumental aggression' may be more closely aligned with the behaviours in the lower half of the plot. These actions are also more in accord with those perspectives that take sociological or social psychological perspectives (e.g., Scully and Marolla, 1983), covering actions that are very impersonal, criminally oriented. Interestingly the social psychological view of Marshall (1989) falls between these two regions.

The closeness of the sexual activity to the violence does lend credence to the view that many sexual offences have a strongly violent aspect. The adjacency of this violence to the impersonal behaviour does reflect rather well the ways in which the one can merge into the other. The criminal behaviour is adjacent to the impersonal behaviour, reflecting the likelihood that criminality is indeed antisocial in the strong sense that it relates to an unpreparedness, or inability, to relate to other people. However, there are offences in which this inability is shown through the inappropriate attempt to form a relationship with the victim, as revealed by the adjacency of the 'intimacy' region. That such actions should be next to the sexual behaviour is also logical in that, on occasion, that implies overlapping motivations.

The sequence of types of activity shown in Figure 1, from sexual activity through criminal behaviour back to sexual activity again is a circular sequence. No simple linear dimension running from one obvious extreme to the other can be identified. This leads to the hypothesis that all five types of activity represent different emphases of the same overall phenomena, rather than providing positions along a continuum. A further test of the validity of this hypothesis of a circular order of activities is provided by considering the frequencies of the actions, as indicated in Figure 3. As has been noted, although there is no statistical necessity for the higher or lower frequencies to be found in a specific region of the plot, it none the less turns out to be the case that the lower the frequencies the further are the actions from the centre of the configuration.

Yet quite independently of the frequencies, it is the nature of an SSA configuration that those actions at the centre of the configuration are the ones that empirically have most in common with each other. Those at the periphery are the most functionally discrete. Therefore, in the present results, as action frequencies become lower so those actions became more distinctly part of the most functionally specific regions of the plot. This means that there are some actions that have a lot in common with each other, providing a core to these sexual assaults, whereas other actions reflect more specific emphases for those assaults. In other words, the distribution of the frequencies support the hypothesis of a coherent system of behaviour that has different emphases to it, adding weight to the validity of the circular order.

The overall combination of the frequencies and the radial elements (a 'radex', Guttman, 1954) all therefore reflects different aspects of the same overall phenomena, differing in their reference around the focus of the victim being treated as a sexual object by the offender, yet in a variety of different ways.

This radex model of sexual offending has a number of heuristic values. For example, examination of it indicates gaps in the empirical space where no variables are found. It can be hypothesised that the current sample does not include actions which would have gone into those locations. Future data can be used to test this hypothesis. One such instance is the occurrence of overtly sadistic aggressive behaviour in which the victim is bound as a form of humiliating and is arousing to the offender. There is no indication that any such extreme form of sexual sadism was present in the sample. If it were it is hypothesised that an SSA would place it at the extreme edge of the plot in the top region of the aggressive behaviour, but close to the boundary with the sexual behaviour. Other researchers will be able to derive many other similar hypotheses.

A further heuristic value derives from the fact that all five aspects of sexual assault contribute to all offences, but there is likely to be different combinations of constituents for different individuals. The differences in an offender's repertoire of offence behaviour can therefore be clearly established. Establishing what these combinations of major classes of behaviour are is an important objective for future research. It could be used for considering how an offender develops over a series of offences or more pragmatically for establishing whether two or more offences were committed by the same person.

Each of these five aspects also has the potential of correlating with different sets of characteristics of offenders. Study of these correlations will be a major step in the furtherance of a scientific base to offender profiling.

Appendix I: Variables used to describe offender's behaviour during an offence as derived from content analysis of victim statements

Coding of variables

Thirty three offence variables were created from a content analysis of available police records and victim statements in order to provide a list of elements common to offences. Variables with a very low frequency were not included. Care was taken to describe the definition of variables so as to eliminate discrepancies in category assignment. All variables are dichotomous with values based on the presence/absence of each category of behaviour. A description of the categorisation scheme is given below.

Offence characteristics

Variable 1. Confidence approach

1 = No   2 = Yes

The style of approach used by the offender in which any ploy or subterfuge is used in order to make contact with the victim prior to the commencement of the assault: this would include any verbal contact - questions asked, false introductions, story told.

Variable 2. Surprise attack

1 = No   2 = Yes

The immediate attack on the victim, whether preceded by a confidence approach or not, where force is used to obtain control of the victim: force in respect of this variable includes threat with or without a weapon. Violence is for the physical control of the victim, i.e., exercised against the victim in order to render her available to the offender, but not the actions covered in variable three.

Variable 3. Blitz attack

1 = No   2 = Yes

The sudden and immediate use of violence, whether preceded by a confidence approach or not, which incapacitates the victim: typically this is the sudden blow which leaves the victim unable to respond or react to the attack. This variable focuses on the extreme violence of the initial assault which leaves the victim incapable of reaction.

Variable 4. Blindfold

1 = No   2 = Yes

The use at any time during the attack of any physical interference with the victim's ability to see: this only includes the use of articles and not verbal threat or the temporary use of the offender's hands.

Variable 5. Binding

$$1 = No \qquad 2 = Yes$$

As above in respect of the use of articles to disable the victim: the categorisation does not include the possible situational effect of partial stripping of the victim, nor the temporary use of manual control of the victim.

Variable 6. Gagging

$$1 = No \qquad 2 = Yes$$

As above in respect of the prevention of noise: this does not include the manual gagging of victims commonly associated with the attack variables.

Variable 7. Reaction (1) Deter/change

$$1 = No \qquad 2 = Yes$$

One of two reaction variables, to examine how the offender copes with, or reacts to, active victim resistance: the resistance of the victim can be verbal or physical but does not include the act of crying alone. The categorisation addresses the offender and not the victim. This variable assigns a 2 to the offender who is deterred or, who changes or negotiates his intended actions upon victim reaction. The category emphasises the change or negotiation of any act as a result of victim resistance.

Variable 8. Reaction (2) No difference

$$1 = No \qquad 2 = Yes$$

As above, but this variable categorises those offenders whose action and/or intentions are not changed by victim resistance; this offender will continue the assault against an actively resisting victim. An offence in which the victim offers no resistance will be found in the categories of 1 on both variables 7 and 8.

Variable 9. Language (1) Compliments

$$1 = No \qquad 2 = Yes$$

The first of five variables concerned with the complexities of what is said by the offender to the victim. This is not necessarily the result of verbal interchange but is focused on the style of speech used by the offender, in the non-violent context.

This variable assigns a category of 2 to those offences in which the offender compliments the victim, usually on some aspect of her appearance.

Variable 10. Language (2) Inquisitive

1 = No   2 = Yes

The second language variable categorises the offender's speech in being inquisitive of the victim. This includes any questions asked about the victim's life-style, associates etc. There are other variables which deal with the identifying of the victim and the requirement, for example, of the victim to participate in the acts committed against her. This therefore focuses on the questions asked of the victim which are those of a non sexual nature.

Variable 11. Language (3) Impersonal

1 = No   2 = Yes

This language variable categorises those aspects of the offender's impersonal/instructive dealings with the victim. The focus is the impersonal style of the offender rather than the categorised differences between personal/impersonal. The personal style of speech will be shown in one or more of the other language variables.

Variable 12. Language (4) Demeaning/insulting

1 = No   2 = Yes

A non-violence language variable which categorises offender's speech with or towards the victim that is demeaning and/or insulting: this would include profanities directed against the victim herself or women in general.

The focus of this variable is the insult and not sexually orientated comment.

Variable 13. Victim clothing disturbed

1 = No   2 = Yes

One of two clothing variables: this categorises the offender's removal of the victim's clothing himself. The alternative category, i.e., category 1, includes the act of disrobing carried out by the victim. This act is always at the instruction of the offender and therefore the same category is used in the circumstances of a naked or semi-naked victim. The focus of this variable is on the actions of the offender and can be seen in comparison with the activities of the offender in the second clothing variable (14). It categorises any act of removal by the offender as 2, regardless of whether the victim assisted or not.

Variable 14. Victim clothing cut/torn

1 = No   2 = Yes

This variable addresses the offender's removal of clothing by particular methods. Although there are obvious differences in the tearing or cutting of clothing, this category deals with the offender who is prepared to use an apparently more violent style in his treatment of the victim. Category 1 covers the disturbance of clothing as well as the undressed victim. The focus is on the removal of clothing and not what the offender does with it after removal.

Variable 15. Control weapon

$$1 = \text{Threat} \quad 2 = \text{Weapon}$$

The categories differentiate those offenders who are prepared to display a weapon in order to control the victim, from those who do not. Threat of the possession of a weapon and threat of physical presence are coded as '1'.

Variable 16. Demand goods

$$1 = \text{No} \quad 2 = \text{Yes}$$

This variable categorises the offender's approach to the victim that includes a demand for goods or money. Importantly the demand categorised in this context is that which is made in the initial stages of the attack. A later variable deals generally with stealing from the victim (V22).

Variable 17. Victim participation verbal

$$1 = \text{No} \quad 2 = \text{Yes}$$

There are two variables dealing with the requirement of the victim to participate in the offence. Both have been found to occur at the instruction of the offender. Those instructions may appear in many forms, therefore this categorisation deals with the offender's requirement that the victim say words or phrases to him at his insistence. The category does not cover the occasions where an offender directs a question to the victim which does not appear to require her to answer.

Variable 18. Victim participation acts

$$1 = \text{No} \quad 2 = \text{Yes}$$

As above, but this is categorised to cover the offender's requirement that the victim physically participate. The acts demanded of the victim are those which may be in association with specific sexual demands made of her but are in addition to those sexual acts. Therefore an example may be the requirement made of the victim to kiss the offender, or to place her arms around him.

In other words, it focuses on the requirements that the victim participate in any act committed against her; in this context the expectation is to differentiate between those offenders who will commit, say, fellatio against the victim and those who commit the same act but accompanied by instructions to do specific acts associated with oral sex.

Variable 19. Disguise

$1 =$ No $2 =$ Yes

Various disguises can and are worn by offenders, categorically the definition of them all would result in an unwieldy variable. The category of disguise in this variable, therefore, deals with those offenders who wear any form of disguise.

Variable 20. Implied knowledge

$1 =$ No $2 =$ Yes

Instances occur within the attacks, at various times, in which the offender implies knowing the victim. This categorisation records the implication that the offender knew or knew of the victim before the sexual assault.

Variable 21. Threat ... No Report

$1 =$ No $2 =$ Yes

This is specific categorisation of the verbalised threat made to a victim that she should not report the incident to the police or any other person. This may take many forms however the specific threat against the victim in this context is plain when made.

Variable 22. Stealing

$1 =$ No $2 =$ Yes

The general category of stealing differentiate those offenders who do steal from those who do not.

Variable 23. Identifies victim

$1 =$ No $2 =$ Yes

This categorisation covers offences in which offenders take steps to obtain or attempt to obtain from the victim the details which would identify her. This may take many forms including verbal approaches, the examination of personal belongings before or after the actual sexual assault, or indeed the stealing of personal identifying documents following the assault. The act is complete if the offender acts in any way that allows him to infer to the victim that he has, or can, identify her.

Variable 24. Violence (1) Control

$1 =$ No $2 =$ Yes

This categorisation of 'violence to control' identifies the use of force which is more than the physical control of the victim and which, situationally, is not the initial attack to obtain control of the victim.

The category in this variable describes the punching, kicking etc of the victim in order to reinforce the control the offender is seeking to exercise on the victim.

Variable 25. Violence (2) Not control

$$1 = No \qquad 2 = Yes$$

This categorisation here deals with the offender who is prepared to use excessive violence in retaliation to perceived resistance or, in some cases, the use of violence apparently for its own sake.

Variable 26. Violence (3) Verbal

$$1 = No \qquad 2 = Yes$$

This variable is distinct from those dealing with the speech types directed at the victim which can be categorised as impersonal (V11), or demeaning (V12). The categorisation in this variable is to address the use of intimidating language in the form of threats to maim or kill which are not necessarily associated with control or resistance. Focus is therefore on verbal violence which is *not* associated with control or resistance.

Variable 27. Vaginal penetration

$$1 = No \qquad 2 = Yes$$

This variable covers whether vaginal penetration was achieved or attempted.

Variable 28. Fellatio (1)

$$1 = No \qquad 2 = Yes$$

This is one of two variables dealing with the forced oral penetration of the victim. The categories of this variable deal only with whether oral penetration was carried out or attempted.

Variable 29. Fellatio (2) In sequence

$$1 = No \qquad 2 = Yes$$

The second variable of fellatio categorises offenders' requirements that their victims submit to oral penetration and are those whose performance of the act is part of a sequence of sexual acts. The offender who does not engage in the oral penetration of the victim will be identified as being categorised as '1' in both variables 28 and 29. Similarly the offence in which only oral sexual activity occurs will be differentiated by being categorised as '2' in variable 28, and '1' in the other sexual act variables.

Variable 30. Cunnilingus

$$1 = No \qquad 2 = Yes$$

This variable deals with the performance of a particular sexual act committed against the victim's genitalia by the offender's use of his mouth. In the present sample there is no sequential variable in this context as to date no cases have been seen where this act is performed alone. There is always some other sexual activity accompanying the act of cunnilingus.

Variable 31. Anal penetration

$$1 = No \qquad 2 = Yes$$

This is one of two variables dealing with penetration *per* anus committed against a victim. This categorisation deals only with those cases where the act was carried out. In the present sample categorised cases the penetration is by male organ only. It includes attempts where there is clear indication of intent.

Variable 32. Anal penetration in sequence

$$1 = No \qquad 2 = Yes$$

The second variable dealing with anal assault: the category addresses anal assault in sequence with other sexual acts. The offence in which anal penetration occurs or is attempted will be categorised '1' on both variables. Similarly the attacks with an anal assault only will be categorised as '2' in variable 31, and '1' in respect of the other sexual act variables.

Variable 33. Apologetic

$$1 = No \qquad 2 = Yes$$

This is a further language variable to deal with the specific apologetic speech used by an offender, most typically at the end of a sexual assault.

Acknowledgement

We are grateful to Milena Kovacik and Katherine King-Johannessen for their contribution to this paper. This research benefited from Home Office Contract No. SC/88/22/247/1 and support from Surrey Police Constabulary.

References

Ault, R.L. & Reese, J.T. (1980), 'A Psychological Assessment of Crime Profiling', *FBI Law Enforcement Bulletin*, Vol. 49(3), pp. 22-5.
Borg, I. & Lingoes, J. (1987), *Multidimensional Similarity Analysis*, Springer

Verlag, New York.

Canter, D. (1985), *Facet Theory: Approaches to Social Research*, Springer-Verlag New York.

Canter, D. (1988), 'To Catch a Rapist', *New Society*, 4 March.

Canter, D. (1989), 'Offender Profiling', *The Psychologist*, Vol. 2, pp. 12-16.

Davies, G.M. (1988), 'Use of Video in Child Abuse Trials', *The Psychologist*, Vol. 1, pp. 20-2.

Foa, U.G. (1958), 'The Contiguity Principle in the Structure of Interpersonal Relation', *Human Relations*, II, pp. 229-38.

Geberth, V.J. (1983), *Practical Homicide Investigation,* Elsevier, New York.

Groth, N.A. (1979), *Men Who Rape: The Psychology of the Offender,* Plenum, New York.

Guttmacher, M.S. & Weihofen, H. (1952), *Psychiatry and Law*, Norton, New York.

Guttman, L. (1954), 'A New Approach to Factor Analysis: The Radex', in Lazarsfield, P.F. (ed.), *Mathematical Thinking in the Social Science,* Free Press, London.

Guttman, L. (1965), 'A faceted Definition of Intelligence', *Studies in Psychology, Scripta Hierosolymitana*, Vol. 14, pp. 166-8, Hebrew University, Jerusalem.

Guttman. L. (1968), 'A General Nonmetric Technique for Finding the Smallest Coordinate Space for a Configuration Point', *Psychometrika*, Vol. 33 (3), pp. 469-506.

Hazelwood, R.R. (1983), 'The Behaviour-oriented Interview of Rape Victims: The Key to Profiling', *FBI Law Enforcement Bulletin*, pp. 1-8.

Holmes, R.M. & DeBurger, J. (1988), *Serial Murder,* Sage, London.

Kocis, L. (1982), 'Posudzovanie sexualnych delikventov', in *Forenzne Aspekty Sexuality, Sexualita zeny*, Zbornik referatov: Kosice, September, pp. 186-94.

Lingoes, J. (1973), 'The Guttman-Lingoes Non-metric Program Series', MA thesis, University of Michigan.

Lloyd, Ch. & Walmsley, R. (1989), *Changes in Rape Offences and Sentencing* (Home Office research study No. 105), HMSO, London.

Marshall, W.L. (1989), 'Intimacy, Loneliness and Sexual Offenders', *Behavioural Research in Therapy*, Vol. 27(5), pp. 491-503.

Mulvihill, D., Tumin, M. & Curtis, L. (1969), *Crimes of Violence. A Staff Report Submitted to the National Commission on the Causes and Prevention of Violence*, Vols. 11-13, US Government Printing Office, Washington DC.

Pinizzotto, A.J. (1984), 'Forensic Psychology: Criminal Personality Profiling', *Journal of Police Science and Administration*, Vol. 12(1), pp. 32-40.

Prentky, R.A., Cohen, M.L. & Seghorn, T. (1985), 'Development of a Rational Taxonomy for the Classification of Sexual Offenders: Rapists', *Bulletin of the American Academy of Psychiatry and the Law*, Vol. 13, pp. 39-70.

Rada, R.T. (1978), 'Psychological Factors in Rapist Behaviour', in Rada, R.T. (ed.), *Clinical Aspects of the Rapist*, Grune and Stratton, New York.

Rossi, D. (1982), 'Crime Scene Behavioural Analysis: Another Tool for the Law Enforcement Investigator', Official proceedings of the 88th Annual IACP Conference, *The Police Chief,* January, pp. 156-59.

Scully, D. & Marolla, J. (1983), 'Incarcerated Rapists: Exploring a Sociological Model', Final Report for Dept. of Health and Human Services, Rockville, Maryland NIMH.

Shye, S. (1978), *Theory Construction and Data Analysis in the Behavioural Sciences,* Jossey Bass, San Fransisco.

Silverman, D.C., Kalich, S.M., Bowie, S.I. & Edbiel, S.E. (1988), 'Blitz Rape and Confidence Rape: A Typology Applied to 1,000 Consecutive Cases', *American Journal of Psychiatry*, Vol.145(11), pp. 1438-41.

Symons, D. (1979), *The Evolution of Human Sexuality,*Oxford University Press, Oxford.

Vorpogel, R.E. (1982), 'Painting Psychological Profiles, Charlatism, Charisma, or a New Science?', *The Police Chief*, January, pp. 156-9.

9 The Environmental Range of Serial Rapists

Abstract

A model of individual sexual offenders' spatial activity was developed based upon 45 British male sexual assaulters who had committed at least two assaults. For each offender a separate map was produced indicating the spatial locations of his offences and residence. A *Marauder* model and a *Commuter* model of offenders' spatial behaviour was proposed. As an elaboration of the Marauder model, the *Circle* and *Range* hypotheses were tested against the sample of offenders. Results of the study support the Marauder model showing that most of the sample (87%) move out from their home base in a region around that base to carry out their attacks. The antithetical Commuter model was not supported within the sample. The Circle and Range Hypotheses were supported demonstrating that offenders operate within a distinct offence region (in 91% of cases) and that the distance they travel to offend correlates directly with distances between offences ($r = 0.93$, p < 0.001). The findings clearly indicate that there is a basis for model of offence venue choice by individuals within the sample. The present study supports the value of a theory of *domocentricity* within offenders' lives and offers potential applicability to the solving of crimes.

Introduction

Many studies have shown that offenders usually do not travel very far from home to commit crimes (White, 1932; Pyle, 1974; Repetto, 1974; Curtis 1974; Kind, 1987). Shaw and McKay illustrated this general trend as long ago as 1942 in their Chicago studies. They established that there is a limited area of zones in which offenders will offend and that these zones were geographically close to the zones in which the offenders lived. However the majority of the research undertaken to date has involved case studies of, for example, classic crime series like 'the Yorkshire Ripper' (Kind, 1987). Alternatively they have considered the aggregate pattern of the spatial activity of a sample of criminals (e.g. Pyle, 1974). Results from such work has provided useful case and population characteristics. In contrast to previous studies of offender movement that have emphasised the aggregate geographical behaviour of offenders, the present study explores directly the psychological question of the extent to which a general model can be developed that is applicable to any individual offender's spatial activity.

Developing a model of the sequential spatial behaviour of offenders requires tests of the validity of various conceptualisations of the psychological processes which determine where an offender chooses to commit a crime. A robust model would also be of practical value to criminal investigators because it could indicate the likely area of the offender's residence.

The starting point for any theory of an offender's selection of the venue of his crime is the hypothesis that the choice of crime venues relates to some kind of home or base from which the individual operates. This hypothesis is based on the view that the offenders for whom an environmental psychology model is developed will not be random drifters of no fixed abode, but will be residing at one or more locations from which they travel to commit their crimes.

Although the environmental cognition literature is not explicit on the point, there is an implicit assumption throughout such studies that a significant determinant of the mental representations of places a person develops is the location of a person's home (as for example reviewed by Golledge, 1987). The proposition is therefore that the 'domocentric' locational experiences of law abiding citizens are a reasonable starting point for building models of criminals' movements. The potential validity of such a proposition is supported by Amir's (1971) finding that even individuals who commit the impetuous crime of rape do operate from a fixed point. Amir's account of Philadelphia police file data (1958-1960) draws attention to the value of understanding more about the psychological processes underlying a criminal's spatial behaviour, raising questions about the significance of the 'fixed point' to the offender and the ways in which it might determine the location of his offences.

In contrast to the 'fixed point' having any personal significance to the offender, Shaw and McKay (1942) of the 'Chicago School' proposed that offenders who operate within city centres are reacting to processes beyond their personal experience. They state that behaviour can be explained in terms of the structure of the urban environment. For Shaw and McKay it is the organisational geometry of cities that gives a pattern to criminal activity. They would thus suggest an arbitrary relationship between offences and between offences and residence other than that the offences are enclosed by a socially recognised 'city centre'.

A somewhat different geographical emphasis is given by Rengert and Wasilchick (1985). They emphasise the importance of the journeys a criminal habitually takes around his home ground. They conducted detailed interviews with 31 burglars, and found a strong likelihood of crime being located on and around the pathways and routes that the burglar habitually used in non-criminal activities. Such journeys through familiar territory are thought to provide information around which an offender could plan his next crime, and that it is this process of information gathering that gives shape to the area in which a person chooses to commit his crimes. They go further to suggest a simple model for offenders' behaviour. The offender in this model is more likely to attack on 'his way home'. Thus the offender will operate within an area which is defined by his home and a base which he frequents, for example his work, local bar or restaurant.

Brantingham and Brantingham (1981) have proposed more affectively based processes for crimes taking place in the area around a criminal's home. They suggest that the security offered by familiarity with the area would outweigh risks of being recognised in the commission of an offence. However, the avoidance of being recognised near a crime scene would lead to the existence of a minimum distance around the home in which the offender would tend not to offend. Brantingham and Brantingham (1981) do provide some aggregate evidence for such a 'safety zone'. Their arguments therefore lend support to the hypothesis that offenders will tend to offend not only within an area around their home but that there will be a maximum and minimum range of distances from home in which they offend.

Capone and Nichols (1975) provide evidence that for robbery, there may indeed be some sort of criminal range. They argue that the offender's goal in crimes of this type are focused on personal gain. Thus the robber will operate within an area which yields the greatest profit and will be looking to identify those areas which have the best opportunities for success. The generality of these findings across different types of crime is an important question. It assumes that an offender in a robbery is maximising his gain for minimum effort and will therefore travel the minimum safe distance that will offer the prospect of a successful crime. Can the same assumption of economic logic be applied to crimes that may have a more overtly emotional nature such as rape, or crimes in which there is a more considered overt risk for larger scale gain, such as armed bank robbery? Capone and Nichols show that there is a significant difference in the lengths of armed and non-armed robbery trips, with armed trips having a greater mean distance. The present study focuses on rape, leaving robbery for future research.

There is some evidence that rapists do have similar geographical patterns to burglars. LeBeau (1987) used centrography (originally developed by Sviatlovsky and Eells, 1937) to defend the idea of a structure to the spatial offence behaviour of the individual rapist. Centrography 'allows one to assess and measure the average location, dispersion, movements and directional change of a phenomenon through time' (LeBeau, 1987). The sample of offenders used was 'all the lone-assistant rapes reported in the San Diego police department in 1971 to 1975'. He suggests that the offender may operate from a clear home or base, presenting evidence for a general geographical pattern of rapes around the home of the rapist.

In a further elaboration of these suggestions LeBeau (1987a) points out that although chronic serial rapists in San Diego that he studied do vary considerably in the distance they travel from their homes, they restrict their 'attacks to within one-half of a mile from his previous attacks' (p. 325). LeBeau (1987a) supports this conclusion with year on year aggregate figures so it is difficult to establish exactly how individual offenders fit into this picture. Furthermore, there is the possibility that many offences are localised in areas that provide special types of target and opportunity. LeBeau's results therefore do raise important questions about the spatial relationships between the residential location of serial rapists and the locations in which they commit their crimes.

Two models: commuter or marauder

In general, then, it seems to be reasonable to assume the existence of a fixed base for men who carry out a number of rapes as for other offenders who commit a series of crimes. There is also some evidence that there will be an area in which the offences are committed that has some non-arbitrary relationship to that base, what might be termed a *criminal range*. The present study test various models of the relationships there might be between an individual's criminal range and the location of their home base.

Two general models may be proposed to characterise the relationship between base and area of crime, as represented in *Figure 1*. The simplest assumption to make about the geometry of a criminal domain is that it is circular as this only requires the determination of a radius, no other boundary limitations are necessary. In Figure 1, therefore, the area around the home (home range) and the area in which the crimes are committed (criminal range) are represented as circles.

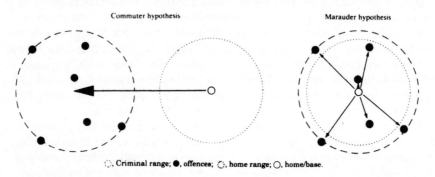

Commuter hypothesis   Marauder hypothesis

◌, Criminal range; ●, offences; ◌, home range; ○, home/base.

Figure 1 Hypothetical models of serial rapists' spatial behaviour

The first model is based on what we have called the *commuter hypothesis*. In this case the offender travels from his base into an area to carry out his crimes. This may be determined by the general geometry of the city, as would be consistent with Shaw and McKay's (1942) proposal of the use of the city centre, or it may be an area determined by regular routes that the offender takes as Rengert and Wasilchick (1985) suggest. However, whatever the particular determinants of the specific area of crime, central to this hypothesis is that although there will be a domain in which the crimes are committed, and this domain will have some distinct relationship to where the offender lives, there will be no clear relationship between size or location of the criminal domain and the distance it is from any given offender's home.

The commuter hypothesis, then, proposes that there is little or no overlap between these two areas and that the offender moves to a district which is outside his home range to offend. This is not to suggest that the criminal range is unfamiliar to the offender, but that it is at an appreciable distance from the area in which he habitually operates as a non-offender.

A second model may be developed on what we call the *marauder hypothesis*. In this case the base acts as a focus for each particular crime. The offender is assumed to move out from this base to commit his crimes and then return. This relates most directly to the research of Brantingham and Brantingham (1981) who see the home as a focus for the crime locations. This hypothesis implies a much closer relationship between the location of crimes and of a criminal's home, such that the further the distance between crimes the further, on average, the offender must be travelling from home.

In other words, the marauder hypothesis proposes that there is a large or total overlap of the home range and criminal range areas. The offender operates from a home/base definitely located within the boundaries of his safe area for criminal activity.

If either of these hypotheses is strongly supported it has implications for further elaboration of the related model. For simplicity of presentation the development of these implications will be left until after the first test of the two hypotheses.

Sample and procedure

Although the general arguments above are applicable to any offences, the present study focuses on sexual assaults. These types of crime are a particularly strong test of the essentially rational models that have been outlined. Sexual assault overtly has a profound emotional component to it and may be regarded by many as containing some strongly impulsive aspects (Amir, 1971). However, when a rapist does commit a series of assaults on women, with whom he has had no previous contact, some pattern is possible in these offences of which the offender may or may not be aware, just as for burglary or drug abuse. Sexual assaults may therefore be seen as an extreme case that tests the fundamental assumptions that an individual criminal's crime venue has some distinct relationship to his place of residence.

To carry out the study details of 45 sexual assaulters were made available by British police forces. These included criminals who had been convicted of crimes legally regarded as 'rape', in which vaginal penetration had taken place, as well as other forms of sexual violence. All offenders had been convicted of two or more offences on women they had not known prior to the offence. A total of 251 offences had been committed by these 45 offenders. The mean rape series consisted of 5.6 offences (S.D. = 3.6) with a minimum of 2, and a maximum of 14 offences. The offenders had a mean age of 26.6 years (S.D. = 8.7) ranging from 15 to 59 years, 21 offenders being broadly classified by the police as 'white' in ethnicity and the other 24 as 'black'. All the offenders operated within the Greater London area and/or the South East of England during the 1980s.

Test of hypotheses

The basic information available to test the hypotheses above is the geographical distribution of the offences in relation to the location of the offender's residence at the time of the offences. For each offender a separate map was produced indicating the locations of offences and his residence. A further summary of this without the underlying base map was produced, as illustrated in *Figure 2*.

The most direct test of the two hypotheses is whether the region covered by the crimes encompasses the location of the residence. In the commuter hypothesis this would not be common, whereas it would be typical of the 'marauder'. A simple test of these possibilities is to examine the area covered by the offences and see whether the residence is within that area.

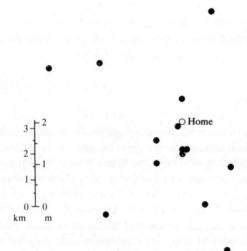

White, 31-year-old, inside serial rapist. ○, Home/base; ●, offences.

Figure 2 Example of rape series

In order to define the area of the offences, the two offences furthest from each other were identified and the distance between them taken as the diameter of a circle that was drawn. Such a circle is likely to encompass all the offences, except for rather unusual spatial distributions. There are therefore more precise geometrical hypotheses that can be derived from the marauder model, *circle hypotheses*. These hypotheses have two aspects:

a)   the offences of a single offender will be encompassed within a circle that is drawn with its diameter as the two offences that are furthest from each other,

b)   the residence of the offender at the time of the offences will be within the same circle.

Clearly such hypotheses make no allowances for variations in local topography, transport routes and so on. They relate to a generalised mental representation of the broad geographical relationships between locations. As such these hypotheses are similar to those relating to the study of distance estimation in cities (Canter and Tagg, 1975). In those studies 'crow flight', direct line estimates of distances around cities were found to have important relationships to actual direct line distances. This was found to be true even independently of travel time between those points (Canter, 1977). The circle hypotheses therefore reflect an assumption about a criminal's mental representations about the area in which he commits his crimes. This assumption is that it is the schematic representation of the location of the crimes that is primary rather than very particular topographical details of those locations. Such details may play a role in addition to the schematic 'image', but the present research explores models that do not include such details.

Results of the tests of the circle hypotheses

a)   It was found that 41 of the 45 offenders had circles which encompassed all their known offences. That is 91% of offenders had all their crimes located within the circular region. Of the 30 offences, within the four cases that did not co-accord, 23 were located within the circle hypothesis area (77%).

b)   When the residential location was considered it was found that the large majority of the offenders, 39 (87%), had a base within the circle hypothesis prediction area.

There were six cases of offenders operating from a base outside the circular region. All of the six spatial patterns showed that the offenders commuted to the offence area. Two of the cases involved picking-up victims and assaulting them in a motor vehicle some distance from home. Two other cases involved the offenders targeting a specific street far away from their home area.

The very high proportions of offenders whose crimes are located in accordance with the circle hypotheses provides strong support for the general marauder hypothesis as being the most applicable to these sets of offenders. The commuter hypothesis therefore does not seem tenable for this sample of sexual offenders, although it may have application where very specific types of targeting, for example on prostitutes, was taking place.

Development of the marauder hypothesis

If offenders are operating within a circular region that also houses their base the question arises as to the relative location of their base within their offence domain. In particular, as the size of their criminal range grows does this change the relative relationship to the domestic focus? One way of understanding and developing this argument is to make the simplifying assumption that the home is at the centre of the offence circle. If this is so then those crimes that are committed far away from each other are more likely to be further from the home than those that are nearer to each other. Such a relationship would hold true for any position that the home had in relation to the crime circle, provided the crimes were distributed around it. This more precise specification of relationships between distances is therefore an arithmetic elaboration of the geometric circle model. It can be summarised as a *Range Hypothesis*: The distance between a criminal's offences will correlate directly to the distance those offences are from his home.

A further development of this hypothesis is that if it is supported, the largest distances between offences will be greater than the largest distance between any offence and the offender's home, otherwise the home would be outside of the circle created from a diameter based on the largest distance between offences. Furthermore if the home was at the centre of the circle then the distance from home to the furthest offence would be half of the maximum distance between offences. In other words, it is hypothesised that regression of maximum distance between offences on maximum distance from home will have a gradient that is less than 1.00 and close to 0.50. A value of less than 0.5 would only be possible if the circle hypothesis was invalid. A gradient greater than 0.5 but less than 1.00 would suggest that the home tended to be eccentrically placed within the crime circle.

The proposition by Brantingham and Brantingham (1981) that there is a safe range around the home in which crimes would not be committed would be supported in the regression equation by a constant value that was positive, but less than the average minimum distance of crimes to home.

Test of the range hypothesis

The scatterplot showing the relationship between the maximum distance between crimes and the maximum distance each crime is from the offender's home is given in *Figure 3*. The correlation for this plot is 0.93 (highly significant at $p < 0.001$). The regression equation is $y = 0.84x + 0.61$. The gradient, at 0.84, does indicate a location within the crime circle, but suggests that it is unlikely to be close to the centre of that circle. This is a finding of some interest which will be discussed later.

The constant is also as predicted. The average minimum distance of crime to home for these offenders was 1.53 miles. The constant of 0.61 miles is well below this. There is, therefore, strong evidence for a minimum distance that the sexual offender is willing to travel from home, in accordance with the hypothesised desire to be at a safe distance away from home.

The criminal's 'safe area' for activity, as defined by this regression equation, is at least 0.61 miles from home but within an area away from all offences which is less than 84% of the maximum distance between offence.

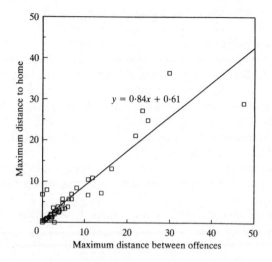

$$y = 0{\cdot}84x + 0{\cdot}61$$

Figure 3 Maximum criminal range: relationship between maximum distance between crimes and maximum distance to home. n=45; r=0.93; p<0.001

Discussion

The clarity of these mathematical results is little short of remarkable for what is regarded as an impetuous, emotional violent crime. They show that, whatever the rapist's experience of committing the crime, there is a basis to his choice of locations that can be modelled from relatively logical environmental psychology principles.

The relationship that a rapist's home has to the location of his crimes has been established for 45 rapists in the South East of Britain who attacked more than one woman; all of the women being unknown to the offenders before the assaults. The indications are that most offenders move out from their home base in a region around that base to carry out their attacks. However the gradient of 0.84 does suggest that there is some bias to commit a number of offences rather closer to home than would be predicted from a simple circular model. In other words, the base is not at the centre of the circle of crimes.

This eccentricity is important because it may reflect a developmental process in which offenders travel further from home at some stages of their offending career than at other stages. The present data set is not large enough to test this possibility thoroughly although there are certainly anecdotal examples of individuals that illustrate it. Such a developmental process could interact with the commuter and marauder models proposed. For although the marauder model was clearly the strongest candidate for describing the present sample there were a few individuals who illustrated a strong commuter process. It seems feasible that the differences between 'commuting' and 'marauding' rapists would be a function of the stages in their development as criminals. With a larger sample this could be tested by the relationship between regression gradient and criminal experience.

The representation of the ranges as circles is, of course, a simplification. The research of both Rengert and Wasilchick (1985) and Capone and Nichols (1975) indicate the possibility that, for North America at least, the expansion of cities from a central down-town may lead to the generation of more elliptical or even sectoral patterns to the geography of serial offending. The grid-pattern of North American cities may also mean that examination of distances between offences is more appropriately carried using city-block metrics rather than the crow-flight measures that were found fruitful for British data.

There are also arguments against the use of more specific models and concrete metrics for the data examined here. The number of offences per offender was relatively small in the current sample. As a consequence very detailed models of the geographical distribution of the offences is difficult to substantiate. Furthermore it seems very likely that the offences recorded are not all those perpetrated by the offender so models that were very restrictive in the spatial structure could be very misleading.

One further consideration is psychological question of what exactly is being modeled in the study. If the view is taken that the model is an approximation to the internal representation of the environment that forms the basis of the criminal's actions, then there is research evidence to suggest that for large complex cities crow-flight distances do capture important aspects of a person's 'cognitive map' (Canter and Tagg, 1975). Indeed Canter (1977, p. 90) reports that crow-flight distance estimates correlate better with both actual distance and actual time to travel around London than do time estimates, suggesting that crow-flight distances may be psychologically more primary than other forms of direct experience. Clearly this is an important issue which future research, with more data than the present, will need to explore.

The fact that rapists reveal strong domocentric behaviour serves further to strengthen the general power of the location of the home in structuring people's lives. It is clearly a process that is worthy of test in many other areas of activity, such as shopping behaviour, recreational activities search for work, or even search for new homes. In the criminal arena it offers direct prospects for practical application in the solving of crimes.

For although the area in which an offender may be living, covered by the circle in the present model, may be very large, nonetheless where detectives are attempting to assign priorities to a long list of suspects the limitations of the circle may still be of utility. It may be possible to reduce the area of the circle by introducing further refinements into the sub-samples of offenders on which the models are based, for example more impulsive offenders may travel shorter distances, or offenders in rural areas may travel further and so on. Research exploring these possibilities has already produced some encouraging results. Investigative suggestions derived from specific studies have also been made available to police investigations with considerable success.

References

Amir, M. (1971), *Patterns in Forcible Rape*, University of Chicago Press, Chicago.

Brantingham, P.J. & Brantingham P.L. (1981), 'Notes on the Geometry of Crime', in P.J. Brantingham and P.L. Brantingham (eds), *Environmental Criminology*, Sage, pp. 27-54.

Canter, D. (1977), *The Psychology of Place*, Architectural Press, London.

Canter, D. & Tagg, S. (1975), 'Distance Estimation in Cities', *Environment and Behaviour*, Vol. 7(1), March, pp. 58-80.

Capone, D.L. & Nichols, W. (1975), 'Crime and Distance: An Analysis of Offender Behaviour in Space', *Proceedings, Assn. Amer. Geographers*, pp. 45-49.

Curtis, L.A. (1974), *Criminal Violence*, MA: Lexington Books, Lexington.

Golledge, R.G. (1987), 'Environmental Cognition', in D. Stokols and I. Altman (eds), *Handbook of Environmental Psychology*, Vol. 1, pp. 131-174, John Wiley, New York.

Kind, S.S. (1987), 'Navigational Ideas and the Yorkshire Ripper Investigation', in *Journal of Navigation*, Vol. 40, No. 3, pp. 385-393.

LeBeau, J.L. (1987), 'The Methods and Measures of Centrography and the Spatial Dynamics of Rape', *Journal of Quantitative Criminology*, Vol. 3, No. 2, pp. 125-141.

LeBeau, J.L. (1987a), 'Patterns of Stranger and Serial Rape Offending: Factors Distinguishing Apprehended and At Large Offenders', *Journal of Criminal Law and Criminology*, Vol. 78.

LeBeau, J.L. (1987), 'The Journey to Rape: Geographic Distance and the Rapist's Method of Approaching the Victim', *Journal of Police Science and Administration*, Vol. 15, No. 2, pp. 129-161.

Pyle, G.F. et al. (1974), *The Spatial Dynamics of Crime*, Department of Geography Research Monograph No. 159, The University of Chicago, Chicago.

Repetto, T.A. (1974), *Residential Crime*, MA: Ballinger, Cambridge.

Rengert, G. & Wasilchick, J. (1985), *Suburban Burglary: A Time and Place for Everything*, C.C. Thomas Publishing.

Shaw, C.R. & McKay, H.D. (1942), *Juvenile Delinquency and Urban Areas*, University of Chicago Press, Chicago.

Sviatlovsky, E.E. & Eells, W.C. (1937), 'The Centrographical Method and Regional Analysis', *Geographical Review*, Vol. 27, pp. 240-254.

White, R.C. (1932), 'The Relation of Felonies to Environmental Factors in Indianapolis', *Social Forces*, Vol. 10, No. 4, pp. 459-467.

Note

1. All the offenders presently being studied are male. The male personal pronoun is therefore intended only to refer to male persons throughout this chapter.

Acknowledgement

We are grateful to Ellen Tsang and Helen Hughes for their assistance on the studies described.

ACTION PLANS

ACTION PLANS

10 Changing Safety Culture in a Steel Works

Background

By the mid 1980s the Fires Research Station that funded my studies of human behaviour in fires decided that it had provided what was needed and that they should not support me to do any further research. So I set about finding other ways of developing that work. An opportunity was provided by the Insurance Technical Bureau who wanted to measure the management contribution to risk in industrial processes (Powell and Canter, 1985). This work did not survive the demise of that bureau but it did open the door to British Steel, who were interested in ways of assessing and ultimately improving the attitude of their workforce to safety.

Like many well managed British Industries, British Steel had been able to reduce accidents considerably over a number of years by technical modifications and the introduction of many safe working practices, but they had reached a point were there were still a number of accidents that were impervious to these processes. They were therefore looking for a radically different way to tackle their problems. My colleague Henryk Olearnik and I approached this issue with a series of studies over two years. Some key findings will illustrate how that research unfolded.

The first finding is illustrated in *Figure 1*. This shows correlations between one year and the next for the accident figures for twelve different departments. As can be seen there is a remarkable consistency in the probability of these supposedly *accidental* events. By comparing the figures with expert opinions of the inherent dangerousness of the processes in each department it was clear that these technical variations were not a major cause of the variations in the accident figures. Something in the 'climate' or 'culture' of the department was probably of more significance.

To test this hypothesis attitude to safety scales were developed and the average score on these scales for each department was correlated with their annual safety figures. *Figure 2* shows one of the remarkably strong correlations that were consistently found between attitudes and safety performance.

These very high correlations, that get close to the reliability levels of both the attitudinal and the safety measures, have since been repeated many times over in many different industrial settings. However, of more significance was the particular pattern of correlations with different aspects of attitudes and the distribution of attitude scores or every particular department. For it was these safety climate

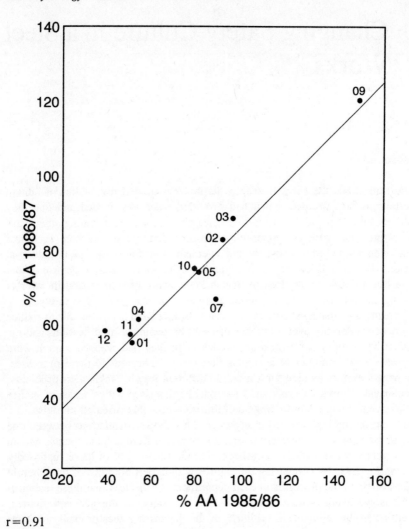

r=0.91

Figure 1 Correlation: all accidents 1985/86 x 1986/87

profiles that provided clear directions in which management needed to proceed in order to improve the climate for each department.

A general framework, however, in the form of an action plan was needed to turn these rather academic ideas into something that could be implemented. The following chapter is a copy of the first few pages of that plan. These pages appear to have become almost a sacred text at the Teesside works where the research was done and together with the detailed recommendations and the departmental attitudinal profiles became a framework that was acted upon in great detail. The resulting change accident rates surprised all of us. An example for one potentially

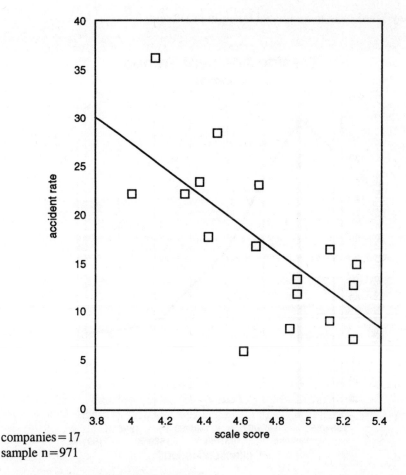

companies = 17
sample n = 971

Pearson's correlation coefficient = 0.09**
** = p < 0.01 (one-tailed test)

Figure 2   Safety attitude scale 6: shopfloor satisfaction correlation with self reported accidents

very dangerous department is given in *Figure 3*. Indeed in some departments the target of zero lost time accidents within five years was reached within the first year of the application of the proposals. Since that time a number of other organisations have supported similar research with good results, although none have been quite so dramatic as those achieved at British Steel.

The work at British Steel was greatly assisted by the one person who could have been most threatened by it, their safety manager Peter Jamieson. Undoubtedly his dedication and expertise contributed tremendously to the success of the whole project. The wholehearted support given by the Managing Director of the site,

Danny Ward, was also a crucial factor in its success.

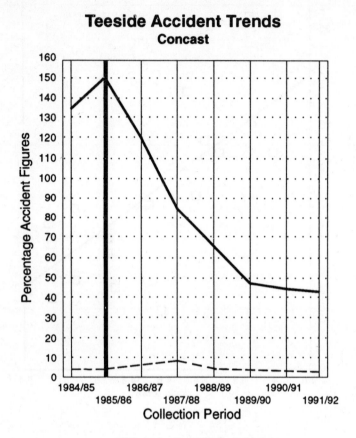

The bold vertical line indicates the point in time at which the Action Plan was introduced.

Figure 3 Teesside accident trends

The zero objective

At present the accident figures at Teesside are much better than some years ago, but there is considerable room for improvement. Recommendations are made with the intention of creating a situation in which there are no accidents within five years.

This report summarises the results of the background research. They show clearly that there are consistent safety performance differences between plants at Teesside and that these can be related directly to differences in attitudes.

From the research conducted at Teesside and other relevant studies, five principles are presented as a basis for an action plan.

A ten point plan is then proposed that will lead to a change of attitudes and the consequent elimination of accidents. Detailed guidance on how these actions may be taken most successfully is provided.

Five basic principles

To change attitudes enough to eliminate accidents five broad principles should be followed:

a.   Encouragement of safe working practices to be as strong as the discouragement of dangerous working.
b.   Provision of strong support for plant level planning and accountability for safety.
c.   Emphasis on the significance of first line supervisor foremen/supervisors in maintaining safe practices and the development of more appropriate training and monitoring for them.
d.   Utilise social processes as the means of changing attitudes to support the exhortation of individuals.
e.   Emphasise the maintenance and fostering of a good organisational climate for safety.

A ten point plan

The principles can be turned into detailed actions following a ten point plan:

1.   Continuously demonstrate commitment to positive safety.
2.   Focus safety accountability.
3.   Derive plant level initiatives
4.   Strengthen work of the safety committees.
5.   Rehabilitate lapsed safe working procedures of production as well as engineering.
6.   Improve contribution of safety representatives.
7.   Develop safety training to emphasise human factors.
8.   Regularly and overtly, monitor attitudes to safety and their relationship to safety performance at plant level.
9.   Establish procedures to check on and improve safety related communication between all groups.
10.   Elaborate and clarify the safety responsibilities inherent in all job descriptions.

An achievable objective

At present there are a great number of separate initiatives that are taken throughout the Teesside works with regard to safety. The effectiveness of these has been clearly demonstrated by the steady fall in the accident ratios over the past decade. However, it is also clear that these actions are no longer very effective in having a major impact on further improvement in the safety record. In broad terms they now appear to be maintaining it at its present level.

A responsive organisation

A number of factors point to the possibility of achieving better safety performance.

One is the fact that earlier measures have been effective so that the organisation as a whole clearly can respond to safety initiatives.

The second is that the attitudinal survey carried out shows widespread support for improved safety, in principle, at all levels of the organisation. Particularly important is the fact that senior management are obviously genuine in their commitment to improving safety performance.

A third is that the research indicates that the very process of surveying attitudes may have modified them and relevant behaviour, supporting the view that a more direct process could have more significant effects.

An overall strategy

A third factor that makes a considerable reduction in accidents an achievable objective is that current safety activities do not appear to benefit form being guided by an overall, detailed strategy. They appear to have grown up in response to many different issues and initiatives. It therefore seems highly likely that if these can be developed into a coherent set of actions that follow an overall strategy for safety at Teesside a real improvement is possible. By taking into account what is now known about the attitudinal basis of dangerous activities a dramatic improvement is possible.

The factors indicating the possibility for improvement all point to the feasibility of eliminating accidents at Teesside.

There is evidence that nearly all accidents are now a product of inappropriate human behaviour at some recognisable stage in the events leading up to the accident. Given that there are many indications that the actions of the work force can be modified at Teesside there are strong reasons to believe that behaviour of relevance to accidents can also be modified.

A clear objective

Making the elimination of accidents the overt objective of the overall strategy also gives it a very clear direction. At the same time it presents as clearly as possible the commitment of British Steel to safe working.

Human factors not technical factors

Workers at Teesside are proud of their skills and the achievements of their industry. They enjoy the technical challenges that their work presents and thrive on debates about processes and products. Within this framework consideration of human aspects of the work situation has tended to be rather limited and mechanical. There is therefore considerable opportunity for developing a more subtle approach to the human factors in regard to safety.

Personal contact

Many years of research on attitude change show that the strongest change processes come from direct contact between people within the context of group support. It is clear that there is considerable opportunity for strengthening these processes at Teesside.

Preservation not compensation

The research indicates that accidents are generally thought of in terms of their threat to the individual. There is also no evidence from our research that anyone considers possible compensation claims as a reason for taking risks. The enhancement of the awareness of the workforce of how they can reduce risks is therefore likely to fall on fertile ground.

Beyond protection to procedures

A further reason why the zero objective is feasible is that the research has revealed that, in general, the wearing of protective clothing is now well established at Teesside. The correlates of accident ratios are attitudes to safety procedures. So, by giving more emphasis to active safe working, improvements in behaviour are possible beyond those achievable by emphasising the more passive response of just wearing protective clothing and using safety equipment.

No magic formula

It must be emphasised that attitudes and consequent behaviour cannot be changed by isolated actions, such as a poster campaign or beefing up training. Behavioural change is brought about by a number of interrelated actions that form a coherent plan. The more these actions can build upon current, worthwhile activities the more chance they have of success.

SCHEMATIC REPRESENTATION OF ACTIONS TO BE TAKEN WITHIN PLANTS FOR ELIMINATING ACCIDENTS

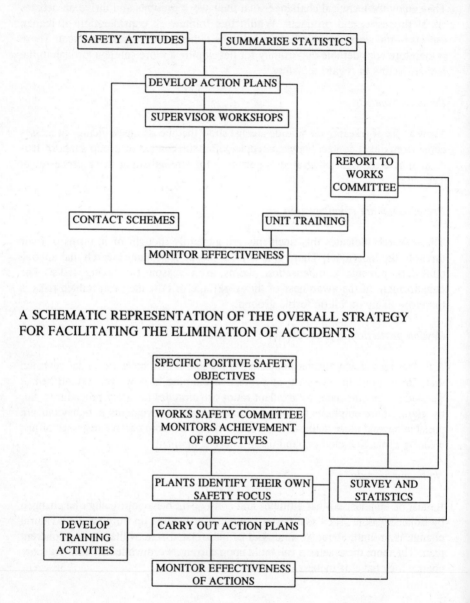

A SCHEMATIC REPRESENTATION OF THE OVERALL STRATEGY FOR FACILITATING THE ELIMINATION OF ACCIDENTS

11 Ward Development Project

Background to Ward Development Project

Shenley Hospital was a large psychiatric hospital on the outskirts of North London. It was undergoing considerable modification as a result of changes in medical practice. As part of these changes attention was turned to providing better facilities for that part of the patient population that it was assumed would continue to need continuous in-patient care, especially its psychogeriatric population.

It had a large psychogeriatric population housed in wards that had been designed for quite other purposes early in the century. The clinical psychologists who worked there recognised the problems of these wards and commissioned me to carry out studies that would lead to design proposals. It happened to be a year when we only had four students on the MSc in Environmental Psychology at Surrey so the project became the focus for their year's study.

As a result of the various projects we were able to make design proposals for how the wards could be redesigned, perhaps the first and only time that psychologists have produced detailed design recommendations without any architectural intervention. The recommendations, of course, also included proposals on the management of the ward, which is virtually unknown in strictly design schemes.

However, we did need to convert these ideas into more detailed plans so that the management team could take them forward for costing and the like. My long standing friend and colleague Arie Peled contributed his architectural skills by interpreting our proposals as plans and drawings, also drawing upon government planning guidelines so that the proposals were within the planning regulations.

The resulting designs were very well received by the hospital management and the staff who saw a number of advantages to the schemes that we had not appreciated. We were thus lead to believe that funding would be forthcoming to redesign the wards according to our proposals. However, we heard nothing for many, many months. Then one day I read in a newspaper that the whole site of Shenley Hospital had been sold to an orthodox Jewish community to convert into housing and other community facilities.

Summary

A five stage programme is outlined. This has the objective of developing and improving the long-stay psychogeriatric wards at Shenley Hospital.

A: Indicative stage

In the first stage four interrelated studies were carried out focusing on ward FA3, drawing upon all personnel who had any contact with the ward.

These studies gave rise to the following conclusions:

1. All staff would like to create a ward that provides the possibility of greater enhancement of patients' activities and experiences.
2. Differences between sub-groups of patients in their demands and dependency could be identified with a high level of staff consensus.
3. The activities in which staff and patients participated had a definite pattern to them which carried design implications, especially in relation to the need for semi-private as well as 'public' spaces.
4. A ward layout that recognised the value of a radial arrangement with clearly central and peripheral spaces would respond to many of the different perspectives staff had on the desired activities on the ward.

B: Preliminary proposals

In the second stage the results of the first stage were used to generate preliminary design/programme proposals.

In essence the preliminary proposals are as follows:

1. The conversion of the main entrance to be directly accessible from the outside via the existing roofed-over verandah.
2. The opening up of the nurses' office to provide a nurses' station.
3. The creation of three/four separate sleeping areas, each with an adjacent small sitting area.
4. The creation of a definite group activities area near the nurses' station, and of a separate dining area.

Subsequent Stages. In order to put these proposals into action a further three stages are proposed.

C: A planning stage

Through further discussions with staff and the collecting of technical information the details needed to produce specific programmes and designs will be obtained.

D: Design stage

Development of detailed design recommendations.

E: Implementation stage

Carrying out the necessary training and building alterations to set the programme in motion.

Research procedures and summary results

Researchers spent a number of days on the ward, throughout a full 36 hour period. During this time they helped with ward tasks and interviewed 40 members of staff associated with the wards. These interviews were structured around an agenda of topics but deliberately allowed staff to raise any issues about the activities on the ward, its layout and use.

In the light of these interviews and the general models of therapeutic environments put forward by Canter and Canter (1979), a structured questionnaire was produced asking about staff objectives for the ward. This was completed by 25 staff.

The interviews with staff and observations of the ward produced various perspectives on the ward. In general staff felt that the ward was unhomely, and depressing. Most staff mentioned a lack of additional activities for patients such as more occupational therapy, an increase of visitors, and more trips. A lack of patient privacy was felt to be very evident. The problem of heavy dependence was also mentioned. Observations supported these statements.

The questionnaire provided a list of care-giving policy concepts that staff felt were of utmost importance for the elderly mentally ill. Issues such as self-respect of the patient and encouraging independence when eating, dressing, walking and going to the toilet were major outcomes. Also included was the provision of aids to help mobility of patients. The overall impression was of providing care which was as normal as possible in a homelike environment with as few institutional features as possible.

A variation of Canter et al's (1985) 'Multiple Sorting Task' was used to examine the consensus held by staff about their patients. The name of each patient known to staff on the ward was written on a separate card. The staff working on the ward and in close contact with the ward were then asked to sort these cards as a way of indicating any important differences between the patients. Fifteen staff carried out these sortings. The combined results of these sortings were analysed and are presented in a Summary MDS representation in Appendix I.

The patient multiple sorting task showed that there were a number of levels of competence amongst patients on the ward. There was an apparent continuum of dependence, running in parallel with stage of dementia in the patient. These results posed the question of segregation or integration of patients of different functioning levels.

In order to understand the conceptualisation of activities on the ward a sorting task of activities was carried out with 15 staff. These were subjected to the same form of analysis as the patient sorting task. The results of that statistical analysis are summarised in Appendix II.

The activity sortings showed a division of activities physically between the front, more public area of the ward, and the back, private regions. There were also clear divisions between social and non-social activities, with social activities seen as rare occasions from observations and interview results. Activities were also clearly separated in staff conceptions as to medical/hygienic activities and enhancing/normal activities. This latter group of activities also fell into the category of rare occurrences.

The staff view on the appropriate spatial relationships between activities on the ward was explored using a location task. The Location exercises were a variation of the Location Task developed by Professor Arie Peled of the Technion, Haifa (Peled, 1976). For this staff were given paper markers with activities on them. Twenty-one staff carried out this exercise and their layouts were combined after content analysis. The summary of these designs, in an overall schematic form, is given in Appendix III.

The design games produced by staff tended to be radial with a centre for either a nursing station, toilet/bathing area, eating area, or more patient centred occupational therapy area. Although not all designs created were radial in shape, the radial design is the best fit to the shape and design of the existing ward. Most designs separated sleeping and night activities from day activities by placing the former at the back of their design and the latter towards the front or main entrance to the ward. Designs that would best improve ward atmosphere and promote a home-like environment would lean towards designs that were normal/enhancement in type.

Organisational changes proposed

The major change suggested by the results of the data would be the commencement of training programmes for the purpose of increasing patient independence. Learning to feed oneself, dress oneself and go to the toilet unaided would be the aim of such programmes. Programmes would be carried out by staff working on the ward and supported by those connected more remotely. These changes would not involve costly procedures, but a reorganisation of care giving procedure.

In the past, Kuller and Mattsson (1984) found that elderly who were previously spoon fed, after their alterations to meantime organisation, were now feeding themselves. Changing the organisation of the present meantime, as Kuller and Mattsson did, might be a worthwhile alteration to be considered.

This increase in patient independence would not only serve to increase patient self confidence and self esteem, but would also make the ward atmosphere less institutional. Initially the work load of staff may be increased, due to the constant effort required to train individuals. However, thereafter work load to staff would be decreased, due to the fact that patients would no longer need as much attention and help with everyday functioning. With patients having an increased level of competence, more response would ensue, also promoting a livelier interactive ward.

Thus while providing training to increase patient independence, existing dependence promoting procedures should be gradually removed, such as using mobile commodes, which make less work for staff, but decrease patient self respect, provide little privacy and encourage dependence.

More activities were suggested for patients. This could be achieved through an increase in the amount of occupational therapy provided. Staff on the ward could elicit participation from patients by, for example, playing music so that even if occupational therapists were not available, patients could still benefit. The use of volunteers could be helpful in this instance, not only for helping staff, but providing the extra stimulation of a visitor to talk to.

One difference of perspective found between departments within the hospital was the amount of stimulation possible in an elderly senile population. Those not working daily on the ward tended to believe that the elderly should live as normally as possible, in pleasant surroundings. They did not think that much response from the patients was possible. If this perspective were changed, more support would be available from outside workers such as social workers and hospital administrators.

The provision of organisational changes away from institutional procedures of care would move the ward away from the current 'custodial' model of care. These programmes would in no way alter the physical environment, and thus would not be costly alterations. As has been shown in the past by Lawton (1980), and Woods and Britton (1985), the senile elderly will respond to programmes designed to increase self esteem and decrease dependence.

Segregation or integration?

Lawton (1980) and Lipman and Slater (1979), both leading researchers with the elderly, have differing opinions as to segregation and integration of patients. In the interviews carried out some senior staff were in favour of having patients of different levels of competence together on one ward. However, nurses working on the ward felt that those patients with very low levels of competence brought the other patients down to their level. Occupational therapists, although generally in favour of the segregation of different levels, thought that those more demented did benefit when present in the same room with other patients having an occupational therapy session. These views, taken together with the other data collected, suggest the value of a ward layout and programme that combines some of the advantage of an integrated ward whilst avoiding the disadvantages.

Physical alteration to the ward

In accordance with the results of the data analysis a number of physical changes to the ward environment would be of value.

In terms of providing a more home-like ward, some features could be added. These would include homely furniture, extra furnishings, such as photographs and pictures. Painting the walls uninstitutional colours like pale blue, yellow or pink may improve the ward. The population under consideration must be remembered. Thus, if plants are suggested, perhaps hanging baskets would be more appropriate so that patients could not eat or ruin them. Old-fashioned furniture should be considered not only because it is fairly easy and cheap to come by, but because of the proven beneficial effect it has had on elderly mentally ill (Kuller and Mattsson, 1984),

The provision of prosthetic aids for the ward is a very important alteration, and hand rails around the ward and in the toilet/bathing area would greatly increase mobility in patients, as well as the provision of wheelchairs and walkers for those more frail, and special orthopaedic chairs for those for whom walking is impossible. It is not thought that these aids would encourage dependence. The elderly may be one of the few sections of the population where there is little hope of learning to walk again if chair bound due to old age. The aids provided would only help to increase the independence of patients, in that assistance now needed to move about would be greatly decreased. However, proper administration of wheelchairs and other aids is necessary, so that those able to walk unaided are not encouraged or allowed to use aids solely to ease staff workloads.

From the patient sortings it was seen that the patients varied along a continuum of dependence and competence. A ward which houses a mixed population should itself be varied. Senile dementia is a condition which can produce varied levels of competence within the same patient, often within the same day; therefore an environment which will meet the needs of a changing population is important. Even if one level of competence or type of patients is to be provided for on a ward, this level will vary within itself due to the nature of their disability. Thus an adaptive environment would be of value.

The creation of an adaptive, flexible ward would need to allow for different types of setting for patients with differing degrees of dementia. It would also need to take account of low staffing levels. This will require some combination of the existing, overall general ward with smaller groupings that will give each group of patients an environment with a distinct emphasis. In effect, this leads to a proposal of smaller within wards.

Each of these 'pods' could have a sleeping area and a semi-public sitting area. In some cases there could also be another area specifically set-up for some other more focused group activities. Access between the different areas would need to be kept open and they would all require ready access to the toilet facilities. It would be important to aid reality orientation by making each of the pods as distinct as possible within the overall design and layout.

In the toilet/bathing area of the ward it was felt by many staff that this was an underheated area, and that very little patient privacy was afforded. Extra features such as a lift to aid patients getting in and out of the bath was suggested. Further privacy could be achieved by the addition of doors on toilet stalls and the installation of more partitions.

To combat one of the major problems of the elderly, confusion, various aids to help orientation can be used. As suggested by Lawton (1980) having different rooms painted different colours can help. Providing large coloured simple maps of the ward can also help patients to find out where they are in relation to other parts of the ward. The use of a personal name to denote one's bed/locker may help in a room full of identical beds. Reality boards with the date, season, and weather on them have been shown to be useful. This idea could be developed to indicate, for instance, the day's TV programmes or other matters of interest to the patients. In the ward under study, there was one in each of the two day rooms. However, they were placed high up on the wall, and patients did not take any notice of them. Other useful features for orientation are clocks, photographs from the war era, and other wall hangings reminiscent of the previous years of the elderly.

Proposed radial design of the ward

Most of the design games produced a radial design of some sort. This is interesting in the light of the existing ward which can be thought of as radial-like in layout. One of the first, and possibly most obvious, alterations in terms of design would be to open up the area currently used by nursing staff as an office. At the moment there is only visibility in one direction from the doorway of the office. This is in the direction of one of the two sleeping areas. If the office were to have windows installed, or walls removed, then the two day areas as well as the other sleeping area would be in clear view.

At the moment, the nurses' office is in the centre area, sharing this centrality with the toilet/bathing area in terms of distance from the rest of the ward. If the theme of care provided would be changed from a custodial/observation/cleaning policy to a more social and enhancing one, then clearly the centre of the ward should be shifted. This could be achieved by the following suggestions.

The main entrance to the ward is currently down a hallway, past the kitchen area, through the double handled door and into the ward. To a patient watching a member of staff leave the ward, it is as though the staff member leaves to another part of the hospital, because the outside world is not in evidence through the door. One enters through one of the day spaces. There is a fire exit at the opposite side of the ward, close to the nurses' office, entering the ward from the outside verandah. If this second entrance were made the main one, the routes established for traffic on the ward could be changed. This would give patients a different direction to watch, and a direct feeling of contact with the outside world. For when the door is opened, there is no hallway, but a direct interface with the elements, protected by the verandah. This would also encourage patients to look outside through adjoining windows near the door and perhaps help to maintain contact with the hospital outside the ward.

The change of main entrance would need to be examined carefully in relation to the other entrances that are used at present, both for staff car parking and for the provision of meals. In one sense, the suggestion of changing the entrance is to give a clear 'front-entrance' and 'back entrance' to the ward. Visitors and others not providing basic services to the ward would then enter into a type of open foyer, close to a nurses' station, with activities, possibly dispersed around the ward, but visible from that entrance. This would be much more welcoming than the current series of doors and the sudden entrance into a patient group.

One of the major criticisms of the ward was its institutional atmosphere and lack of homeliness. This could be altered by repainting the walls and by lowering the ceiling height. The present tall ceilings tend to give the ward a gymnasium feeling, and add to patient confusion. In addition, the lighting levels could be changed in a manner similar to that proposed by Lawton (1980), so that good lighting would be available, yet it could be adjusted for various reasons.

To make the ward literally a brighter place, the south facing position of the ward could be used to the fullest. There is already a verandah, which, if covered by plastic or glass, could be a bright extension to the ward. If covered in, it could be used all-year-round. Outside verandahs were often suggested in design games, as were gardens outside. At present the hospital does have well kept gardens; however, often patients cannot get close enough to the windows to see out of them. Often, too, from a sitting position, it is not possible to see much out of the windows, which although large are not low enough for a sitting population.

Conclusion

If these relatively simple changes are introduced, then the environment will become a much healthier one in all respects. Staff approve the proposed alterations which would include increased patients' self esteem, improvements in ward atmosphere, and redecoration, provided that staff are kept well informed and are felt to have had a major part in the formation of changes.

Technical appendices

I   Summary analysis of sorting of patients
II   Summary analysis of sorting of activities
III   Schematic summary of location tasks
IV   Schematic design proposal
V   Bibliography

Appendix I: Instructions for the multiple sorting task with patients' names

Each of these cards shows the name of a patient presently on this ward. Do you recognise all these names? I would like you to think about your feelings about these people in this task.

Can you sort these cards into different piles so that all the cards in each pile have something in common, but are different from the other piles? Think about how these people are similar and different from each other. You may have as many or as few groups as you like; however, usually people find between five and seven groups is adequate. You may sort the cards as many times as you like.

The participant was presented with the 24 cards randomly shuffled. After groups were formed the participant was asked why cards were put together in the same pile, and how the other piles were different. Labels for each pile were elicited from the sorter. Notes were taken as the participant sorted the cards, with encouragement given to the participant 'thinking aloud'.

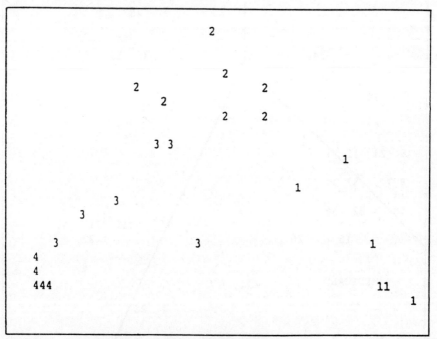

MSA of patients based upon staff categorisations.
  4, highly dependent/bedridden - demented;
  3, very dependent/chair bound - demented;
  2, fairly dependent/mobile sometimes - dementing;
  1, fairly dependent/more mobile - sometimes lucid.

Appendix II: The same instructions as given in Appendix I were used with 40 activities instead of patients' names to be sorted

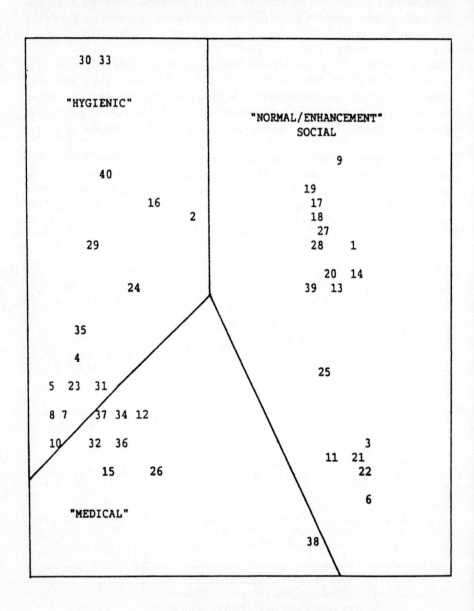

MSA of staff conceptions of activities occurring on the ward.

List of 40 activities used in activity sorting

1. Sleeping in chairs
2. Sleeping in bed
3. O.T on ward
4. Making Beds
5. Bathing
6. Physiotherapy on ward
7. Cleaning patients
8. Toileting
9. Visits from relatives
10. Cleaning patients after meals
11. Visits from chaplain
12. Doctor visits
13. Listening to records
14. Reading/looking at papers
15. Patient tea-time
16. Staff tea-break
17. Sitting alone
18. Watching T.V
19. Talking to other patients
20. Sitting in a group

21. O.T trips and outings
22. Visits to O.T centre
23. Feeding by spoon
24. Eating
25. Parties for patients
26. Changing bandages/dressings
27. Patients looking out of windows
28. Patients walking around
29. Preparing drinks for patients
30. Cleaning dishes after meals
31. Staff serving food
32. Patient count
33. Cleaning floors
34. Patient observation
35. Staff changeover
36. Medicine round
37. Patient observation and checking during day
38. Admission of new patients
39. Patients sitting outside
40. Laundry duties

Appendix III:

This list of 23 activity/place names was compiled from activities observed to occur on the ward, and from interviews with staff both on and connected to the ward. Other non-activity/place areas were added from the results of the sorting tasks. These activity/place names were then hand written in capital letters across a diamond shaped (square) white paper disk. The activity/place 'markers' were deliberately designed to appear 'home-made', so as not to seem too professional and inhibit participants. The squares measured approximately 5.0 cm by 5.0 cm.

A place for patients to sit quietly

A place for Chaplain visits

A place for admission of new patients

A place for patient examination

A place for storage

A place for medicine storage

A place for staff breaks

A place for doctor visits

A place for preparing drinks/food for patients

A place for O.T activities

A place for patients eating

A place for patients sitting in a group

A place for visitors

A place for watching T.V

A place for patients to listen to records

A place for sleeping

A place for laundry

A place for cleaning dishes

Patients sitting outside

Nurses' office

Staff changing room

Bathing

Toileting

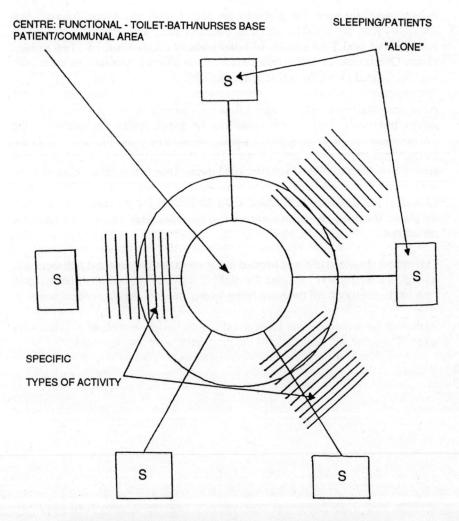

CENTRE: FUNCTIONAL - TOILET-BATH/NURSES BASE
PATIENT/COMMUNAL AREA

SLEEPING/PATIENTS

"ALONE"

SPECIFIC

TYPES OF ACTIVITY

SCHEMATIC REPRESENTATION OF SPATIAL RELATIONSHIPS DESIRED

Appendix IV: Instructions for the design game

The participant was presented with a large circle drawn in black on a large white piece of paper, labelled 'front' at one side. The participant was told that the circle represented the 'inside' of the ward and that outside of the circle represented 'outside' the ward, or the near vicinity. Then the markers were shown, and any activity/place areas not understood were explained.The participant was then instructed to arrange the markers both inside and outside of the circle so as to represent their ideal long-stay ward for elderly senile-dementia patients.

Active encouragement was given to the use of imagination and fantasy. Any additional activities could be added by the participant, and similarly any of those provided not used.Thus doubles of activity/places could occur, i.e., two bathing places. Overlapping of activity/place markers was allowed, although the participant was encouraged to use the whole space available.

After rearrangements were completed and the participant was satisfied with the design produced, marks were made on the paper where the centre of the activity/place was according to the participant-designer, and the labels from the markers transferred to the design board. Then the participant was asked to section areas if possible into rooms, and then label these. Then connections between these such as doors, corridors, and screens were asked to be drawn onto the board. Any additional features were then added if the participant felt it necessary, such as a fireplace. Windows and main entrance/s to the ward were also elicited from the participant.

Throughout the exercise it was stressed that it was a design game and that there was no right or wrong way of doing the task. It was also stressed that the designer remove themselves from the ward being studied so as to design an ideal ward.

At the end the participant was asked to explain the design created, while notes were taken. The name and profession of the participant were also recorded.

Appendix V: Bibliography

Canter, D.V., Brown, J. & Groat, L. (1985), 'A Multiple Sorting Procedure for Studying Conceptual Systems' in *The Research Interview*, Academic Press, London.

Canter, D.V. & Canter, S. (eds) (1979), *Designing for Therapeutic Environments*, Wiley, Chichester.

Kuller, R. & Mattsson, R. (1984), The Dining Room at a Geriatric Hospital. Presented at the 8th IAPS Conference, July, West Berlin.

Lawton, M.P. (1980), *Environment and Ageing*, Brooks/Cole Publishing Company, Monterery, California.

Lipman, A. & Slater, R. (1979), 'Homes for Old People: Towards a Positive Environment' in D.V. Canter and S. Canter (eds), *Designing for Therapeutic Environments*, Wiley, Chichester.

Peled, A. 'The Strathclyde Location Test', in *The Behavioural Basis of Design, Book 2*, P. Suedfeld and J.A. Russel (eds) (1976), Dowden, Hutchinson and Ross.

Woods, R.T. & Britton, P.G. (1985), *Clinical Psychology with the Elderly*, Croom Helm, London.

Acknowledgements

We are grateful to Linda Shattock and Pearl Chow for their assistance in collecting and analysing the data. Arie Peled's valuable contribution in converting the schematic plans into design proposals is also greatfully acknowledged.

12 Designing a Research Centre

Introduction

Thornton Research Centre (TRC) is a major research site for Shell, housed at the base of the Wirral Peninsula about 20 miles south west of Liverpool. During 1993 it was decided that the existing rather extensive mixture of buildings should be refurbished, some pulled down, with new more coherent buildings to replace them being needed. This was to be part of a general plan to rejuvenate research activities in preparation for the 21st Century and the many emerging technological developments. It was decided that the planning of the whole new site and the design of the new research laboratories should benefit from environmental psychology input. I was approached before any architects were appointed, but after preliminary planning had taken place, to carry out a series of studies that would provide the strategic basis for the planning and design.

The projects had to be completed over a period of a few months in a context that I knew, from previous experience, would change during our involvement. In fact one set of architects came and went during the project and a research centre in the South of England, at Sittingbourne, was brought into the plan and had to be included in the study.

I decided to turn the potential problems into strengths by inviting two long established colleagues and friends to join me. David Stea flew over from Mexico to oversee the design participation exercises and Arie Peled flew from Israel to supervise the location tasks. They both subsequently contributed to the preparation of the planning and design proposals. The remainder of the work was managed with my colleague Ian Donald. However, the day to day running of the project and the writing of the first drafts for the reports for Shell fell to a young student of mine who had just completed her MSc in Environmental Psychology, Margaret Scott. I like to think this was an appropriate reward for the fact that it was her personal contacts that had first brought Shell and me together.

A great deal of information had to be analysed and collected in a short period of time. Once again a group of willing students studying on the MSc in Environmental Psychology provided the intelligent field workers to carry out many of the interviews and questionnaire surveys, including an architect on the course, Richard Blaise, who did the drawings for the picture questionnaire. Unfortunately the MSc course no longer had the flexibility of earlier years so this unique opportunity could not become a major focus for the students and instead had to be slotted into their very tight course structure. The lengthy reports that were produced and the discussions in many meetings were acted on by Shell and

I have since seen something I never expected, actual buildings rising from the ground, influenced in part but directly, by the results of our research.

The chapter that follows is an edited version of the final report that was produced. It has been edited to give a flavour of the ideas behind the work as well as the methods employed and the summary, strategic framework that was incorporated into the detailed design.

Objectives

The objectives of this report are to give an account of the research which has been carried out at Thornton Research Centre and Sittingbourne Research Centre with respect to the redevelopment and redesign of the Thornton Site. It aims to articulate the design aspects that are salient, and to identify the appropriate characteristics for the developments at Thornton Research Centre.

The recommendations made in this report are general trends rather than individual statements or requirements and it is not intended as a simple description of what people say they want.

The report has three sections. The first is a review of what is currently known about laboratory and research centre design. The second section outlines the methodological basis for the research which is reported, and the methods which were employed during this research. The third section reports the results of the research and how they relate to the design of the laboratory blocks and the site design.

Theoretical basis of the research

Theory of place

Canter (1977) presented a model for the issues which need to be addressed during design research. The basic assumption is that whatever is being designed, is a series of places, each with its own identity and experiences. Canter describes places not as collections of independent elements, but elements which combine to create places. The elements are integrated so that although they are definable as separate elements, to create a place, each must be present.

Canter's model identifies the major constituents which amalgamate to form places.

The constituents of place are:

- the behaviours associated with a given locus, or which are anticipated to be within a given locus
- the physical parameters of that setting
- the conceptions which people hold about that setting

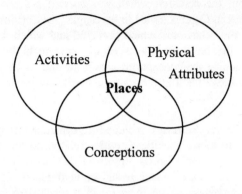

Canter's (1977) Visual metaphor for the nature of places (p.158)

These three elements are the constituents of places. Each is present in any setting defined as a place. Each can be considered separately, but each is entwined with the others. As a result, a place has not been fully identified until each of the elements for that setting are known. At the same time, exploration of one of the elements can be the starting point for research even if the other elements have not been fully developed. For example, the conceptions held about the activities at Thornton were explored even though the physical structure was not known at this time.

The research at Thornton was structured using this theoretical perspective.

- Behaviours - researched through design exercises in which teams produced simplified models of the building, location tasks in which the preferred spatial relationships between architects was explored and an importance questionnaire that asked how important it was for the design to acheive certain objectives and interviews
- Physical attributes - researched through design exercises, location tasks, pictures questionnaire in which people were asked to comment on line drawings of possible designs, importance questionnaire and interviews
- Conceptions - researched through design exercises, location tasks, pictures questionnaire, importance questionnaire and the sorting task.

Clearly, many of the research tools addressed several elements of place, but some were specific. For example, the sorting task explored the conceptions which the staff at Shell Research hold about the activities which occur at Thornton. It examined the conceptions held about the nature of the work involved in the activities and the place experience which each activity affords. The pictures questionnaire looked at the relationship between physical attributes of buildings and the images which they are interpreted as possessing.

In essence then, the research which was carried out at the Thornton and Sittingbourne Research Centres aimed to investigate the constituents of place. It sought to identify the behaviours which occurred and which were anticipated to occur, to look at the physical aspects of the current buildings and the new designs, and to examine the conceptions which the staff hold about the research centre and its activities. Each of these aspects will now be considered in a little more detail.

Activities.   The design exercises included information about behaviours by asking participants to locate specific activities relative to one another and gave reasons for that. For example, in the design of the research centre as a whole, many groups included an area which would be landscaped. They explained that staff would like somewhere to go to at lunch times and to take breaks. They gave examples of the activities of walking, resting and relaxing.

The location tasks highlighted similar concerns, but also examined more closely the relationships between different activities and their associated objectives. For example, activities which were considered to involve similar features such as safety were located together.

The importance questionnaire clarified with a larger sample some of the issues which had been raised in previous sessions. With regard to activities, it clarified the design for the office by asking about the behaviours which staff would expect to be able to do there. For example, questions asking the importance of 'having a space around your desk to hold meetings with your colleagues to discuss work', and, 'there is peace and quiet at your desk for you to be able to work.'

The interviews explored in open ended questions some of the issues which had been identified as important to the new research centre and laboratory design. Examples of this included discussions about changes to car-parking arrangements, and encouraging interaction and communication between people.

Physical attributes.   To explore the physical attributes of the buildings which would be appropriate, design exercises, location tasks, pictures questionnaire, importance questionnaire and interviews were used.

The design exercises provided the staff with opportunities to raise aspects about the physical design which they considered important. These included the architectural style of certain buildings currently on site which were considered to be inappropriate, the style and placement of windows and building height. The laboratory design exercises provided the participants with the opportunity to design and build their ideal laboratory building, including the internal and external design. This led to specific guidelines from the participants concerning the physical design of the laboratory block.

The location tasks allowed the participants to design, in an abstract form, the site and the laboratory blocks. For the laboratory blocks in particular, this meant that participants could include specific physical features. These included the physical layout of the inside of the laboratory blocks, such as laboratories, offices and communal areas. On the site, landscaping and route layouts directives were also given.

The pictures questionnaire approached directly the issue of what the architectural style of the new buildings at Thornton should be. This provided clear themes which could be applied as guidelines to design and as criteria for evaluation. The research did not present the results as a style of architecture which should be adhered to, rather that whatever style(s) are chosen, that they should take into consideration the themes which were found to be salient by the staff.

The importance questionnaire again was used to explore with a larger sample some of the issues raised in earlier sessions. Questions included, 'the building you work in looks efficient', and 'the site looks as if it has been designed economically'.

The interviews explored in open ended questions the aspects of building design which should be included. This resulted in being aware of the overall effect being more 'frugal' than 'extravagant'.

Conceptions. Exploring the conceptions which are held by the staff of Shell Research used design exercises, location tasks, pictures questionnaire, importance questionnaire and the sorting task.

The design exercises highlighted the relationships which exist between various activities, and also the nature of activities which are considered appropriate. For example, there was a clear distinction between safe and hazardous activities which are performed within a laboratory block. This was supported by the location tasks, and linked to the sorting tasks. The dirty and more hazardous activities were located to the rear of the buildings and of the site, being separate from the clean, quiet and safe activities.

The sorting task researched the conceptions in the most direct way. It looked specifically at the conceptions which the staff held about the activities which are done at Thornton and at Sittingbourne. The data clearly revealed the distinction between the activities according to 1) the type of activity and 2) the nature of the place experience where that activity is done. This was useful in providing information on the relative location of activities and in the organisational structure of Shell Research at Thornton.

The pictures questionnaire explored the salient conceptions which are held in terms of 'appropriate to Thornton' and various architectural styles. The importance questionnaire clarified certain issues such as what is the purpose of an office by looking at what is important through questions like, 'a person's office or work space gives you some sense of their status' and 'you have a secure place around your desk to keep your work'. The answers to these questions showed that office security is important but images of status are not important for staff of Shell Research.

These examples show how the research which had been carried out has been structured using the Theory of Place, and that the elements have been investigated as separate but integrated elements. The resulting work describes the place of Thornton and the places within Thornton.

Hierarchy of places

Within Canter's (1977) formulation of places there is not just one place which is called Thornton, but many places within the research centre as a whole and more within each of those. Places are not defined solely by size, and as a result, a centre like Thornton is composed of many places, each with their own identity, experience, physical features, behaviours and conceptions.

The places within Thornton can be identified in ways which are easy to understand and which constitute various 'modules' for the design. Within the Research Centre, there is the Laboratory Block. Within that are individual blocks. Within those are areas shared by large groups. Within those are smaller, group areas. Within those are offices. Each of these are places, and each have their own experience. However, because there is a hierarchy of places, many of the recommendations resulting from the research can be applied to more than one level. For example, the nested spatial hierarchy is applied to groups, buildings and the site as a whole. It suggests the grouping of people, groups and buildings around a central resource/relaxing area. The idea is applied to several levels of place hierarchy. Another example is the locating of hazardous activities at the rear. This can be of both the site as a whole, the laboratory block and individual laboratory blocks.

The Theory of Place provides for research to cover the whole of a design and not just small individual aspects of the design. By using the concept of a hierarchy of places, it is easier to identify the themes which develop during the course of the research, and to apply them in the creation of the design.

Methodology

The research on which the design recommendations are based was carried out at Thornton Research Centre between 27th October and 1st December 1993, and at Sittingbourne Research Centre on 16/17th December 1993. Additional material was collected on the landscaping on 3rd March 1994 at a workshop organised by Shell in collaboration with John Tierney of Wilson/Mason.

All the material collected was treated in confidence, with only general trends being reported to Shell management rather than individual comments. Participants were drawn from the whole of the staff at Thornton through advertising for volunteers and by direct recruitment by supervisors. The participants from Sittingbourne were invited to attend by their supervisors.

The activities were carried out at Thornton over a period of six weeks. Some members of staff took part in one or more studies. In total, 196 different people took part in the process at Thornton. This included:

- 14 Focused Interviews
- 52 Questionnaires researching attitudes and opinions towards the site
- 54 Questionnaires researching conceptions about building styles
- 24 Design Exercises
- 30 Location Tasks
- 26 Individual sorting tasks
- 3 Group location tasks
- 11 Group discussions
- 15 Landscape Designs

The sorting task, importance questionnaire and pictures questionnaire were completed at Sittingbourne in two days. Fifty-one people took part at Sittingbourne. This included:

- 51 Questionnaires researching attitudes and opinions towards the site
- 51 Questionnaires researching conceptions about building styles
- 51 Individual sorting tasks
- 4 Group location tasks

This section of the report will list the type and range of data collection activities which were used during the research, and describe the nature of some of the analysis.

Initial interviews

Interviews were held with the Director of Thornton, four of the Department Heads at Thornton and seven Group leaders from Thornton plus two other senior people. These interviews explored broad issues concerning plans for the site and the laboratories, and were the first stage in understanding the salient aspects in the designs.

Design workshops

Two design workshops were held at Thornton, each lasting a day. The first day focused on the design for the laboratory, and two groups of four people took part. For this session, the participants were laboratory staff holding any position up to group leader. The second day focused on the site, and four groups of four people took part. They were from the whole of Thornton, again, holding any position up to group leader.

Both days started by asking the individual groups to discuss aspects which they would wish to see included or avoided in the new designs. These were discussed with the whole group to clarify and assess the level of agreement. The individual groups were then asked to build a model of the new laboratory or site, so that it would be their ideal laboratory or site. No restrictions such as underground piping or cost were imposed on these designs. Finally, the designs were discussed by the whole group.

The design workshops were a particularly rich source of data. The sessions provided reasons and criteria for the designs, plus the models and many comments. The data was content analysed, and the major themes were identified.

Interviews

Further interviews were held with laboratory staff to gather more information about design issues in a laboratory.

Multiple sorting task

Twenty-seven people in four groups took part in the sorting task (Canter et al, 1985) at Thornton. Fifty people in four groups took part at Sittingbourne. A list of the activities which occur at Thornton had been compiled and the aim of the exercise was to explore the links which the staff perceived between parts of the organisation and the environmental experience in which each activity takes place.

The members of the groups were invited to look over the list of activities and add any which they felt were missing. At Sittingbourne, many of the activities which occur specifically at that centre were added. The activities were written on to pieces of card, which had a unique number printed on the back. Each person had an identical set of cards. The participants were asked to look at the cards, and then to sort them into groups in such a way that the cards in any group were similar to each other in some way and different from those in other groups. Each card could be in one group and one group only. There could be as many groups as they liked, and as many cards in each group as they liked. It was emphasised that there were no right or wrong answers, and that it was their opinions which counted. The common factors identified by each participant for the cards in each group were then written down by the participant, together with the numbers of the cards which were in each group.

The exercise was repeated two or three times, or until the participant could think of no more categories. The participants were then asked to think about the experience of being in the place where each activity occurs, and to sort according to this place experience.

The participants were also asked to work as a group and to sort the items into groups as they had done as individuals, but this time to arrive at a group consensus. It was emphasised that this did not relate to actual locations.

The data from the sorting task was analysed using Multidimensional Scalogram Analysis (MSA). In this type of analysis, the groupings imposed by the participant on the cards can be represented by a row of data or 'profile', which can be compared with the profiles for all the other cards. The more frequently cards have been grouped together, the more similar their profiles and, therefore, the closer the points are to each other in the computer generated space. The more distant points are from each other the less likely those activities were considered to be similar to each other in some way.

The plots can be divided into areas by reference to the original data supplied by the participants, and lines drawn to best represent the categorisations of the participants. A line drawn between two adjacent points indicates that although the points are physically close together, the overall structure of the participants' categorisations shows that they belong in separate sections of the plot. It is indicative of a factor which is pulling these items together, but which is not as strong as the factors which have created the divisions.

The titles of the areas in the plots come from the names given to the groups in the sorting. These are the aspects of the cards which those in a group have in common.

The data was analysed to show the basic conceptualisations which staff at Thornton and Sittingbourne hold about the various activities, and to show the types of place experience which they associate with each activity.

Importance questionnaire

Fifty-two people from across the Thornton site, and 51 people from Sittingbourne completed a questionnaire. None of the participants from Thornton had been involved with any previous data gathering. The questionnaire sought to clarify issues which had been raised through the research, and to assess the level of support which some possibilities had.

Members of staff at Thornton completed the questionnaire with a researcher. 67 questions covered a range of issues, and asked the participant to say how important the issue being addressed was to them. In addition to this, the researcher gained background information about the participant including job title and department, and asked for their reaction to the consultation process.

The participants at Sittingbourne were asked to complete the questionnaire themselves, and background information was obtained at another stage.

The data was analysed by calculating the means for each question, SSA and ANOVA. The results clarified which issues were important to the staff of Sittingbourne and Thornton, and whether there were any differences in the opinions of staff depending upon their department.

Pictures questionnaire

Twenty drawings of buildings covering a wide range of architectural styles, in two groups of ten, were shown to 54 staff at Thornton. They were asked to pick one as being their most preferred, and one as their least preferred, giving reasons for their decision.

Ten of the drawings were shown to 51 participants at Sittingbourne. The drawings were chosen to represent the range of preference expressed at Thornton previously. They were asked to chose their most preferred and to give reasons. Background information about the participants was gained at this point.

Location tasks

Three location task sessions were held. The first focused on the laboratory and the 10 participants were all laboratory staff. The second and third sessions focused on the site as a whole and the 20 participants were drawn from all of the site.

The Location Task (Peled 1976a, 1976b) is a technique through which a person can make explicit both the way in which they would like to position, partition and orientate the spatial regions of a place, and the meanings attached to this place. It was designed so that users would not be constricted by the complexities of actually designing a place, nor would it be too abstract to consider.

The participants are asked to think about the place as they would like it to be and to make a list of the places they would like to have in the immediate vicinity of, or be able to see from the place. They are then provided with a 'square-circle'[1] drawn on a piece of paper. The region surrounding this is the outside of the place, and marked on the paper are four major directions; Front/Back, Right/Left and Core/Periphery. They are asked to locate the items they have listed so that the best place as they would like it is created. The participant is asked to mark groups of places or regions of space on the paper and to describe the place they have tried to create.

The task enables the participants to relate simultaneously to inside and outside places, and to relate each place to another and to the system of places as a whole. It is this holistic approach that allows the participants to use all of the parameters in an attempt to create a spatial representation of the place's identity.

For the site location task, the participants were provided with the list of activities used in the sorting task. They were invited to add more activities if they wished, then to write down the activities onto stickers and locate the activities on the 'square-circle'. A discussion was held about each location task and the points it made.

The data was analysed using content analysis.

[1] This is a rounded square drawn on a piece of A3 paper.

Landscape workshop

Two landscape workshops were run with 14 volunteers from the Thornton site. They were asked to consider the experiences and activities they would like to include in the site design. The first exercise included a visit to the main area to be developed, and the volunteers gained an understanding of the size of the area which will be approximately the size of two football pitches. They were asked to list activities and experiences, and to make a rough drawing of locations. After a group discussion, they were asked to think about the ideas in more detail and to locate activities and features on a map of the proposed site plan. They were not restricted only to the central area, and could include the areas between buildings, the perimeter and the front entrance. There was a further group discussion and clarification of the landscaping ideas created in the workshop. Content analysis revealed themes for the preferred landscape design.

Design principles

The results of the research can be summarised in the following design principles.

International research centre

Thornton Research Centre should reflect in its design, the site as an International Research Centre and to support research of the highest standard.

Visitors. The design should facilitate contact with visitors, and provide quality accommodation for their visit.

Landscaping. Landscaping should be used to provide a variety of experiences on the site.

Building design. The building style should reflect Thornton as a World Class and International Research Centre.

Identity

A sense of identity should be provided to each building. Two design issues can promote this;

1. Building style - whilst maintaining a sense of uniformity across the site, each building should incorporate unique design features.
2. Landscaping - should promote distinct identities for each group of buildings.

Front stage and back stage.   The design should incorporate 'public' and 'private' areas to enable people to be in control of what is 'presented' about their activities and what is 'backstage'.

Nested spatial hierarchy

The design should combine individual privacy with interaction and communication. This should occur on three levels; group level, building level and site level. This can be achieved by application of the idea of a nested spatial hierarchy.

Safety and security

The site design should improve the physical quality of the site and incorporate elements of security in the design.

Ring road and parking.   The design should remove traffic from the centre of the site to improve the quality of the site. Security can be improved by the separation of vehicles from the site centre.

Clear demarcation of areas.   This will ensure that visitors are readily recognised and facilitate security.

Comfort and efficiency

The site design should improve the efficiency within which the site operates. This includes raising the standards of comfort and convenience for visitors and staff.

Rationalised buildings.   Fewer buildings will improve communication and interaction between staff, and provide a sense of identity to teams.

Activity layout.   Logical location of activities relative to one another will improve communication and interaction between staff.

Orientation.   Logical layout of the site will improve way finding for staff and visitors. This will add to the efficiency of the site.

Site layout recommendations

Central focus

The site has a central focus. It is surrounded by individual buildings, and is accessed from all points of the site.

Ring road

The central focus creates a natural ring road which contains all main buildings and separates the site from the car parking.

The centre of the site can therefore be a pedestrian region.

Car parking and access. The car parking can be around the periphery of the site. This allows access from the back of the site, and reduces fears of personal safety.

Focused buildings

The buildings are arranged around the central area. Whilst keeping their individuality, each focuses on and shares this central area. This improves the interaction and communication between the buildings.

Visitors

The Visitor Centre is located at the front of the site, but within the central area. Visitors can thus be brought immediately into the centre of the site. This helps them to understand the structure and orientation of the site.

Landscaping

The site landscaping should be strong, with emphasis on a natural appearance rather than a 'park' approach. Native plants which encourage wildlife should be used.

The use of landscaping can improve the individuality of each building by providing unique views to each building.

Landscaping can provide a relaxing atmosphere of contemplation, and a change of environment from offices or laboratories.

Overall, variety is required to provide several different experiences around the site.

Security demarcation

The centrality of the Visitor Centre allows a demarcation of security so that grades of security can be applied. Visitors will be directed to the visitor centre in the first instance, and then suitable security measures applied depending upon which area of the site will be visited and the nature of the visit.

Front stage and back stage. The site and buildings can have areas which are open to all. These are 'front' regions, and contain public facilities and information. Hazardous and sensitive activities and information can be located in the 'back' regions. These are at the back of buildings and the site, and are not visited by either staff or visitors unless they need to go to that specific area.

In this way, a natural security demarcation is formed which can be reinforced by physical measures.

Progression through the site. The progression through the site with regard to the activities should be: Visitor Centre → Support Services and Site Facilities → Research and Development → Hazardous Activities.

Buildings

Focus. The buildings focus on the centre of the site, and within the buildings there are central points and areas.

Communal. There are communal areas within buildings where communal equipment is located and which serve as areas in which staff can meet informally, and therefore should not just be a storage area. These areas provide opportunities for communication and interaction.

Social. On a smaller scale, groups within the building have social areas in which to meet and talk. These are accessed directly from offices, so combining privacy and individual control with interaction and communication.

Connections. Connecting buildings preserves individual identity whilst maintaining links between groups. Covered connections can provide protection during inclement weather.

Building style

The style of the building designs should encompass a range of characteristics such as height, extent of uniformity and connections to other buildings in addition to the style of the external design

Building style dimensions. Buildings which are appropriate to Thornton would give an impression of a World Class Research Centre and which are impressive to visitors.

The designs should appear to be more frugal (but not cheap) than extravagant, and should incorporate the following features:

- Simple designs
- Many windows

- Some interesting design features
- Roofs which are not flat
- A design which is more 'classic' than futuristic.

Uniform/individuality. Each building should be designed to be unique. This needs to be balanced with the sense of uniformity around the site.

Height. The buildings should not exceed 2/3 storeys. To improve the experience of the buildings, plenty of external light should be allowed into all areas of the buildings. In laboratory blocks, the third storey should not be used for laboratory purposes.

The height of the buildings can be used to create differences in the design of the individual buildings. Variation in height and third storey design will provide external and internal individuality.

Labelling. Each building should be labelled with a number and/or a name which describes the activity which occurs within. A unique number and/or name will differentiate between buildings and improve a sense of individuality. The numbering system should be logical.

Activity groupings

The activities at Thornton need to be located on the site in ways which improve interaction and communication between related disciplines and which improve the working experience for the staff.

Place experience. The activities have different place experiences such as noisy, dirty, clean and quiet. Where possible, noisy and dirty activities should not be placed close to clean and quiet ones. This is unlikely to occur since the noisy and dirty activities tend to be research and development, while clean and quiet activities are generally the support services and site facilities.

Risk reduction. To reduce risks, hazardous activities should be located towards the rear of the site and at the rear of buildings.

Clustering. Activities which are similar in nature should be clustered together. Research activities should be together, and development activities should be together, etc.

Laboratory layout recommendations

Components

The laboratory should be composed of the following:

- Offices
- Communal Area
- Laboratories
- Laboratories for specific activities
- Storage
- Visitor Reception

Linking laboratory blocks

The laboratory blocks should be linked by the communal activities

Hazards

Hazardous materials should be kept away from public areas, and preferably on the ground floor to reduce the problems of any leaks.

Hazardous activities should be located away from public areas, preferably at the rear of buildings

Progression through the building

The progression through the building should be:

Entrance

↓

Visitor Reception

↓

Information Point

↓

Administration Facilities

↓

Formal and Informal Meeting Points for Staff

↓

Refreshment and Facilities Area

↓

Offices

↓

Laboratories and Offices

↓

Laboratories for Hazardous Activities

References

Canter, D. (1971), *The Psychology of Place*, Architectural Press, London.

Canter, D. (1977), *Multiple Sorting Task*.

Peled, A. (1976a), 'The Strathclyde Location Estate', a Project Technique for Eliciting the Constructs of Spatial Division of an Experienced Environmental Event' in the Suedfeld, P. and Russel, J.A. (ed.), Book II, *The Behavioural Basis of Design*, Hutchinson and Ross, Dowden.

Peled, A. (1976b), 'A study of the Appropriation of a Secondary School's Space by a Sample of 34 Pupils in Korosec-Serfaty', P. (ed.), *Appropriation of Space*, pp. 88-89.

COMPLEMENTARY MEDICINE

13 How Do We Know It Works? Approaches to the Evaluation of Complementary Medicine

Some starting points

Complementary medicine is a term used to cover a vast array of treatment procedures as wide ranging as aroma therapy, iridology, acupuncture, homeopathy and osteopathy. It is sometimes known as alternative or even folk medicine. These complementary therapies exist because people find them helpful. Research must, therefore, be directed at asking 'Who?', 'What?', and 'How?'. In the following chapter ways of answering these questions are examined. Emphasis is given to the need for a variety of different research strategies and tactics. A preliminary outline of an overall approach which would hold together the strands in a fruitful way is proposed, based on facet Meta-Theory.

In considering the emerging research prospect for the study of complementary medical practice it is important to clarify some initial premises.These provide a framework within which to consider a great variety of research possibilities.They also point towards areas of study that might not otherwise be apparent.

Complementary medical practice exists and thrives

Fulder's (1984) review of over 250 organisations and colleges for practitioners, taken together with the more recent survey by Wharton and Lewith (1986), showing the extensive use made of those services through referrals from medical general practitioners, serves to illustrate the vast need there seems to be for complementary medicine.

This fast growing network of alternative services means that research cannot proceed on the basis that there are some novel untried procedures that must be proven, before they can be released to an unsuspecting public. The researcher is not faced with the recent discovery of some purported new cure that will not be taken up unless research proves that it works. The situation is more like that of a committed, scientific atheist, who wishes to understand the values of religion.

This chapter is derived from papers that were greatly influenced or indeed co-authored by Ceri Roderick and Lorraine Nanke. I am happy to acknowledge their contributions to the thinking behind the present chapter as well as their detailed research input.

Religions of many forms exist on a large scale. Their destructive potential cannot be denied, but many will speak up for their fundamental, essential value in society. The task of research is to understand the strengths and weaknesses of these existing approaches to the promotion of human wellbeing. To develop that understanding we must examine the logic upon which the different complementary practices operate and study closely the conditions under which successes and failures occur. Above all, the very existence of complementary medicine demands that research establishes exactly how and why it exists. Merely proving or disproving the specific effects of the agents (needles, pills or manipulations) used in complementary medicine, will have as little effect as Marx's arguments about the illogicality and evil of religion.

Metaphors for disease processes

The need to broaden our approaches to the study of complementary treatments is illuminated when it is realised that we cannot see diseases; they are an invented notion. We may see their consequences but not the disease process. So, in order to talk about a disease we have to develop ways of referring to those processes, particularly if we want to talk about possible outcome and treatment and what is being done to control or eradicate the disease. To do this, metaphors have to be used to describe what is going on.

For example, a common metaphor is warfare. We are 'attacking' the disease. This is one way of talking about the process between doctor and patient. In fact it is quite an interesting and rich metaphor. There are even local 'guerrilla battles' that are being fought. These contrast with, say, somebody in intensive radiotherapy or chemotherapy where it becomes a total war in which the individual accepts total involvement.

Another metaphor may be thought of as horticultural. The idea that there are natural processes that with enough light and effective watering and so on, will come to fruit. This is just as much a metaphor and just as necessary to use as any of the others.

Other metaphors that are very common are a variety of mechanical metaphors, not just in relation to the body. The idea that you can localise the seat of action of a particular antibiotic, for example, and thereby nudge the offending component out of the way in order to change the system. Another sort of metaphor that is related but rather different is the hydraulic metaphor of pushing forces along a pipeline. Acupuncture speaks of energy and forces and so uses these ideas overtly, but there are many other practices which are similar in their vocabulary. One that is often used in surgery, is the plumbing metaphor. It is often very powerful for the individual to know that his 'pipes are blocked' and that they can be unblocked.

There is another fascinating metaphor that is sometimes used today, yet it is difficult to find a word for it. Perhaps 'acrobatics' is a good term because it helps to explain why people are so hesitant in certain areas, especially in psychotherapy. The business of 'getting hold of yourself', of 'coming to terms with yourself', of developing a way of thinking about yourself, about gaining control over your own actions, the whole issue of agency and the individual being a dominant performer in his own display, is often presented in a way that involves all sorts of psychic contortions, and on occasion also physical ones. That is one of the reasons why I think people find the psychotherapeutic encounter so difficult to understand, so threatening, because it does involve going through mental gymnastics that they might feel they are not up to.

One further metaphor is really close to magic and witchcraft, especially the idea of exorcism. This seems to be still a very powerful idea in many areas; the idea of driving the evil out, 'If you take these magic pills they will make the disease go away'.

I have deliberately chosen metaphors that are equally applicable to complementary and allopathic/conventional medicine. All are used as part of the process of negotiating and discussing the nature of the problem that the individual is facing.

Returning to the general framework, the problem of generating ways of measuring outcome and deciding whether treatment actually works, is a problem of finding measurement devices that will connect with the sort of metaphorical explanations that are at the heart of our dealing with patients.

The question 'How do we know it works?' is a very powerful mechanical metaphor. It enshrines the idea of a machine rolling on, and of bits falling off or being broken somewhere. We replace a part or fix it in some way. Then we ask 'How do we actually know whether it is still working?' We accept that the person is such a complicated machine that you cannot actually look at it and see that it is working in the same way that it was, and that in a few years time the weakness may show up again somewhere.

If we had asked the question 'How do we know that it has gone?', it would have been more of an exorcist form; 'How do we know that the individual has got it under control?' would be more acrobatic; 'How do we know when we are winning?' would be military; and 'How do we know that channels are unblocked, or fluids are in balance' a hydraulic form of question. Each has equal legitimacy. But each draws attention to different ways of considering the whole system of experiences that go to make up the treatment process. If research ignores this complexity and seeks only to examine bio-medical processes it may make some small-scale discoveries, but it will miss the overall picture.

Conventional research activities are frequently flawed

The first volume of the *Journal of Complementary Medical Research* was devoted to the strengths and weaknesses of the controlled, randomised experimental trial. It is clear from that discussion and many other considerations of research procedures that it would be unduly limiting to restrict complementary medical research to the experimental research strategy. But it is also important to realise that, as with all activities conducted by human beings, all research is subject to many different biases and flaws. Furthermore, any given study involving people as the subjects of the study is more open to error than might often be realised. This is because the study of biological, psychological and social processes is particularly difficult and, especially where practitioners are carrying out the studies, because practitioners, even though sophisticated in theory, are often not expert in research methodologies. Many purely technical infelicities have been pointed out in the published literature on research on people, even before the philosophical and ethical problems involved are considered.

No one study or research strategy will reveal the untrammelled truth, and inevitably a variety of strategies will be needed. Attempts should be made to identify the biases in any one strategy and deliberately complement that approach with others that are not so open to that bias.

The scientist-practitioner model

One common approach to therapeutic research has been termed the scientist-practitioner: the clinician who not only helps relieve patients' problems using the expertise of their own discipline, but also carries out research into their own practice. The model is based on the idea of a continuing dialogue between theory and practice. Clinical work provides a source of insights and hypotheses about the effects and effectiveness of particular interventions. These are then subjected to more systematic evaluation in individual cases and larger scale group studies, eventually contributing to the development of collective knowledge and improvements in practice.

In relation to psychotherapy, Strupp(1981) suggests that the scientist-practitioner model provides: 'the opportunity for oscillation between the observation and participation, between taking part and standing back, between feeling and thinking, between (controlled) abandonment and study. It is this process of oscillation, the unique human ability to resonate, identify and therapeutically respond to themes in the patients' experience that is essential ... It should be possible to encourage research that is both rigorous and relevant to clinical and social issues' (p. 563).

Advantages of the model

Overcoming the clinical/research split. A major advantage of the model is that it overcomes the sterile split between clinicians and research scientists, potentially avoiding the narrowness of thought and rigidity of action which are often associated with exclusive focus on either. Scientific researchers are often criticised for producing results which seem irrelevant to clinical practice using measures and strategies which are beyond the scope and resources of clinicians. Conversely, clinicians are criticised for not using the insights acquired as a result of their experience as a basis for research, development of cumulative knowledge, or training, trusting solely on their clinical experience to evaluate their practice. The model is intended to overcome this problem by combining clinical and research functions in the same individuals where possible.

Accountability. The increasing stress on accountability in the provision of services means that particular therapeutic disciplines cannot avoid the necessity of describing and empirically validating the effects of their work. This requirement is likely to become increasingly important to patients who wish to make an informed choice between the wide diversity of treatments available. In this context, all clinical disciplines have an obligation to carry out some type of empirical research into their methods of treatment.

Lack of dependable knowledge. Perhaps the most important consideration underlying the scientist-practitioner model is the lack of dependable information currently available about the reliability and effectiveness of many diagnostic and therapeutic techniques. In 1950, Raimy stated that: 'psychotherapy is an undefined technique, applied to unspecified problems, with an unpredictable outcome. For this technique we are recommending rigorous training' (p. 93). It is disappointing to recognise how much this comment is still applicable to psychotherapeutic practice and it may be useful to consider the extent to which it is also relevant to complementary medicine. Clinicians of all disciplines are best placed to recognise and study the important aspects of real life clinical intervention and change; indeed most rely on their own experience as validation of their particular theoretical approach and techniques. Though such personal conviction may be valuable to the individual clinician and their patients, it is of little help in contributing to collective, dependable knowledge about the process and effects of different types of therapy. This requires systematic empirical investigation producing objective results which can be evaluated by others within the discipline and the wider scientific community.

Problems of the model

A salutary lesson from clinical psychology. Unfortunately, the scientist-practitioner model remains more of an ideal than an accurate description of normal practice, even in clinical psychology which is explicitly based on this approach. Despite a thorough grounding in research methodology, very few practising clinicians actually carry out research after qualification, and many state that they would prefer less emphasis on research methodology in training. Some consideration of this issue may help complementary practitioners avoid a key pitfall of the scientist-practitioner model, and help establish the research enterprise on a more productive footing.

The clinical context and experimental science

One of the major problems facing clinicians who wish to carry out research has been identified as the mismatch between the demands of clinical research, and the requirements of experimental science. This was the conclusion drawn by Bergin and Strupp (1981) from a survey of leading psychologists and psychiatrists. They state that: 'among researchers as well as statisticians there is a growing disaffection from traditional experimental designs and statistical procedures, which are held inappropriate to the subject matter under study. This judgement applies with particular force to the area of therapeutic change, and our emphasis on the value of experimental case studies underscores this point. We strongly agree that most of the standard experimental designs and statistical procedures have exerted, and are continuing to exert, a constricting influence on fruitful inquiry, and they serve to perpetuate an unwarranted emphasis on methodology' (p. 440). This mismatch has often been dealt with by attempting to adapt clinical questions to the Procrustean bed of experimental science. As such, it is often accepted as axiomatic in medical, psychological and biological research that the only genuinely scientific strategy is the experimental design, in which people are randomly assigned to different conditions and subjected to blind or double blind trial in order to measure the influence of a key independent variable. The independent variable in such studies is characteristically seen as the main single causal agent producing the effect, which is the observed difference between groups. The limitations of this approach have been well documented elsewhere, (e.g., Heron, 1986) but it is worth noting some of the main difficulties encountered in a clinical context here.

Conflicting priorities

A clinician's first priority is almost always the wellbeing of individual patients, and this may conflict with the requirements of strictly experimental research design. For example, treatment strategy may normally be decided on the basis of ongoing therapeutic dialogue with the patient, changing in response to the patient's reaction, and reformulations of the problem. Yet, controlled comparison between two specific techniques often requires that the treatment, or lack of treatment in the case of a control group, is determined by the requirements of the research design rather than patient need. The scientist-practitioner model is likely to be most effective when the primary clinical priority is recognised, and means found to help clinicians carry out research into what they actually do in the course of normal practice rather than tailoring practice to the experimental design.

Moral concerns

Closely related to the issue of clinical priorities are the moral problems which can be encountered using the standard clinical trial. Firstly, there is the difficulty of obtaining patients' informed consent, as this kind of study is ideally carried out double blind, without patient or practitioner knowing which patient is receiving which treatment. Secondly, many clinicians express concern about patients in the control group being untreated, given a placebo, or receiving a treatment which may be less effective than the experimental treatment.

Single versus multiple factors

The experimental method is designed to address questions which can be answered in terms of simple cause-effect mechanisms.The clinical trial is only able to compare simple alternative causal agents, i.e., the variable which differs between control and experimental groups, to explain observed variation in effect. This kind of question is perfectly appropriate where there are clear theoretical reasons to predict that treatment agent A will cause outcome B; for example, that a particular antibiotic will remove infection and associated symptoms, or that any difference in outcome is likely to be due to the single factor on which the control and experimental groups differ, e.g., type of treatment received. The clinical trial is particularly well suited to the traditional disease focus of orthodox medicine, in which the search for single pathogenic agents and remedies has a strong theoretical basis. However, it is less applicable to the holistic approach, which is based on a theoretical framework stressing the importance of multiple interacting factors relevant to treatment effects in each individual patient.

Clinical and statistical significance

Associated with the clinical trial methodology has been an over-reliance on statistical probability measures to compare group differences. These measures are often used inappropriately, and lead to impoverished interpretation of results, particularly in relation to small sample sizes. Statistical significance is frequently confused with clinical significance, and all too often studies report only data on the probability that differential treatment outcomes are a result of chance, and assume that the treatment which produces a reliably different outcome is better. Yet, it matters little if one therapy produces effects at a statistically significant level more than other therapies, if these changes are not of sufficient magnitude to be experienced as meaningful by the patient. Even statistically significant results often account for only a small proportion of the observed variance, indicating that in such cases the single cause explanation provides an inadequate account of obtained results.

Practical difficulties

The practical requirements of setting up clinical trials, including obtaining large numbers of matched subjects, control groups, possibly external blind raters, and large scale standardisation of treatment, can place excessive and possibly unmanageable demands on practising clinicians who might otherwise be prepared to contribute to research. Further, 'blind' administration can easily be applied to pharmacological treatments in which active and placebo substances can be made to appear identical. However, it is impossible to administer many other forms of physical or psychological treatment 'blind', for example massage or acupuncture; such treatments an be incorporated into standard clinical trials only if an apparently equivalent but theoretically inert form can be devised and administered to the control group.

Group versus individual differences

The practice of using group averages to compare patient groups obscures potentially important individual differences in treatment response. Kiesler (1965) has described this practice as based on 'the patient uniformity myth', that is, the assumption that the variables being studied are the only relevant differences between groups. This assumption is not warranted on empirical grounds, as there is much evidence that some patients in every study improve, some stay the same, and some get worse (see for example, Garfield, 1981). Barlow et al (1984), point out that the roots of the problem lie in traditional experimental research methodology, and particularly the improper use of sampling techniques.

According to sampling theory, a random sample of the population of interest must be studied if adequate generalisations are to be made about the whole population. In a clinical context, this would mean drawing a sample in which all individual differences potentially relevant to treatment outcome are represented. If the treatment applied to all of these individuals produced a statistically significant effect compared to a control group, the treatment would be judged effective. However, Barlow et al add that applied researchers have long recognised firstly the practical impossibility of obtaining a patient sample in which all potentially relevant factors are adequately represented, and secondly the theoretical problem that the sample would be so heterogenous that few if any treatments would be likely to show statistically significant effect.

An alternative strategy consistent with experimental methodology and the clinical trial has been the selection of homogenous patient groups to minimise sources of individual variation which may confound results. This approach is also subject to the practical problem of obtaining an appropriate sample; for example, finding a group of anxiety patients who also have similar personalities, backgrounds, life circumstances and any other factors of potential relevance to treatment. Further, the results of such studies can only be generalised to patients with similar characteristics, and so are of limited value to practising clinicians. What is needed is an approach which can go beyond the comparison of group averages, to help identify which patients respond in which way to which treatment.

Experimenter distortion

Experimenter distortion in research is a double-edged sword. On one hand, the most productive research is usually carried out by those with a strong interest and expertise in the subject area. On the other hand, science is based on the ideal of objectivity and freedom from personal bias. Though a study may be designed on the basis of personal interests, the results should be reproducible by other independent researchers with different interests. One potent way in which the researcher can distort or influence data obtained is by inadvertently conveying their expectations to patients. Orne (1962) suggested that subjects are usually so keen to please the researcher that they actively search for and act on clues as to how the researcher wants them to behave. These clues and hints are collectively referred to as the 'demand characteristics' of a situation. 'Demand characteristics' are clearly involved in any clinical or research enterprise involving human beings. However, tailoring treatment to fit strictly experimental research design may so alter the perceived demand characteristics for patients that results obtained may not easily generalise to the different perceived demand characteristics of the normal clinical consultation. Experimenter distortion may be one reason for the fact that one of the few reliable generalisations that can be drawn from the wealth of psychotherapy outcome research is that most studies provide some degree of support for the orientation of the researcher.

Quantitative and qualitative data

One fallacy often associated with reliance on experimental methodology is the assumption that easily quantified factors are inherently more scientific than those which are not so easily assigned to numbers. This has been likened to the fable of the drunk looking for his key under the light rather than where he lost it, because he can see under the light. The important point here is a that a research study should be designed to assess the factors which are likely to be relevant to the original question, rather than those which are easily measured. This applies in particular to clinical research, where qualitative changes, for example sense of wellbeing or relationships, may be of overriding importance. The goal of objectivity and replicability is central to any type of measurement, but different types of measurement are appropriate for different types of variable. The task is to identify ways in which relevant factors can be most reliably assessed, rather than trying to build research questions around factors which can be easily quantified.

Temporal changes

Finally, many experimental studies compare treatment outcome at one particular point in time, classifying patients in terms of extent of recovery. The usefulness of this approach may depend partly on the condition being studied; for example it makes considerable sense in relation to acute conditions such as an infection, or emotional crisis reaction, but is perhaps less applicable to chronic or lifestyle-related conditions, in which longer term changes, and maintenance after treatment are more significant.

The need for a meta-theory

Once these assumptions are recognised, it is apparent that a plethora of unconnected non-cumulative studies is likely. In the complementary arena such diffusion of effort is even more likely because of the many different theoretical formulations from which hypotheses can be derived. The significant concern that variations between individuals should be fully accounted for serves only to add complexity to an already potentially confusing situation.

There are a number of ways out of this possible morass. One is to identify and focus attention on high priority areas, especially those with political significance, and focus attention on those. Unfortunately, priorities today may be irrelevant tomorrow. This is unfortunate in research terms because research initiated today will certainly not report until tomorrow, if not the day after. Another approach is to provide a framework within which the theories and methods of all research can be accommodated. Such a framework must be value-free and neutral as regards particular theoretical stances, but will allow comparisons between different studies.

This might seem a great deal to demand of any framework, until it is realised that what such a framework is being called on to provide is simply a coherent logical system for describing research. Such a system needs to provide the intellectual tools for summarising the particular theories under study and for establishing the links that those theories have with recorded data. In other words, the approach that will provide a framework for a variety of different studies, drawing on different theories, without forcing them all into the same theoretical straitjacket, will be a theory about how theories are constructed and tested, a meta-theory.

An effective meta-theory would enable researchers to cast, say, acupuncture and homeopathy into the same logical mould, together with conventional medicine without the need to interpret all the data as energy lines, or as pharmacological changes, or whatever. Of course, eventually it would be expected that one explanatory system would become dominant, because of its power and fruitfulness, but in the best scientific traditions there would be no need to assume, in setting up the research, which theory is the most powerful.

The level of abstraction of this argument is so great that it is worth giving a concrete example of the essential logic of this approach. Consider homeopathic prescribing on the basis of the identification of the patient as relating to a particular polycrest. A strongly theory-driven research project would, typically, try to find some existing classification of the patients being treated, say, in conventional medical terms and either try to 'validate' the homoeopathic prescription by relating it to known pharmacological effects, or by trying to convert the polycrest into the conventional medical diagnosis and extrapolate the results.

If a meta-theory can be drawn upon, however, the homoeopathic procedure can be examined initially in its own terms. It will reveal that certain relationships between what happens to patients, how they are initially classified and the treatment prescribed will be predicted by the theory. A conventional medical approach will also generate an interrelated set of predictions. Both approaches can therefore be examined to see which is the most fruitful in the consideration of the treatment and its outcome.

It is important to note that in the example no reference is made as to which treatment is the most 'successful'. Success is a higher-order level of analysis and may be made irrelevant by the earlier level of discourse, for example by the fact that the homoeopath, or GP, cannot specify what outcome should be characteristic of the treatment given. As this example shows, the meta-theory requires to be quite robust and logically powerful if it is to make any significant contribution.

A brief outline of facet meta-theory

The value of a meta-theory also depends upon how flexible and fruitful it proves itself to be. Mathematical procedures are generally the basis of any meta-theoretical approach, but in the area of complementary medicine many of the issues to be studied will not lend themselves readily to advanced mathematics. One approach that is gaining in acceptability, facet meta-theory, derives from elementary mathematical ideas. This has been applied to studies ranging from distinguishing malicious from non-malicious false alarms to the fire brigade to the prognosis of thyroid cancer, from research on the provision of hostels for alcoholics to explanations of slimming behaviour. In essence the facet approach sees any scientific theory as consisting of four components:

1. The first, and most central, is the recognition that all theories are in essence derived from ways of classifying observations, incorporating some clear definitions of what the classifications are. This is known in facet theory as a 'definitional system'.
    Darwin's theory is based on the classification of plants and animals, etc. Bacteriological theory is derived from categories of disease, symptoms and bacteria. Acupuncture is derived from classes of energy imbalance, osteopathy from classes of position of bones and so on. Any mutually exclusive, exhaustive set of categories is known as a 'facet'. Facets are assumed to be only qualities, unless there are particular reasons why some order or quantification can be given to the 'elements' of which they are composed. The colours of the spectrum make up the qualitative elements of a colour facet, unless they are defined in the quantities of wavelength. This fundamentally qualitative basis to facet theory is what gives it its power and flexibility.
2. The second component is the identification of patterns in any observations made. An elementary pattern would be the observation that those assigned to one treatment group all have measured levels that are distinct from those assigned to another group. The notion of a 'pattern' in the observations is, however, a very rich one that can accommodate notions as complex as multivariate relationships or as simple as differences in percentages.
3. The third component is the establishing of a correspondence between some aspect of the definitional system and some critical aspect of the patterns in the observations. People described as having been treated with a particular drug and whose responses have been classified according to how much better they are, would be expected to have a different sub-set of responses to those who were not described as having been so treated.
4. The fourth component is a logical explanation or 'rationale' as to why the correspondence between definitional system and observations occurs.

Definitional system, pattern in the observations, correspondence and rationale are all directly recognisable in any good science, whether it uses the language of facet theory or not. In that respect facet theory is simply a systematisation of the general scientific approach. But by being so systematic and theory-tolerant, it does provide opportunities for research in complementary medicine that are hidden when less overt systems of science are utilised.

A general data matrix

In order to see how the facet approach can define a research agenda there is one helpful technical device, the data matrix.

In essence, all therapeutic research can be viewed as the exploration of patients and their attributes. The simplest way of thinking of this is that data is collected that can be represented as a number of rows, one row for each patient, and a number of columns, one column for each facet that characterises the patients. The cells of the matrix indicate the value any given patient has achieved on any given facet. For example, in its most elementary form a drugs trial of 20 people could produce a matrix of twenty rows and two columns, one classifying the patients in terms of the drug they received, the other in terms of its effects. The pattern looked for is one that matches the two classifications. If there is no discernible match then nothing clear can be said about the effect of the drug.

Matrixes of greater complexity can, of course, be constructed. They can mix together, for example, the many psychological and physiological variables that a holistic approach would suggest should be combined. The data matrix knows and cares nothing of such miscegenation! The rows need not be different people but can be the same person at different points in time, or some combination of the two. In other words, like the facets to which it relates, the data matrix makes no assumptions about the most appropriate theories or methods for the research in question. It is a neutral vehicle for carrying out research. But, as will be seen, it helps to define a number of otherwise rather vague research objectives. Of course, as the matrix becomes more complex so more demands are made on the analysis procedures to find the critical 'patterns'. New developments in computing and statistics greatly facilitate the matrix analysis, but elaboration on these more technical aspects is not appropriate here.

Objectives for research

Having established a context for considering complementary medical research and a framework within which to specify such research, it is now possible to elaborate some of the main objectives for research and indicate how that research might be structured.

Research priorities in complementary medicine

On this account of science, the most important task facing complementary medicine is to define key research questions. This involves clarification of conceptual systems used in different disciplines into a form which can be evaluated by empirical data.

Reliability of clinical judgements

When measuring stable characteristics such as personality, measurements must be stable, consistent and free from random error or chance fluctuations. For example, if a different result was obtained each time a particular individual's height was measured, something would be seriously wrong with the measuring device. The issue is more complex with regard to unstable changing characteristics such as health status which are more often the subject of clinical concern. In such cases, reliability can best be assessed in terms of inter-rater agreement in clinical judgement, or the extent to which trained clinicians will make approximately the same judgement of a particular individual characteristic. In many areas of complementary medicine fundamental questions concerning the reliability of particular clinical judgements, diagnostic tools, patient classifications, or treatment effects have not been addressed by empirical research. On this basis alone, it is in many cases premature and misleading to draw too close analogies with orthodox medical research, where trials are often based on very specific research questions which have been shaped up by a wealth of accumulated data, and a coherent theoretical rationale.

Such work on the reliability and validity of basic clinical tools and techniques is an essential theoretical and empirical ground-clearing exercise, which needs to be carried out on a large scale to provide a meaningful context in which to undertake and interpret more sophisticated studies such as clinical trials. Unless we know that clinicians are talking about the same thing when they refer to, for example, particular homoeopathic types or cranial rhythms, studies based on such classifications will be very difficult to interpret. Similarly, it is essential to determine how much each of these classifications corresponds to clinically important differences between patients, which make a real difference when taken into account in treatment planning.

Such data is best obtained by trained clinicians carrying out studies to check the types of clinical judgement made in their own area of expertise. For example, Dove's*study of osteopathic assessments is an impressive example of a clear research question, i.e., 'can practitioners regularly and reliably agree with each other about clinical judgements they are making about a particular cranial rhythm?'. This was checked using simple, relevant and easily obtained information. Even apparently negative results showing low reliability can potentially lead to a re-shaping and refining of the research question; for example, is the inter-rater reliability of clinical judgements affected by the original training received by practitioners? or by type of cranial rhythm? or by transient patient factors? Even if subsequent studies show low reliability this is still useful in helping to stimulate the search for better diagnostic tools, and refine practice and training.

---

* Personal communicaton

Basic clinical questions

Kazdin (1980) has identified a range of questions which have provided a useful basis for psychotherapy outcome research, and which may also be of relevance to complementary medicine. I have elaborated on his ideas below.

Does treatment work?

The question here is whether patients change for the better as a result of treatment; would it make any difference if the patient was simply left alone? This simple question is often lost in a range of complex statistical manipulations yet it is the most fundamental issue in clinical research.

Patel (1987) has proposed that multidimensional cost benefit analysis is the most useful approach to treatment evaluation. This should include the cost of treatment required to produce particular therapeutic effects, in terms of time, money, other resources, and possible negative consequences for the patient. Clearly, all other things being equal, the least costly treatment alternative is to be preferred. Similarly, many different aspects of outcome should be taken into account in treatment evaluation. Patel suggests that holistic practitioners may see a higher proportion of positive treatment effects that are gradual and relatively intangible in nature, such as emotional and physical wellbeing, healthy lifestyle, and more satisfying relationships. Though such factors may be more difficult to assess than specific symptom reduction, they must be included in any comprehensive evaluation of treatment outcome and effectiveness.

Patient deterioration

Do some patients get worse as a result of treatment? This possibility is often obscured by the use of group averages which do not differentiate between those patients who do particularly well, and those who do particularly badly as a result of a particular intervention. There may also be a reluctance on the part of therapists of all persuasions to examine treatment failures. Though this tendency is understandable it may well be based on a fundamental misunderstanding.

Any effective intervention is likely to have the potential for causing negative as well as positive consequences depending on context. In the case of complementary medicine and psychotherapy, as with much of orthodox medicine, the question is to identify those applications which maximise positive and minimise negative consequences, rather than abandoning the treatment. The identification of deterioration in individual patients in response to treatment is an essential part of mapping out the optimal range of applications for particular treatments and specifying contraindications.

Durability

The temporal aspects of treatment and recovery are often overlooked in comparisons of outcome in patient groups at a particular point in time. This approach is most useful in relation to acute conditions which can be described as 'cured' or otherwise following a limited period of treatment. For patients who do not fall into this category, closer examination of the nature of changes occurring over periods of time may help to clarify the processes involved in recovery. For example, some treatment approaches, such as homoeopathic medicine and psychoanalytic psychotherapy, predict temporary exacerbation of problems in some cases as part of the process of genuine recovery. These exacerbations are therefore not contraindications for treatment, but signs that it may be having a longer-term therapeutic effect.

Conversely, there is the important question of durability of treatment effects. There are real clinical and practical difficulties involved in producing and evaluating long-term effects, but they are an important aspect of comprehensive treatment evaluation. For example, research into the addictive disorders has shown relatively good short-term effects following treatment, followed by consistently high relapse rates within three months following treatment. It would be of interest to determine whether positive lifestyle changes are adopted as a result of complementary medical treatment, and if so whether they are equally ephemeral or more enduring.

Comparative effectiveness

The question here is which of a range of treatments is most effective for a particular condition; there are two related issues involved here. Firstly, there is a need for direct assessment of the nature and extent of effects produced by different treatments. Secondly, there is a need for conceptual clarification. Complementary medicine includes a wide diversity of disciplines, each of which share some basic common features such as concern with treating the whole person, as well as unique conceptualisations of human disease and distress, and associated interventions. Complementary disciplines are derived from diverse cultures and historical periods, often related to more primitive ideas and practices. An important part of comparative research must be the appraisal of the conceptualisations and procedures of each discipline, both in their own terms, and in relation to each other in order to provide a meaningful context within which comparative outcome studies can be designed and interpreted.

Causal mechanisms

What aspects of treatment are necessary, sufficient or facilitative of therapeutic change? This is a more focused question about the effects of particular components of the therapeutic package. It has attracted increasing attention in view of meta analyses of psychotherapy outcome studies, which tend to show fairly similar results despite differences in therapist, theoretical approach, and type of intervention. These findings strongly suggest that treatment may not always work for the theoretical reasons that therapists believe. Comparison of differential outcomes following treatment does not by itself answer the question of what were the 'active ingredients' of treatment.

This question is usually addressed by identifying the main components of treatment, and assessing outcome in patient groups receiving systematically different combination of these components. For example, in homeopathy it would be possible to compare three groups of patients receiving only constitutional, only pathological, or both types of remedy. Similar studies could be carried out, including, for example, different lengths of consultation, advice on health maintenance, and physical examination, in combination with other treatment techniques. Often such research showing that particular aspects of treatment are associated with particular effects is accepted as adequate justification of clinical practice, though there may be considerable debate about the precise causal mechanisms involved.

Which therapist factors are important?

Within complementary medicine there has been much debate about the relative contribution of personal and professional qualifications to the therapeutic process. For example, homoeopathic medicine is practised by both medically qualified and lay clinicians, though the clinical importance of this difference remains unclear.

Psychotherapy research has shown that a wide range of practitioner qualities can affect the process and outcome of therapy including personality, interpersonal style, beliefs, gender, power, attractiveness, socioeconomic status, and length and type of professional experience. Of particular relevance is the fact that studies carried out in this area have shown little evidence that theoretical orientation of psychotherapists influences treatment outcome. On the basis of these findings, it could be hypothesised that diversity of theoretical orientations and techniques associated with complementary medicine obscures a greater similarity in types of personal qualities and approach relevant in the treatment process. The questions here are: what influence do the personal qualities of therapists have on treatment outcome, and do they bear any systematic relation to professional discipline or training?

Patient factors

As with therapists a wide range of patient characteristics have been shown to affect treatment outcome. One particularly interesting finding in psychotherapy research is that patients' perception of therapist qualities, specifically warmth, empathy and genuineness, are predictive of treatment success or failure in a variety of therapeutic contexts. By contrast, direct measures of therapist verbal and non-verbal behaviour ought to be expressive of these qualities, but they have not shown consistent links with outcome.

On the basis of such findings, Kendall and Norton-Ford (1982) proposed the hypothesis that patients' perceptions of therapy may have a more important influence on treatment than specific therapist actions or interventions. Put another way, the patients' perception of therapy may be an important mechanism accounting for treatment effects.

Partly as a result of its search for objective and easily quantifiable effects, and partly due to the influence of therapist expectations, psychological research has only recently begun to take account of the patients' perspective. However, as Joynson (1977) has pointed out, one of the unique and most important characteristics of human beings is their capacity for self understanding and control. Any approach which tries to understand or predict human response without taking this important source of data into account is bound to meet with limited success.

Alternative strategies

Any research activity has two components which jointly contribute to defining the meaning of the research question. The *strategy* or design refers to the overall plan of campaign, according to which the study will be carried out and data collected. The *tactics* refer to more detailed methodology employed to achieve the wider objectives including how the researcher will interact with patients in order to study them, the precise data to be obtained, and the type of analysis to be carried out. Tactical issues are well documented in most research methodology texts, and will not be dealt with further here.

The clinical trial described above is only one of a range of potential research strategies, each of which has a different optimal range of application and different associated advantages and disadvantages. The following list is intended to give an idea of some alternatives to the clinical trial which have proved useful in psychotherapy research and may be of value to complementary medicine.

Single case design

It is often useful to ask what is happening to this patient? what am I doing to them? what experiences are they going through? how do they understand what is happening to them? are any events in their lives relevant to my intervention? The detailed analysis of individual cases can be used to illustrate certain principles, provide accounts of descriptive procedures, provide a focus for debate about the way in which particular problems can be managed, and generate hypotheses about significant factors in treatment response which could form the basis for subsequent studies using larger samples. This type of clinical vignette is commonly used for teaching purposes, though its potential in written form has been less well exploited.

This type of research may be particularly useful for holistic practitioners, who are concerned that the important role played by individual differences in treatment is obscured by use of standardised measuring techniques or average scores. It allows more detailed inclusion of the experience of both therapist and patient during treatment. A range of tactics can be used in the single case study, ranging from a narrative biographical format, to a controlled study in which the individual is used as their own control, and response compared at different stages of treatment, and to different types of intervention.

The main limitation of this approach is that it may be unrepresentative and reflect the idiosyncrasies of a particular therapeutic intervention in a way which cannot be generalised to other contexts. This does not invalidate single case studies provided they are not used to address general questions such as the efficacy of particular treatments.

Questionnaires

Given the importance of subjective and experiential factors to the treatment process, the development of questionnaires to assess such material can potentially make an important contribution to research. However, they also introduce a range of new problems. It is a very common occurrence for researchers to mistake substantive questions about what they are intending to study for practical problems about the phrasing of questionnaire items. Partly for this reason, it is often preferable to find other ways of obtaining this data where possible, such as direct observations or measurements. William James, one of the founders of modern psychology, recognised this point as long ago as the 1890s in his statement, 'because of its ease of use, the questionnaire is the bane of modern society'.

The questionnaire is a complex and subtle instrument and nothing is more cost effective when you get it right, but getting it right is often a tedious process which involves precise definition of the focus of research interest, eliminating sources of potential ambiguity and bias, and a design which is clear, simple, easy to use and interesting to complete.

Field study

This involves careful analysis of an ongoing situation into which some kind of change is introduced; for example, changes in referral rates from other practitioners following provision of different types of information. The stress here is on examining naturally occurring changes and developments, rather than introducing changes for the purpose of research. The main advantage of this strategy is its focus on authentic real life events in the clinical situation. Conversely, the main disadvantage is the researchers' lack of direct control over the events being studied, so that it may be difficult to identify the nature and direction of causal relationships.

Laboratory model

This involves setting up experiments in carefully controlled situations, such as the clinical trial. The main question which this strategy is designed to address is the extent to which a particular causal agent is responsible for a particular effect. The limitations have been described above.

Consultancy activities

In this situation the question is 'how can I facilitate or improve a particular intervention process? What can I do to make it more effective?'. As with field studies, the main advantage of this approach is its close contact with real life situations where the researchers' main aim is to improve a particular situation.

De-constructing the therapeutic process

Throughout the consideration of the study of complementary research we regularly return to the need to understand exactly what is going on in any therapeutic practice. This, in many ways is the central question for research.

Most therapeutic practices are described in general, broad terms. Frequently some central procedure, whether it be manipulation or the insertion of needles or prescribing herbs or pills, is regarded as characterising the whole treatment process. Yet practitioners of all persuasions will insist that these procedures are only a small part of a broad therapeutic intervention. Research therefore must begin to unravel the different components of therapy, break it down into its critical constituents. In terms of a data matrix, the proposal here is to develop matrices in which the facets that make up the columns are drawn from all the stages of therapy - how the patient chooses a therapist, or has one chosen for him/her, the nature of the initial contact with the practitioner, the types of information elicited and so on, right through to the various types of therapeutic outcome.

Another elaboration of therapeutic practice requires that differences between practitioners are considered. In matrix terms this implies thinking of the rows as falling into sets according to the practitioner the patient in that row sees. In other words groups of patients could be examined in order to see whether the patterns in their area of the matrix differ from patterns in other areas. Provided the columns carry information on the practitioner, then further analysis could reveal differences between practitioners that are important for the patient's experiences and treatment outcome.

Developing an understanding of holistic systems

A further development of this central question is the explanation of the concepts used in complementary practice. In the discussions of complementary practices and their theories considerable obeisance is made to the concept of the patient as a whole person, but research activities do little to identify exactly what this entails or to set up studies that are consciously 'holistic'. The problem appears to be that little recognition is given to the assumptions about the nature of the whole patient, in making the relevant measurements. For example, when measuring the galvanic skin response the patient is dealt with as an electro-chemical organism. Identifying the angle of parts of the skeleton implicitly regards the patient as a mechanical device and so on. If a patient is to be treated as a whole then measurements should include the mechanical, pharmacological, biological, psychological and social aspects.

In terms of the data matrix the facets that make up the columns should include examples drawn from all the different frames of reference for considering people. Of course, this is a demanding requirement to be applied to every single study. But at least the range of measures should be included in the full agenda for complementary research. An important emphasis here is that all the measures do have potentially equal weight. The idea that there are 'objective' measures that have a special place and supposedly 'subjective' ones, only of relevance for interest or background information, is completely at variance with the principles and theories articulated in most writings on complementary practices.

The central problem of reliability

So far it has been assumed that all the activities of medical practitioners are carried out with a crisp scientific precision, that the judgements made and diagnoses reached are incontrovertible amongst practitioners of a particular school of thought. Daily conversation suggests that this is not the case. Indeed an account of the many subtle cues which an acupuncturist or osteopath, for example, is called on to distinguish, leads to the conclusion that such skills are fruitfully open to scientific scepticism.

The establishment of relationships between facets across people requires that the values that are put into the columns of the matrix are robust and stable enough to allow important correspondences to emerge. In other words, if one of the columns was the practitioner's judgement of, say, strength of a particular pulse, but the practitioner was not exactly sure about that judgement, to the extent that the same pulse had an equal chance of being categorised as very strong or moderate, then categorisation of pulse strength may not be reliable enough itself to relate to any other measures made. All measurements potentially suffer from the problem of low reliability and so they must be developed so as to minimise the problem.

In essence, there are two related procedures for improving reliability of any categorisation scheme or measurement. The first is to be as clear and precise as possible about what exactly is being measured. In facet terms this means specifying as effectively as possible all the categories, the elements, of a facet. This greatly increases the likelihood that the person making the measurement (a patient by self-reporting, the practitioner by making an observation, or researcher using a measuring device) does indeed measure the same entity whenever it is present. It also increases the probability that two people will have a shared understanding of what they are measuring and record the same thing.

The second procedure is to make each measurement a number of times and in a number of different ways. Some summary or averaging of the measurements can then be made. This will increase reliability, provided all the measurements are of the same phenomena. This latter caveat turns out to be more problematic than might be immediately apparent, as will be shown in the following consideration of validity. But for the present the point that can be made is that it does not matter, and is actually helpful, if the data matrix contains columns that in various ways repeat themselves. In the initial stages of research there is some value in having redundant facets. These help to establish the basic reliability of the measurements. The relationships between similar measures not only helps to clarify what is being measured, but also helps to establish what the minimal reliability of the measurements are likely to be.

Validity and sensitivity

The consistency with which any measurement is made, usually discussed under the label of 'reliability', is distinguished in the research methodology literature from 'validity'. This is taken to be the extent to which a measurement measures what it is purported to measure. A measurement that was supposed to assess muscle tone, but actually measured blood pressure, would he quite misleading, no matter how reliable it was. The problem is, though, establishing what any system of categories of numbers is actually measuring. Pupil dilation, for example, has been discussed in the popular press as an indication of interest or excitement, but it may be more of a general autonomic arousal response that can be induced by fear, anger, joy or whatever.

The only way to establish what a measurement does reflect is by a scientific process. This requires understanding as to what other measurements it should relate to according to the theory and then demonstrating that data show those relationships do hold. In this framework all studies using the various measurements are part of the process of validating those measurements. The relationship between the facets that is explained by the theory is a test of the validity of those facets. From a facet perspective the establishment of a correspondence between some aspect of the definitional system and the observations plays two parts; it contributes to establishing the validity of the theory and also to demonstrating the validity of the method of making the observations.

Reconsidering the problem of reliability, it will be recalled that this derived from establishing the relationship between clearly defined similar measures. But validity has just been shown to be about such relationships as well! The inevitable conclusion is that validity and reliability are both part of the same scientific process. Their difference is one of emphasis. In the early stages of a study it might be questioned as to whether people who declare themselves as worthless, say, do also consistently reveal themselves as unprepared to face challenges. Some psychological theory may suggest that a measure of one should relate to a measure of the other. If such relationships are found then their validity is enhanced. But then both may be taken as indicators of self esteem, their relationship being an indication of the reliability of that measurement.

This discussion may be taken one important step further. A very precise, closely defined measuring procedure must still be shown to relate to some other procedures for its reliability and validity to be established. But consider, for example, the measure of blood pressure as a general indication of the stressful state of the individual. Some of the unreliability of this indicator of stress comes from the relationship of blood pressure to age, to recent physical exertion and many other aspects of the individual. It is sensitive to other things than just stress. However, if it were only related to stress (assuming there is a clear definition of that) then it would he of little value. It would not be possible to relate stress to anything else *but* blood pressure.

The point here, and it is critical for all research in complementary medicine, is that a measurement can be *too* reliable, its sensitivities can be too focused. All scientific activities grow out of the establishment of relationships between different facets, continually generating superordinate facets that encompass previously distinct ones.

Understanding the role of patient variation

All the matrixes and facets discussed so far have focused on groups of patients and comparisons between them. However, much of the discussion of the differences between people and significance of that difference for treatment is really derived from the notion that comparisons between people even on a number of facets misses the important qualities of their essential uniqueness. This idea can be given a much clearer scientific definition by casting a matrix for each individual. By treating the same person at different points in time as the rows, or by taking different aspects of their problem as the rows, a variety of facets can be generated. This will enable the particular structure of the individual's illness to be examined. The special quality of that person's illness can then be explored, but comparisons with other patients is not ruled out. The comparisons can be made of the internal, numerically established patterns. This will give a comparison of the structure of the relationships between the different problems as manifested in different patients.

The psychological literature is full of such studies and many of the questions raised by Heron and Reason (1986) in the first issue of *Complementary Medical Research* were concerned with developing parallel studies in the medical arena.

Hypothesis generation as well as testing

When the nature of the research activity is discussed at the level of abstraction and in the degree of detail presented here the novice and expert are both likely to express horror at its complexity and the difficulty of knowing where to begin. There is certainly little doubt that discovering fruitful starting points are some of the most valuable contributions of any research activity. The discovery of the structure of DNA did not, of itself, have immediate practical implications, but it opened the doors to many others.

One of the objectives of complementary medical research should therefore be to find effective future starting points, i.e., finding ways of thinking about problems. In the language of science it means carrying out studies that will generate hypotheses as well as studies that test them.

The idea of hypothesis generation research can be thought of by considering as an example a study in which a number of patients have been treated by a variety of practitioners and the effects of that treatment have been recorded in a number of different ways. If some means could be found of representing all those patients so that previously unthought-of aspects of the differences between them could be related to their treatment experience, and brought to light, then this might suggest directions for more detailed research.

Having attention drawn to previously unconsidered aspects of people may seem a very demanding procedure, but once again the faceted data matrix helps to make the task manageable. Instead of starting with a set of facets and seeing whether the patterns in the data matrix support the validity of those facets, essentially a hypothesis testing procedure, the reverse is proposed. The matrix is examined to see if it reveals any interesting patterns and the researcher/practitioner is then challenged to see if those patterns suggest any possible explanations, generate any hypotheses. Computer based procedures now exist that help to indicate which patterns in the data may be of interest.

Strategies for context manipulation

Like a war on ignorance, research can be thought of in terms of the overall plan of campaign, the strategy, and in terms of the particular ways in which battles are fought, the tactics. A full range of both strategies and tactics must be drawn upon to have some hope of making progress in the war. The variety of tactics available has already been discussed in terms of the measurements to be made, the facets that define the columns of the data matrix. It has also been emphasised that any such research tactic carries with it assumptions about the type of organism that is being studied. A truly holistic approach therefore requires that the full range of tactics be employed.

By contrast, the strategies used make assumptions about the types of research questions being asked. In terms of the data matrix, research strategies are ways of thinking about the analyses to be performed on that matrix, or the types of patterns in that matrix that will be of significance. For example, if the efficacy of a known causal agent, for instance a drug, is in question then the researcher needs to be confident that s/he has direct control over who receives that particular agent and who does not. The only way to do this is for treatment agents to be randomly distributed among a reasonably homogeneous set of patients. This is the randomised experiment. Clear differences between measurements in one set of rows when compared with another set in the data matrix will be evidence for the effects hypothesised. As can be seen, the strategy is concerned with what aspects of the context under study need to be manipulated in order to answer a particular type of research question.

Often the precise question of causality is not at issue. Rather the researcher wishes to know whether there is convincing evidence that some approach to treatment has recognisable consequences. In this case, rather like the legal attempt to provide proof of guilt, the researcher will attempt to amass information from different sources, comparing various possibilities, attempting to corroborate and validate the effects of the treatment. Rather than answering *causal* questions as in the experiment, the attempt in this strategy is to answer *probitive* questions.

Beyond the questions of treatments and their outcomes there are a variety of questions, possibly the majority in the medical area, that are really concerned with establishing the pattern of relationships between the variables that exist, This third, relational, strategy is the one drawn upon most usually by epidemiological studies. Here the matrix is examined for the pattern of relationships it reveals and possibly for changes in relationships over time. Frequently this can be a hypothesis-generating procedure.

A fourth strategy, already mentioned in relation to research objectives, is important to record. This is the comparative case study. In many areas of medical activity it is very important to try and establish what exactly is going on in specific cases. Here the broad relationships across individuals is less a question than the particularities of individual cases. In the history of medicine such detailed studies of individuals have often been of great significance. There are now detailed guidelines available for the conduct of case studies beyond the conventional medical context (Bromley, 1986). Any research programme may well move back and forwards between different strategies as the research questions being asked change and unfold.

Recognising the restrictions on research resources

The discussion above has thrown a broad net over many possibilities. Clearly resources are limited for doing all this work. It is therefore worth, finally, considering the nature of these limitations and the opportunities available for overcoming them.

The major limitations may be listed as follows:

(a)   Readily available, reliable and robust data collecting procedures.
(b)   The data collecting and analysis skills necessary to use these procedures.
(c)   The opportunities for collecting and analysing information about patients and treatments.
(d)   The development of clear, testable accounts of the principles involved in complementary practice.
(e)   The difficulties inherent in obtaining the patients' experience of complementary practices.

A broader view of science

One major problem with the scientist-practitioner model has been identified as excessive reliance on strict experimental methodology in the clinical context. The history of science shows that this approach of transferring methodology from one field to another is rarely productive, and genuine progress is more likely when attention is first centred on the questions which need to be asked; only then can an appropriate methodology usefully be identified. In support of this suggestion, some commentators have noted that social work seems to have produced more relevant and applicable research than clinical psychology. This has been attributed to the fact that social workers, unlike clinical psychologists, do not receive a prolonged training in experimental research methodology. As a result, more emphasis is placed on asking the right questions first, and then using whatever methods seem most appropriate to finding the answer.

One of the motivations underlying the tenacious hold of experimental methodology on clinical research has been the legitimate desire to carry out genuinely scientific work. The problem here is to define what 'science' really means. It has long been recognised that science does not mean building grand metaphysical systems to explain the world; that is, or at least was, philosophy. More recently, it has become apparent that science is not about collecting all the information and ending up with huge piles of data, or following a particular methodology, or using complex statistical techniques either. Rather the discipline of science consists of looking at the correspondence between the research question and the empirical data. This depends on establishing a clear question, and a methodology for obtaining data of direct relevance to the question. Data can then be used to further refine the question, leading to genuinely cumulative development in empirically-based knowledge. It is the 'goodness of fit' between the question and the data that forms the basis of good scientific research.

One example of how empirical observations can lead to clearer conceptual classification schemes is the discovery that some types of material leave marks on photographic plates, which led to the classification of materials in terms of whether or not they emit radiation which can be recorded. This way of thinking implies that there is some conceptual way of dividing up whatever it is you are studying, such as remedy types, acupuncture points or types of illness. The observations which are made, and the data obtained are ways of classifying the answers. Statistics is of course concerned with technical ways of classifying the data, and should ideally be used to assess the degree of correspondence between the conceptual divisions made in the research question, and the patterns which emerge from the data.

It is in the nature of science always to have a balance between precise confidence in any key concept and sceptical questioning of exactly what is the focus of concern. Research should therefore be seen as an unfolding, clarifying and defining activity that has no obvious end point. There is no logic to looking for *the* cure for a given illness. The research activity is concerned with an ever-greater elaboration of what is the nature of the cure and the nature of the illness and the relationships between these two. On the strictest scientific grounds the study of complementary medicine is essential for the scientific development of orthodox medicine.

References

Barlow, D.H., Hayes, S.C. & Nelson, R.O. (1984), *The Scientist Practitioner*, Pergamon, Oxford, pp. 3-33.

Bergin, A. & Strupp, H. (1972), *Changing Frontiers in the Science of Psychotherapy*, Aldine, Chicago.

Bromley, D.B. (1986), *The Case-study Method in Psychology and Related Disciplines,* Wiley, Chichester.

Canter, D. (1985), *Facet Theroy,* Springer-Verlag, New York.

Comber, M. & Canter, D. (1983), 'Differentiation of Malicious and Non-malicious Fire Alarm Calls using Multidimensional Scaling', *Perceptual Motor Skills,* Vol. 57, pp. 460-2.

Fulder, S. (1984), *The Handbook of Complementary Medicine*, Coronet, London.

Garfield, S.L. (1981), 'Evaluating the Psychotherapies', *Behaviour Therapy*, Vol. 12, pp. 295-308.

Gough, G. (1985),' Reasons for Slimming and Weight Loss', in Canter, D. (1985), *Facet Theory,* Springer-Verlag, New York, pp. 245-56.

Henkel, R.R. & Morrison, D.E. (1970), *The Significance Test Controversy*, Butterworths, London.

Heron, J. (1986), 'Critique of Conventional Research Methodology', *Complementary Medicine*, Vol. 1, pp. 12-22.

Joynson, R.B. (1977), *Psychology and Common Sense*, Routledge and Kegan Paul, chapter 1.

Kazdin, A.E. (1980), *Research Design in Clinical Psychology*, Harper and Row, New York.

Kendall, P.C. & Norton-Ford, J.D. (1982), 'Therapy Outcome Research Methods', *Handbook of Search Methods in Clinical Psychology,* by Kendall, P.C. and Butcher, J.N., Wiley, New York.

Kiesler, D.J. (1965), 'Some Myths of Psychotherapy Research and the Search for a Paradigm', *Psychological Bulletin*, Vol. 65, pp. 110-136.

Levy, S. & Guttman, L. (1985), 'The Partial Order of Severity of Thyroid Cancer with the Prognosis of Survival', *Data Analysis in Real Life Environment* by Marcotorchino, J.F. et al, North Holland, Amsterdam, pp. 111-12.

Orne, M. (1962), 'On the Social Psychology of the Psychology Experiment with Particular Reference to Demand Characteristics and their Implications', *American Psychologist*, Vol. 17, pp. 776-83.

Patel, M.S. (1987), 'Evaluation of Holistic Medicine', *Social Scientific Medicine*, Vol. 24(2), pp. 169-75.

Raimy, V.C. (1950), *Training in Clinical Psychology* (Boulder Conference), Prentice Hall, New York.

Strupp, H.H. (1981), 'Clinical Research, Practice and the Crisis of Confidence', *Clinical Psychologist*, Vol. 49, pp. 216-20.

Tyerman, C. & Canter, D. (1983), 'A Taxonomy of Small Hostels for Alcoholics', *Drug and Alcohol Dependence*, Vol. 11, pp. 225-31.

Wharton, R.L. & Lewith, G.T. (1986), *Complementary Medicine and the General Practitioner*, report to the RCCM.

14 In Summary

In summary

The putting together of this book coincided with my moving to a Chair in Psychology at The University of Liverpool from Surrey University where I had been for 23 years. This return to my *alma mater* after 30 years provides both an opportunity for new developments as well as a curious feeling of completion and consolidation. Reading through and editing the material for this book, all originally written while I was at Surrey, I can see that a particular style of research and of psychological thinking did evolve through these many studies (and of course the many others not covered here). There is still the need to give as full and coherent an account of that approach as is possible rather than the demonstration by example which is currently the main way the approach has been explored. Of course, it is not a fixed framework. In particular it is now evolving rapidly through use with many colleagues in application to the emerging area of *Investigative Psychology* which I identified and named shortly before I left Surrey. This book thus can be taken both as a review of the past and a sketch plan for a future more elaborate examination of a particular approach to psychological research.

In summary, for the present then, it may be helpful if I list the characteristics of this research 'style' as I see it.

Perhaps the first characteristic of my work is to recognise that research, like all other human activities does have a particular 'style' to it. There will never be one biting logic that will identify one dominant research pathway and drive out all other forms or research, leaving one particular 'paradigm' with a monopoly. The pretence in some text books that there is only one true path to scientific knowledge is challenged by the fact that no two text books agree on what that path is! But against that background it is important that scientists, especially psychologists, are as clear as possible about what their assumptions are upon which their approach is based. Probably as much as a third of the present volume attempts to articulate those bases in my own work, to show the principles out of which my own research 'style' has emerged. This may provide too self-conscious a psychology for many people's taste, but I will leave it to others to search for more profoundly psychological explanations for why I carry out research the way I do, confident that such explanations can be found and are relevant to understanding the work described on previous pages.

The second characteristic of my research appears to me to be the interest in the structure of relationships between psychological phenomena. That is an examination of systems of thought and action, rather than an interest in sequential causal mechanisms. This often requires a high tolerance for ambiguity, but is rewarded in providing honest reflections of real-world (as opposed to invented) phenomena that do offer practical implications.

This interest in psychological systems must have its roots in the work which I devoured as an undergraduate in Liverpool, of Charles Osgood and George Kelly as well as the psychometricians in intelligence and personality theory that so impressed me as a student. But I always combined that with a third characteristic, a fascination with individual uniqueness and the significance of the person. That has always had a small but verbose following in psychology from the days of William James through Gordon Allport onto Rom Harre and their followers today. Much of my research can be seen as an attempt to model general patterns of actions and cognitions in ways that derive from their context yet that enable us also to recognise the uniqueness of each person, not just as points on general dimensions but as a unique perspective on a particular set of experiences.

From this approach a fourth quality of the studies described usually emerges. This is the recognition that in any domain there will be issues and experiences that are common to everyone in that domain, whether it be patterns of actions in a building on fire, uses of a place or the way an attacker carries out a rape. These, typically, are what gives the domain its identity, but there will also be aspects of action or experience that distinguish between people in that context, some of them being unique to an individual. This framework provides the equivalent to the adjustment of the strength of magnification for the consideration of any issue. Without the need for radically different models we can compare the psychology of any domain by focusing on what the participants in each domain have in common, or we can adjust our sights to look at rare occurrences that will relate to sub-groups. Or we can use an even finer magnification and look at what is unique to individuals.

I suppose all of this provides a fifth characteristic that many will see as fundamental to my work, the recognition of the importance of context and the need to study any psychological phenomena in relation to how and where it naturally occurs, an almost anthropological stance. If the context defines the phenomena then it is feasible to consider how much detail to seek out about that phenomena. The adjustment of the 'focus' of a study is only possible because the actions and experience have a fixed setting in some conceptual 'place'.

The rather static view of humanity that emerges from this is something I have always struggled with, but it is only in studies of environmental transactions, notably human behaviour in fires, and some of the considerations of criminal development in which I have been able to introduce a little dynamism into my thinking. Recent attempts at modelling criminal actions over time have lead me to explore a way of thinking that is fundamentally dynamic, the narrative. The future will show how powerful that is and how far the framework is applicable.

The broad range of topics I explore is both a personal quirk, an undoubted aspect of my style, and an inevitable product of my fascination with the outer reaches of the realms in which psychology has been applied. It has become almost axiomatic for me that if there is a pressing human concern to which psychologists have not made a contribution then I am intrigued by the possibilities for such a contribution, and how the challenge of that new domain can illuminate central, more academic questions. Alternative medicines, behaviour in emergencies, the detection of crime and the design of complex buildings are all areas that illustrate a particular fascination with new fields that have not been well ploughed by other psychologists in the past.

The interest is in what these areas of human endeavour can teach us about people. But, almost inevitably because the problems for study are defined in relation to the context in which the actions occur there are a set of practical issues that arise. Whether psychological study can assist those practical concerns always has to be an open question. In most cases of even the most applicable psychological research there is little uptake of the findings. I have often wondered why the results of my research get applied when so much other research does not. The answer lies in the difference between the early studies I did on schools and hospital design, working with architects, that had no obvious applications and the later work on behaviour in fires and criminal behaviour that clearly does.

The difference in uptake must have some relationship to the other disciplines that would incorporate and act on the findings from psychology. There are, indeed, surprisingly few areas of professional activity that are under the sole control of psychologists. Even the heartland of clinical psychology often require collaboration if not actual authorisation from medical practitioners. But in the areas in which I have been involved it is more typically the case that the actions that are recommended must actually be carried out by non-psychologists. The willingness of those groups to respond to psychological guidance may be rather limited. Architecture is a good case in point. During the late sixties and early seventies there was a sizeable minority of architects who took an active interest in environmental psychology, but that group virtually disappeared during the eighties. A contrasting example is industrial management. In Britain at least during the sixties and seventies, industrial/organisational psychology was looked on with some general suspicion, but my own experience is that by the early nineties most major industrial directors would feel that they were not doing their job properly if there were not some psychological expertise active somewhere in their organisation. So although the uptake of psychology is not entirely out of the hands of psychologists it is only realistic to recognise that the readiness of the recipients for whatever largesse we have to offer must play a significant role.

The recipients will nonetheless be more or less amenable to the psychologists' message depending on how that message is expressed. Perhaps one of the clearest lessons I have learnt is that the closer the expression of the findings can come to specific interpretations of the relevance of the research to the recipient the more likely are they to take any notice. I was always reticent of such interpretation, naïvely thinking that the professionals with whom I was communicating were better informed in their own area and therefore better able to see the implications of my studies. But it was only after considerable experience that I realised that the detailed knowledge that I and my colleagues had of the topics we had studied put us in a strong position to make sense of that material in ways that others could use. This was demonstrated most dramatically in the guidance I gave to the Trinity police enquiry. I stuck my neck out and described the person they were looking for rather than giving them statistical tables and an account of the hypotheses open to test. The senior investigating officer did take my suggestions much more seriously than I would ever have expected, with very good results.

The other aspect of my more recent work that also contributes, I think, to the possibility of practical uptake is the preparedness to build arguments around illustrative case studies. Few people are prepared to act on the basis of general trends no matter how statistically sophisticated but if they can have that trend elaborated by reference to an actual person or department then they can gain confidence. I was brought up academically to distrust the case study and so it still takes an act of courage to prepare an argument around a solitary example, but I have found that whether it be the Kings Cross underground fire or a particular threat letter there is often much to learn from their detailed consideration, provided one is careful not to fall into the trap of believing that example exhausts the possibilities.

For journalists the one-off example is their stock in trade. As a consequence once you are prepared to comment on particular cases, especially if they are exotic or bizarre you then have to face media interest. Dealing with Radio, TV and newspaper journalists is an activity that I have often likened to riding a tiger. For some of the time you might have the impression that you are in control and have the exhilarating feeling that you may be travelling somewhere, but it is very probable that you will end up as just another lunch.

The media fascination with the excesses and extremes of human behaviour presumably reflects a more general human interest in these matters? I suspect that this is driven by a personal desire to understand and explore the more exotic aspects of human existence that are paralleled in my interest in broadening the boundaries of psychology and testing theories central to psychology in the crucible of actual life and work. The minutiae of short term memory or selective attention as studied with students in a laboratory, have never had me in their thrall, but what people notice when caught in a fire, or remember about an assault do seem to me interesting and important. Although, with the mellowness of my maturity I am prepared to accept that the answers to both sets of questions can inform each other. The question my own research brings me back to again and again is how much it is the theories, the ways of thinking, that are the contribution to daily life and how much it is the methodologies that psychologists develop that provide procedures for solving practical problems? My view is that it is the theories and concepts that feed applicability but that these need to be turned into practical methodologies open to solving local, focused issues.

I find the facet approach that guides so much of my work, so attractive because it bridges the theory methods divide so elegantly. Future developments, especially in the information technologies will I believe, further reduce the boundaries between theory and method in psychology. It is from these developments that future applications of psychology are most likely to grow.

Developments in the applications of psychology

I am of the generation that grew up with information technology. We used slide rules at school, but by the time I was doing my PhD it was necessary to have some programming skills in order to complete the data analysis. My research group was one of the first in the University to use desk-top computers on a regular basis, and when I was Head of Department I was instrumental in introducing one of the first integrated local area computer networks into a departmental office. I was around in the late sixties when many predictions were made about the future of these new technologies. I have survived long enough to see that many of the major predictions have failed to come about (such as the widespread use of the video telephone) and a few of the most significant developments (notably the fax) appeared on the scene virtually unheralded. So I know how parlous is the prediction of developments in the information technologies and their likely impact. As an applied psychologist, though, I see major developments emerging not from the creation of new technologies but from the great increase in the ease of use of all the existing ones. Once we can all actually use spreadsheets and graphics packages, e-mail and on-line interactive data bases then there will be great developments in research and the applications of psychology.

This will mean that there will be increasing pressure to convert psychological theories and results into computer based systems. There are already clear indications of this trend in the demand from our safety work for a computer based attitude analysis system, a pilot version of which has already been made available to one company. The studies of criminal behaviour has also already spawned a sophisticated data base that has been drawn upon to contribute to criminal investigations. These days the term 'expert system' is often (rather loosely) applied to these types of system and although that term may be somewhat inappropriate it gives a gloss of futuristic science fiction that makes such packages so attractive to senior management.

The consequence of this sort of development is to nudge applied psychologists away from a pure science base to their work towards what might be regarded as an engineering framework. This framework is evaluated in terms of the utility and efficiency of the system rather than the profundity and validity of the science on which it is based. This will put even more emphasis on the need for clear statements of what the psychological base is of the systems developed. Indeed there are already many examples of software technicians chasing off with limited understanding of the behavioural phenomena they are modelling. As a consequence they are producing systems that have a dubious and certainly short life span. Perhaps the most widespread example of this is the building of supposed readability formulae into many word processors when there is no clear evidence that such formulae do indeed measure the readability of a piece of text.

The building of effective decision support tools based on psychological formulations will therefore, I believe, put even greater emphasis on the need for powerful concepts and models, robust theories. This somewhat paradoxical demand for stronger, clearer theories comes about in part because of the pressures on people building computer systems to modify their objectives to accommodate the technical possibilities and limitations of the software, or to fit within established ways of doing things. It is the challenge of these demands that I see the facet approach responding to. The end result of a good facet study is a set of clearly defined concepts that are usually related to specific data handling activities. As our computer systems become more useable the boundaries between the methods of psychology and the theories can become much more permeable so that the science can effectively drive the engineering.

Turning process into product

This book has brought together examples of my work that have attempted to put psychology into action. It is therefore appropriate to conclude by trying to encapsulate what it means to take the university based scientific discipline of psychology and bring it into connection with the world beyond the groves of academia. How it is possible to take such abstract ideas as humans being active agents who make sense of their world and act on that sense, constructing their reality through the use of biased and limited although extremely subtle capabilities. The challenge comes from the predilection of psychologists for studying and describing processes. Perhaps that is all that can be readily established independently of a particular context. But to use the knowledge gained of those processes it is necessary to turn them into some form of product that can be made available for use. The demand in a nutshell, it seems to me, is to convert ideas into action. If this book helps us to put psychological ideas into action it will have become a process with a worthwhile product.

Bibliography of the Writings of David Canter

Books and special issues

Moore, J., Canter, D.V., Stockley, D. & Drake, M. (1995), *The Faces of Homelessness in London*, Dartmouth, Aldershot.

Canter, D.V. (1994), *Criminal Shadows: The Inner Narrative of Evil*, Harper-Collins, London.

Breakwell, G. & Canter, D.V. (eds) (1993), *Empirical Approaches to Social Representations*, Clarendon Press, Oxford.

Canter, D.V. (1990) (ed.), *Fires and Human Behaviour: Second Edition*, David Fulton Publishers, London.

Canter, D.V, Comber, M. & Uzzell, D. (1989), *Football in its Place*, Routledge, London.

Canter, D.V. (1988), *Environmental Psychology*, University Studio Press Company. (Trans, Kosmopoulos), Saloniki, Greece.

Canter, D.V., Krampen, M. & Stea, D. (1988) (eds), *Ethnoscapes:Current Challenges in the Environmental Social Sciences. Volume 1 - Environmental Perspectives*, Avebury, Aldershot.

Canter, D.V., Krampen, M. & Stea, D. (1988) (eds), *Ethnoscapes:Current Challenges in the Environmental Social Sciences. Volume 2 - Environmental Policy, Assessment and Communication*, Avebury, Aldershot.

Canter, D.V., Krampen, M. & Stea, D. (1988) (eds), *Ethnoscapes:Current Challenges in the Environmental Social Sciences. Volume 3 - New Directions in Environmental Participation*, Avebury, Aldershot.

Canter, D.V., Jesuino, J.C., Soczka, L. & Stephenson, G.M. (1988) (eds), *Environmental Social Psychology*, Kluwer, Dordrecht.

Canter, D.V., Jesuino, J.C., Soczka, L. & Stephenson, G. (1986), *Environmental Social Psychology*, Kluwer Academic Publishers.
Canter, D.V. (1985) (ed.), *Facet Theory: Approaches to Social Research*, Springer-Verlag, New York.

Brenner, M., Brown, J. & Canter, D.V. (1985) (eds), *The Research Interview: Uses and Approaches*, Academic Press, London.

Canter, D.V. (ed.) (1982), 'Assessing Environmental Quality', *International Review of Applied Psychology*, Vol. 31, No. 2, Special Issue.

Canter, S. & Canter, D.V. (1982) (eds), *Psychology in Practice: Perspectives in Professional Psychology*, Wiley, Chichester.

Canter, D.V. (1980) (ed.), *Fires and Human Behaviour*, Wiley, Chichester.

Canter, D.V. & Canter S. (1979) (eds), *Designing for Therapeutic Environments: A Review of Research*, Wiley, Chichester.

Canter, D.V. (1977), *Psychology of Place*, Architectural Press, London.

Canter, D.V. & Lee, T.R. (1974), *Psychology and the Built Environment*, Architectural Press, London.

Canter, D.V. & Stringer, P. (1975), *Environmental Interaction*, International Textbook Co., London.

Canter, D.V. (1974) (reprinted 1982), *Psychology for Architects*, Applied Science, London.

Canter, D.V. (1972), 'A Psychological Analysis of the Royal Hospital for Sick Children: Yorkhill Glasgow', *Architects' Journal,* 6th September.

Canter, D.V. (1970) (ed.), *Architectural Psychology*, RIBA Publication.

Social psychology

Breakwell, G.M. & Canter, D.V. (1993), 'Methodological Contributions to the Theory of Social Representations', in Breakwell, G.M. & Canter, D.V.V. (eds), *Empirical Approaches to Social Representation*, Oxford University Press, Oxford, pp. 331-335.

Canter, D.V. & Monteiro, C. (1993), 'The Lattice of Polemic Social Representations: A Comparison of the Social Representations of Occupations in

Faveolus, Public Housing, and Middle-class Neighbourhoods of Brazil', in Breakwell, G.M. & Canter, D.V. (eds), *Empirical Approaches to Social Representations*, Oxford University Press, Oxford, pp. 223-247.

Wilson, M. & Canter, D.V. (1992), 'Shared Concepts in Group Decision Making: A Model for Decisions Based on Qualitative Data', *British Journal of Social Psychology*.

Canter, D.V. (1988), 'Environmental (Social) Psychology: An Emerging Synthesis', in Canter, D.V. et al, *Environmental Social Psychology*, Kluwer, Dordrecht, pp. 1-18.

Canter, D.V. (1988), 'Environmental (Social) Psychology: A New Synthesis', in Aragones, J. & Corraliza, J.A. (eds), *Comportaminento y Medio Ambiente*, Consejeria de Politica Territorial, Madrid, pp. 103-120.

Canter, D.V. (1986), 'Putting Situations in Their Place: Foundations for a Bridge between Social and Environmental Psychology', in Furnham, A. (ed.), *Social Behaviour in Context*, Allyn and Bacon, London.

Canter, D.V. (1985), 'Intention, Meaning and Structure: Social Action in its Physical Context' in Von Cranach, M. Ginsburg, G.P. & Brenner, M. (eds), *Discovery Strategies in the Psychology of Action*, Academic Press, London.

Brown, J. & Canter, D.V. (1985), 'The Uses of Explanation in the Research Interview', in *The Research Interview: Uses and Approaches*, Academic Press, London.

Canter, D.V., Brown, J. & Groat, L. (1985), 'A Multiple Sorting Procedure for Studying Conceptual Systems', in *The Research Interview: Uses and Approaches*, Academic Press, London.

Canter, D.V. (1982), 'Crowding', in *International Encyclopedia of Psychiatry, Psychology, Psychoanalysis and Neurology*, Aesculapius Publishers, New York.

Canter, D.V. & Brown, J. (1982), 'Explanatory Roles', in *The Psychology of Ordinary Explanations of Social Behaviour*, Antaki, C. (ed.), Academic Press, London, pp. 221-242.

Canter, D.V., Brown, J. & Richardson, H. (1979), 'First-time Buyers are only Part of the Story', *Housing Review*, pp. 168-169.

Canter, D.V., West, S. & Wools, R. (1974), 'Judgements of People and Their Rooms', in *Brit. Jour. Soc. Clin. Psych.*, Vol. 13, No. 2, pp. 113-118.

Medical/clinical psychology

Crassa, M. & Canter, D.V. (1993), 'Nurse's Conceptualisations of Cancer', to be published in *Health Psychology Journal*.

Canter, D.V. (1993), 'The Wholistic Organic Researcher: Central Issues in Clinical Research Methodology', in Powell, G., Young, R. & Frosh, S. (eds), *Curriculum in Clinical Psychology*, BPS, Leicester, pp. 40-56.

Canter, D.V. & Nanke, L. (1993), 'Can Health be a Quantitative Criterion? a Multi-facet Approach to Health Assessment', in Fulder, S. & Lafaille, R., *Towards a New Science of Health*, Routledge, London, pp. 183-204.

Nanke, L. & Canter, D.V. (1990), 'The Multivariate Structure of Treatment Practices in Complementary Medicine', *Complementary Medical Research*, Vol. 4, No. 3, September, pp. 1-8.

Canter, D.V. & Nanke, L. (1989) 'Emerging Priorities in Complementary Medical Research', *Complementary Medical Research*, Vol. 3, No. 3, pp. 14-21.

Canter, D.V. (1988), 'How Do We Know That It Works? Therapeutic Outcome as Negotiation', *Complementary Medical Research*, Vol. 3, No. 1, pp. 98-106.

Canter, D.V. & Booker, K. (1987), 'Multiple Consultations as a Basis for Classifying Patients' Use of Conventional and Unconventional Medical Practice', *Complementary Medical Research*, Vol. 2, pp. 141-160.

Canter, D.V. (1987), 'A Research Agenda for Holistic Therapy', in *Complementary Medical Research*, pp. 104-116.

Booker, K. & Canter, D.V. (1987), 'Measuring Differences between Individuals - Psychological Measurements: The Surrey Experience of Treatment (SET) Battery', in *Complementary Medical Research*, pp. 94-103.

Canter, D.V. (1983), 'The Environmental Context of Nursing: Looking Beyond the Ward', in Skevington, S. (ed.), *Social Psychology and Nursing*, Wiley, Chichester.

Tyerman, C. & Canter, D.V. (1983), 'A Taxonomy of Small Hostels for Alcoholics', *Drug and Alcohol Dependence*, Vol. 11, pp. 225-231.

Kenny, C. & Canter, D.V. (1979), 'Evaluation Acute General Hospitals', in Canter, D.V. & Canter, S. (eds), *Designing for Therapeutic Environments: A Review of Research*, pp. 309-331.

Canter, D.V. (1977), 'Children in Hospital: A Comparison of Behavioural Maps and Cognitive Maps of Children's Hospital Wards', *Journal of Architecture and Planning Research*.

Facet theory

Donald, I. & Canter, D.V. (1990), 'Temporal and Trait Facets of Personnel Assessment', in *Applied Psychology: An International Review*, Vol. 39, No. 4, pp. 413-429.

Wilson, M.A. & Canter, D.V. (1990), 'The Development of Central Concepts during Professional Education: An Example of A Multivariate Model of the Concept of Architectural Style', in *Applied Psychology: An International Review*, Vol. 39, No. 4, pp. 431-455.

Canter, D.V. (1985), 'How to be a Facet Researcher', in *Facet Theory: Approaches to Social Research*, (ed.) D. Canter, Springer-Verlag, New York, pp. 265-275.

Canter, D.V. & Comber, M. (1985), 'A Multivariate Approach to Multiple Sorting', in *Sequence Analysis: Surrey Conferences on Sociological Theory and Method 2*, Gower, Aldershot.

Canter, D.V. (1983), 'The Potential of Facet Theory for Applied Social Psychology', *Quality and Quantity*, pp. 35-67.

Canter, D.V. (1983), 'The Purposive Evaluation of Places: A Facet Approach', *Environment and Behaviour*, Sage Publications, Vol. 15, No. 6, pp. 659-698.

Canter, D.V. (1982), 'Facet Theory', in *International Encyclopaedia of Psychiatry, Psychology, Psychoanalysis and Neurology*, Aesculapius Publishers, New York.

Canter, D.V. (1982), 'Facet Approach to Applied Research', *Perceptual and Motor Skills*, Vol. 55, pp. 143-154.

Canter, D.V. & Kenny, C. (1982), 'Approaches to Environmental Evaluation: An Introduction', in *International Review of Applied Psychology*, Vol. 31, pp. 145-151.

Canter, D.V. & Rees, K. (1982), 'A Multivariate Model of Housing Satisfaction', *International Review of Applied Psychology*, Vol. 31, pp. 185-208.

Canter, D.V. & Kenny, C. (1981), 'The Multivariate Structure of Design Evaluation: A Cylindrex of Nurses' Conceptualizations', in *Multivariate Behaviour*

Research, Vol. 16, pp. 215-236.

Kenny, C. & Canter, D.V. (1981), 'A Facet Structure for Nurses' Evaluations of Ward Designs', *Journal of Occupational Psychology*, Vol. 54, pp. 93-108.

Canter, D.V. & Tagg, S. (1980), 'The Empirical Classification of Building Aspects and their Attributes', in Broadbent, G., Bunt, R. & Llorens, T. (eds), *Meaning and Behaviour in the Built Environment*, John Wiley and Sons, Chichester.

Canter, D.V. & Walker, E. (1980), 'Environmental Role and Conceptualizations of Housing', *Journal of Architectural Research*, pp. 30-35.

Information technology

Wishart, J. & Canter, D.V. (1988), 'Variations in User Involvement with Educational Software', *Comput. Educ.*, Vol. 12, No. 3, pp. 365-379.

Canter, D.V., Powell, J., Wishart, J. & Roderick, C. (1986), 'User Navigation in Complex Database Systems', in *Behaviour and Information Technology*, Vol. 5, No. 3, pp. 249-257.

Canter, D.V., Rivers, R. & Storrs, G. (1985), 'Characterising User Navigation through Complex Data Structures', in *Behaviour and Information Technology*, Vol. 4, No. 2, pp. 93-102.

Canter, D.V. (1984), 'From Knobs and Dials to Knowledge', in *Design*, August 1984, pp. 31-33.

Storrs, G., Rivers, R. & Canter, D.V. (1984), 'The Future of Man-machine Interface Research: A Discussion and a Framework for Research', in *Applied Ergonomics*, Vol. 15.1, pp. 61-63.

Canter, D.V. & Davies, I. (1982), 'Ergonomic Parameters of Word Processors in Use', *Displays*, pp. 81-88.

Environmental psychology

Canter, D.V. (1995), 'The Facets of Place', in Moore, G.T. & Marans, R.W. (eds), *Advances in Environment, Behavior, and Design, Volume 4, The Integration of Theory, Research, Methods, and Utilization*, Plenum, New York.

Canter, D.V. (1991), 'Social Past and Social Present: The Archaeological Dimensions to Environmental Psychology', in *Social Space: Proceedings of an*

Interdisciplinary Conference on Human Spatial Behaviour in Dwellings and Settlements, Odense University Press, pp. 10-16.

Guardia, J., Valera, S., Pol, E. & Canter, D.V. (1991), 'Estudio comparativo Entre el analisis de Correspondencias Multiples y la Teoria de Facetas en un Cuestionario para la Evaluacion del Grado de Satisfaccion con la Vivienda', *Psicologia Ambiental: Intervencion y Evaluacion del Entorno*, Arquetipo Ediciones, Sevilla.

Canter, D.V. (1990), 'Understanding, Assessing and Acting in Places: Is an integrative framework possible?', in Galing, T. & Evans, G. (eds), *Environmental Cognition and Action: An Integrated Approach*, Oxford University Press, New York, pp. 191-209.

Canter, D.V. (1990), 'In Search of Objectives: An Intellectual Autobiography', in Altman, I. & Christensen, K. (eds), *Intellectual Histories in the Environment and Behavior Field (Human Behavior and Environment)*, Vol. 11, Plenum, New York.

Canter, D.V. & King, K. (1990), 'Ward Development Project', presented at The European Seminar Building for People in Hospital: Workers and Consumers, Dublin, 12-14 October 1988. *Building for People in Hospital: Workers and Consumers*, Dublin: The European Foundation for the Improvement of Living and Working Conditions, pp. 137-153.

Canter, D.V. (1988), 'Action and Place: An Existential Dialectic', in Canter, D.V. et al (eds), *Ethnoscapes: Current Challenges in the Environmental Social Sciences Volume 1 - Environmental Perspectives*, Avebury, Aldershot, pp. 1-17.

Canter, D.V. & Donald, I. (1986), 'Environmental Psychology in the United Kingdom: Origins and Current Trends', in Stokols, D. & Altman, I., *The Handbook of Environmental Psychology*, Wiley, New York.

Canter, D.V. (1985), 'Environmental Psychology', in Kuper, A. & Kuper, J. (eds), *The Social Science Encyclopedia*, Routledge and Kegan Paul, London, pp. 258-259.

Canter, D.V., Craik, K. & Brown, J. (1985), 'Psychological Aspects of Environmental Risk', *Journal of Environmental Psychology*, Vol. 5, Academic Press, London, pp. 1-4.

Canter, D.V. (1984), 'Beyond Building Utilisation', in Powell, J.A., Cooper, I. & Lera, S. (eds), *Designing for Building Utilisation*, Spon, London, pp. 41-47.

Canter, D.V. (1984), 'Vandalism: Overview and Prospect', in *Vandalism: Behaviour and Motivations* edited by Claude Levy-Leboyer, North Holland publishers, pp.345-356.

Canter, D.V., Craik, K. & Griffiths, I. (1984), 'Environment Bridge Building', *Journal of Environmental Psychology*, Vol. 4, pp. 1-5.

Canter, D.V. (1983), 'Phases et Roles de la Participation des Sciences Humaines a L'elaboration de Projets', in *Research Sociologues*, No. 3, pp. 273-296.

Canter, D.V. (1982), 'Psychology and Environmental Design', in Canter, S. & Canter, D.V. (eds), *Psychology in Practice: Perspectives in Professional Psychology*, Wiley,Chichester, pp. 289-310.

Canter, D.V. (1982), 'Psychology and Signposting', in Easterby, R. (ed.), *The Presentation of Visual Information*, Wiley, Chichester.

Canter, D.V. & Craik, K. (1981), 'Environmental Psychology', *Journal of Environmental Psychology*, Vol. 2, pp. 313-321.

Canter, S. & Canter, D.V. (1979), 'Building for Therapy', in Canter, D.V. & Canter, S. (eds), *Designing for Therapeutic Environments: a Review of Research*, pp. 1-27.

Groat, L. & Canter, D.V. (1979), 'Does Post-Modernism communicate?', *Progressive Architecture*, Vol. 12, pp. 84-87.

Canter, D.V. (1978), 'Environment Design and Behaviour', in *International Encyclopedia of Neurology, Psychiatry, Psychoanalysis and Psychology*.

Canter, D.V. (1975), 'Buildings I Use', in D. Canter (ed.), *Environmental Interaction*, Surrey University Press, London, Chapter 6, pp. 165-213.

Canter, D.V. (1975), 'Coping with Environmental Change', in Honkimn (ed.), *Responding to Social Change*, Hutchinson and Bass, Downden.

Canter, D.V. & Tagg, S. (1975), 'Distance Estimation in Cities', in *Environment and Behaviour*, Vol. 7, March.

Canter, D.V. (1974), 'Empirical Research in Environmental Psychology: A Brief Review', *Bull. Brit. Psy. Soc.*, Vol. 27, pp. 31-37.

Canter, D.V., Benyon, M. & West, S. (1973), 'Comparisons of a Hologram and a Slide of a Room Interior', in *Perceptual and Motor Skills*, Vol. 37, pp. 635-638.

Canter, D.V. (1972), 'Attitudes to Housing: A Cross-cultural Comparison', *Environment and Behavior*, March, pp. 3-32.

Canter, D.V. & Canter, S. (1971), 'Close Together in Tokyo', in *Design and Environment*.

Canter, D.V. (1968), 'Office Size: An Example of Psychological Research in Architecture', *Architects' Journal*, pp. 881-888.

Applications to professional activity

Canter, D.V. & Breakwell, G. (1986), 'Psychologists and the Media', in *The BPS Bulletin*.

Canter, D.V. & Donald, I. (1986), 'Psychology in the United Kingdom', in Gilgen, R. & Gilgen, C.K. (eds), *International Handbook of Psychology*, Greenwood Press.

Canter, D.V. (1985), *Applying Psychology*, Inaugural Lecture, University of Surrey.

Canter, D.V. (1983), 'Way-finding and Sign-posting: Penance or Prosthesis', in Easterby, R. (ed.), *Information Design: The Design and Evaluation of Signs and Printed Material*, Wiley, Chichester.

Canter, D.V. (1983), 'The Physical Context of Work', in Oborne, D. (ed.), *Environment and Productivity*, Wiley, Chichester.

Canter, S. & Canter, D.V. (1983), 'Professional Growth and Psychological Education', in *Bulletin of the British Psychological Society*, British Psychological Society, Leicester.

Canter, D.V. (1982), 'Psychology and Tourism Management', *Tourism Management*, Butterworth, London, pp. 193-195.

Canter, D.V. & Canter, S. (1982), 'Professional Psychology', in Canter, S. & Canter, D.V. (eds), *Psychology in Practice: Perspectives in Professional Psychology*, Wiley, Chichester, pp. 1-22.

Frost, A. & Canter, D.V. (1982), 'Consumer Psychology', in Canter, S. & Canter, D.V. (eds), *Psychology in Practice: Perspectives in Professional Psychology*, pp. 249-269, Wiley, Chichester.

Human behaviour and emergencies

Canter, D.V., Donald, I. & Chalk, J. (1992), 'Pedestrian Behaviour during Emergencies Underground: The Psychology of Crowd Control under Life

Threatening Circumstances', (Basel Paper).

Donald, I. & Canter, D.V. (1992), 'Intentionality and Fatality during the King's Cross Underground Fire', *European Journal of Social Psychology*, Vol. 22, pp. 203-218.

Donald, I. & Canter, D.V. (1992), 'Psychological Issues in Preventing Emergencies From Becoming Disasters', in Tony Taylor et al. (eds) BPS, *Psychological Aspects of Disasters*.

Donald, I. & Canter, D.V. (1990), 'Behavioural Aspects of the King's Cross Disaster', *Fires and Human Behaviour*.

Donald, I. & Canter, D.V. (1990), 'How the Behaviour of Passengers and Officials Contributed to King's Cross', *Fire*, Vol. 83, No. 1024, pp. 20-22.

Donald, I. & Canter, D.V. (1988), 'Behavioural Continuity under Fatal Circumstances during the King's Cross Fire', *British Psychological Society Annual London Conference*, BPS, London, December 19-20.

Canter, D.V., Donald, I. & Wood, P. (1988), *'Behavioural and Psychological Aspects of the Fire at King's Cross Station'*, Invited report to the Fennell Investigation into the King's Cross Underground Fire, University of Surrey, Guildford.

Canter, D.V. & Powell, J. (1986), 'The Management Factor Technique as an Aid to Decision-Making by Industrial Safety Management', in H. P. Willumeit (ed.), *Human Decision Making and Manual Control*, pp. 289-298.

Canter, D.V. (1985), *Studies of Human Behaviour in Fires: Empirical Results and their Implications for Education and Design*, Building Research Establishment Report, Fire Research Station, Borehamwood.

Powell, J. & Canter, D.V. (1985), 'Qualifying the Human Contribution to Losses in the Chemical Industry', in *Journal of Environmental Psychology*, Vol. 5, pp. 37-53.

Tong, D. & Canter, D.V. (1985), 'The Decision to Evacuate: A Study of the Motivation which Contribute to Evacuation in the Fire', in *Fire Safety Journal*, Vol. 9, No. 3, pp. 257-265.

Wishart, J. & Canter, D.V. (1985), *Assessment of Informative Fire Warning Systems: A Simulation Study*, Building Research of Establishment Report, Fire Research Station, Borehamwood.

Powell, J. & Canter, D.V. (1984), 'Studies in Development of Method to Assess the Management Factor in Industrial Loss', published in *Ergonomics Problems in Process Operations*, The proceedings of an Institute of Chemical Engineers Symposium, Aston, Birmingham July 1984, I. Chem, E. Symposium Series No. 90, Pergamon Press, London.

Canter, D.V. (1981), 'Fires and Human Behaviour', *Fire Prevention Journal*, Wiley, Chichester, Vol. 145, pp. 28-31.

Sime, J. D., Canter, D.V. & Breaux, J. J. (1981), 'University Team Studies Use and Success of Extinguishers', *Fire Journal*, pp. 509-512.

Canter, D.V. (1980), 'Fires and Human Behaviour: Emerging Issues', *Fire Safety Journal*, Vol. 3, pp. 41-46.

Breaux, J., Canter, D.V. & Sime, J. (1977), 'Human Behaviour in Domestic Fires', in S. Burman and H. Genn (eds), *Accidents in the Home*, Croom Helm, London, pp. 38-57.

Investigative psychology

Canter, D.V. (in 1995), 'Psychology of Offender Profiling', in Bull, R. & Carson, D. (eds), *Handbook of Psychology in Legal Contexts*, Wiley, Chichester.

Canter, D.V. & Kirby, S. (1995), 'Prior Convictions of Child Molesters', *Science and Justice*, Vol. 35, No. 1, pp. 73-38.

Canter, D.V. & Gregory, A. (1993), 'Identifying the Residential Location of Rapists', to be published in the *Journal of the Forensic Science Society*.

Canter, D.V. & Larkin, P. (1993), 'The Environmental Range of Serial Rapists', *Journal of Environmental Psychology*, Vol. 13, No. 1.

Canter, D.V. (1992), 'An Evaluation of the "Cusum" Stylistic Analysis of Confessions', in *Expert Evidence*, Vol. 1, No. 2, pp. 93-99.

Canter, D.V. & Heritage, R. (1990), 'A Multivariate Model of Sexual Offence Behaviour: Developments in Offender Profiling', *Journal of Forensic Psychiatry*, Vol. 1, No. 2.

Canter, D.V. (1989), 'Offender Profiling', *The Psychologist*, January, pp. 12-16.

Canter, D.V. (1988), 'To Catch a Rapist', *New Society*, 4 March, pp. 14-15.

Comber, M. & Canter, D.V. (1984), 'Differentiation of Malicious and Non-Malicious Fire Alarm Calls Using Multidimensional Scaling', in *Perceptual and Motor Skills*, Vol. 57, pp. 460-462.

A selection of conference presentations

Martin, L. Wilson, M. & Canter, D.V. (1992), 'Just Task Feedback: An Exploration of the Wider Impact of Providing Groups with Additional Information', British Psychological Society London Conference (Winter), London, December.

Wilson, M. & Canter, D.V. (1992), 'From "Layman" to Architect: A Metamorphosis', paper presented at the Proceedings of IAPS 12th International Conference at Chalkididki, Greece on 11th July 1992.

Canter, D.V. & Donald, I. (1991), 'Changing Safety Attitudes in Industry', a paper presented at the Seminario Europeo, El Factor Humano en Los Accidentes Conference at Oviedo, Spain on the 30th October 1991.

Canter, D.V. (1991), 'The Emergence of Investigative Psychology and the Limits of Criminal Behaviour', paper presented at the British Psychological Society Conference at Guildford, 20th September 1991.

Canter, D.V. (1991), 'Offender Profiling Fact and Fiction', British Association for the Advancement of Science, Plymouth, August.

Canter, D.V. (1991), 'The Development of Offender Profiling', Investigative Psychology Conference, Guildford, July.

Canter, D.V. (1991), 'Developments in Offender Profiling and their Contribution to Criminology', British Criminology Conference, York, July.

Canter, D.V. (1991), 'Attitudes to Safety in Industry', Meeting of the Joint Research Committee on Safety in the ECSC Industries, Burgundy, France, July.

Canter, D.V. (1991), 'Facet Approach to Decision and Policy Making', paper presented at the Third International Facet Theory Conference at Jerusalem, Israel on the 16th June 1991.

Canter, D.V. (1991), 'Safety, Health and Environmental Design: Exploring and changing rules of place through cognitive ecology', paper presented at Edra Conference, Mexico on the 12th March 1991.

Canter, D.V. (1991), 'Consistencies in Offender Behaviour', paper given at the Annual Conference of the Criminological and Legal Division of the British

Psychological Society at Canterbury on 3rd January 1991.

Canter, D.V. (1991), 'Accident and Intention: Creating a Safety Culture', Positive Safety Management Conference, Ebbw Vale, Wales, January.

Canter, D.V. (1991), 'Psychological Contributions to Criminal Investigations: The Emergence of the New Discipline of Investigative Psychology', New Horizons for Architectural Psychology, Athens, Green, October.

Canter, D.V. (1991), 'Saving Life: New Horizons for Psychology', Drever Lecture, Edinburgh, October.

Canter, D.V. (1991), 'Behavioural Science Contributions to Police Investigations', Surrey Probation Service Conference, Egham, September.

Canter, D.V. (1991), 'Football', The Football Licensing Authority, Safety Inspectorate, London, May.

Canter, D.V. (1991), 'Using Psychology to Save Lives', Barcelona, Spain, April.

Canter, D.V. (1991), '"Facet Theory", Cognition in Context: Where did it all go wrong?', Facet Theory, Brazil, South America, April.

Canter, D.V. & Donald, I. (1991), 'Changing the Safety Culture: Attitudes and Accidents', The Second Health and Safety at Work Conference: The Human Factor, Esher. February.

Chalk, J., Donald, I. & Canter, D.V. (1991), 'The Structure of Safety Attitudes and Safety Culture: A Cross-Cultural Study of Human and Organizational Factors in Industrial Safety', paper presented at the Third International Facet Theory Conference at Jerusalem, Israel on the 16th June 1991.

Donald, I., Canter, D.V. & Chalk, J. R. (1991), 'Measuring the Safety Culture', paper presented at the International Conference on Health, Safety and Environment Conference, at The Hague, Holland on the 11th November 1991.

Moore, J.M. & Canter, D.V. (1991), 'Home on the Street: An Exploration of Street Homelessness in London, Mab-Unesco Symposium on Perception and Evaluation of the Quality of the Urban Environment: Toward Integrated Approaches', in the European Context, Rome, Italy, November.

Moore, J. M. & Canter, D.V. (1991), 'Home and Homelessness, Housing and Design Education Conference, International Association for People and their Physical Surroundings', London, July.

Wilson, M. & Canter, D.V. (1991), 'Modelling Group Decision Making', Third International Facet Theory Conference, Jerusalem, Israel, June.

Guardia, J., Valera, S., Pol, E. & Canter, D.V. (1991), 'Estudio Comparativo Entre el Analisis de Correspondencias Multiples y la Teoria de Facetas en un Cuestionario para la Evaluacion del Grado de Satisfaccion con la Vivienda', Psicologia Ambiental: intervencion y Evaluacion del Entorno.

Canter, D.V. & Donald, I. (1990), 'Accident by Design', Environmental, Attitudinal and Organizational Aspects of Accidents, paper presented to Culture, Space, History: 11th conference of the International Association for the Study of People and their Physical Settings, Ankara, Turkey, 8-12 July.

Canter, D.V. & Donald, I. (1990), 'Accident by Intention', Attitudinal Aspects of Safety, paper presented at the Science 90, Swansea.

Moore, J.M. & Canter, D.V. (1990), 'Designing for Therapy: Testing a Design Theory', paper presented at the Culture Space History, 11th International Conference of the International Association for the Study of People and their Physical Settings, Ankara, Turkey on the 8th July 1990.

Canter, D.V. (1989), 'Engineering Appraisal of Sports Grounds', one day seminar, London, October.

Canter, D.V. (1989), 'Accident and Intention: Attitudinal Aspects of Industrial Safety', (1989), presented at The Ergonomics Society 1989 Annual Conference, University of Read, 3-7 April.

Canter, D.V. (1986), 'An Environmental Psychology of Prisons', presented at the 18th Cropwood Conference Long-Term Imprisonment, Cambridge, 19-21 March to be published by Gower in conference proceedings.

Canter, D.V. (1984), 'Action and Place: The Existential Dialectic', paper given at the 8th International Conference on Environment and Human Action, West Berlin, July 25-29, 1984, pp. 16-26 and published in the conference proceedings.

Canter, D.V. (1979), 'Y A T-IL Des Lois D'Interaction Environmentale?' in Jules Simon (ed.) Conference Proceedings of Louvian-le-Neuve.

Canter, D.V. & Lee, K.H. (1973), 'A Non-Reactive Study of Room Usage in Modern Japanese Apartments', presented at Psychological and Built Environment Conference, University of Surrey, September, published in Conference Proceedings.

Index